MW01194994

HARD CANDY

PLATE ONE
CHARLES A. CARROLL (LEFT) AND ROBERT L. CARROLL
C. 1948
POMPTON LAKES, NEW JERSEY

HARD CANDY

Nobody Ever Flies
Over the Cuckoo's Nest

A True Story
by
Charles A. Carroll

CHAMPION PRESS, LTD.
FREDONIA, WISCONSIN

CHAMPION PRESS, LTD.
FREDONIA, WISCONSIN
Copyright © 2005 by Charles A. Carroll
All rights reserved. Published 2005.

Printed in the United States of America
10 9 8 7 6 5 4 3 2 1

ISBN: 1-932783-34-2
LCCN: 2004115191

For more information contact:
Sara Pattow
Champion Press, Ltd.
4308 Blueberry Road
Fredonia, Wisconsin 53021
262.692.3897
sara@championpress.com
http://www.championpress.com

FOR MY BROTHER, ROBERT L. CARROLL

I WILL ALWAYS LOVE YOU

AND FOR ALL THE ABUSED CHILDREN OF THE WORLD

CONTENTS

ILLUSTRATIONS

FOREWORD

I MET CHARLES A. Carroll when he was about eleven years old, some fifty years ago, while completing a summer psychological internship program needed for state certification. It was immediately apparent to me that he was not mentally retarded. I no longer recall what was told to me, if anything; however, the absurdity of his placement in that environment was obvious.

With my wife's approval, I started bringing Charles home with me on weekends, hoping to overcome some of the institutional sterility and offer him more interesting and wholesome experiences. We maintained this relationship for a time after my internship was completed. My wife and I had a new baby, and I was starting a new job. While in retrospect that was insufficient reason to discontinue my relationship with Charles, I nevertheless did not give much thought to the impact of that decision on Charles.

[Forty] years later, Charles rediscovered me, and I have been gradually learning firsthand what survival was like for him at that institution. Why did I not learn what life was like for him while working there? Apparently I did not ask the right questions; I was focused on learning how to administer tests, not on the residents' overall living situation. Nor did it occur to me to question Charles about living conditions and treatment at the institution. Again, I must ask, why not?

I never heard any discussion among the professional staff about treatment of the residents. As a young intern, I put them and a renowned superintendent on a pedestal, assuming they were running a caring and humane organization. I like to think that, had I known about the sexual and physical abuse taking place under the noses of the officials, I would have fought against such mistreatment. At the time, however, knowing nothing, I did nothing. I am ashamed of my naïveté and insensitivity to the lack of protection offered to the residents, in particular, to Charles.

When I questioned Charles about conditions today, he remarked: "Like years ago, it's still about inadequate protection, unqualified management, and an uneducated staff, particularly those closest to the children. So unhealed is this social sore that no child is ever to be left alone with any one employee or older resident, ever! The point is, if we look into what happened to others and me then, and insist it no longer exists, I'm afraid we are deluding ourselves. Clearly the abuses continue, only today such improprieties are better hidden, a fact that is indisputable in the evidence presented in *HARD CANDY's* appendices."

It is my hope that this moving story will bring help to those too helpless to fend for their own lives. The public must assume greater responsibility for: (a) prodding legislatures to adequately fund these institutions and (b) insisting that institutional employees truly care for and protect their defenseless residents, and that they do so with a "gentle hand" of respect.

Charles has handled a difficult theme with great skill and produced a narrative of absorbing interest. While reading like fiction, it is clearly not; it is a hair-raising personal account of what too often happens to children caught up in the callous, institutional mismanagement of their lives. *HARD CANDY* is a "must read" for both lay people and those connected with government and social agencies, if essential improvements are to be made in the humane treatment and physical protection of children and adolescents placed in state institutions, foster homes, and related agencies. Moreover, *HARD CANDY* may well serve as an outstanding reference in the social science curricula of higher education in understanding child abuse and its effects on the human spirit.

HARD CANDY is an absorbing story, not only in Charles's descriptions of his life under the so-called care of agencies and institutions, but in his eventual triumph as an articulate, caring, and sensitive human being. It is a moving and inspiring memoir of adventurous achievement and human survival. Read this book. I highly recommend it.

Stanley I. Alprin, EdD (Retired)
Cleveland State University

PREFACE

HARD CANDY IS A TRUE STORY, a human portrayal of an uncommon nature. No one thing contributes more to its value than its authenticity. But be forewarned—you will not find literary frills, polite language, soft corners of prose, soothing seams of dialogue, happy jingles, or joyful songs. You will find, however, a thread of love that weaves together this entire story—a story about a special devotion shared between my brother and me and how we cared for each other when no one else would, how we understood each other when no one else did, and how we desperately clung to the needed components of love and friendship to survive—together—the horrific reality.

This book will give you a glimpse into the bleak world of institutional "bad guys"—administrators, monitors, and teachers—who stood side by side with idiots and madmen and who deliberately committed atrocities against these children, causing many to flee into an unconventional brand of protection, a futile attempt to gain some semblance of refuge.

HARD CANDY is also about hope, human triumph, courage, and the ultimate victory from systemic governmental and bureaucratic misconduct. Within the scope of this alarming tale, you will hear bones breaking—and the children breaking them. You will witness lunatics within a kaleidoscopic of madness beyond the comprehension of most "civilized" people. You will encounter helpless children—many trembling with fear, others suffering with miserable loneliness, unable to mend their broken hearts. You will see and hear institutionalized children crying out with torn and bleeding rectums, many separated from God and mankind, unable to hold onto delusions of life ever getting better, for it only worsened.

HARD CANDY shines a light on pathetic souls forced to remain in darkened basements, many of them drained of their childhood vigor between the ages of five and sixteen—and many of whom eventually became the further victims of a mass eviction into the community, where they were left to carry their emotional wounds for the rest of their lives. This was the coup de grâce, the state's final blow.

HARD CANDY took seven years to write, but it took a lifetime to assimilate the emotional conflicts caused by having been repeatedly abused. Only when I summoned this strength was I able to muster the unrestrained clarity needed to write this book. It must be remembered that child abuse is insidious. It is long lasting. And, for me, it carries an indelible recollection—sometimes a near-photographic memory—harboring an uncanny ability to remember things in minute detail. Sadly, those who were abused as children undergo an emotional struggle that continues throughout their lives. And while we may improve psychologically over time, once abused, there is no escape from its tragic consequences.

Be forewarned, I tell this story without the usual restraints tied to self-consciousness, personal embarrassment, and ego. In writing it, I do not suffer the discomfiture of looking bad, weird, queer, or whatever else one might conclude of me because of my insistence on authenticity and honesty. In the end, it is my hope that the candid and straightforward depictions in this book will be somewhat instrumental in protecting children who are still dreaming of having their lost sense of humanity restored; still rocking on sore tailbones, alone and afraid; still trying to mend their miserable loneliness and tarnished hearts; and still quivering from bone-cold fright because there is no legitimate protection for them.

When you read *HARD CANDY*, I hope that the forthright portrayal of actual events will ignite in you a need for justice and deliverance for those too helpless to fend for themselves—and I hope that, in a positive way, your conscience will never again be the same.

Charles A. Carroll
June 2005
Southern California

ACKNOWLEDGMENTS

I AM INDEBTED to the following friends and colleagues for their advice, support, and unselfish contributions, all of whom never stopped believing in me.

In alphabetical order, they are:

Stanley I. Alprin, EdD (Retired), a childhood friend, Cleveland State University; Harry Blitzstein, a Los Angeles artist, friend, and caring confidant; Nina Catanese and Beth Skony, content editor and line editor, respectively, of Launch Pad Media, Chicago, IL; Alison Cohen, editor, no one better, Huntington Woods, MI; Rachelle Cohn, a career counselor at Santa Monica Collage, a dear friend of many years; Mary Farmer, a journalist and friend, *News Tribune*, Perth Amboy, NJ; Sheridan Gibney, a Hollywood screenwriter and trusted friend, Missoula, MT; Kristi J. Golden, who went out of her way for authenticity, Office of the Attorney General, Trenton, NJ; Craig Huen and Michael Gulan, for their literary assistance and thought-provoking help, Presence Press USA, Saukville, WI; James Kenneday, a special friend from the state of Ohio; Art Kunkin, a gentle soul, friend, and teacher, founding publisher-editor of the *Los Angeles Free Press*; Joe McCaffery, *Star-Ledger*, Newark, NJ; Shirley Mitsunaga, RN, a lovely human being, friend, and confidant, Los Angeles, CA; Brook Noel, publisher and president of Champion Press, Ltd., my publisher, a special friend with a colorful spirit, a gentle soul, and a dynamic, professional publisher,

Fredonia, WI; Sara Pattow, who worked tirelessly, is an endearing friend, and is president of sales and marketing for Champion Press, Ltd., Fredonia, WI; Regis and Joy Philbin, *Live with Regis and Kathie Lee*, Buena Vista Television, NY; William Plummer (1945-2002), senior editor, *People* magazine, Time Inc., NY; Nancy Rosenfeld, a warm, considerate soul who worked tirelessly on my behalf insisting on excellence, literary agent and principal, AAA Books Unlimited, Chicago, IL; Neil Rosini, a libel attorney and friend whose expert advice this book could not have done without, New York, NY; Bea Sandler, a devoted, lifelong intimate friend, Board of Education, Los Angeles, CA; Salvador Scalia (1965-1989), a friend beyond words, Bronx, NY; Harry J. Searer (1927-2002), an advisor, dear friend, and supporter whose faith in me withstood the test of time, of The Zubin Mehta Estate, Brentwood, CA; Joyce Standish, editorial services, Las Vegas, NV; Ruth Wurtzel (1907-2004), a fine woman who was willing to cross the line in the name of justice, wife of Charles Wurtzel, vice president of the New Jersey Association for New Lisbon Boys, New Lisbon Developmental Center, New Lisbon, NJ.

HISTORY

NEW LISBON DEVELOPMENTAL CENTER
NEW LISBON, NEW JERSEY

DURING THE INCEPTION of New Lisbon, founders battled the wilderness of Burlington County, New Jersey. The area was covered with forest trails and swamps, and endless amounts of brush had to be cleared and stumps pulled to make way for the institution's "grand birth." Workers also had to get by without electric lights and, at times, even water. Despite these obstacles, construction was soon completed for a barn, water tower, chicken house, and three woodframe cottages.

On July 8, 1914, New Lisbon opened as an experimental venture to house a handful of boys transferred from The Training School at Vineland, another institution for the mentally retarded located an hour or so away. In fact, New Lisbon's first name was: The Burlington County Colony of The Training School at Vineland.

In 1916, with about fifty residents, the Colony became a state institution. New Jersey's state emblem was added to its sign and it was given a new name: The New Jersey State Colony for Boys (though it was sometimes referred to as the State Colony for Feeble-Minded Males at New Lisbon).

The state determined that private contributions from county citizens could not sufficiently fund the institution. Thus, a board of managers was appointed and the first annual appropriation was $25,000—a considerable sum at that time.

As for the residents, the children who had originally been transferred from Vineland were more emotionally deficient than mentally ill. The founders thought this kind of child could readily be exploited and molded to the ideals of a new concept; they were right.

Over time, the Colony started accepting boys with a multiplicity of mental illnesses and deficiencies. When state funding made it feasible, they also took in the community's most deranged boys, some of whom were just short of being legally dangerous. The men came later.

By 1926 New Lisbon was recognized as a "training center," and by World War II it housed nearly 800. When I was sent there in 1951, the population had grown to 900 and many resident cottages were uncomfortably overcrowded. At that time, many shades of abuse and neglect had escalated to unfathomable levels.

PLATE TWO
NEW JERSEY STATE COLONY FOR BOYS SIGN

To the best of my recollections, the events I describe in *HARD CANDY* all took place and the "characters" are real. Please be aware that I have re-created some dialogue to reflect, as accurately as possible, conversations and people in my life as I remember them. Some incidents may have been moved and juxtaposed with others in the interest of keeping this book to a reasonable length, and I hope the reader will forgive any slight errors that may exist due to the not-always-perfect memory of a child as well as the scanty (and sometimes nonexistent) documentation that often hindered my research.

All names in *HARD CANDY* have been changed in order to protect the privacy of individuals, with the exception of: Dr. Stanley Alprin and his wife, Marilyn; Robert L. Carroll and myself; Mr. Fein; Robert Fleming; Dr. Kahn; Thomas J. Kelly; Governor Robert B. Meyner; Mr. Mitchell; Dr. Parnicky; Mr. Peak; Stanford Remington; Aunt Shea; Mrs. Shepherd; Clarence Shepherd; Dr. Stevenson; Rudolph Stranard; Mr. Westly; and Dr. Yepsen.

Part One

There is no absolute freedom from sexual, physical, emotional, or verbal abuse, because with every abused child, there is a life sentence to be served, one that is paid by the innocent for the guilty—a tragic, but true, indelible hallmark of the world's abused children.

Charles A. Carroll

CHAPTER ONE

Sane Kids in
Insane Places

I LANDED A nasty blow to Rawbone's eye, blood spurting from it like a severed artery, but it didn't weaken him. He returned a smashing right hook to my jaw. I went down, falling flat on my back. Mr. Pring broke from the ropes and began the count:

"ONE . . . TWO . . . Get up, boy, get up! THREE . . . FOUR . . . FIVE . . . Dammit, kid, get up! Want Blacky to win? SIX . . . SEVEN . . ."

Half-dazed and drained of all energy, I staggered and stumbled as I tried to stand. I could hardly carry my own weight, but when I finally did manage to get on my feet, the crowd went wild. Applause erupted throughout the room.

Mr. Pring came up to me. "Do you wanna go on, kid? You look shaky."

I slurred an answer.

"What was that?" Mr. Pring asked, his hand cupping his ear.

"I said I'm okay. I'm tired, that's all."

"Do you think you can go on?"

"I . . . I've got to, Mr. Pring."

"Then pull yourself together."

"I'm okay now."

"Okay, we'll do it your way. I just don't want to see you get your brains kicked in. He's a big kid. One thing's for sure, ya got gristle, kid. Get back to your corner."

Less than a minute into the next round, Rawbone clobbered me good, delivering a solid left hook to the side of my head. It left me momentarily stunned, but I managed to shake it off. This time I went back into him with everything I had, landing another smashing blow to the open wound of his right eye, blood again sliding down the side of his face onto the ropelike veins of his neck. Unaffected, he returned a solid punch and bloodied my nose.

The bleachers went wild over the sight of more blood. It was the perfect elixir to assure the madness of the crowd. We continued at each other nonstop, punching and jabbing left and right hooks, some missing, some landing.

We remained merciless. I connected a left hook to Rawbone's jaw. That did it. He went down as if dropped from a two-story building. The roar of the crowd was deafening. Mr. Pring broke from the ropes.

"ONE . . . TWO . . . THREE . . . FOUR . . ."

Though still dazed, the resilient Rawbone came out of it, mumbling to Mr. Pring as he stumbled to his feet.

"I didn't get that," said Mr. Pring. "Speak up."

"I slipped."

"Slipped? Is that what I heard you say?"

"Yeah, I slipped."

"Bullshit! The kid gotcha, and you know it."

"No, no, I slipped."

Mr. Pring didn't buy it. He turned to the howling crowd, waving his arms for them to shut up. The room quieted.

"Hey, listen up. Blacky said he slipped!"

The room thundered and swelled with boos and stomping feet.

Mr. Pring turned to Rawbone. "They think you're full of shit, and so do I. Get back to your corner."

Instead, Rawbone stood his ground. Pointing at me, he grumbled, "That pussy-ass mothafucka ain't shit. I'll get 'im this time."

"I said go back to your corner. I'm tired of your lip, and I'm not telling you again."

"Okay, okay, I'm goin'," Rawbone obeyed, returning to his corner with the gait and attitude of a badass hipster.

Moments after we were settled in our respective corners, Mr. Pring gave us the eye. "You two boys ready?"

We nodded.

"On the count of three, come on out with your dukes up. May the best man win."

Near the end of that round, my energy was gone. Rawbone's punishing blows had whittled me down to a sloppy fighter. My arms felt like lead and my legs unsure. Rawbone, catching me off guard, connected. I went down hard. As I laid there, I began slipping in and out of consciousness, only now and then hearing the count: "ONE . . . TWO . . . FOUR . . . SEVEN . . ." I began seeing images of my tormented childhood flickering before me, much like a runaway movie projector operating out of control, rolling hellish clips of a cruel and enduring past. Then the mental images slowed to a trickle and stopped on a 1951 frame, on the very day the nightmare began nearly a decade earlier.

PLATE THREE
CHARLES A. CARROLL
C. 1951
SHORTLY BEFORE BEING WRONGLY SENT TO A MENTAL INSTITUTION
POMPTON LAKES, NEW JERSEY

CHAPTER TWO

Thrown Out of the Twentieth Century

I WAS EIGHT years old in 1951 when we reached the front entrance of the institution. A man slid off a stool and lazily approached our car, gripping a tattered copy of *Reader's Digest* in one hand and a clipboard in the other.

"Hello, Mrs. Johnson," he greeted. "So nice to see you again. You haven't been here for a while, have you?"

"A while," grunted Mrs. Johnson, as she turned her large frame to face the man. "How are you, Mr. Biddlemier?"

Clearing his throat, he answered, "Fair to middlin'. You know, I'm nearing retirement, and—"

"Retirement? But didn't you tell me the last time I was here that you were only fifty-five or so?"

"I'm fifty-six now and I have almost thirty years in. Time tends to spin out of control at my age. It goes fast. Before you know it, I'll be resting in my easy chair."

"Oh, phooey, Mr. Biddlemier, you've got lots of time."

"I hope you're right," he responded, sticking the magazine under his arm and inspecting a page on the clipboard. He raised his eyes over the rim of his spectacles. "You must have the Carroll boy."

"He's the one."

"Didn't you bring his older brother here about a year or two back?"

"That's right."

"Let me take a closer look at him." He leaned forward and peered in. "Gee, what a handsome boy," he said, his wrinkled, battlefield face breaking a smile. "Now that's a cute little lad. Hey, did you know it's Governor's Day today?"

"Today?"

"Yep, the governor just left not more than ten minutes ago. Although there's still some picnic left, I'm sure. Hungry?"

"I'm famished."

"Well, I won't hold ya, then. What about his paperwork?"

"I have it right here." Mrs. Johnson handed the papers to the man.

"Let me get your approval. Be right back."

A few moments later the tired, old man returned with the papers. "Here," he said. "Everything's in order. You have a good day now, ma'am."

As we drove forward, I looked up at the words on a large, dark sign hanging from a tall pole:

STATE COLONY

The New Jersey State Colony for Boys, commonly known as New Lisbon, was one of the state's largest mental institutions for the nonviolent insane and mentally retarded. However, oblivious to the significance of the day's events, I couldn't help but be enchanted by the acreage before me; it was alive and dotted with vibrant floral colors. The trees and bushes were pruned to perfection, the entirety of the scene exuding an air of tranquility and complete peace. Impressed, I turned to Mrs. Johnson and expressed my wonder.

She remarked, "Yes, it is pretty, isn't it? The patients do it all. They're master artisans. It's so lovely here."

           CHARLES A. CARROLL

"What do you mean, 'patients'? Are they sick?"

"They're just the people that live here. They even have cottage contests every year to see which patients can produce the prettiest areas around their living quarters. If you think all this is pretty, wait 'til you see what's ahead. It gets even lovelier."

"You mean nicer than this?"

"Yep."

Both sides of the roadway were dotted with various mounds of fall flowers, each exploding with dazzling color. The gardens included colorful asters and chrysanthemums, all standing strong like windbreaker guardsmen. And beyond the flowery mounds were spans of lush lawns, all precisely mowed and edged, with sprinklers creating bright-colored rainbows and chattering rainbirds bobbing in and out of watery mists.

"Roll down your window and smell the air," suggested Mrs. Johnson.

"It smells like . . . like flowers. I'm gonna like it here."

"See-ee, I told you."

Suddenly, up ahead, my awe blackened to utter disbelief as Mrs. Johnson stopped the car at the white lines marking a pedestrian crosswalk.

"Who are they, Mrs. Johnson?" I asked as a line of strange-looking men crossed the roadway, some bowlegged and pigeon-toed, walking on the balls of their feet, most with flat affects.

Looking over at me, Mrs. Johnson replied, "They live here. And look at you, white as a sheet, as if you've seen a ghost."

"But they . . . I mean, why do they look so different?"

"We all look different, silly."

"But they . . . they . . . they look funny, Mrs. Johnson."

"Funny? Like how?"

"Ugly."

"Ugly? Watch your mouth! They can't help the way they look."

I sat watching them with spellbound curiosity. They were circuslike, as if from a sideshow, many with crooked postures and odd-looking faces. Some were drooling, some limping and shuf-fling along with slumping gaits, their shoes without tongues; many had pant legs hanging well above their ankles. One of the men stopped in the middle of the road and faced us, waving a well-mean-ing hello in infantile openness, his wide smile revealing missing teeth. Then, out of nowhere, an attendant appeared and butted the man in the back with a club, ordering him to move along.[1] When the last man crossed over, the attendant faced Mrs. Johnson. He tipped his hat, muttered an apology, and motioned for her to move on.

Mrs. Johnson shoved the gearshift into first and sped off.

"This is where I'm gonna live, Mrs. Johnson?"

"Yep! This is your new home."

"I'm scared. They look like the boogeyman."

"Boogeyman? Don't get uppity with me, Carroll."

"But, I—"

"Just hush that mouth, Carroll."

"But Mrs. Johnson?"

"Now what?"

"Why don't you call me Charles anymore?"

"Get used to it. In this place, a lot of people have the same first name. So to make it easier, we call everyone by their last names. It's simpler. Now stop the questions, Mr. Carroll."

"I ain't no mister, Mrs. Johnson," I said, giggling.

"Don't get cute. If you weren't such a smarty-pants, you'd still be with your foster parents. They were nice people, but you always had to run away. Why?"[2]

"But I never ran away, Mrs. Johnson. Honest."

"I guess Mrs. Whipple is a liar?"

"I almost did once. Did my mommy tell you that?"

"Now I guess I'm a liar too."

"No, no."

"Then hush your mouth before I give you the back of my hand. Mrs. Whipple would never lie about anything."

Mrs. Johnson pulled up to the Administration Building and parked. Off to the side of the steps leading to the front door was a group of boys, none of whom looked like those I had seen on the road. They were younger, in their teens.

"Who are they, Mrs. Johnson?"

"They're the lockdown crew from Cedar. They help with the gardening. They're being punished for being bad."

"Why are they looking at us?"

"Get used to it," she said, gathering her files. "Let's go."

The Administration Building was a majestic structure. It stood tall, making a dignified statement of decency and protection in its solid facade and wide expanse.

We climbed the granite steps, entering the building through two hand-carved, eight-foot doors, the inside air swooshing in our every step of the way to the receptionist's desk.

"Hi, Millie," greeted Mrs. Johnson.

"Oh, hi, Mrs. Johnson. I'll bet he's Carroll's brother. My, my, my, what a handsome boy."

"Mr. Biddlemier said the same thing. He is a cutie, isn't he? Is the picnic over?"

"It just finished."

"Ah, shucks. That's what I thought." She handed the receptionist the court papers and authorization documents from Mr. Biddlemier. The receptionist leafed through the pages, initialed them, and handed them back to Mrs. Johnson.

"Here. Just take these to Hospital Admissions."

Mrs. Johnson turned to leave.

"Wait a minute," alerted the receptionist. "What about his things?"

"Oh, shoot! I nearly forgot. Thanks, Millie. They're in the trunk. I'll go and—"

"No, no, I'll take care of it," Millie said. "Just leave me your keys and I'll have one of the boys outside bring 'em in. You can pick up your keys when you're ready to leave. Meanwhile, I'll call over to the hospital and let them know you're on the way."

"Thanks, Millie, you're a doll. Come on, Carroll."

"Bye, handsome," said the receptionist, smiling.

I shyly waved. When we reached the bottom steps, one of the boys from the lockdown whistled at me, as if I were a girl.

Mrs. Johnson, tugging me along, scolded, "Don't you boys have anything better to do?"

We crossed the grounds using a sidewalk that led directly to the hospital. Along the way, we passed several cottages. From the windows, I saw patients watching us, some waving, some just gawking. Others were popping in and out of bushes, sneaking peeks with silly grins on their faces, a number of them mumbling garbled words as if trying to tell me something. One patient was wearing shoes on the wrong feet with mismatched socks, and some wore no socks at all.

When we passed the hospital annex, men stared from behind curtains with noses pressed against windowpanes, gazing with questioning expressions.

At the bottom of the hospital steps, a man in a white orderly's uniform was waiting for us.

"Hi, Mr. Alvarez. Here he is." Mrs. Johnson gave the man my hand as she turned over the records. "See ya." And with that, she was gone.

I turned my attention to the man. Alvarez was a tall Latino with a pencil-thin mustache who spoke with a broken accent. He wore a black leather belt with a large, shiny buckle, the word "Mexico" written across it. A pair of pointed alligator boots punctuated his feet.

"Come on, Carroll," said Alvarez. "Let's go inside."

We climbed the broad, wooden steps of the aging building. When we entered, I was immediately hit by the hospital odors—disinfectants, rubbing alcohol, dirty bandages, sour mops—and the distinct smell of brown lye soap. At the front desk, Alvarez handed the records over to a young nurse with washed-out blond hair and a dusting of freckles that swept across the bridge of her nose and rosy cheeks. The lady reviewed the contents of the folder, rubber-stamped the file's jacket, and handed them back to Alvarez.

"Get him showered," said the nurse, "then take him to Admissions on Ward 3."

Alvarez led me to a door marked "Stairwell," and we climbed three flights. When he finally opened the door onto the fourth floor, the world on the other side horrified me. The halls were filled with men, sorry-looking creatures with sad, deep-set eyes on tired, drooping faces. Some were hobbling about with crippling deformities; others were wrapped in sheets and sitting on oak benches along the wall; still others were secured by heavy, buckled straps into high-back wooden wheelchairs. One patient stood masturbating in front of the men on benches, his pupils unequal as he ejaculated; he was completely oblivious to the patient at his feet who choked on his own vomit and gasped for breath.

Alvarez passed by them, unconcerned. A short time later, he stopped at a door, removed a huge set of jailor's keys, and unlocked it.

"What's in there?" I asked.

Alvarez pointed at a sign above the door. "What's that say?"

"'Shower Room.'"

"Hey, that was pretty good. You can read. Not bad. Come on, let's get you showered."

As we stepped inside the room, Alvarez locked the door behind us and led me to the middle of the room to a husky oak table with three stacks of folded towels.

"Take everything off," he said.

"Everything?" I asked.

"Yes, everything. You sure as hell can't shower with 'em on."

"Can you turn around?"

"Come on, come on, get 'em off."

I began undressing, the wet ceiling dripping on my back. Once out of my shoes and socks, the concrete floor felt cold and damp under my bare feet. The room had a musty odor, as if the air had been breathed too much, and the walls and windows seemed to be sweating from the last patient's shower. I removed my pants and dropped them to the floor at my feet, leaving my underwear on. I looked up at the man, feeling self-conscious.

"Yes, the underwear too," he ordered. "Now then, what brings you to this place?" The radiator on the far wall clanged, hissed, and spat steam and water.

"My foster parents didn't want me no more."

"How come?"

"Because they . . . ah, nothin'. Hey, why do those people in the hallway look so funny?"

"Now, don't tell me you don't know what kind of place this is?"

"I don't."

"You're in a nuthouse. Where did you think you were?"

"What do you mean, a 'nuthouse'?"

"A place for crazy people . . . you know . . . people screwed up in the head."

"But I . . . I ain't crazy!"

"Sure, sure, kid. I never knew one who admitted it."

"But I ain't, honest."

"Now look. They don't send people here for nothin'. Come on, get that shit off. I ain't got all day."

"Can you turn around?"

"No, no, no . . . I gotta check ya over."

I took off my shorts and, in a feeble attempt to be modest, covered my privates with my hands.

Smiling, the man said, "Think that's gonna help, huh? Go over there and take the third shower stall."

When I entered the stall, I was surprised to not find any hot or cold knobs. I looked back at Alvarez.

"Just stand there," he said, eyeing me. He walked over to a wall with a number of valves, turned on one—and, suddenly, water shot out of the showerhead above me, first spitting and coughing air,

CHARLES A. CARROLL

then, finally, delivering a fine stream of nearly scalding water.

"Ouch!" I yelled, jumping out of the shower stall. "That's too hot!"[3]

"Oops! Sorry, kid. There. How's it now?"

I felt the water with my hand.

"Is that better?" he asked.

"That's better."

"Here." He kicked a bar of soap into my stall, and as I reached down to pick it up, he remarked, "Damn, boy, you got a pretty-lookin' ass."

"What?" I asked, over the noise of the shower.

"Never mind. Get movin'. I gotta get you back. Start rinsin' off."

"Now?"

"Yes. Hurry up. I'm shuttin' off the water."

I began rinsing. Just as the last soapsuds circled down the drain, the water stopped. After drying off, I returned to my clothes.

"Hold it," he said, coming over to me. "Put this on."

He handed me a nightgown and kicked my clothes into a nearby corner. I slid into the gown, much of it clinging to my still damp body as it fell to my knees.

"Here, put these on." He handed me paper slippers. "Okay, now come with me. It's time to get you admitted."

As we started down the hall, I saw a patient being wheeled on a gurney. He was shaking, as if in the throes of an epileptic fit, with no one doing anything about it. The hallway echoed with the sounds of insanity. Patients in nightgowns staggered about as if in trances. Many had zigzagging lines of gentian violet smeared over odd-looking sores and blemishes, some resembling the erratic splashes of a Jackson Pollock canvas.

When we finally reached Admissions, we were met by a nurse who had a nose shaped like a wedge of cheddar and eyebrows shaved in permanent arches. She held her hand out for my chart.

After leafing through the pages, the nurse looked up at me and

PLATE FOUR
GOVERNOR'S DAY ANNUAL PICNIC
YEAR UNKNOWN

said, "Millie called over and told me you were a good-looking boy. She wasn't kidding. You're a doll. Tell me, do you have any Italian in you, Carroll?"

"I don't know."

"How come you don't know?"

"I don't know."

"That's funny, usually that's the first thing a kid learns . . . Okay, Alvarez," she said, initialing various pages in the folder, then handing it back to him. "Get him to the doctor, and be sure to give him this." She handed him a stethoscope.

"Yes, ma'am," he said, sticking the stethoscope in his back pocket. "Come on, Carroll, it's time to see the doctor."

"Oh, and Alvarez, don't forget to close the door on your way out this time."

In the hall, Alvarez complained, "I can't stand that arrogant bitch."

"How come?"

"Because she thinks her shit don't stink."

On the way to the doctor's office, a single-file line of scrubby-looking individuals was coming our way. Some patients were waltzing with their arms around imaginary people as others kept up in slow-motion tandems; one was doing a jig. When I looked down at their feet, I noticed that the tile floor was worn away, sometimes down to the concrete, from years of the monotonous boredom of similar walks; a shiny path of erosion ran the entire length of the hallway.

At the doctor's office, I was cheerfully greeted. "Hi, son. I've been waiting for you! I'm Dr. Steinberg." The man extended his fat hand.

The doctor looked as though he weighed upwards of three hundred pounds, his tight-fitting clothes revealing every dimple, bulge, and ripple of his plump body.

"Come on over here and hop up on this," he said, patting the examining table.

I climbed up.

"Now then," he continued. "Let me get a look at your ears. Yes, they're clean . . . and healthy too. Take that thing off. Alvarez, where's my stethoscope?"

"Here it is."

"Wait outside, Alvarez."

After Alvarez left the room, I hopped off the examining table and removed my nightgown, feeling less self-conscious with this man.

"Okay," said the doctor. "Hop back up there and lie down. I wanna have a look at you."

He began prodding, probing, poking, and pressing various parts of my body, then shoved his thick finger into my groin. "Cough, son . . . again . . . once more . . . good! Now let's see if your lungs and heart are in good shape. Breathe in deep and let it out . . . again . . . good. I think you'll live another day. In fact, I think you're fit as a fiddle. Do you have any ailments, son?"

"Ailments?"

"Do you feel sick?"

"No."

"Good. By the way, have you had a chance to see your brother yet?"

"You know him?"

"I ought to. I'm his doctor."

"Is he sick?"

"No, no, no, nothing like that. He's fine. You'll probably be seeing him before long."

"You mean today?"

"I'm afraid not. I'll have to quarantine you first, then maybe after that."

"What's 'quarantine' mean?"

"It means that you have to stay here for a couple of days. Hey, Alvarez," the doctor shouted through the door. "Come in here."

Alvarez stuck his head in the door. "Yes, Doc?"

"Get me that syringe on my desk, will you?"

"Sure, Doc."

Alvarez quickly returned with a cellophane-wrapped syringe and handed it to the doctor.

"Put your arm out, son. You'll feel a little sting. Ready?"

"Ouch!"

"Now, now, now, it didn't hurt that badly, did it? Okay, son. Alvarez, this kid needs an enema. I'll call Nurse Reeves to get him a bed ready. Good luck, son." He turned to me and handed me my nightgown, which I quickly put back on.

Alvarez took me to a room with two cubicles, each with a bathtub, toilet, and deep, industrial sink.

"Take your nightgown off and go over there," said Alvarez, pointing to a bathtub with a wooden plank flopped over it.

"Take it off again?"

"Yes, everything. I ain't got all day."

I removed my nightgown and entered the cubicle. As I sat there, Alvarez began preparing a soapy solution in a porcelain kettle over the sink. When he finished, he placed the kettle on a hook over the tub and began lubricating the hose's tip with Vaseline.

"Okay, lie down on your side and bring your knees all the way up to your chest."

"Like this?"

"Perfect. Ever get one of these?"

I turned to look. "What is it?"

"An enema. It makes ya go to the bathroom. Now turn around. Stay on your side and face the wall."

I hesitated.

"I said turn around and face the wall. I ain't got all day . . . and stop lookin' at me. If ya look at me while I'm doin' it, it'll hurt. You don't want it to hurt, do ya?"

"No."

"Then do as I tell ya."

I rolled over and did as he ordered.

"That's it. Now, just keep your face to the wall. It won't hurt, I promise."

"What are you gonna do?"

"I already told ya. This'll make ya go to the bathroom. Now be quiet and stop askin' so many goddamn questions."

"But I don't need to go to the bathroom."

"You will," he said, inserting the tip into my rectum.

"Ouch!" I bellowed, turning my head.

"I said face the goddamn wall! I ain't tellin' you again."

I turned to the wall and watched his shadow lean over. He began fondling my rear end.

"What are you doing?"

"Just shut up."

The shadow on the wall leaned back, masturbating. A few moments later, like broken-winged shadows in mindless flight, the image ejaculated, its sperm sliding down the wall in front of my face.

Pointing at the wall, I asked, "What's that stuff?"

"Never mind that," he said, reaching over his head and releasing the hose-clamp.

I jerked from the unexpected sensation of warm water filling my colon. When the hose finally gurgled its last drop of fluid, he removed the lubricated tip from my rectum and told me to sit on the toilet. I knew he had done something wrong, terribly wrong, but my youth and inexperience didn't know how to define it. All I knew was that I wanted to defecate his sin.

In bed that night, I tossed and turned, restless, feeling caught between God and sin, flanked by right and wrong. I prayed to a God I didn't love or understand because I was suddenly too afraid *not* to believe in something—prayed that I might awaken the next morning to find it had been nothing more than a bad dream.

1. "In every institution where the discredited principles of 'Restraint' are used or tolerated, the very atmosphere is brutalizing. Place a bludgeon in the hand of any man, with instructions to use it when necessary, and the gentler and more humane methods of persuasion will naturally be forgotten or deliberately abandoned." Clifford Whittingham Beers, *A Mind That Found Itself: An Autobiography*, 7th ed. (New York: Longmans, Green & Co., 1908; Garden City, NY: Doubleday, 1962), 124. Page reference is to the 1962 edition.

2. In 1985, during my search to come to terms with the past, I contacted New Lisbon requesting information. They mailed back a scanty document. One paragraph read: "The boys were committed to the State Board of Child Welfare on January 29, 1946. The S.B.C.W. then placed them with . . . [a] foster mother [who] complained the boys would run away when unsupervised."

3. See Appendix A.2.1/Shower Scalding and Resident Abuse/1991. A New Lisbon employee was accused of burning a Yucca Cottage resident with hot water, causing second-degree burns over twenty percent of the resident's body.

CHAPTER THREE

The Gatekeepers
of Hell

THREE DAYS LATER, a runner from Pine Cottage lumbered into my hospital dormitory.

"Are you Carroll?" he asked.

"Yes," I answered.

"My name's Desarino. I'm supposed to take you to Birch Cottage. Mrs. Steele wants you to get into these clothes, and ya better be quick about it. She gets pissed when somebody holds her up."

"Is my brother there?"

"Your guess is as good as mine. Hurry up."

As I stepped out of the hospital, I felt glad to be rid of the deafening shrieks of the patients. But I began to notice, when we got deeper into the institution's grounds, that the Colony's floral color was disappearing. So, too, were the bright green lawns and manicured shrubs. By the time we neared Birch Cottage, about all that was left were patches of dandelions, balding lawns, and broken sidewalks lifted by stubborn tree roots.

At an intersection in the road, all four street corners displayed knee-high, black-lettered signs that listed cottages with red arrows pointing the way. Birch Cottage was straight ahead. As we were about to step off the curb, a tractor hauling a trailer passed.

"Desarino, what's in those barrels that stinks so bad?" I asked.

"Slop! The shit people won't eat."

"What do you mean?"

"It's from breakfast this morning. They're takin' that shit to the pig pen."

"You mean they have pigs here?"

"Lots of 'em. You should hear them pigs squeal when they hear that tractor comin' toward the farm."

"But why don't the people eat it? My mommy made me eat everything. She said it's a sin to waste food."

"Because the food's bad."

"Like how?"

"How 'bout animal skin, ears, and hair for starters? You have to watch what you eat in this hellhole."

"How does it get in there?"

"Because the people doin' the cookin' don't give a shit."

"Is there a real farm here?"

"A big one. They have cows, chickens, goats . . . and they grow corn, onions, peppers, strawberries—you name it. They even take that stuff to the state fair."

"Where's the farm at?"

"Way the hell out and gone."

"Are we gonna pass it?"

"No, it's too far. Heck, there's Birch right over there," he said, pointing to one of cottages ahead.

I studied Desarino as we walked. He was an eighteen-year-old, olive-complexioned boy with a muscular build. He had black, wavy hair and a strong, Roman nose. Desarino showed no signs of being retarded and revealed no symptoms of mental deficiency; he looked completely normal, much like the boys I had seen at the steps of the Administration Building when I first arrived.

"What are those?" I asked, pointing at two smokestacks that stood tall over the institution.

"That's the laundry, where they erase what's goin' on around here."

"What do you mean?"

"Never mind. You'll find out soon enough. Listen, kid, I've seen a lotta shit in this place."

"You use lots of bad words."

"Did you ever see a pissed guy that didn't?"

"I don't know." I thought a moment. "Are you crazy too?"

"No, but they think so. God, boy, you're sure one for questions! How old are you, anyway?"

"I'm eight. Almost nine. Why?"

"Just askin'."

"Why does everybody tell me that?"

"What's that?"

"That I ask a lot of questions."

"Because you do, I guess."

"Hey, Desarino, will you ever get out?"

"If they let me."

"Think they will?"

"Yeah, when they wise up and stop puttin' the normal people in with the nuts. Hey, Carroll, I think I like ya already. Too bad you're so young."

"What do you mean?"

"Maybe ya could be my Kid some time. I know I could love ya one day."

"But you're a boy!"

"Listen, kid, love in this place is spelled with the same four-letter word."

"What's that mean?"

"Never mind."

"Golly, you talk funny. Hey, Desarino, how come it ain't as nice around here like it is back there?"

"Ya mean the plants and stuff?"

"Yeah."

"Because the visitors who come back this far don't matter."

"Why not?"

"Because they ain't the ones forkin' over the money. They only want to impress anyone belongin' to the state. They're the ones puttin' up the money. Wise up, kid. Hey, ya know somethin'? I like you. If anybody ever bothers ya, let me know."

"Bothers me how?"

"Like hits ya and stuff. Here's Birch." He pointed to the next cottage. "I'll bet Old Bag Steele's watchin' from one of the windows. She don't miss shit."

"Do you mean Mrs. Steele?"

"Yep."

"But a nurse told me yesterday that she was a nice lady."

"Don't believe it. Steele's a bitch."

"Like how?"

"You'll find out. Hey, do me a favor, though."

"What?"

"Don't tell her I said anythin' about anythin'."

"How come?"

"Just don't. Promise?"

"I . . . I won't if you don't want me to."

"Now I know I like ya. Well, this is it. This is your cottage."

"Where's everybody at?"

"God only knows. Hey kid, remember, if anybody ever bothers ya, just let me know. Come on, we better get up there before the old bag shits a brick."

Just as we reached the top step, the door swung open.

"Hi, Mrs. Steele. This is—"

"Shut up! I know who he is. Gimmie that." She snatched the folder from Desarino's hand. "Get movin' before I find a reason to have you shipped to Cedar."

"But, I was only—"

"Don't you dare argue with me!" Her features twisted into a maddening sneer. "Get back to Pine Cottage where you belong."

Blood filled Desarino's face. Without another word, he turned and left.

CHAPTER FOUR
Thrown into the Belly of the Concrete Beast

"YOU COME WITH me." Mrs. Steele grabbed my wrist and hauled me inside, immediately taking me to the sewing room.

Betty Steele was a fat, purple-haired, aging woman whose only hint of femininity was her blood red fingernails. She wore a side-arm of keys that slapped against her thigh every time she walked. The keys dangled from a foot-long chain that hung from a wide leather belt circling her midriff. Her body appeared off center, as if her stuffing had shifted to one side.

"Sit there," she ordered, pointing to a chair next to her desk. Taking her seat, she began leafing through my folder, then raised her eyes and said to me, "Ya better not be like that brother of yours."

"He's here?"

"Never mind that!" she yelled, putting an arthritic finger up to my face. "Because if you're anything like him, I'll have your ass in a sling like I have his right now. We understand each other?"

"Yes."

"It's 'yes, ma'am' and 'no ma'am' around here. Understand me?"

"Yes, ma'am."

"That's better. Stand up. I wanna have a look at ya." She stood over me, looking me up and down. "Your sleeves are maybe a little short, but what the heck, nobody's gonna see ya anyway." Her eyes narrowed with suspicion. "What did that brat kid say to ya?"

"Nothin'."

"He was talkin' to ya about somethin' at the bottom of the steps. So what was it about?"

"Oh, about the farm."

"Anything else?"

"No."

"It's 'no, ma'am.' Don't make me tell ya again. Are you sure you're not lyin' to me?"

"I'm not, ma'am."

"I can't stand a liar! Don't try it with me. I can always tell when somebody's pullin' a fast one over on me."

"But, I ain't lyin', Mrs. Steele. He was talkin' about the pigs and cows and—"

"Shut up! I don't need to know all that. I'll tell ya one thing. That boy's headed for a bruisin'. He's too damn smart for his own good. Come with me." She took me into the dormitory. "This is Birch One, where you'll be sleepin'."

The room held fifty beds, twenty-five lining each wall military style. The corners of each bed were folded and tucked neatly with delicate, white linens and blankets pulled so tightly as if to intentionally remove all traces of comfort. And while the flapping curtains at the open-mouthed windows gave the dormitory a heartbeat of its own, they in no way diminished the cold and impersonal environment of the room. It emitted the aura of a funeral parlor, and a foreboding chill entered my young system, telling me that this was not a bedroom for the living but a resting place for the dead.

Then Mrs. Steele led me into the day room. The open windows were ushering in sunlight and, like the dormitory, the curtains fluttered in the wind. The floors were buffed to a gleaming shine. But there was one troubling fact: the room looked more like a store display than a space used by kids.

Mrs. Steele pointed me toward a stairwell that led into the basement. At the top of the steps, she cupped her mouth with her hands and shouted, "JACKSON! Get up here, quick!"

A few moments later, the door at the bottom of the steps opened, its hinges squeaking. Like a well-oiled machine, a black boy climbed the steps.

"Yes, Mrs. Steele?"

"What took ya so long?"

"I tripped in the hall," he answered, his bronze forehead glistening with sweat.

"Here, take him," she ordered, giving him my hand. "He gets Seat 4. Carroll, you do as he tells ya. Understand?"

"Yes, ma'am."

The black boy looked at me. "Hi, my name's Nathaniel Jackson, but everybody calls me Jackson."

"I'm Charles Carroll."

The six-foot, thirteen-year-old boy led me down the steps.

"It's dark down here," I said.

"I know. Just stay with me."

"What's that smell?"

"You'll get used to it. Come on."

Once my eyes adjusted to the darkened basement, I began seeing partial images: isolated puddles of water on the floor, cobwebs dangling like asterisks from the corners of the walls, and rows of tubular runners along the ceiling, suspended by pencil-thin, steel hangers. Straight down the middle of the ceiling was a drainage pipe about four inches around, dripping water from its lead fittings and giant elbows.

"It's spooky down here, ain't it?" I asked.

"You'll get used to it."

Suddenly, a deafening blast sounded.

"What was that?"

"The boiler. Wanna see it?"

"I . . . I guess."

He led me to an open doorway and snapped on a light.

"Is that what did it?"

"Yep. That's the boiler. It does that sometimes."

"What's it for?"

"It heats water and sends steam to the radiators."

The portly boiler was wrapped in three inches of asbestos. Its huge belly rested on four ornate, cast-iron legs and its fittings were spouting hisses and spraying mists from its improperly sealed valves.

"Come on. Everybody's waitin' to meet ya."

When we finally made it to the lighted room at the other end of the hall, what I saw and smelled traumatized my boyhood sensibilities. The children were seated on one continuous wooden bench that wrapped around three walls, all peeling from neglect. It looked as if each paint job had been a futile attempt to disguise many years in the basement's cycles of gloom. The wall was heavily veined from water seepage, and the room gave off a musty, mildewy odor.

Over time, the children's buttocks had sanded down each spot on the bench in the shape of their rear ends, the squirming of each child having worn away the wood's original character. Under each boy's assigned seat was a wooden box where he stashed his nightgown during the day and his outer clothing at night.

Unlike the men I had seen in the hospital or the teenagers outside the Administration Building, these were very young boys, ages five to nine, their faces scribbled with yawning youth. They were still in the early stages of growth, their feet not even touching the floor as they hadn't yet matured into the hideous, idiosyncratic postures of their adult counterparts.

They looked like wax museum figures, their expressions drooping with miserable aloneness, their awkward bodies listless, their expressions heavy with despair, and their lazy eyes absent of childhood wonder.

They sat mannequin-like, elbow to elbow. Many faces were bruised; three boys had black eyes and several others had swollen lips. And many had feces clinging to their chins, noses, hands, and clothing, contributing to the room's overwhelming smells.

Pushed up against the fourth wall was a desk, which, I would soon learn, was Jackson's usual perch. From there he could view everyone, his legs always dangling over the side, watching, as if lying in wait to pounce with predatory accuracy on anyone who caught his attention. Jackson ruled the basement with an iron fist, emotionally and physically, hog-tying all the children within a strait-jacket of fear.

Leaving me at the doorway, Jackson flew into a rage at one of the boys who was talking. "You were talkin', weren't you, Shienbaum?"

One kid called out, "He was just talkin' to himself."

Jackson, paying no mind to the kid's comment, yanked Shienbaum out of his seat and shoved him to the floor. Before the boy had a chance to move into a defensive curl, Jackson kicked him in the gut with all his might. The boy uttered a throaty, hawkish sound.

"Get up!"

Shienbaum, deformed with twisted, bony arms and spindly legs, caught his breath and clumsily rose to his feet. He ran to his seat, holding his stomach, then stuck his thumb into his mouth and be-gan sucking, tears streaming down his cheeks. Drool cascaded un-broken from his lips to the floor.

Jackson hopped on his desk, turned to me, and said, "Don't just stand there in the fuckin' doorway. Come in here next to me."

I joined him beside the desk.

"Tell everybody your name."

"Charles," I said nervously.

"No, dummy, your real name."

"C-C-Carroll, sir."

"Sir? Do I look like a fuckin' sir? Spell it!"

"C-a-r-r-o-l-l."

When Jackson began laughing, the others joined in, most of them cackling like barnyard animals.

"You sissy! You got a girl's name!"

As everyone continued to laugh, I lowered my eyes to the floor, hating my name for the first time.

Putting his black, waxy finger to my face, he warned, "Tonight, I'm fuckin' you, sweetie."

Shouting and laughter continued to fill the room, knocking me off-kilter. After the mirth had calmed down, Jackson ordered everyone to say hello to me. Their well-meaning "hellos" were exhibited by grunts and squeals.

"Shut up!"

The room fell silent, everyone resuming a stiff posture and looking straight ahead. The only movements were those of dust particles suspended within the beams of sunlight slipping through three small windows below the ceiling line of the third wall.

"Come here," commanded Jackson, sliding off his desk. "I want you to meet some of 'em." He shoved me to the far corner of the room.

The stench of the place made my stomach heave. I turned from the boys and looked at Jackson, holding my belly. "I think I'm gonna get sick."

Jackson fluffed it off as nothing. "You'll get used to it." He turned to a boy on the bench. "This is Drake. Ugly, ain't he?"

Feeling uncomfortable for the boy, I found myself at a loss for words.

"He ain't shit. Meet Angelo."

This boy looked normal, different from all the rest.

"Hi," I said, holding out my hand. He shook it, but held onto it. I instinctively pulled my hand away.

Jackson had a grin on his face. "Ain't he pretty, Angelo? But you ain't gettin' him. I am. Now, Carroll, I want you to meet Skinner." He took me over to another boy. "Ain't he fucked-up lookin'?"

The boy was mongoloid.

"Shake his hand."

I put my hand out to Skinner. "Hi," I said, immediately noticing the boy's foul breath.

"Come here. This is Long-Tongue."

The next boy was a retarded Native American, a small, knock-kneed seven-year-old with crippled legs. His last name was Tenderfoot, but he was nicknamed Long-Tongue for obvious reasons: he continuously licked his lips with an exceptionally long tongue.

I put my hand up to my mouth at the mere sight of the badly deformed boy.

"Cut that shit out!"

Removing my hand, I suddenly felt as if I were going to throw up. "Jackson," I said, "I don't feel good. My stomach hurts."

"Ah, you'll get used to it. Say hello to him."

"Why's he like that?"

"He's a mute. Always does that with his tongue. Cute, ain't he?"

"I . . . I guess. What's 'mute' mean?"

"He's a dummy, dummy. He can't talk and he can't hear."

"Why say hello to him if he can't hear me?"

"No problem. You can do it by kissin' him."

I puked. Vomit gushed from my mouth all over the boy and myself.

Jackson jumped back, mortified by my reaction, and shouted, "What the fuck you doin', asshole?"

I emptied two more heaves. Jackson drop-kicked me. I fell into my puke. Then Jackson picked up one of my feet and began dragging me through my own vomit.

Screaming and crying, I begged him to stop. "I'm sorry, I'm sorry, I'm sorry! I didn't mean to do it!"

Jackson thrashed me about like a human mop while the others encouraged him with idiotic laughter. Then he released my foot and ordered everyone to shut up.

"Get up, Carroll!" Jackson screamed. He disappeared into the hall, then returned with a mop and bucket. "Clean that shit up!" he demanded, shoving the mop handle into my hand and dropping the bucket at my feet.

After a while, Jackson, perturbed with my progress, came running over from his desk. "See that?" he asked, pointing to the dividing lines in the concrete floor. "You're missin' shit. Do it right."

Still standing over me, he watched my every move. I had to barf again, this time covering my mouth, my cheeks swelling like a balloon.

"Swallow it!"

I hesitated. I could hear laughter filtering through the room again.

"I said, swallow it!"

Painfully, I gulped it down.

"Mop it, sissy!"

Again, the room became still as I resumed mopping.

"Now wring it out."

I turned and looked at Jackson. "But . . . but there's no water in there," I said, pointing to the bucket.

"Oh, you want water, do ya?" He ran over and grabbed my arm. "I'll show you what water is," he yelled, jerking me out of the room and into the darkened hallway. "Stay there and don't move." He waved his finger in my face. "If ya do, I'll kick your fuckin' ass. Understand?"

"I . . . I won't move," I told him.

"Better not."

Moments later he returned, holding the nozzle of a fire hose. "Turn it on, Angelo!"

The force of the water hit me in the gut. I fell backwards on my butt, the water pressure sending me down the hall. I pleaded, "I'm sorry, I'm sorry!"

"Okay, shut it off, Angelo!"

Coughing up water, I stumbled to my feet and turned around.

"Turn it back on, Angelo!"

The force of the water slammed into my back, my ears filling with the sounds of kettledrums. Unable to withstand the pressure, the force of the water knocked me off my feet, shoving me into a spin. Around and around I spun like a top.

"Shut it off, Angelo!"

I got up and I entered the room, dripping with water. Everything was eerily quiet, as if nothing had happened.

"Sit over there," ordered Jackson, pointing to the designated seat assigned by Mrs. Steele.

I wiggled into my spot and sat elbow to elbow with everyone else, staring straight ahead with the same mannequin-like precision, soon to learn that nighttime belonged to another world.

CHAPTER FIVE
Where Even the Boogeyman Cried

THAT EVENING, MRS. Steele shouted from the day room staircase, "SHOWER TIME!" The boom of her voice crashed through the basement like an unwanted intruder, not like a gentle instruction that might guide a child and soothe the spirit.

Jackson jumped off the desk and reiterated Mrs. Steele's order, "You heard her. Everybody get 'em off!"

We all stood and began undressing. As I watched others go through the process of disrobing, I began to notice the terrible extent of Jackson's violent rampages. Their naked bodies revealed evidence of stark brutality. Many wore black-and-blue marks like badges of victims, tattoos that never went away. The bruises were the handiwork of Jackson's whimsical, strong-arm bidding that forced the children into absolute submission.

I saw in these boys mutilated torsos of living flesh—anatomy knitted together by crooked spines, seemingly mismatched limbs that looked like spindly stilts attached to stumps of torsos, club feet and joints gnarled like rotten kindling. They were conglomerates of twisted bones that held together a tragic existence—an existence that was clearly no nightmarish dream but a horrific reality, as if God had forgotten to complete each body's basic human form. The children were not His fixer-uppers but unwanted hand-me-downs, sent from God's heavenly place into a hellish reign where their discarded minds and bodies languished in the hands of brutal caretakers. These kids were the lame and the ugly—tossed out by a so-called conscionable, "civilized" society. They were the real Humpty-Dumptys who could not be put back together again, by God or man.

I folded my clothes and stuffed them into the box under my seat. Retrieving my nightgown, I shoved it under my arm and joined in line with the others. The floor felt cold and damp and, like the others, I cupped my hands over my privates. As I stood there, I noticed more dried feces clinging to rear ends, backs, legs, and between toes. Though the basement already smelled bad, it became even worse upon undressing. And so, the room took on the sudden odor of a countryside outhouse. The stench was unbearable.

Each time Jackson passed by, I could feel his eyes cutting into my body as though he were wielding a knife, his stare reminding me of Alvarez's shadowy insult. When I finally made it halfway up the stairway that led to the first floor, I was overcome by the gush of fresh air from the open day room windows. In contrast to the basement below, the air above smelled like a wave of pure oxygen.

From the top landing, a glaring 200-watt light bulb shot onto the boys in front of me, further exposing the jumble of mutant flesh. As I approached the shower room, I saw a short, stubby man whose left cheek was swollen with a wad of chewing tobacco. The man's name was Beany. His bosom bulged with his personal possessions, consisting mostly of packs of cigarettes and saved sandwiches from the mess hall. Beany was from Cedar, and the showering task was his sentence for minor institutional infractions. He was clearly retarded.

In each hand the man clutched large terrycloth rags, which he dunked into the bathwater to scrub each boy standing with arms raised over his head. Beany periodically spat black tobacco juice into the potbelly wooden barrel with soapsuds sliding down its side, then sent the scrubbed-down boy to a shower stall for rinsing.

"Okay, the next six," ordered Jackson, counting aloud as the boys moved forward.

Twelve unsteady legs attached to wobbly torsos climbed the steps, each boy clearly leaning on gaunt dignity and tarnished hope as if, when they reached the top, a better reality might somehow break them out of the straitjacket environment of the basement below.

While in bed that first night, I found myself unable to sleep, tossing and turning, unable to rid myself of the hospital images and what had happened since arriving at Birch. After about three hours, amid snores and mumbled moans of troubled minds, I finally felt sleep ensnaring me in its grip. As I began drifting off, I was suddenly pulled back by the night man's routine count. I opened my eyes and watched the beam of his flashlight rolling over the beds, one by one, the man whispering numbers as he passed each one. It was Mr. Westly.

Mr. Westly was a stocky, large-boned man who always wore a heavy woolen overcoat that slapped his knees when he walked, be it summer, winter, spring, or fall. And while I wondered if he was always cold, one thing was clear: he was a warm and gentle soul. He was nicknamed the "Peppermint Man" because he gave each child two pieces of peppermint upon waking them in the morning. He was not disposed to hurting anyone and was considered by the other kids, except for Jackson, as one of the "nicer" attendants at Birch. Jackson didn't like Mr. Westly because he knew he couldn't get away with anything around the man, particularly abusing the kids. But whenever Mr. Westly was not around or when he finally got off duty, Jackson's ruthless personality would once again emerge.

As Mr. Westly whipped his flashlight about and whispered bed numbers, he finally passed me. When he reached the other end of the dormitory, he stopped at a turnkey station and punched a time clock slung over his shoulder from a wide leather strap. Then he resumed the count on the other side of the dormitory and disappeared into the darkened hallway that joined the two sides of Birch.

Once more unable to sleep, I laid in my bed thinking about my foster parents, trying to figure out what I had done so wrong as to warrant this kind of punishment. Unable to come up with a reasonable explanation, my thoughts landed on my brother. And again, I was unable to forgive myself for withholding what I'd heard from the house window the day Mrs. Johnson came to take him away. That day, long ago, I had sworn to myself to never again betray him and to uphold our Indian blood-brother pact at any cost. Finally, I turned over the cool side of the pillow and coiled myself into a fetal position.

Then, from below my bed, I heard rustling sounds. My eyelids snapped open. I rose up on my elbow to see what was going on. The glaring streetlight, shining through the window, revealed it was Jackson. He had come to collect on his promise.

"Sh-hh," he warned, his black finger held up to his large lips. He lifted my covers and climbed in, whispering, "I've been thinkin' about you all night. I ain't gonna hurt ya. Gimmie a kiss."

"But you're a boy."

"Shut up," he said, pressing his thick lips against mine.

I spat out his kiss and wiped my lips. "I don't like that."

"Sh-hh," he again warned, pulling me under him and kissing me again. "You're the prettiest boy here."

"But—"

"Shut the fuck up. I told you to be quiet. Now lie on your stomach."

"But why?"

"Just do it. You and your fuckin' questions."

"Do I have to?"

"Just do it, goddamn it."

"But I don't wanna."

"See this?" He produced a balled-up fist. "This is what your brother's gonna get if you keep fuckin' with me. I'll kill his ass, mothafucka!"

"Okay, okay. I'll do it," I said, already scared to death of him or, worse, what he might do to my brother. While on my stomach, he pushed his legs between mine, his knees deep into the mattress. From the corner of my eye, I watched him move back until his face reached my rear end.

"What are you gonna do?"

"Sh-hh." He spread the cheeks of my buttocks and spat.

"What was that?"

"Shut up," he whispered, adjusting his penis at my rectum.

Then, without warning, another boy's head popped up from between the beds; it was Angelo.

"Need some help?" asked Angelo.

"Yeah. He's gonna wake up Mr. Westly if I don't get him to shut up."[1]

"What's-his-name's at the day room door peekin' again."

"I know. Fuck that Peepin' Tom. He ain't gonna say shit. Cover his freakin' mouth so Mr. Westly won't hear 'im."

As Angelo raised his arms and wrapped them around my mouth, the man in shadow tiptoed to the foot of my bed and began masturbating.

"Okay," said Angelo. "Punk 'im."

When Jackson thrust his penis into my innocence, I bit into Angelo's arm and then screamed. Mr. Westly, hearing the ruckus, came running, his chair crashing to the floor. As the mystery man's silhouette quickly vanished from the dormitory, Jackson and Angelo dove for the floor and crawled to their beds. Mr. Westly's flashlight sliced through the darkened dormitory in every direction. Twice, he walked up and down the full length of the room, the high beam of his flashlight bouncing from bed to bed. Finding nothing amiss, he retreated into the darkened hallway, where he resumed sleeping with the back legs of his chair leaned against the wall, a newspaper draped over his lap.

About twenty minutes later, Jackson was back, this time without Angelo. I was still trembling and fighting back tears from his first assault.

"P-ss-t, stop cryin' before Mr. Westly hears ya." Jackson climbed into my bed as if he belonged there, shoving me to one side. "I won't hurt ya this time. I promise, okay?"

"But that hurts."

"I said I wouldn't hurt ya this time, didn't I?"

"But I don't like that."

"Turn over on your stomach. I'm only gonna put it between your legs this time."

"Will it hurt?"

"I told ya, no. Roll over."

"You won't hurt my brother?"

"I oughta, after what you did to Angelo. Now turn over."

I rolled onto my belly, my body trembling with fright.

"That's it," said Jackson. "Spread your legs."

"Like this?"

"Yeah, like that."

Jackson straddled me at my ankles, leaned over and spat between my legs, then flopped on top of me, his legs forcing my legs closed around his penis. He began humping me as a dog would a bitch in heat. After he ejaculated, he picked himself up, wiped his penis on the sheets, then leaned over and whispered in my ear, "See? I told ya it wouldn't hurt this time, didn't I?"

"Who was that man at the day room door?"

"Shut up about that. That's for me to know."

"Can I ask you another question?"

"What?"

"Why do you like to do that stuff to me?"

Avoiding an answer, he said, "I get a treat tomorrow. Do you like candy?"

"What kind?"

"Christmas candy. You know, hard candy."

"Okay."

"Keep your trap shut about this, ya hear?" he said sharply, wagging his finger in my face.

"But what about my brother?"

"What about 'im?"

"You won't kill him, will you?"

"Oh, shut up! I gotta go." He slid onto the floor, crawled under the beds, and slithered away into the darkened night.

Unable to sleep, I laid in bed, crying to myself, wishing with every fiber of my being to be out of there—to be home again—to be free and just be a kid. Confused, scared, disgusted, and dueling it out with my masculinity, fear overran my courage; it gripped me in the palm of its hand with a stern warning that telling what happened was not an option.

ENDNOTES FOR CHAPTER FIVE

1. See Appendix A.1/U.S. Department of Justice Investigation of New Lisbon/ 2003 and 2004. "From January 1, 2002 through . . . early May 2002, over a half-dozen New Lisbon staff were caught sleeping while on duty."

   Also see Appendix A.2.2/Employee Sleeping While on Duty/2001. A New Lisbon employee was charged with sleeping while on duty at Dogwood Cottage.

   Also see Appendix A.2.3/Sleeping on the Job; Endangering Residents; Assaulting Resident and Coworker/2001. An employee of New Lisbon's Quince Cottage was accused of leaving his work area and falling asleep while on duty, missing dispensing medications to residents, showing a disregard for residents' needs, and striking a resident in the stomach.

Plate Five
Birch One (right) and Two
1923–1965
The center building, connecting the two sides of Birch,
housed the sewing room and the Steeles' apartment.

CHAPTER SIX
Synthesis of Brotherhood

"YARD TIME!" SHOUTED Mrs. Steele.

Forgetting myself, I snapped to my feet, but quickly sat back down. As I shrank into my seat, Jackson's face focused on me, his expression a perpetual leer. I lowered my eyes as he stared through me, uncertain what to expect from him next.

Jackson, apparently forgiving me, turned to the others.

"You heard her. It's yard time!" He jumped off his desk and corralled all of us into a single-file line around the three walls. Jackson went to the back door and opened it. "Let's go," he ordered.

I followed the boy in front of me out the door, climbing the concrete steps into the harsh sunlight that caused most of us to either squint or cover our eyes with our hands until they adjusted to the brightness.

The backyard was a large square, like a giant sandbox containing tons of white sand, running the entire length of both sides of Birch. The play area had two sets of swings and a row of six see-saws. It bordered a cornfield that ended at a dirt road, which eventually led to the institution's rear entrance and was often used by attendants as a shortcut. A fence ran along the far side of the road, marking New Lisbon's property line and separating us from the woods beyond.

As I roamed the yard that day, it didn't seem as though I were joining the others in their activity; rather, I became a spectator of their "play." And while I didn't have all the words for it then, my instincts told me everything.

I felt the failure of the system in that backyard, seeing the children not playing, but groping about within a meaningless existence. Many seemed to walk aimlessly on falsehoods of hope while others hobbled about on dreamy crutches of anticipation. They were frightened, tragically wrapped in bandages of utter terror and covered with a patchwork of civilized dressings and bureaucratic gauzes—frightened because of an unjust administrative protocol that allowed their restricted lives to deteriorate into a complete subjugation of their human spirit. They were all a goddamn shame.

For them—not for me—my inner childhood sank in sorrow. It was often easy to ignore my own misery with so many victims before me, knowing that the oxygen of human dignity had been sucked from their souls and that I was utterly helpless to do anything about it. Seeing their tragedy plagued my visceral sensitivity, from which there was no escape. That was my cross.

But *they* actually had one advantage I lacked: while their minds could sometimes go in and out of an ignorant and, hence, blissful state—because so many were not right in the head—mine could not. I was cursed with deep feelings no normal boy should ever have to endure. Though young—so young—I had a strong inner sense of justice, of right and wrong. And because I understood all this internally and was able to remain focused on that wrong, I was never self-blaming. I know this is what saved my sanity.

Though growing weary with yearning for my brother, I kept a constant vigil for him. I found my way to a corner along Birch Two's side and sat with my back to the wall, knees curled up against my chest, hoping I might get a glimpse of Bobby. The blazing sun soon sedated me and, before long, I was in a dreamlike state.

Sometime later, a tugging on my pant leg startled me. Groggy and hot, I wiped the sleep drool from my mouth and sweat from my

CHARLES A. CARROLL

forehead and opened my eyes into the blinding sun.

"Hey, Chuckie, wake up! It's me."

Blocking the sun from my eyes, I asked, "Who?"

"It's me. Your brother, dummy."

"Bobby? It's . . . it's really you?"

"Yeah, dummy. Heck, yeah, it's me."

"I've been lookin' all over for you."

"I ain't here because Mrs. Steele sent me to Cedar."

"Cedar! Ain't that the jail?"

"It's a playhouse. It's better than Birch. Cedar ain't shit. Why did that foster mother send you here? I thought they liked you better than me."

"She just did, that's why."

"I never trusted her. She didn't love us, huh, Chuckie?"

"I don't think so."

"Did ya miss me?"

"I sure did," I said, reaching out to hug him.

"No, no, no!" he scolded. "Don't!" He pushed away my outstretched arms.

Befuddled by his reaction, I asked, "But why not? I'm your brother . . . and . . . and I missed you. What's wrong with that?"

"Because somebody might think somethin' nasty, that's why." He turned around to see if anybody was looking.

I fixed a silent stare on him, not understanding the problem. As I studied him, I knew something was different, but I couldn't quite put my finger on it.

"Hey, Chuckie . . . two days before you came, I got mad and busted a chair in the day room. Mrs. Steele sent me to Cedar, but fuck her. She ain't shit."

"Bobby, you curse a lot, and—"

"That ain't shit around here," he interrupted. "Hey, Chuckie, they're gonna let me outta Cedar pretty soon. Then we'll be together."

"You mean back here?"

"I guess so. Hey, Chuckie, I can't stay long. I fuckin' snuck over here to see ya, and I gotta get fuckin' back."

"You shouldn't curse, Bobby."

"So what? We ain't home, ya know?"

Having a relapse of Catholicism, I thought for sure Bobby would be sent straight to hell on the next elevator down.

Afraid for my brother, I asked, "Bobby, if they catch ya here, will ya get in more trouble?"

"Yeah, but fuck 'em. There's a way outta Cedar, but they don't know how. Look over there." He pointed to a man standing at the edge of the yard. "See that guy? I'm his Kid. He's at Cedar too. He helped me break out. Don't worry, we can get back in without anybody seein' us."

"You broke out?"

"Yeah! It ain't shit. It's easy. My Kid's smart."

"Kid? He ain't no little kid."

"In this place, 'Kid' means a good friend. Nobody fucks with him. And nobody fucks with me either—not with him around. He's a bad motherfucker. Look at his muscles." He pointed again in his Kid's direction.

Instead of looking at the man's muscles, I stared into Bobby's eyes, wondering what was so different about him. Bobby caught my quiet stare.

"What's the matter, Chuckie? Why you lookin' at me like that?"

"I'm . . . I don't know, I'm . . . I'm just glad to see you, that's all. But . . . you changed a lot."

"Like how?"

"I don't know . . . just . . . you're just different, that's all, Bobby. Is it really nice at Cedar?"

"Yeah. I told ya, it's a playpen, and I'm the youngest one there. I'm almost ten, ya know."

"I know. How come you're the youngest one over there?"

"Because they didn't have any other place to put me. Mrs. Steele did that. She said I was too much trouble. I'm smart, Chuckie. They think I'm a nut, but I'm smart. I ain't no nut, huh, Chuckie?"

"No, Bobby. You ain't a nut."

A shout from Bobby's friend interrupted us from across the yard. "Come on, honey! We gotta go."

"Honey? He called you *honey*."

"Don't pay that no mind. He was a fighter until he got his brains knocked out. There's another one like him at Cedar. His name's Beany."

"You mean the guy that washes us at night?"

"That's him. He's from Cedar too. But my Kid's bad. Nobody fucks with him."

"What's his name, Bobby?"

"Simpson."

Simpson still stood and waited. He was a light-complexioned, handsome black fellow in his midthirties. His clothes looked like they were ironed onto him, and his hair was combed straight back. He had a thick, broken nose that pushed off to one side and dark eyes deeply set into his head.

"I better go," said Bobby, "before they figure out I'm gone."

"I'm gonna miss you, Bobby. I wish you were here with me."

"Sh-hh! Not so loud. Somebody'll think somethin' bad."

"Bad? Like what?"

"Be quiet. Hey, Chuckie, if I—"

"Bobby, Bobby, there's Jackson!" I warned. "You better hide."

"Fuck him! He ain't gonna do shit, not with my Kid around and—"

"Come on, honey!" interrupted Simpson. "We gotta go!"

"Why's he callin' you honey all the time?"

"Don't pay him no mind."

Bobby scrambled to the corner of the building, then turned and waved, shouting, "Hey, Chuckie, if I can, I'll come and see ya every week 'til I'm out. See ya!"

Moments later, Mrs. Steele's throaty voice rang out from one of the dormitory windows. "Jackson, get 'em inside! Yard time's over!"

CHAPTER SEVEN

Kisses

IN THE BASEMENT, after we all returned to our frozen positions, Jackson said from his desk, "Carroll, you must think I'm a stupid nigger or somethin', huh?"

"You mean me?" I asked, pointing to my chest.

"You heard me. C'mere."

I stood in front of him. "Don't look at me like you don't know what I'm talkin' about. I saw your brother outside. I should tell Mrs. Steele."

"But he'll get in trouble if you do."

"'*But he'll get in trouble if you do*,'" he mimicked in a feminine manner, sliding his hands into my pants and pulling me into his open legs, clasping his hands around the small of my back.

"Forget it. I'm not gonna say nothin'. Look, I got somethin' for ya." He reached into his shirt pocket. "Here, this is for you." His closed fist was outstretched in front of me. "Go on, take it."

"What is it?"

"Just take it . . . go on."

I put my hand out and he dropped four colorful pieces of Christmas hard candy into my hand. "See, I told ya I'd save ya some, didn't I?"

Recalling the promises from the night before, a sharp sting ripped through my sense of morality. I felt my face turning red as I pictured him raping me all over again. When I recognized the lust showing on his face, I said, "But I don't want 'em for that."

The kids behind me began snickering, as if they knew the true significance of the candy offering.

"What do ya mean you don't want 'em? They ain't poison."

Swallowing hard, I stood my ground. "No, I just don't want 'em."

"You stupid mothafucka!" Jackson suddenly leaned back and shoved his foot into my chest. I landed on my back. He hopped off the desk and stood over me, angrily shouting, "For that, I got a big surprise for ya." He turned to the others. "Hey, you guys, want a kiss?"

Laughter, giggles, and kissing sounds instantly filled the room.

"Get up!" Jackson extended his hand.

As I reached for the hand, he flipped it backwards, like one of those "Hit the road, Jack" gestures.

"Fuck you!" he said. "Get the fuck up yourself."

Once back on my feet, he grabbed me by the arm and led me to one of the boys.

"Kiss 'im," he ordered.

"Him?" I asked, suddenly filled with revulsion as the boy extended his arms to me.

"You heard me . . . kiss the mothafucka!" he yelled, shoving me into the boy's arms.

I closed my eyes and forced myself to touch the boy with my lips. After I kissed him, mixed catcalls and howls reverberated through the room. The boiler down the hall belched, as if punctuating the insult.

Next it was Spitty's turn. He was a nine-year-old with a normal-looking face, but he was badly crippled. He cried a lot, often cupping his hands to collect the tears as they dripped from his chin. I hesitated.

"Kiss Spitty, goddamn it!"

Resigned to his treacherous whims, I leaned over and kissed

Spitty. Again, laughter filled the room. As I pulled myself out of Spitty's arms, I slipped and fell to the floor.

"Get up!" ordered Jackson, kicking one of my legs. "I ain't through with you yet."

As soon as I got up, he took me to another boy who was slobbering all over himself. I turned to Jackson, begging that he not make me do it again. My plea for relief was refused.

"Kiss 'im!"

I kissed him.

"Okay, c'mere." He took me over to Angelo. "You owe 'im one. Kiss 'im."

Again, I turned to Jackson, begging him not to make me do it.

"Don't gimmie no shit, I said kiss 'im!" he yelled, shoving me against Angelo.

Angelo took me in his arms, leaned me over, and French-kissed me, as if I were his sweetheart. Spitting out the kiss, I wiped my mouth.

Jackson pulled me out of Angelo's arms, telling him, "Don't get carried away, mothafucka!"

Jackson led me to Long-Tongue. "Kiss 'im!"

"Not him!"

"I said, kiss 'im, goddamn it!" Jackson hollered, pushing me into Long-Tongue's lap. The retarded boy's tongue was hanging over his chin and dripping with saliva.

"No, don't make me, Jackson, please . . . please don't make me, please." I looked up at Jackson, begging.

Jackson grabbed a clump of my hair and shoved my face into Long-Tongue's.

The boy withdrew his tongue back into his mouth, wet his lips, and then kissed me, sending his disgusting tongue deep into my throat. I pulled away, gagging and spitting out his saliva. Everybody roared with laughter. I looked around at the others and then back at Long-Tongue, his face illuminating a silly grin.

The rest of the children continued to egg on Jackson, some begging to be next. Jackson finally led me to a boy nicknamed Football because his head was shaped like one.

"Stand up, Football," ordered Jackson.

As the boy rose to his feet, I turned to Jackson. "Not him too. Please, not him."

Football threw his arms around me and gave me a long kiss, jamming his tongue into my mouth. Repulsed, I pulled away, but my efforts to withdraw from his muscular grip were futile. Jackson pushed me deeper into Football's arms. Football acted on the opportunity and kissed me again, this time really hard, his teeth crushing against my lips and causing my lower lip to bleed. Jackson pulled me out of Football's arms, ordered him to sit down, and led me to the mongoloid boy.

"Stand the fuck up, dummy!" demanded Jackson of the pathetic-looking boy.

The boy hesitated.

"Yes, you. Get up."

The boy stood up, but instead of kissing me, he placed his hand over my bleeding lip and wiped it, his eyes welling with tears. Then he sat down, a tear sliding down his left cheek.

"What the fuck ya call that?" asked Jackson.

The mongoloid boy didn't move. He just stared straight ahead.

"Ah, fuck 'im!" said Jackson, shoving me over to the next boy. "That idiot don't know his ass from a hole in the ground. He's a stupid mothafucka!"

Next, it was Slue-foot, a driveler with stinky breath who walked slightly stooped with one foot dragging behind him. As I stared at him, his blank face turned into a childlike blush, his eyes sparkling with desire.

"Stand up, Slue-foot," ordered Jackson.

The deformed and clumsy boy stood up.

I kissed his slobbering lips and quickly withdrew from the foul odor of his mouth.

"Hey, Sterling," shouted Jackson to a boy across the room. "Want one?"

"Fuckin' ay!" he replied. "But that mothafucka needs to wipe his mouth. I ain't kissin' him after Slue-foot."

"Wipe your mouth and come with me," ordered Jackson, finally putting me in front of Sterling, who was picking his nose with two fingers. Nevertheless, Sterling seemed different. He didn't appear as severely retarded as some of the others. He was a big boy for his barely nine-year-old frame.

"Take your fingers outta your nose and wipe your mouth, mothafucka! Stand up. Think he's cute?" Jackson nodded toward me.

"Yeah," Sterling said happily. "He's . . . he's the best. I like 'regulars.'"

"Kiss 'im, Carroll."

I did as Jackson ordered, withdrawing my lips in absolute disgust. "God, not the tongue again!" I exclaimed in continued disgust.

Clapping and catcalls filled the room. Jackson doubled over and laughed as I stood there spitting the slobber from my mouth. Sterling took his seat and laughed his guts out.

The next boy became giddy when he realized it was his turn, revealing chipped and decaying teeth from a silly, grinning face. But as soon as Jackson ordered me to kiss him, his smile quickly wilted into a red-faced blush. After leaning over and kissing the boy, Elephant was next.

Elephant was an ugly soul. His feet were as big as his head, and he had huge arms, like legs, and large, oversized pink lips. Compelled to obey Jackson, I bent over and kissed him. But when I withdrew from his embrace, Elephant clambered to his feet and surprised me with a powerful punch to my face that bloodied my nose. I went down. Elephant bent over and began punching me again and again without any hint of a conscience. I curled into a ball and covered my face.

"That's enough, Elephant!" Jackson pulled him off me. "Go back to your seat . . . and what the fuck did ya hit 'im for? It was just a kiss, you stupid mothafucka!"

I came out of the curl, pounding my fists on the floor, sobbing and screaming, "Mommy! Mommy! Mommy! I want my mommy!"

"You sissy mothafucka! Shut the fuck—"

"SUPPERTIME!" shouted Mrs. Steele from the day room landing.

"Get up and get in line, Carroll, before you get me in trouble with Mrs. Steele."

We lined up, and the basement became eerily quiet. As I followed the line to the doorway, all that could be heard were the scuffling of shoes on the concrete floor and the crackling of Christmas hard candy underfoot.

Part Two

Indifference . . . is not only a sin, it is a punishment.

Elie Wiesel
Speech on "The Perils of Indifference"
1999

PLATE SIX
BIRCH ONE DORMITORY
C. 1952

CHARLES A. CARROLL (STANDING BY DOORWAY) BEING PUNISHED WHILE MR. STEELE LOOKS ON.
NOTE: TO GIVE THE "RIGHT IMPRESSION," THE BOYS WERE ALWAYS CHANGED
FROM THEIR NIGHTGOWNS TO PAJAMAS BEFORE ANY VISITS BY THE MEDIA.

CHAPTER EIGHT
The New Man

ONE AFTERNOON, ABOUT a year later, I was sitting on a bench outside the sewing room. As punishment for not making my bed correctly, I had to stay with my arms crossed and my back against the wall until suppertime. From my position, I could see Mrs. Steele through the hinged opening of the door, which was slightly ajar; she was darning socks at her sewing machine. Suddenly, the recently installed doorbell at Birch's front door rang. Still unfamiliar with the sound of the bell, Mrs. Steele jerked, throwing both open hands to her chest.

Startled, she said to herself, "Ah, crap! Who could that be?" She abruptly rose to her feet and a dozen or so socks fell from her lap, her chair falling backwards to the floor. She made a mad dash for the front door. Upon passing me, she warned with a thimble-capped finger, "If you move a muscle, I'll boil you in oil."

As soon as she disappeared, I quietly got up, tiptoed to the hall that led to the front door, and peeked.

Mrs. Steele looked through a slit in the small, curtained door window and snarled, "Who are you? You're not supposed to be here without clearance from the Administration Building. What do you want? I'm busy!"

The man mumbled something.

"Louder!" she insisted. "I can't hear you."

"It's me, Melvin."

"Who?"

"Melvin Wheeler. Bill Fein's friend."

"Oh, it's you, Mr. Wheeler," resigned Mrs. Steele, opening the door. "Come in. You caught me off guard. How are you?"

"Fine, Mrs. Steele. I hope I'm not interrupting anything."

"Not at all. I was just darning some socks . . . and forget the 'Mrs. Steele' stuff. Call me Betty. We can discuss matters in my sewing room, but I must tell you, it's a mess. I hope you don't mind."

"I'm not much of a housekeeper myself."

"It isn't that, it's just that I have socks all over the place right now. Sometimes I can hardly keep up with the task. There's a lot of hard play with these kids. They wear everything out fast."

"I see."

"Follow me."

I hightailed it back to my seat.

I figured the tall, handsome man to be in his forties. As they passed by me, he nodded, smiled, and greeted me.

"Hi, son. How are you today?"

"Don't pay him any mind," snapped Mrs. Steele. "That brat is being punished. He'll never learn. What that boy needs is a good sturdy piece of willow taken to his fanny."

"Really?" asked Mr. Wheeler, as they entered the sewing room.

"You bet. Have that seat beside the sewing machine."

I could still see into the room from my place on the bench. As Mr. Wheeler took his seat, Mrs. Steele bent over, her large rear end in his face as she picked up socks that had fallen to the floor. She brought the upset chair upright and sat down, pulling herself into the sewing machine and continuing with her darning through-out the conversation.

"Now then," she said, blood draining from her face, "Billy Fein said you worked up in Alaska. I have a brother up there."

"Yes, I recall him telling me that."

"You were up there a number of years, I heard."

"Ten, to be exact."

"That long? I had no idea. And you worked on a highway?"

"That's right. In fact, I supervised a crew on the Alaska Highway for the Army Corps of Engineers just after the outbreak of the war. And, boy, is it cold country up there, although the locals and the mounted police seemed to like it, and my wife was no different. She loved it up there too. It was 1942 when I started, and I decided to stay after the war, 'til just a few weeks ago."

"Oh, that recently? Do you miss it?"

"Not really. It's good to be back in these parts. Of course, when my wife died, it got me thinking about my mortality, and it was time to return to my roots. I was homesick."

"Was, uh . . . was she ill?"

"Yes. It was cancer."

"I'm sorry."

"I am too. I'm still not over it." He placed his hand over his heart, his face grimacing. "I was with her to the end. I saw her spirit wrench free from her body." Then, pointing a finger at himself, and with a slightly raised voice of conviction, he said, "I'll never forget it."

"I'm sure you won't."

He held up four fingers. "Four days before she died, they had her on life support. Poor thing couldn't breathe on her own. They had a darn tube shoved down her throat for oxygen. And in spite of all her misery and pain, she tapped on the bed railing and motioned for a pencil and paper. I went to the nurses' station to get them, then I placed the pencil in her hand and held the pad up for her. What do you think she scribbled?"

"I haven't the slightest."

"Without looking down, she wrote . . . excuse me, but it breaks me up every time I think about it."

"No, no, no." Mrs. Steele shoved the chair back with her feet, leaning over on the edge of her seat. "I understand."

Collecting himself, he muttered softly, "She wrote, 'I love you.'

Imagine that. And it was the last thing she ever wrote. What do ya think of that?"

"Touching, that's what I think. Very touching, indeed."

"And I still have that note."

"You do?" asked Mrs. Steele, squirming back in her seat, brushing away darning lint from her dress. "What did you do with it?"

"I framed it! It's hanging . . . excuse me." He cleared his throat. "It's . . . it's hanging on my wall over the bed." He was visibly shaken.

"You poor thing," comforted Mrs. Steele, reaching over and tenderly placing her hand on his shoulder. "I can see it hasn't been easy on ya, has it?"

He removed his glasses, his face wrinkled into a near cry. "Christ, I wept like a woman," he said. "Death is a terrible thing for the living. I haven't been the same since."

"I understand perfectly, Melvin."

"Do you? Do you really, Betty?"

"Of course I do, Melvin, of course I do."

"You know, Betty, I've tried getting back to myself, but I guess you never do totally. It's like a futile tug of war with a broken heart."

"It can be that way with great losses," said Mrs. Steele, sympathetically.

"The mourning process . . . it . . . it can't be rushed . . . it has its own schedule. You go with it until it spits you out, treating you more like a used candy wrapper than a hurting human being filled with grief."

"Candy wrapper?" asked Mrs. Steele.

"Yes, it throws you away when it's done with you! I doubt I'll ever be the same. You do know what I mean, don't you, Betty?" he asked, putting his glasses back on.

"I most certainly do."

"I want to say one more thing and then I'll cut all this out."

"Sure, Melvin . . . you just go right ahead."

Pushing his glasses further up the bridge of his nose, he said, tearfully, "I know this going to sound silly, but every morning, and before I go to bed at night, I hug my wife's empty dresses. Does that sound dumb to you?"

"Not at all! I think it's a sweet thing to do. Can I offer you a Kleenex?"

"No, thank you. I'm fine, really." He lifted his glasses and wiped away a tear. "And, Betty," he said softly, leaning over and putting his hand to the side of his mouth. "Frankly, I really don't give a hoot who knows it, because it's the only thing in life that gives me comfort anymore."

"How sad," remarked Mrs. Steele.

"In a way, I guess it is, but that's life, isn't it? One has to go on, right?"

"That's true."

"I'll never stop loving her."

"I can see that. I'm so sorry for your loss. Maybe we should change the subject. I understand you and Billy Fein are the best of friends."

"We are."

"You should know, I don't take nobody unless they're highly recommended. It's my boys. I take good care of them and want to make sure people I recommend for hiring do the same. I love my boys and they love me."

"Yes, ma'am."

"Some applicants try to get one over on me . . . ya know, like slipping through the cracks. But I catch 'em in my net. Nobody puts anything over on me."

"Yes, ma'am."

"They gotta be special. So tell me, were you and Billy child-hood chums?"

"Not quite. Actually, we met in the army."

"That's right, he did tell me that, now that you mention it. My memory isn't as sharp as it used to be, although if ya wanna know the truth, I hate admitting it. It comes with age, they say. Billy told me you're from Pennsauken too."

"That's right. We grew up—"

"What was that?" interrupted Mrs. Steele. "Did you hear that?"

"I didn't hear anything."

"I'll bet that brat's up to something. Be right back."

I immediately sat up and closed my eyes as if not paying them any mind, but I knew Mrs. Steele was at the doorway looking at me. I held my breath and could feel her presence, her daggerlike stare and nasal breathing. I didn't move a muscle.

"Wake up!" she ordered. "No sleeping!"

I squirmed and began breathing again. "I wasn't asleep, Mrs. Steele."

"Don't sass me."

As soon as she returned to the sewing room, I crossed my eyes, raised my thumbs to my ears to bend them forward, and stuck out my tongue at her.

"Now that's a brat for ya," I heard her tell Mr. Wheeler. "His brother's worse. Sorry about that interruption. Now then, where were we?"

"We were talking about Pennsauken."

"Oh, that's right. Go ahead."

"Billy and I grew up there, but our paths never crossed—that is, until we met in the army. He was a good soldier . . . a lieutenant, although I just made sergeant. If you don't mind my asking, it seems very quiet. Where are all the children?"

"They're around."

"I see."

"Billy Fein's been sick a lot lately. He's more off duty than on. That's why I asked him if he knew anyone that could fill in for him. He speaks very well of you, Melvin."

"Thank you, Betty. Nice of you to mention it."

"I'm finding it harder and harder to find anyone to stay. It seems nobody wants the graveyard shift. Would you have any objections to working late at night?"

"Not at all, Betty."

"I have two other men on the graveyard shift right now, Mr. Peak and Mr. Westly. What I need is somebody to take their shift if they're off or out sick. And other cottages may need you sometimes too. What do ya say?"

"Terrific! When would you—"

"Just a minute, I've gotta get this one sock darned before I forget it."

She tramped on the treadle, filling the room with the unpleasant sounds of a worn-out motor. Having seen her sew before, I knew she was zigzagging a running stitch over a sock hole with the confidence of an expert seamstress. Then she switched off the machine.

"There," she said with satisfaction. "That's that. Melvin, you're hired."

"I'm delighted. When would you like me to start?"

"You'll go on salary immediately. Billy Fein was right. You're gonna be fine. Do you have any children, Melvin?"

"Four boys."

"Really? We had four girls . . . you with your boys and me with my girls. How 'bout that! Ya know, Melvin, I've been a mother to these boys for more than . . . Jesus, how many years is it now? Eight? Nine? It's around that. And all during that time, I've grown very close to them. Of course, I'm very proud to say they love me too."

"Billy Fein told me how close you are to the boys."

"He said that about me?"

"He did, really."

"He's a dear."

I was sure Mr. Wheeler was patronizing Mrs. Steele. I figured if they were really good friends, Mr. Fein would have told him what he told Jackson one night, that Mrs. Steele was as batty as a fruitcake and that the board of trustees should can the bitch.

"So you've been here that long?" questioned Mr. Wheeler.

"Yes. My husband retired from the navy ten years ago and . . . wait a minute. It's been, my gosh, about fifteen years now. Anyway, we learned about New Lisbon through a friend. When we checked into being cottage parents, I jumped at the chance. This job helps supplement his retirement and gives me some pin money. Besides, this place gives us good benefits. I wouldn't be here if it weren't for that. In fact, without the benefits, I wouldn't put up with half of these kids. It's not easy handling a hundred or so children."

"I'll bet that can be a chore," remarked Mr. Wheeler.

"I love my boys, though. To be honest with ya, when it comes to the bad ones—ya know, when they really get outta line—I first hand 'em over to my monitors. If that fails, out they go to Cedar. For all I care, they can pull stumps all day."

"So where exactly are all the children?"

"In the basement with my monitor. You'll like Jackson. He's dependable. You can count on him."

"A good kid, is he?"

"You bet. Poor guy, he's had it tough."

"What do you mean?"

"Oh," sighed Mrs. Steele. "When he came to me four years ago, he was a mess. His parents, they said, abandoned him way back. The police found him wandering about in a park. Imagine that."

"Which park was that, Betty?"

"The big one in Mt. Holly. The authorities figured he'd been in that park for a few days with nothing to eat or drink. He was barefoot, for heaven's sake . . . his clothes were tattered, and he soiled his pants. He was malnourished and near death from exposure. It was in the middle of winter."

"How old was he at that time?"

"Three or so. As it turned out, they never could locate his parents, but they did manage to find some uninterested relatives. What a shame! So, after a few years in foster homes, the courts decided to send him to us. It wasn't easy, but he turned out fine. He's a sweet colored boy and he'll do anything for me. Anything. He's a grateful kid. A good kid. And he's good with the boys. He'll be a big help to you, Melvin. Trust me. Come on, I'll show you around . . . oh, wait

. . . it's almost three o'clock. I have a three-thirty appointment. You do plan to live on the grounds, don't you?"

"If there's something available."

"There is, and I'll arrange it. Can you move in right away?"

"No problem. I don't have much. My belongings are pretty meager."

"I'll take care of it."

"Thank you, Betty. You sure do a lot around here."

"A little help is what I need. It's my husband. My Henry's gonna be seventy. He's been so ill. He's upstairs with the flu."

I thought to myself, What a liar! He's a drunk.

"Does he need a doctor?"

"He'll be fine. I often have to do some finagling to shift employees around, but now I have you and that solves everything."

"I'll do my best," reassured Mr. Wheeler.

"Gee, I love that blazer you're wearing. Wool, isn't it?"

"It's gabardine."

"Of course. How could I have missed a firm, durable fabric like that. I like a twill weave. You're a smart dresser. Your attire blends well." Mrs. Steele pulled her attention from the blazer. "Now then, back to business. You'll be working the graveyard shift—unless, of course, I need you to fill in on one of the earlier shifts. For now, you'll be on call."

"That's fine."

"Mr. Peak's on tonight. If he doesn't make it, I'll contact you to fill in. I'll call over to the Administration Building to have your room ready. By the time you get there, they'll tell you which one is available. See Millie at the front desk. Welcome aboard."

"Thank you, Betty."

"I'll tell Millie you're on your way."

"Thanks again."

"Not at all."

As they headed for the front door, the new man turned, smiled, and winked at me. I immediately liked him.

CHAPTER NINE

The Stone Age
of Insanity

"CARROLL, GET UP here, on the double! Jackson, get his ass up here right now! I'm in a hurry! Do ya hear me, Jackson?"

"Yes, Mrs. Steele," shouted Jackson from the basement. "I'm coming!"

Once we reached the top of the steps, she began to scold Jackson, her upper dentures dropping to her lower jaw. Thumbing them into place, she admonished, "Jackson, you know I don't like to be kept waitin'. Here, take this list. Carroll and these other boys are gonna be transferred to Side Two because we're gettin' five new ones from Admissions."

Jackson glanced at the list. "You mean Long-Tongue too, Mrs. Steele? But he ain't even nine yet."

"Never mind that. He's close enough."

"Yes, ma'am," said Jackson, sheepishly.

"That's better. Now, I want all of them ready to go at four o'clock this afternoon. Understood?"

"Yes, ma'am."

"Carroll, you come with me."

Mrs. Steele took me to Birch Two. There, at the top landing that led into the basement, she said, "I would've just sent you over here with the others at four, but I wanted to have a word with you in private." She gave me a serious look and put her finger in my face. "Now listen. You've been here a year already and you should know all the rules. They're no different here than they are on the other side. Rawbone is your monitor at Birch Two. You do whatever he tells ya. Now, the reason I brought you over here is to tell you your brother was released from Cedar today. He's down there. I don't—"

"My brother's here?"

"Yes, he is. And don't interrupt me. When will you learn? Now then, any crap outta you two, I'll send you both to Cedar where you can pull stumps and chop down trees all day. Ya got me, boy?"

"We'll be good, Mrs. Steele, honest. I'll make sure."

"Atta boy," praised Mrs. Steele, reaching down and patting me on the cheek with an air of affection and a smile. "Go on. He's waitin' for ya."

I ran down the basement steps as fast as I could, through the darkened corridor, then to a room where everybody was sitting. Just as I arrived, everybody began singing a song, one that would normally be sung to a girl, only my name was substituted for hers. When they finished, Rawbone ordered them to sing it again.

As I listened, I knew then that no boy should ever be given a name resembling a girl's. And what made it worse, of course, was that we were always addressed by our last names, so I was unable to escape the all-too-often ridicule of catcalls and whistles whenever my name was called out.

The floor plan of Birch Two was an exact copy of Birch One. Like Jackson's desk on the other side, Rawbone's desk was situated against one wall. The other three walls had the same flaking paint and were lined with the same backless benches, with carbon-copy boxes for clothes under each boy's seat. The basement air was no different; it stank down there too. The foul odors filled my nostrils with a familiar stench, one that would now hold a whole new round of spooks and goblins. Identical shadowy drainage pipes leaked at rusted-out elbows. The entire atmosphere all but smothered my love for freedom and sunshine long before I even entered the room.

I looked around for my brother, eventually seeing him in a corner with his feet up on the bench, hugging his bent legs. His face was buried in his knees with his hands up to the sides of his face, deliberately avoiding eye contact with me. He was rocking back and forth, crying.

While I was still at the doorway, Rawbone slid from his desk and came over to me. He wrapped his arms around me and began grinding his hips against mine. I was too afraid to repel him. I just stood there numbly, my arms limp at my sides.

"Come over here with me," ordered Rawbone, breaking his hold and leading me by the arm to his desk, where he proceeded to sit and pull me into his open, dangling legs. The singing stopped. All body movements ceased. All eyes were fixed. Like Jackson, Rawbone had turned his boys into puppetlike dummies, pulling their strings to twitch at will.

"Hey, everybody, ain't he cute?" He suddenly shoved me backwards. No one stirred. "Go sit down over there," he ordered, pointing to an opening between two boys. "Fleming, stand up!"

Eleven-year-old Robert Fleming was severely retarded. His face looked like an overblown balloon. He was thick fingered, flat-footed, pudgy, fat lipped, and growth stunted. His head was larger than normal with flaming, amber eyes. When he spoke, his words were not crisp or deliberate but, rather, slurred and slow in coming.

"Me-ee?" he garbled. "Wh-what me do?" He pointed at his chest.

"You didn't give me your cake last night, that's what! You ate it, mothafucka. Now it's time to pay up. On your feet."

The boy hesitated, his face turning red.

"I said, stand the fuck up!" Rawbone again ordered.

Slowly, the boy rose to his feet, remarking, "I do nothin'."

Rawbone went over to him, spun around, and landed his foot on the side of the boy's head. Fleming fell to the concrete floor, knocking out his front teeth, blood from his mouth puddling on the floor. He didn't move.[1]

"Check that out," boasted Rawbone, pointing down at the boy. "I just knocked that mothafucka out! He's out like a light."

Everybody remained where they were, not budging an inch.

Standing over Fleming, Rawbone raised his foot back and kicked the boy in the ribs. Fleming's thick lips expelled air like a deflating balloon, and after a moment or two, he began to move slightly.

"Get the fuck up!" commanded Rawbone. "Get up, get up, get up! Goddamn it, you just won't mothafuckin' listen." He bent over the boy, grabbed one of his arms, and twisted it like the limb of a downed tree.

CRA-A-A-CK!

The break sounded like a wet towel smacking a concrete wall. Rawbone dropped the boy's fractured arm and walked away, boasting, "That'll teach ya! Next time you'll—"

"TREAT TIME!" shouted Mrs. Steele, her heavy bulk lumbering down the basement steps.

Rawbone sprinted to his desk and sat on it, acting as if nothing was wrong. As soon as Mrs. Steele entered, Rawbone spoke. "Look, Mrs. Steele, as soon as he heard you comin', he got up and tripped over his stupid feet."

"Again?" asked Mrs. Steele, grimacing. "Where'd all that blood come from? Get up, Fleming."[2]

As the battered boy came out of it, Mrs. Steele snarled, "Dammit, when are you gonna learn not to trip over your own feet? Help him up, Rawbone. Better get him to the infirmary."

As Rawbone assisted the boy to his feet, a clear fluid leaked from Fleming's eyes.

Rawbone turned to Mrs. Steele. "Holy cow! I think he broke his arm too!"

"Oh, crap! Not again. Get him outta here. Somebody mop up that mess."

"I'll do it, Mrs. Steele," volunteered Slue-foot, who had been transferred from Birch One a few months earlier.

"Then hop to it."

As Rawbone led Fleming out of the room, Mrs. Steele stopped him.

"Rawbone, come see me when you get back from the infirmary."

"Am I in trouble, Mrs. Steele?"

"No, silly."

"But what about my treat?"

"Never mind that right now. Get Fleming outta here. I'll have your treat for ya when ya get back. Okay, boys, put out your hands." Mrs. Steele opened a large tin of Christmas hard candy, which she always hoarded over the holidays.

ENDNOTES FOR CHAPTER NINE

1. See Appendix A.2.4/Physical Contact Causing Resident's Death; Falsifying Statements/2002. A New Lisbon employee was accused of inappropriate contact with a resident of Birch Cottage, resulting in the resident's death, and then falsifying his statement about the incident.

2. See Appendix B.1/Abuse of Patient Causing Broken Arm; Neglect of Duty/2001. An employee of Trenton Psychiatric Hospital was charged with pushing a patient into a chair, resulting in a fractured arm, and then failing to report the incident or seek medical care for the patient.

CHAPTER TEN

The Lady in the Grey Flannel Suit

IT WAS VISITING day, an event that fell on the last Sunday of every month. Parents came with loving and open arms, often comforting and giving solace. But such consolation gave the children only a short reprieve from their dreary existence; they were soon returned to the blight of New Lisbon's secrecy, cleanups, and cover-ups.

Not all children received visitors. In fact, visiting day for them, and for me, was one of the most dreaded times each month, because it once again confirmed we were unwanted. I, like so many others, never had a visitor.

The preparation process required us to satisfy Mrs. Steele's cleansing obsession. And be mindful, these sessions were not just confined to visiting day. The same performance was repeated for "special guests," particularly state or institutional bureaucrats who might otherwise be scheduled to come through Birch on any given day.

The first phase of preparation began the day before. This entailed scouring the entire inside of the building, especially all areas visible to guests. As we scrubbed, Mrs. Steele often demanded that everything be "fresh looking" or, as she warned, "I'll have all your asses in a sling." We heeded that warning, often scrubbing until our hands became raw from the harsh detergents.

Phase two meant dressing in our best, but not before Mrs. Steele doused us with an aromatic, sweet-smelling concoction she had put together from cloves, water, and dried rosebud petals. That solution filtered out the lie of our usually smelly reality; it was a false mixture that delivered its pretense on a shiny platter.

Phase three was floor buffing, a job that had to be completed only an hour before visitors were due. Our task was to bring a high luster to the day room floors as well as the hallway that joined both cottages. No one was exempt from this process. Of course, Rawbone and Jackson were the ringmasters of the sham, always snapping orders and whipping into submission the spastics, the bowlegged, the cripples, the hunchbacks, the midgets, and those with every mental and physical variable in between.

The monitors first dragged a large box of rags from the sewing room into the day room, dumping the entire contents in the middle of the floor. Every limper, drooler, and hobbler broke from the line along the four walls with the hope of getting the better rags first. We dropped to our fannies and tied them onto our feet, knotting them at the ankles. Then we rag-tied the mouths of the droolers so there would be no evidence of saliva smears after the shining process was completed.

Once everybody was ready, we formed two circles: the outer ring went one way, the inner ring the other way. It was a pathetic procedure that converted all of us into human buffing machines— a pitiful display of crooked legs and shuffling feet tottering about in lopsided circles of mundane despair, going nowhere. The kaleidoscope of madness fit Mrs. Steele's mindset perfectly; we produced her highly polished lie, putting a false shine on sins and masking the systematic destruction of human souls with a sublime outward appearance.

That December day, after the final buffing chore, we were no sooner sent back into the basement to await the visitors than Mrs. Steele's voice alerted us from the top of the day room steps: "I want the Carroll brothers up here this instant! Let's go! Get up here on the double."

"Carroll? A visit?" Rawbone taunted, his attention directed at me. "Who the fuck would visit you? Don't forget me, mothafucka. Bring me somethin' back."

"I will," I said, snapping to my feet. I could hardly believe my ears about having a visitor. Bobby followed me.

We ran down the darkened basement hallway to the steps leading up to the day room. One look at Mrs. Steele and I gasped. She was in her best finery, wearing a gaudy lavender dress that draped to her ankles, with an oversized white corsage attached at the cleavage of her breasts. As she looked down at me, the petals of the large flower brushed her lower chin flab. Her thin lips were accented by ruby red lipstick and her cheeks were dusted with pink rouge, giving life to her otherwise cadaver-like face.

"Dammit, you two! I ain't got all day," she said, tapping the railing with her freshly painted fingernails. "Visitors'll be here soon. Ain't got no time for any crap."

I asked, "We have somebody comin' to see us, Mrs. Steele?"

"You never learn. I ask the questions around here. Get your asses up here," she spouted, the petals of her corsage moving in tandem with her windy mouth. "Go over there and have a seat." She pointed to a table in the day room. "I don't want either of you touchin' the decorations or that Santa Claus in the corner. Is that understood?"

"Yes, ma'am," we said.

"Good. Because if I hear one peep outta either of ya, I'll pull your visit—and I mean it. Is that clear?"

"Yes, ma'am," we both answered.

"Rawbone! Up here on the double!"

Rawbone came running. "Yes, ma'am."

"Go to my sewing room and bring me that box sitting on the floor next to my desk. Be quick about it."

Once we took our seats, Bobby turned to me and whispered, "Who's comin' to see us?"

"I don't know, Bobby. How should I know?"

Mrs. Steele scowled at us. "I told you, not a peep. Now take those toys and scatter them over the floor," she ordered while leaving the room.

"Look, Chuckie, toys."

"I know. What a phony bitch."

"Yeah. Where's the visitors, anyway?"

I looked out the window. "I can see them comin' down the sidewalk now. See them?"

"You're right. They're comin'. Let's go in the back and watch 'em come in the door."

"Good idea. Let's go."

From the back of the room, we watched people pairing off with their loved ones. The last lady who came through the door stopped and began looking at each table. Her eyes finally rested on us.

"Maybe that's our visitor. Do you know her, Chuckie?"

"Nope."

The lady coming toward us was dressed in a grey flannel suit with padded shoulders, and she carried a package under each arm. She looked stuffy and overdressed for the occasion. Her suit was tailored tightly to her body, and she walked with the sophistication of a socialite, her pencil-thin heels tapping every step of the way. She wore a fashionable hat with a veil that fell over her face, the wide brim neatly framing off her heavily painted eyes.

"Well now." The lady pointed at Bobby, her hands in skin-tight gloves. "You must be Lester."

"Lester? No, I'm Bobby."

"Of course. And you must be Allen?"

"No, my name's Chuckie."

"That's funny. That was your father's name."

"It was? I didn't know that."

"Allen's your middle name. And Robert, your middle name's Lester. Are you telling me you two didn't know either?"

"No, we didn't know that," I answered.

"Who are you?" asked Bobby.

"I'm your aunt."

"How do you know us?" asked Bobby.

"Because I'm Josie Shea, your mother's sister."

"You know our mother?" I asked.

She smiled and removed her hat. "Certainly."

"Why didn't she come?" asked Bobby.

"She couldn't. So I came." She unwrapped one of the packages. "Lester, this is yours. It should keep you nice and warm. Do you like it?"

"For me?"

"It's a lovely coat. It's yours. And Allen, here's one for you too." She tore open the second package. "There," she said, holding it up. "Do you like it?"

"I guess it's okay." I sat there looking at the coat, not really liking it as much as my brother's.

Suddenly beside myself, a sense of contempt stirred within me. I raised my eyes to hers and snapped, "We want our mother!"

Leaning back, as if startled by the outburst, she awkwardly softened her rigid frame, leaned slightly forward, and replied with suspicious understanding, "Of course you do. It's just that she . . . well, she just couldn't make it, that's all."

"What?" I said belligerently. "For all of our lives?"

"That's not nice, Allen," she scolded.

"My name's Chuckie, not Allen."

"Be nice, Allen, please. Come on, try them on—both of you. I just know you're going to look cute in them."

We stood, put on the coats, and displayed the fit, while the price tags dangled from the sleeves.

"Mine fits nice," said Bobby. "Can we take 'em off now?"

"Sure Lester, take it off if you like."

"Ma'am," I growled. "The coat is nice and all, but I don't need a coat. I need my mother. We both do."

"Why couldn't she come to see us too?" asked Bobby.

"Maybe next time, boys. You can remove your coat now, Allen, if you want to."

We laid the coats on the table and took our seats.

Bobby leaned over and smelled her tweed coat, then leaned back in his chair and said, "You smell like mothballs."

I kicked Bobby's leg under the table.

"Stop it, Chuckie. Smell her. She smells like mothballs. There ain't nothin' wrong with the truth, is there, Mrs.—what did you say your name was?"

"I'm your aunt, Lester. Just call me Aunt Shea."

"Would you mind calling us by our real names, ma'am?" I asked.

"Mind your manners, Allen," she scolded.

"You smell like mothballs," Bobby repeated.

"I do, don't I, Lester? I should've taken the coat to the cleaners after I removed it from the cedar chest. I didn't have time to do that, so that's why you can smell the mothballs. By the way, I've heard some very nice things about Mrs. Steele. I hear she's wonderful to you boys. It's so nice to know that both of you are so well taken care of. I'm so glad."

Bobby and I looked at each other, knowing what the other was thinking.

At the end of that uncomfortable hour, our aunt asked if she could take some pictures of us, insisting that we wear the new coats for the shots.

"Come on," she said. "We'll go outside. It's cold, but it's a lovely day and perfect for those coats. And the sun's sparkling white."

As we rose to our feet, Bobby asked, "How can a sun be white? The sun's yellow."

"What a lovely boy you are, Lester. You've always been my favorite. Let's go. It won't take but a few minutes." She removed a camera from her oversized alligator purse and led the way.

After taking the snapshots, she escorted us back inside where Mrs. Steele was waiting. We removed our jackets.

"I'll take those," said Mrs. Steele. "Why don't you two boys go back to your seats while I have a little talk with your aunt."

We complied.

They talked while we tried reading their lips from our table. Making nothing out of their words, we turned to talk to each other. About five minutes later, our aunt returned to say goodbye.

We never saw her, or the two coats, ever again.

PLATE SEVEN
CHARLES A. CARROLL (LEFT) AND ROBERT L. CARROLL
C. 1952
WEARING COATS BROUGHT BY THEIR AUNT, JOSEPHINE SHEA

Part Three

You spoke about the masses and their reluctance to become involved with the horrors to people and other creatures. I may have told you that I believe the Lord's great error was creating the human species, a species so capable of such mindless and terrible treatment of Earth and all her creatures.

Stanley I. Alprin, EdD
From a letter to Charles A. Carroll
December 16, 1991

CHAPTER ELEVEN

Dr. Alprin

"RAWBONE!" SHOUTED MRS. Steele from the staircase landing. "I want Carroll's ass up here right away. Do ya hear me?"

"I heard you, Mrs. Steele. I'll be right up."

When we emerged from the basement, Mrs. Steele ordered, "Get him over to Diagnostics. Leave him there with Lady Ann and then get right back here. I'm in no mood for those kids today. I've got a headache."

"Yes, ma'am," answered Rawbone dutifully. "Come on, Carroll, let's go."

"Where are we goin'?"

"To the nut doctors."

"But I'm not nuts."

The Diagnostics Building was just across the street from Birch. It was an unassuming building with no main entrance—unlike the Administration Building and those buildings closest to it, with their grand entrances. We entered from the side and followed a long corridor that eventually led to a reception desk, where an odd-looking lady welcomed us.

"Hi, Rawbone. Is that Charles you have there?"

"Yes, ma'am."

The lady's bright clothing and unusual manner immediately drew my attention, as did the name tag attached to her bright yellow sweater that read: Lady Ann. Her lips were unevenly smeared with bright red lipstick, both painted larger than her lip line. She looked like Bette Davis in *Whatever Happened to Baby Jane?* And, like the pathetic character in the film, the rest of her makeup was flaky and poorly applied. Her smile exhibited smoke-stained teeth.

"Take a seat over there," she directed, pointing a finger that boasted a cheap, oversized ring. "Yes, that bench over there. No, wait . . . better yet, come over next to me. This is where the handsome boys sit."

I cut a half smile.

"Oh, a blusher, huh?" She strained to look at my face, then turned to Rawbone. "Rawbone, you can go now. Oh, and be sure to tell Betty I said to take it easy. I know how hard she works over there. Poor thing. She's got a hard job. It's not easy to manage so many children. Don't forget to tell her now."

"I won't, Lady Ann."

As soon as Rawbone left, Lady Ann turned to me. "So, you're the good-looking boy I've heard so much about."

"Me, ma'am?" I asked, a surprised look on my face.

"Dr. Alprin and I know quite a bit about you. He'll be seeing you before long. Right now, he's busy with another client. As soon as he's finished with him, he'll see you. Okay, handsome?"

Shyly, I answered, "Yes, ma'am."

"Would you like a magazine . . . a book . . . or—"

"A book? You mean a real book?"

"Why, sure, honey. They're over there." She pointed to a table with reading material. "Why do you look so surprised?"

"I didn't know they had books in this place."

"What do you mean?"

"I haven't seen a book since I've been here."

"Are you telling me that Birch has no comic books or magazines or—"

"Nothing like that."

"Well, there's a bunch over there. Pick out what you want and then come back and sit next to me."

"It's . . . it's really okay?"

"Go on. It's okay." She shooed me with the back of her hand.

I went over to the table and stared at the bonanza of reading material. I had difficulty choosing which one to take, but one book in particular caught my eye. It was titled *Somebody Up There Likes Me*.

I returned with the book and took a seat next to Lady Ann, when suddenly her face soured.

"Yikes! That's bitter!" she said, removing a pencil's eraser end from her mouth. "I just had that stupid thing in my ear."

I giggled.

"Oh, laughing at me, are you? I'm about to come around my desk and tickle the daylights out of you."

Laughing hard, I said, "You're a funny lady."

"Go on, laugh at me if you want. I deserve it. And you know what?"

"What?"

Her face lit up with charm. "Gosh, you're a real handsome sweetie, ya know that?"

I turned serious. "I . . . I hate it. I wish I could disappear."

"Disappear. What on earth for?" Her expression revealed puzzlement and concern.

"Because I hate being handsome. I wish I was a scarecrow so everybody would run away."

"You do? But, why in the world would you ever want to be a scarecrow, sweetie?"

"Because . . ."

"What do you mean by that, sweetie?"

"Just because, that's all. I'm gonna read my book now."

Lady Ann exuded sympathy and understanding. "Why . . . why, of course, honey. You . . . you just go right ahead and read to your heart's desire. If you don't want to discuss it, that's your privilege, and I understand. Okay, honey?"

"Yes, ma'am."

I buried my face in the book. As I turned the pages, the words before me began morphing into images from the basement, taking me on a rendezvous with the macabre and filling my head with shrieking murmurs and soured breaths. I tried blocking these disturbing thoughts, but could not.

Internally, I lost my composure. My mind went wild creating abstract adjectives and twisted concepts, etching out dirty rhymes and idiotic sonnets, horrible riddles that invariably threatened my sanity. More and more, I felt like the fractured Humpty-Dumpty whose cracks couldn't be mended and whose broken heart could never again be retrofitted with a prosthesis of normalcy, never again recapture any semblance of what was once my God-given innocence.

I sat there, with the book on my lap, feeling like a thrown-away paper whistle, my hope crowned with a crinkled, pointed hat and my spirit tormented by the gloom of abandonment. And, worst of all, it was my normalcy that was the biggest predator of all.

Suddenly, my thoughts were interrupted.

"Charles . . . Charles . . . Charles, are you all right?"

I jerked out of my trance.

"Boy," said Lady Ann, "were you daydreaming or something? What were you thinking?"

"Terrible things."

"Like what, honey?" She leaned forward with sympathetic eyes.

"Oh, nothing. I'll be all right."

"You were crying."

"I was?" I placed my open hand to my cheek. "I . . . I guess I was." I looked at my hand. It was wet.

"Are you sure you're okay, Charles? The doctor wants to see you now. Are you up to it?"

"Yes, ma'am."

"I'll take you to his office. Come on with me, cutie."

Upon entering the doctor's office, an oak of a man rose to his feet. His hair was thick and wavy, a thatch of black. And, above the knot of his tie, stringy hair curled out of the neck of his shirt. He was well dressed, in good collegiate taste, but not overdone or dramatic.

"Thank you, Lady Ann. I'll call if I need you. Be sure to get the door on your way out."

"Of course, doctor."

"Hi, I'm Dr. Alprin." He extended a large, thick hand. "You must be Charles."

"Yes, sir."

"Why don't you sit here." The doctor directed me to a chair in front of his desk.

Taking his own seat, he asked, "So what do you think of my secretary?"

"She's nice."

"We think so too. Charles . . . you don't mind my addressing you as Charles, do you?"

"I guess it's okay."

"Good. I don't like using last names. I know they do that here, but I'm not in favor of it; it's too impersonal. Now, let's see," he continued, looking down at my chart. "Charles Carroll. That's a nice name."

"I hate it."

"You hate it? Why?"

"Just because."

"I'll bet there's a good reason why you might feel that way. Perhaps you'd like to tell me about it?"

"Just . . . just because, that's all."

"Well, if you decide you want to talk about it, I'm all ears. Fair enough?"

"Yes, sir."

Dr. Alprin, without saying another word, began leafing through a folder. Looking up, he said, "I see that you have a brother . . . Robert, is it?"

"Yes, sir."

"You were both born in 1942, your brother in February and you on November twenty-ninth. Do you know anything about your mother or father?"

"No."

"It says here you were placed in a Catholic orphanage in September 1943, when you were less than a year old. Would you like to talk about that?"

"I hated it there."

"Charles, you can relax with me. There's nothing to fear, and anything you say to me stays in this room." He looked at the papers again. "Now then, after more than two years they were unable to place you with adoptive parents. Do you remember any of that?"

"Some of it."

"They also say that on January 29, 1946, both of you became wards of the state, and the courts ordered that you two were never to be separated. Do you remember that?"

"No."

"Looks like neither of you has had it easy. Would you like to discuss any of that with me?"

I shrugged. "Maybe a little."

"We can put it off if you want."

"No, I guess it's okay."

"You left the orphanage in June of 1946. Do you remember that?"

"Yes."

"Who took you out of there?"

"A state lady. Her name was Miss Bea. She was nice to us. We liked her a lot. I'll always remember Miss Bea. She bought us ice cream, and we laughed a lot."

"I'll tell you what. Why don't you go over to that couch. It'll be more comfortable for you. Then you can tell me all about it."

I went over to the couch and sat on it.

"No, not like that. I'd rather that you lie down."

"But I ain't tired."

"Let's try it. We'll try it that way and see how it goes. Fair enough?"

"Like this?"

"That's it. Now I want you to relax. Let go of your worries. Forget where you are and just go back to that day."

I let out a tormented sigh and began relaxing. "Like this?" I asked.

"Good. That's it. Are you comfortable?"

"Yes, sir. But I feel funny to be lying down when I ain't tired."

"Charles, I'm going to sit just behind you. I'll be right here all the time. Relax. Let go. You're getting tired, very tired. You're getting sleepy. Forget all your worries. Forget all your troubles. That's it. Close your eyes. Picture that day when Miss Bea came to get you and your brother. You're doing fine. You're feeling lighter, relaxed. That's it. Loosen up and let go. Deeper into the past, deeper . . . deeper . . . you're fully relaxed. Where are you, Charles?"

"At St. Walburga. We're leaving."

"What's St. Walburga?"

"The orphanage."

"Tell me about that day when Miss Bea came to get you and your brother. Feel like doing that?"

"Yes, sir."

"Very good. Okay, begin whenever you're ready."

"COME ON BOYS, it's time to go to your new home." Sister Bernadette extended her hands for each of us to take. Following behind us were three duty-bound nuns who were ordered by Mother Superior to wave us off.

Sister Bernadette, a kind and gentle disciple of St. Walburga's, had a fetishlike habit of fiddling with her wedding band, often boasting that she was the bride of God. She could spiel off Bible verses as if she had written them.

Sister Agatha was the meanest member of St. Walburga's Catholic might, an arrogant soul who stood square-shouldered. She could quickly break her piety whenever she whacked the heads, backs, and legs of children with a red yardstick, applying such measures on those she thought worthy of her discipline. We called her Sister Bluebeard.

Sister Peters was short, barely five feet tall. She was the most revered—a kindly woman, but a bit wacky, insisting that "sister shoes" were the best footwear made for the human foot. She was different from the other nuns. Many children loved her because her "sister shoes" stood firmly on a platform of down-to-earth morality. She was mostly kind and never refrained from hugging us, but was also known to occasionally apply "the stick."

Sister Mary Margaret, who wore a pair of square, rimless spectacles that never sat straight on the bridge of her nose, was a fascinating lady. She not only wore gloves at the dinner table but was a divine nut over cleanliness, fastidiously removing specks of imaginary dust from her holy garb.

When we reached the state car, Miss Bea ordered, "Boys, say your goodbyes to the holy sisters."

We turned to the nuns standing at the rear of the car and waved them our goodbyes.

"Robert," said Miss Bea. "You take the back seat. Charles, come up here with me."

"Hey," objected Bobby. "That ain't fair! I wanna be up front too."

"You'll get your turn, honey. Come on, Charles, get in."

We took our places. When Miss Bea turned over the motor, the car backfired, the blast sending a puff of black smoke into the faces of the nuns. They all scurried to the curb, coughing and gasping, their hands waving away the noxious fumes.

Bobby, laughing, said, "Hey, Charles, the car farted in their faces!"

"Robert! Hush!" scolded Miss Bea, quickly getting out of the car to assist the startled nuns. "I'm so sorry, Sisters. Are you all okay?"

"It frightened us!" said Sister Agatha. "That little brat, Robert . . . he was . . . he's laughing at us!"

Bobby, holding his stomach from laughing so much, tried to muffle his hysterics by burying his face into the car seat.

Excusing herself, Miss Bea went to Bobby's open window. "Robert," she scolded. "Please stop laughing!"

"I can't help it, Miss Bea. It was funny," he answered, still shaking with laughter.

Miss Bea turned to the nuns. "Sisters, I should've forewarned you. This car sometimes backfires. Forgive me. I should've asked you to stay on the curb."

"Never mind that now," said Sister Peters. "It wasn't your fault. That boy needs a good lickin'."

"And you, Sister Agatha, is there anything I can do?"

"No, no, Miss Bea, but you can get those kids out of here."

"Sister Agatha's right," agreed Sister Mary Margaret, straightening her spectacles. "We're fine. We've got the Lord with us, you know."

"I know, Sister Mary Margaret. I've heard that when the Lord's with you, who can be against you?"

"Those two boys can," retorted Sister Agatha. "What insolence! It's absolutely intolerable!"

"I'm so sorry, Sister Agatha. I assure you, they won't be of any trouble to you anymore."

"I thought that boy would've learned something by now. It's scandalous, I tell you! Outright scandalous!"

"You're right, Sister Agatha. I understand. Are you sure there's nothing else I can do? Maybe I can—"

"Never mind that," barked Sister Agatha. "We're fine. We're a bit ruffled, but fine. Now, please go."

Miss Bea returned to the car and restarted it, gunned the engine, and sped away.

Bobby and I looked through the back window. The four nuns had already drawn their dainty, white handkerchiefs from their arm slings and were waving them. But before the car disappeared around the first corner, the aging clunker expelled one more burst of anger, all eight cylinders delivering one last blasphemous boom that expressed our sentiments with surprising accuracy.

Once out of sight, Miss Bea eyed Bobby through the rearview mirror, guilt written all over his face.

Miss Bea broke the silence. "That was so funny back there."

"You mean . . . you mean you're not mad?"

"Certainly not, Robert."

"You really mean it?"

"Sure!"

"Gosh, Miss Bea, I like you."

"You do?"

"We sure do, don't we, Charles?"

"Yeah," I said. "You're our best friend."

"I am?"

"We ain't lying," insisted Bobby.

"I know you're not, but don't say 'ain't.' Say instead 'aren't' or 'are not.' There's no such word as 'ain't.'"

"Okay, but I'm still glad we ain't there anymore."

"Well, maybe you've got a point. They can be a bit stuffy at times."

"What's 'stuffy' mean?" I asked.

"It means not being down-to-earth."

"Sister Agatha acts like she's from heaven. What a witch!"

"Now, now, now, that's not nice."

"But, she *is* a witch."

"Hush that kind of talk. Sister Agatha's a good psychologist with excellent credentials. I'll tell you what. I've got an idea."

"Like what?" asked Bobby.

"You'll see. Charles, you're first," she said, pulling over to the side of the road and yanking on the hand brake. Miss Bea turned in her seat and faced me. "So, you two like laughing at nuns, do you? How about some of this?" She wiggled her fingers in my underarms.

"Stop it," I laughed, not really meaning it. "You're tickling me."

Miss Bea stopped and looked at Bobby. "Want some?" she asked, wiggling her fingers in the air.

"Can I?"

"You bet. Come on up here."

Climbing over the seat, Bobby landed between us. The tickling extravaganza sent waves of excitement through our subdued systems. We couldn't remember ever laughing so hard.

After a few moments, she stopped the tickling and asked, "Now, wasn't that fun?"

"It sure was," I replied.

"Well, I had fun too."

"You did, Miss Bea?" asked Bobby. "Do big people have fun?"

"Certainly. What a question! Okay, Robert, back in your seat."

As soon as Bobby returned to his seat, Miss Bea released the brake and sped off.

"Miss Bea, you're a lotta fun."

"So are you, Charles."

"What about me?" asked Bobby.

"You too, Robert."

"At least you ain't like those crab apples, Miss Bea. I hate those nuns."

"Now, now, be nice."

"Miss Bea," I asked, "what's it like to have a mother?"

"It's great, if you're lucky enough to have a good one."

"There's bad ones?"

"Sure."

"Why are they bad?"

"Because some are. Just because God gives a mother a baby doesn't mean she's always qualified to be a good mommy. I run into a lot of bad mothers all the time."

"But why does God give babies to bad mothers?"

"There you go with all those questions again, Charles."

"I'm sorry, Miss Bea . . . Miss Bea, what about your mother? Was she nice?"

"The best!"

"What about fathers? Are there bad ones too?"

"Look, Charles, there's good and bad people in every walk of life. You'll come to understand that when you get a little older."

"Was your father nice?"

"He's in heaven."

"He is?"

"Yes, he died before you two were born. It happened a long time ago when I was nineteen. He had cancer and he was only forty-four."

"Do you miss 'im?" Bobby asked.

"I'll always miss him, Robert. He used to always hold my hand, no matter where we went. My mother wasn't as affectionate, but she was a good person."

"I wish we had a mommy and daddy."

"You're gonna get them today. Hey, you two, I've got another idea. Want some ice cream?"

"Ice cream! You mean it?" we shouted.

"I sure do. We'll stop as soon as we find a place."

"Miss Bea, are you married?"

"My, my, my, you're an inquisitive little boy, aren't you, Charles?"

"That Sister Agatha used to hit me with a long, red ruler when I asked her questions. I hate nuns."

"I don't think they hit you that hard—hey, look, boys! There's an ice cream parlor! Let's go." She turned into the driveway.

"Yippee!" I cheered.

"Ice cream! Yummy!" added Bobby.

"Okay, boys, what kind will it be?"

"I want chocolate, and Bobby wants strawberry."

"Good. Sit tight, and I'll be right back."

Miss Bea returned with three double-dip cones. After we finished the ice cream, Miss Bea looked at her map and read aloud, "Okay, we need to keep heading to Morristown, then take Route 202 north to Pequannock, and . . . ah, yes, that's it! Then to Pompton Plains, and then Pompton Lakes." She folded the map and tucked it into her glove box.

"Miss Bea?"

"What is it, Charles?"

"Thanks for the ice cream."

"You're welcome, Charles. Ready boys?"

"Heck, yeah," answered Bobby.

Miss Bea turned over the engine and sped off. A little while later, she announced, "This is Pompton Lakes. We made it. Now we need to find the street. Just be patient, boys. I know we're going in the right direction. We go down here and turn onto Ringwood Avenue, and then . . . oh, heck, not again. I need to look at that map."

She swerved to the side of the road, retrieved the map, and spread it across the steering wheel, her finger following the lines on the paper. "There," she said, tapping the spot. "That's Sunfair Road. I always get lost when I come this way, but I've got it now."

"How far is it, Miss Bea?"

"It won't be long now," she answered, tossing the map into the glove box.

The mere thought of arriving at our new home invoked a sudden sadness in me. I looked at Bobby, attempting to read what he was thinking too. We frequently communicated this way. Often, when our eyes met, we immediately sensed what the other was thinking, especially when we were restricted from saying anything aloud because someone else was within earshot.

"Why're you cryin', Charles?" he asked.

"Hush, Robert!" interjected Miss Bea. "He's not crying."

"But he is, Miss Bea! Look at his face."

Miss Bea turned to get a better look at me. "You are!" she cried out. "What is it, honey?"

"Maybe they'll be a bad mommy and daddy."

"Oh, honey." She put her arms around me. "Never mind all that."

"Will we ever have to go back to the orphanage, Miss Bea?"

"No, no, no! Not ever again. You two are my miracle boys. Mr. and Mrs. Whipple will adore both of you." My face was buried in her lap, and she rocked me back and forth in her arms. "Go ahead, honey. Have a good cry. It'll make you feel better."

"You crybaby!" barked Bobby.

"Oh hush, Robert. Let your brother be."

"But, Miss Bea, Sister Agatha said it's a sin to cry."

"Baloney! I say it's okay. Go ahead, honey, let it out."

I looked up at Miss Bea and said, "I like you, Miss Bea. Can you be our mother?"

"Do you mean that?"

"We both do," said Bobby.

"What a sweet thing to say. I wish I could. But I'll tell both of you one thing. I'll never let anything bad happen to you boys ever again. Both of you have been through enough. I'll never let you go back to St. Walburga, okay?"

"Yippee!" shouted Bobby. "No more nuts—I mean nuns!"

"Now that was a Freudian slip, Bobby," laughed Miss Bea. "Here, Charles." She reached into her purse. "Dry your eyes, blow your nose, and join in the laughter."

I looked back at my brother and burst out laughing. He was sticking his tongue out at me with crossed eyes. Miss Bea looked at him and began laughing too. Before long, we were all overwhelmed by silliness.

"Hey, look at what you did to me, Charles." Miss Bea pointed to her lap.

Bobby leaned over and looked. "Miss Bea, did you pee?"

"Of course not," bellowed Miss Bea with the delight of good humor. "Your brother's tears did that. Stop acting silly, Robert. Okay,

CHARLES A. CARROLL

you two, here we go." She released the emergency brake and sped off.

"Hey, look!" alerted Bobby. "It's startin' to rain!"

"By golly, it is," said Miss Bea, switching on the windshield wipers.

Within seconds, what had begun as a fine mist turned into a thunderstorm, but it was over as quickly as it had started. Miss Bea switched off the wipers, and I opened my window to have a better look. The air smelled of earth and leafy mulch. The sun stuck its head through the dark cloud high overhead, sending ribbons of magnificent hues up and down the town's grassy slopes. And clear across the sky, there was a brushstroke of a rainbow that delighted us.

The roads meandering through the hills were melting like fairytale chocolate paths, a muddy ooze collecting at the bottom of the surface streets.

When we reached Sunfair Road, Miss Bea made a right turn, crossed a wooden plank bridge, and began the ascent up the muddy road.

"See that house?" she asked, pointing further up the road.

"You mean that green one?" I asked.

"Yes, Charles, that's the one. That's your new home."

That was our signal. I looked back at my brother. This was the moment we'd longed for, and though Bobby's nose was pressed against the window, he felt my stare and turned to look at me. Our eyes registered with each other: it's time.

Because we were never parented, we were already filled with early syndromes of rejection and deep pockets of loneliness. In our bellies, we held a duffel bag of mixed tricks, containing three cases of put-on smiles, six tins of forced giggles, and a stash of reserved manners. This moment meant we had to bury deep inside us our worn-out frowns and pieces of broken hearts, our disappointment over dreams that had never come true. We had to be particularly careful to keep these sad feelings hidden from those who could do us harm, careful to always project the guise of happy little children, like those often depicted in Grandma Moses's paintings.

The cinder-block-and-mortar house was an unassuming, single-story structure set off from the road on a hill and embraced by patches of wilderness. A steep driveway was cut into the hillside and, as soon as Miss Bea turned into it, the wheels began spinning and sinking into the mud, causing the car's back end to swerve. Then the engine quit.

"Ah, shucks!" complained Miss Bea. "It stalled!"

"What now?" asked Bobby.

"We'll try it again, that's what. Ready, boys?"

After several attempts to restart the engine, it finally turned over. The car sputtered and jerked, its back end fishtailing again, the rear tires sinking deeper into the mud. Miss Bea continued to gun the engine. The car bucked violently, sending our heads back and forth. Then the wheels took hold and shot the car forward, only to stall again and come to a dead stop about midway up the driveway.

"Oh, heck! All we need now is to get stuck in the mud. Let's see if it'll start up again."

The car huffed and puffed as the engine attempted to turn over without firing. After a couple more tries, it coughed a cranking sound, then came to life and finally calmed to a stable hum.

"Yippee! You did it!" shouted Bobby.

"Okay, here we go. This time we'll give it the old college try. Hang on, boys."

The car lurched again, refusing Miss Bea's command, its back wheels swerving.

"Keep going, Miss Bea!"

"I'm doing my best, Charles."

"Yeah, Miss Bea!" insisted Bobby. "Don't stop now!"

The car gained traction, its tires sinking and spitting mud, as Miss Bea tightened her hands around the steering wheel with a white-knuckle grip. Then the car shot ahead and leveled off at the top, its front wheels sliding into a concrete tire stop.

"We made it!" shouted Bobby. "Hey, look, a lady's comin'."

"That's Mrs. Whipple. She's your new foster mother."

"CHARLES," WHISPERED DR. Alprin, "let's hold it right there. You're now back in the present. You'll feel completely rested. On the count of three, you'll be fully awake and entirely rested. Ready? One . . . two . . . three. Open your eyes, Charles. How do you feel?"

"Fine."

"You're a very good subject, Charles."

"What's that mean?"

"That you did very well. We'll do it again, if you'd like."

"Yippee! Right now?"

"You're just raring to go, aren't you?" Dr. Alprin chuckled. "I'll have you come back another time. Will that be all right with you?"

"Heck, yeah."

"That's good, but it'll be a while. I have a lot of testing to do, and I'm behind schedule."

"But you won't forget, will you?"

"No. I promise. Next time, if you want, you can tell me about your foster home and what it was like there. Maybe, if there's time, we can also get the IQ test out of the way. Would that be all right with you?"

"What's an IQ test?"

"To see how smart you are."

"I already know I'm smart!"

"I have little doubt about that, Charles. Let's call it a done deal. Come on, I'll have Lady Ann call Mrs. Steele so somebody can escort you back to your cottage."

PLATE EIGHT
BIRCH ONE DAY ROOM
C. 1952

THOMAS J. KELLY, PRESIDENT OF THE NEW JERSEY ASSOCIATION FOR NEW LISBON BOYS, PRESENTING BIRCH ONE BOYS
WITH THEIR FIRST TELEVISION. THIS PHOTO APPEARED IN LOCAL NEWSPAPERS TO PROMOTE NEW LISBON'S IMAGE.
CHARLES CARROLL IS IN THE CENTER OF THE ROOM (INSIDE THE CIRCLE), WITH DARK HAIR, IN A PATTERNED SHIRT.

CHAPTER TWELVE
A Peace Offering
at the Window

ABOUT A WEEK later, I was in the day room taking advantage of our two hours of allowable television time each evening. Television was a new technology in the early fifties. For the kids, it was an effective tranquilizer—a true pacifier—and it gave them all some relief from their hardships. And though many children had, by then, already lost their capacity to dream, television gave so much of it back, allowing them to imagine the unimaginable, to pretend and wonder, to make believe, and, even if only for a moment, to "leave" New Lisbon for an alternate, more peaceful dimension. Television touched them in a divine way, as if the gentle wand of technology had intervened on behalf of their mangled minds and instilled a calm usually uncharacteristic of them.

Television also captured Rawbone's imagination, giving him and us two hours of reprieve from each other, a brief interlude where we were not being strong-armed or hog-tied. Rawbone took the first row on the floor and watched with his nose all but to the screen, sometimes hogging the picture, forcing everyone else to rubberneck around him. When nine o'clock came, the previously switched-off day room lights were snapped back on and, once again, we were faced with the glaring reality of bedtime.

That night, I got bored with whatever program was on and went into the dormitory. There, Bobby stopped me.

"Hey, Chuckie, I was just comin' to get you. Desarino's at that window." He pointed to the window at the far left end of the room. "Go see 'im. Hurry up."

"Who?" I asked.

"Desarino! You know who he is. You told me he brought you to Birch when you first got here. Remember him now?"

"That guy? Yeah, I remember him. What's he want?"

"How should I know, Chuckie? But he's the baddest motherfucker here. Go on, he's waitin' to see ya."

I stood motionless.

"Don't just stand there, dummy. Hurry up. He likes you."

"Okay," I told Bobby. "I'll go see what he wants."

When I reached the open window, an early summer breeze was wafting in and Desarino was perched on an outside ledge, his hands hanging onto the windowsill, exhibiting a flirtatious smile.

"Remember me?" he asked.

"Yeah, I remember you. You're the one that came to get me at the hospital a long time ago, huh?"

"Then you do remember me. Hell, that was more than a year ago. I thought you'd forget all about me." He reached into his pocket. "Here, take these."

I looked down at his open hand. "Raisins! For me? Gosh, we never get those. You really don't mind?"

"I brought 'em for you," he said, still holding them out to me.

"Gee, thanks." I took them from his hand and quickly hid them under the pillow of the bed next to me.

"I think of you all the time."

"How come?" I asked.

"Because you're the prettiest motherfucker here, that's why."

"Pretty? Girls are pretty, not me. I'm a boy."

"Maybe. But that's how I see you. Hey, I want to ask you somethin'. I heard an attendant's gettin' close to you—you know, actin' friendly and all."

"You don't mean Mr. Wheeler?"

"Yeah, that's the guy. What's he up to?"

"What do you mean?"

"He may be all right, but watch out."

"But he likes me, and he's really nice. He spends time with me when he works at Birch. I like him."

"Half the sons of bitches workin' in this place are either scumbags or people that like to mess around with kids. They have a fancy name for guys like that. Peda-somethin' . . . I don't know . . . it's a funny word. All I know is that those bums like little kids. The married ones are the worst. Is that Wheeler guy married?"

"He was, but she died."

"Just watch it, because they look all right on the outside, but inside they're creeps. Just be careful who you trust. There's lots of guys workin' here that are like that. I oughta know, 'cause they tried that shit with me—and I don't just mean here in Birch, but in other cottages where they transferred me."

"Like who?"

"You don't know them. This one guy used to work at Birch when I was around twelve."

"You used to be here?"

"Yep."

"What happened?"

"I caught that creep playin' with my peter."

"You mean your thing?"

"Yeah, while I was sleepin' one night. When I woke up, he took off. I only saw his back, but I knew it was him—it had to be him, because he was the only one on duty that night. But since that night, he quit."

"How come?"

"Because I think he got scared when he figured I knew it was him that night. Now there's one like him workin' at Juniper Cottage, and he was a supervisor at the Administration Building before he went to Juniper. I never imagined he was like that, but he fucked around with me too. And now there's one in Pine Cottage too. I swear this place gives me the creeps."

"Did the guy at Pine Cottage do anything to you?"

"Damn right he did, or at least he tried."

"Like how, Desarino?"

"He's been comin' onto me a long time. Get this—when I take a shower, he's always standin' there waitin' for me to come outta the stall so he can get another look at my dick."

"That ain't anythin', is it?"

"That creep makes me sick. Anyway, I went to the Administration Building and told on him.[1] Guess what they told me?"

"What?"

"They said I was twistin' things around, and he was one of the best attendants they had, and I should have my mouth washed out with soap. They wouldn't believe me. They said I was makin' it up because they heard we didn't get along. That's the shits, if ya ask me."

"They really wouldn't listen to you?"

"Oh, they listened, but that's it. They said I was crazy. They love throwin' around that word. And that stinks."

"You mean they didn't even talk to him about it?"

"Shit no, or at least I don't think so."

"Is there anybody like that, you know, that's still in my cottage?"

"Don't know. What about Mrs. Steele? Is she still up to her old tricks?"

"She ain't never gonna be nice . . . and they call her a cottage mother. I hate her."

"Ya know what, Carroll?"

"What's that?"

"I've been thinkin' a lot about you, but when I heard about this Wheeler guy bein' friendly with you and all, I knew I had to talk to you. But you think he's okay, huh?"

"I know he is. Guess what he said to me once?"

"What did he say?"

"That he liked me more than his own sons."

"He said that?"

"He did! Cross my heart. And he's teachin' me to read better too. He's a really, really nice man. Hey, can I tell you a secret?"

"Sure."

"You won't tell nobody?"

"You can trust me."

"He sneaks me newspapers. When he ain't on duty, he gives them to Mr. Fein to give to me. Nobody knows, so don't say nothin'."

"You mean Mrs. Steele doesn't let ya have books and stuff anymore?"

"Did they use to?"

"Shit, yeah."

"I heard her say we couldn't have 'em because some kids used to stuff 'em in the toilets and clog 'em up."

"You're so cute. Ya know that?"

"You keep sayin' things like that to me. Even when you brought me to Birch, you told me that. I don't like it. I mean, you know, it makes me feel funny."

Desarino's friend called from below.

"What's up, Jacobsen?" he asked, leaning back and looking down. "Is somebody comin'?"

"No, but we better go soon," answered Jacobsen. "The patrol's makin' their rounds. I just saw them pass Pine."

"Keep an eye out."

Desarino turned his attention back to me. "Do ya need anything? I work in the kitchen. I mean, just tell me what you want and I'll get it for you. How 'bout some cake? Want me to bring you some cake the next time I come by to see ya?"

"Cake? Heck, yeah."

"Gosh, you're a pretty motherfucker."

"I wish you wouldn't say that. You talk like I'm a girl or somethin'."

"Don't get mad, okay?"

"I'm not mad. Hey, Desarino, did you really mean that stuff about the attendants and all?"

"Just don't trust any of them. Mr. Peak and Mr. Westly are okay. They're the only good guys around this place. And watch out for Wheeler. Did he really tell you that he liked you more than his own kids?"

"He really did. I swear. But he ain't that way. I just know it."

"Maybe not. Just take my advice and watch out, especially with nice attendants, okay?"

"Okay, I will."

"Hey, I gotta go. Can I ask you a favor before I leave?"

"Like what?"

"Can I," he said softly, "have a little kiss before I go?" His face radiated bolts of desire with a half smile.

"A what?"

"A little kiss, that's all. Just one."

"But that's for girls. I ain't no—"

"Hey, Desarino!" called out his friend. "Come on, man."

"Okay, I'm comin'." He looked back at me. "Hey, Carroll, I love ya anyway. See ya, sweetie. I gotta go," he said, abruptly dropping to the ground.

I stuck my head out the window and watched Desarino fade into the shadows of the night.

When I pulled my head inside, I felt morally challenged, but by this time, my inner moral fiber was wearing thin. The blight of the basement's gloom, the inability to gain legitimate protection, and Rawbone being the equivalent of a brontosaur in a bassinet worked away at the best of me.

Each punch in the face, each kick in the ass, and each rape ate away at me until I began rationalizing a new set of plans to protect myself. Could I sell out the God in me for a wingless angel? One thing I did know unequivocally: if I didn't do something soon to ease the burden of the daily trauma, I would go mad or die.

1. See Appendix D/National Child Abuse Hotlines and Reporting Information by State.

   Also see Appendix F.4/Websites for Child Abuse Awareness and Prevention.

CHAPTER THIRTEEN
Ruby and Dustin

I HAD BEEN at New Lisbon nearly two years and nothing had changed. My nerves were frayed and my confidence had dwindled to mere remnants of my former self.

A couple of months had passed since that disconcerting night with Desarino at the window. We were all in the basement doing Rawbone's bidding when Mrs. Steele shouted from the day room landing.

"Carroll, get up here! I wanna talk to you! You too, Rawbone!"

When we reached the top of the steps, Mrs. Steele snapped at me, "Dr. Alprin wants to see you again. I thought he forgot all about you. Rawbone, I'm sending him over by himself. He knows the way. And there go those kids. Get back down there and quiet them. Tan their hides if they need it. Do it, before I lose my temper and thrash 'em myself."

"Yes, ma'am."

"Carroll, take the day room door. When they're finished with you, get your butt back here. Ya hear?"

"I will, Mrs. Steele."

"Good boy. Now get a move on."

On the way, I wondered why Dr. Alprin hadn't sent for me all summer. I was deeply troubled by the long wait; it seemed like forever. But I had a high regard for this man and I reasoned that I couldn't let my true feelings get in the way, however reserved I might be about him. He was my one solid piece of reality! I needed to be legitimized, declared officially "normal," if there was any chance of getting out of there. And so, my hope was renewed; I was now all but convinced that this just might be the most important day of my life.

When I finally reached the receptionist's desk, Lady Ann greeted me like an old friend. She hadn't changed a bit; she was dressed like a palm reader. Smiling, she displayed her familiar, smoke-stained teeth.

"It's good to see you again, Charles. My, my, you're more handsome than ever. I like the way your hair's combed. Oh, and I think Dr. Alprin's ready to see you. Let me check with him."

Moments later, Lady Ann returned. "He's ready, Charles. Come on, I'll show you in."

As we entered the room, Dr. Alprin greeted me warmly.

"Hi, Charles. Sorry I took so long to see you again. How have you been?"

"Fine, Dr. Alprin."

"Doctor," said Lady Ann, politely excusing herself, "I'll let you two get on with your business. See you later, handsome." She winked one of her long, artificial eyelashes at me.

After she left the room, Dr. Alprin began, "Suppose we just go over to the couch. I'd like you to tell me about your foster mother. Let's start where you left off last time."

"Where's that?"

"When you arrived at the foster home. Are you up to it?"

"Oh, that. If you want me to."

"Good!"

I laid down on the couch and got comfortable, and Dr. Alprin led me into the past.

"Uh-oh," said Bobby. "There she is. I think she's mad."

"Oh nonsense, Robert. Behave yourself," Miss Bea said, rolling down the window and waving. "Hi, Mrs. Whipple. Boy, that was a humdinger of a downpour . . . and your driveway . . . for a minute there, I didn't think I'd make it up all the way to the top. How are you?"

"I'm doin' fine," Mrs. Whipple answered. "Sorry about the driveway. It gets like that every time it rains. My husband's been meaning to pave it. Oh no, it's startin' to drizzle again. I'm goin' inside. Need any help?"

"No, no, you go ahead. My papers flew all over the front seat. I've got to get them together. I'll be there in a second."

The foster mother wore a wrinkled, see-through raincoat around her shoulders and soiled jeans rolled up below her knees. A pair of black-and-white sneakers accented her feet.

"Miss Bea?"

"What is it, Robert?"

"She doesn't look like a foster mommy."

"Oh really, Robert? What's a foster mommy supposed to look like?"

"Like a foster mommy, I guess. What's those papers for, Miss Bea?"

"Mrs. Whipple has to sign them."

"She's mad, ain't she, Miss Bea?" asked Bobby.

"What makes you think that, Robert?"

"I feel it in my bones."

"Your bones?" chuckled Miss Bea. "Now that's a good one. And what would you know about bones?"

"Sister Agatha said that to us all the time, huh, Charles?"

"Yep, she did."

"Oh, so that's where you got it. Now look, you two, it's time to get serious. Mrs. Whipple is a good person, and so's her husband. Give them a chance. Okay?"

"Uh-oh, look!" alerted Bobby. "She's comin' back."

"Hush." Miss Bea turned her attention out the window. "Is something the matter, Mrs. Whipple?"

"Not really, but since it just stopped raining again—"

"By golly, you're right. It did stop," Miss Bea interrupted. "I'm sorry, you were saying?"

"I thought the boys could go to the backyard for a while."

"You mean now?"

"Yes. I just thought a private get-together would give us a chance to work out the details. Would you mind?"

"Sure, not at all. Boys, go to the backyard and play for a bit."

"They can play with our dog, Wiggie."

"Oh, that's right, your dog—and what a sweetie she is. Yes, boys, that's a good idea. Go play in the backyard and meet Wiggie. We'll call for you when we're finished."

We got out of the car and tiptoed through the muddy driveway onto the flagstone pathway that led alongside the house to the backyard. Wiggie was a beautiful collie, greeting us like old friends, her bushy tail wagging like a feather duster. She was attached to a sliding chain strung from the back corner of the house to her doghouse. We knelt on the wet grass, and she lifted her paws onto my shoulders and began licking my face while Bobby hugged and petted her. When we stood up and looked down at her, she rested on her hindquarters, looking back up at us. Her tongue was hanging out of the side of her mouth like a limp rag over a clothesline, saliva dripping from it as she panted. Her eyes begged for more petting.

"She likes us, Bobby."

"I love her. She's nice, Charles."

Mrs. Whipple shouted from one of the rear windows. "Come on inside, boys."

We unleashed Wiggie and came running with the dog at our heels, but just as we were about to turn the front corner of the house, we heard a noise from the driveway. It was an old, rusted Packard sedan, its back wheels spitting and its front bumper hanging and rattling every inch of the way up the rain-stricken, earthy mess. The Packard finally made its way to the top and came to an abrupt halt at the tire stop next to Miss Bea's car.

A man got out of the car and walked toward us. I immediately noticed an off-center pimple near the tip of his nose. He was wearing a New York Yankees baseball cap, red plaid shirt, green khakis, and a pair of thick-soled construction boots.

Mrs. Whipple and Miss Bea exited the house and joined us.

"Hi, Ruby!" greeted the lanky, six-foot man, waving a metal lunch box.

"Hi, honey! You're just in time! They just got here."

"Hello, Miss Bea. Did you have trouble getting up the driveway?"

"I'll say I did! How are you, Mr. Whipple?"

"Fine, Miss Bea, but what's with the two of them?"

"Not now, honey," intervened Mrs. Whipple. "I'll tell you all about it inside. Honey, would you mind taking Wiggie to the back and leashing her for me?"

"Sure, thing. I'll be right in."

Bobby and I made our way into the house.

When Mr. Whipple returned, he placed his lunch pail on the table, went into the living room, and plopped into an easy chair. "God," he complained, letting out a tired breath, "I'm beat."

"Did you have a hard day, honey?"

"I sure did. You know that new boss I told you about? What a creep."

"What did he do now?"

"He thinks he's better than everybody else. What're your names, boys?" he said, addressing us. He removed his shoes and placed his feet on the ottoman.

"This one's Robert," said Miss Bea. "And this one's Charles. Go on, boys, shake Mr. Whipple's hand."

I walked over and extended my hand.

"Hi, Charles. You look like a Chuckie to me. Can I call you Chuckie? It's short for Charles."

"Sure, that's okay."

"Oh, goody!" exclaimed Bobby. "Can I call you Chuckie too?"

"Sure, Bobby," I said.

"Then Chuckie it'll be," bellowed the man, with a hearty voice. He turned to my brother. "How are you, Robert?"

"Okay, sir."

"Sir? First, let's get something straight, boys. Call me Dustin, and call my wife Ruby. Forget all that 'sir' stuff. We got a deal?"

"Yes, sir," I answered.

"And Robert, what about you. Is it a deal?"

"Heck, yeah."

"Charles, Robert," beckoned Miss Bea from the kitchen, "come in here with us."

Dustin looked at Ruby. "So tell me, honey, what's up with the two boys? I thought there was only—"

"Please, dear, I told you, not now. Oh, and you should've seen them with Wiggie. It was like a reunion. They had a terrific time with her."

"Good! Honey, bring me my paper, will you?"

"Sure, honey."

After taking the newspaper to Dustin, Ruby said, "Don't just stand there, boys. Have a seat."

Bobby and I sat across from each other at the kitchen table. Ruby and Miss Bea sat opposite each other.

"I'll bet you two are hungry," Ruby remarked.

"I'm hungry," said Bobby.

"Well, Robert's not bashful. What about you, Charles?"

"A little," I answered shyly.

"I've got just the thing. How about peanut butter and jelly sandwiches to tide you two over 'til supper?"

We stared at her with blank faces, having no idea that she was about to add a great piece of childhood to our memories.

"Honey! You're gonna spoil their supper," offered Dustin from the other room.

"Never mind, honey."

"Mrs. Whipple," interjected Miss Bea, "they've never had them before."

"Did you say *never*?"

"That's right, never."

"Is that right, boys?" asked Dustin, his head cocked around the newspaper.

"That's right, Mr. Whipple. This'll be their first time."

"I don't believe it!" exclaimed Ruby. "I never heard of such a thing. Why, I don't think there's a kid in the world that hasn't had a peanut butter and jelly sandwich by their age. What gives with them, Miss Bea?"

"The nuns say it's too worldly."

"Worldly? If you ask me, somebody's got a screw loose at that orphanage. So, since that's the case, you two are in for the treat of your lives. I wouldn't miss this moment for anything in the world." Ruby pulled a loaf of Bond Bread from a cupboard, along with two plates. From the icebox, she brought out a bottle of whole milk and placed everything on the table in front of us.

Bobby and I looked down at the spread, in awe.

"Mrs. Whipple, you don't lock up the icebox?" I asked.

"Lock the icebox? Why on earth would I do that?"

Miss Bea cut in. "They padlock everything at the orphanage— the icebox, the cupboards, everything."

"But why?" asked Ruby.

"To keep the kids out, I guess."

"Well, there's gonna be none of that here. A locked icebox! Imagine! See these?" Ruby held up two jars from the table. "This one's jelly. And this one's peanut butter. And this is what they look like," she demonstrated, removing the lid from the peanut butter jar and tilting it. "Really funny-looking stuff, huh?"

We giggled.

"And this is jelly. When you put both together . . . oh, forget it. It's time for the taste test. I'm gonna make two sandwiches right now. Then you'll know what the fuss is all about."

We watched her, our faces twisted with curiosity.

"There," she said, sliding two plates in front of us, along with two tall glasses of milk. "Now eat to your heart's content."

All became quiet.

"Well, what's the matter?" asked Ruby.

"Ruby, don't we have to say grace?" I asked.

"Grace? Not over peanut butter and jelly sandwiches. Forget it. Dig in, boys!"

We felt an unfamiliar surge of liberty run through us.

"Go ahead, boys, you're entitled."

Once we started, we ate like gluttons, gobbling down the sandwiches quicker than Ruby could make them. The gourmet extravaganza delighted us—and when it was over, all that was left were two empty jars, a crumpled-up bread wrapper, an empty milk bottle, twenty sticky fingers, and two milk mustaches.

"So, how was it, boys?"

Bobby belched.

Laughter erupted.

"I don't blame you, kid," said Dustin. "I do it all the time!"

"Oh, phooey," said Ruby. "Don't listen to him. He's a big kidder. Did you boys know that the Chinese—or Japanese, I can't remember which—belch out of respect when they eat?"

"They do?" I asked.

"That's right. In their country, it's impolite not to belch at the dinner table."

"That's not what Sister Agatha told us," I said.

"Is she one of the nuns at the orphanage?" asked Ruby.

"Yes, ma'am," I answered. "She hit us if we did that in front of her."

"Forget that place, Charles," said Miss Bea. "That's all behind you now."

"Here, boys," said Ruby, reaching into the sink behind her. "Wipe your hands and faces with this." She handed us a wet towel.

After we finished cleaning up, Ruby asked, "Now, tell me, boys, do you two think you could be happy here?"

Bobby and I glanced at each other.

Bobby finally broke the silence. "Heck, yeah!"

"And what about you, Charles?"

"Y-y-yes, ma'am," I answered emphatically.

Ruby took a deep breath and exhaled it through her nose. Only the ticking of the cuckoo clock could be heard.

"Miss Bea," said Ruby, "I think we need to talk."

"In private or—"

"In private."

"Surely. I'm sorry, boys. Go out and play again," said Miss Bea. "When we're through talking, we'll call you back inside."

While playing in the backyard, Bobby drew my attention to the sounds coming from the house. We were on the embankment closest to the back window.

"Hear that?" he asked.

"What?"

"Somebody's mad. I can tell by the way they're talkin', Chuckie." He paused. "Listen, Chuckie. There they go again."

"Nah, I didn't hear nothin'."

"No, no, listen! Hear them?"

"You're hearin' things. C'mon."

"Okay," agreed Bobby. Then, just as we were about to engage in a game of hide-and-go-seek, he stopped. "See, there they go again. Listen!"

Bobby was right. I could hear them now, because this time somebody was shouting. There was definitely some arguing going on. I turned to Bobby.

"You think it's about us, Bobby?"

"I don't know, but I told you they were fightin'. Wanna move closer?"

"Nah, they might see us."

"You chicken. C'mon."

We moved to the very edge of the embankment.

"Hey, Chuckie, I—"

"Sh-hh! That's Miss Bea. She's mad, I think. Why would she be mad?"

"How would I know, Chuckie?"

"Hey, that's . . . that's our foster mother, but . . . why's she mad too?"

"I don't know. We didn't do nothin' wrong, did we?"

I shrugged my shoulders. "I don't think so."

"Listen, Chuckie, I got an idea."

"Like what?"

"C'mon." Bobby grabbed my arm. "Let's go listen by that window."

"Not me!" I said, pulling back my arm. "We'll get in trouble."

"Let's find out if they're mad at us."

"No," I said. "You do it."

"I'm too big. They won't see you. You're smaller."

"Not me!"

"Want me mad at you?"

"No."

"Well then, go on!"

"Yeah, but—"

"C'mon, don't be chicken."

"But . . . okay, just this time," I said, letting out a frustrated sigh. "But it's all your fault if they catch me."

"That window! It's open."

"Which one?"

"That one there." Bobby pointed to the window from which Ruby had called for us earlier.

"Oh yeah, I see it."

"Go on!"

I slid down the embankment, getting mud all over my new clothes, and slowly inched my way to the back window. About ten feet from the window, I turned and looked up at Bobby. He motioned with his hands to keep going.

Remaining crouched down, I made it to the window. At first, I heard soft murmurs, diffused sentences, and diluted words. But as things heated up, the words distilled to perfect clarity. Too afraid to peek, I sat down with my back to the wall and listened.

"I want a baby, but the doctor says I can't have one. I'm so confused, Miss Bea. I don't wanna be stuck with somebody else's kids, particularly two grown boys."

"Grown boys?" barked Miss Bea. "They're just babies."

"Yeah, but you know what I mean."

"Look, Mrs. Whipple, they need you. They . . . they need someone to love them. Now, we've been through this before."

"I know, but—"

"But what? Do you think I have the heart to take them back to that orphanage after all this? Besides, I wanted to place them before I close up shop. I'm moving out of state."

"Yes, I know. You mentioned moving when we talked on the phone. It's just that I've been unable to get pregnant. That's why I thought having a baby around would, you know, give me some relief. When I came into your office and told you I wanted to adopt somebody's kids, I didn't mean kids this old."

"Yes, but Mrs. Whipple, I distinctly remember telling you their ages and the emotional makeup of those kids at St. Walburga and that love—lots of it—could help them. Remember what you said when I told you all that?"

"What was that?"

"That it didn't make any difference to you."

"Yeah, I guess, but . . . but I thought you people gave away babies, not . . . not just grown kids. That's why I went to your office in the first place. Everybody wants a baby!"

"Their mother didn't!"

Those words left me with a new sense of hopelessness. I felt betrayed, like a piece of unwanted human leftovers. I hugged my bent knees and cried into my hands, knowing my duffel bag of tricks to hide my true feelings was low on fixes.

CHARLES A. CARROLL

"P-ss-t!"

I looked up. Bobby was motioning to me to come and join him, pointing to the driveway. I got out of there as quickly as I could and climbed the embankment.

"What's the matter?" I asked.

"I called ya because somebody's comin'. Look." He pointed to the road.

We watched the car as it passed the house and sped away, up the adjoining hill.

"So, what happened, Chuckie?"

"Nothin'."

"Nothin'? But I saw you cryin'. Did they say somethin' bad about you?"

"I wasn't cryin'. I got somethin' in my eye, that's all. Leave me alone, Bobby."

"What're you mad at me for?"

"Ah, nothin'."

Ruby shouted from the open window. "You can come back inside now, boys!"

We went running. I opened the front door and entered, gingerly approaching Ruby, who was standing in the middle of the kitchen floor waiting to receive us.

"My God, Charles!" she exclaimed. "Look at the mud all over you. What were you doin', rolling in it?"

My eyes welled with tears.

"What . . . what's the matter, Charles? You're crying." She got down on one knee and leveled her eyes to mine. "How come?"

"I ain't cryin'."

"Then what are those?" She extended her hands and wiped the tears from my face. "This has gone far enough. Boys, welcome home."

"CHARLES, ARE YOU all right?" asked Dr. Alprin softly.

PLATE NINE
ROBERT CARROLL WITH WIGGIE
C. 1948
POMPTON LAKES, NEW JERSEY

"I . . . I guess so."

"Here," he said, handing me a tissue. "You're quite a young man. Let's do this. The next time I see you, we'll take up where we left off—that is, if you're up to it."

"You mean . . . you won't mind?"

"Not at all. Feeling a little better now?"

"Yes. Dr. Alprin, is there something wrong with me? I mean, like is there any chance I'm slow? You know, retarded?"

"Retarded? You? Of course not. Let's go see Lady Ann." He led me out of the room with his arm around my shoulders.

CHAPTER FOURTEEN
A Popeye-Bluto Duet

"FIGHT DAY!" YELLED Rawbone.

This was the kind of day one could never forgot. Fight Day was the most gruesome of Rawbone's escapades. It was his most enjoyable pastime, and we were the pawns.

Rawbone pointed to a clumsy-looking fourteen-year-old who sat a few seats from me.

"Hey, Biddle, you're fightin' Bozo."

"Finestein?" shouted Biddle. "I've been waitin' for his ass. Yeah, I'll fight 'im!"

Everyone broke from their ordered, stiffened positions and began stomping, whistling, and clapping. The howl was deafening.

"Sh-hh. Not so loud," warned Rawbone, pointing to the ceiling. "I don't want Mrs. Steele comin' down here!"

The room became silent, Rawbone again taking charge. "Okay," he said. "Get up here, Biddle! You too, Bozo."

Finestein was completely out of Biddle's weight league. His arms were thinner than the tendons of Biddle's neck and he was horribly retarded. But, though thin and seemingly outclassed by his opponent, he had no scruples when scrapping with others and was capable of being dangerous when antagonized.

Finestein was stricken with two noticeable deformities. The first was a bulbous nose the color and size of an apple, blanketed with raw, inflamed pimples; it was a nose that did not graduate into his face but looked as though it had been pasted on—thus the "Bozo" nickname. He also had oversized feet, measuring fourteen inches, making him a clumsy-walking fifteen-year-old.

Biddle was meaty chested and big boned, clearly lacking the frail look of Bozo. But these boys did have one trait in common: both had identical temperaments and were full of contempt for each other. If not refereed, one of them could end up dead. It was a Popeye-Bluto duet that needed careful monitoring—truly a masterpiece in the theater of the absurd set in an arena of madness.

They stood nose to nose, snot spitting from Biddle's angry nostrils and a drizzle of drool hanging from Bozo's mouth, glistening like a cellophane swirl.

"Are you two ready?" asked Rawbone.

"Me ready," replied Bozo.

"And what about you, Biddle?"

"I'm ready to fuck him up."

Rawbone turned to the others. "Okay, you guys, you can loosen up. Just don't be too loud or you'll have Mrs. Steele mad at all of us," he warned, spreading the two boys apart. "Get 'em up."

Biddle raised his fists.

"Higher, Biddle. Yeah, like that. Now go at it, mothafuckas!" he yelled, backing out of the way.

Biddle smashed his fist into Bozo's face. Bozo shrugged off the blow and began jabbing and punching. As the fight progressed, they began channeling their own anger and throwing more violent punches at each other. Before long, it became their fight. Rawbone was getting just what he wanted: a complete transference of personalized anger to a fight that generated its own steam. Now, with both participants sufficiently motivated, Rawbone took his seat on the desk while the others whooped and hollered at the goings-on.

Bozo landed a fine punch to Biddle's jaw that knocked him dizzy. A tooth from Biddle's mouth flew into the air; one of the seated boys caught it and tucked it into his shirt pocket. Like Bozo, Biddle shook it off, and they went at it, each playing his own hand. It was a violent display of guts with a full deck of lunacy, a scrambling frenzy of swinging limbs and pretzel-like configurations of two bent and broken kids.

Biddle's face was cherry red from punches, a nosebleed accenting the hurt, though he didn't falter and bravely kept throwing jabs. But he was weakening and, at one point, he let his tired arms drop to his waist. Bozo saw this opening and landed a fierce uppercut to his chin. Biddle dropped to the floor looking half-dead but, within moments, came out of it. He rolled over and leaned on his elbows. As he started to get up the rest of the way, Bozo snuck a punch with such a force that it knocked Biddle flat. But Biddle wasn't through yet. He got up and returned fire, wildly throwing blows, blood from his nose smeared all over him. Bozo connected a right hook to Biddle's jaw. Biddle again landed on his back and laid motionless. Everybody jeered, showing disappointment, while Rawbone relished every second of the fiasco, jumping off his desk.

"Get up, Biddle, get up!" Rawbone yelled.

Biddle, on his back with his eyes open and fixed, didn't move.

"Get up, Biddle!" Rawbone again ordered. "Don't just lay there, you stupid mothafucka!"

Bozo leaned over Biddle and drew back his fist.

"No, no, Bozo." Rawbone pulled him away by the arm. "Let 'im get up and *then* kick the shit out of 'im. Get up, Biddle!"

Biddle, coming out of it but no doubt delirious, rocked his head back and forth.

"You ain't knocked out. Get up, Biddle, up!"

Biddle, with what little energy he had left, clumsily made it to his feet, mumbling, "That motherfucker sucker-punched me. I'll get 'im this time."

They went back at each other like madmen. Bozo delivered harder punches, Biddle sometimes deflecting them. Biddle, now completely pissed off, socked Bozo in the belly. Bozo fell to his knees, holding his stomach, groaning and mumbling, before finally collapsing on his face.

"Get up!" yelled Rawbone. "Christ, I thought you had this son of a bitch! Get up!"

Everybody was yelling.

"Sh-hh," ordered Rawbone. "Not so loud. If you guys bring Mrs. Steele down here, I'll fuck ya all up. Now, keep it down. Bozo, get up."

All the boys were on the edges of their seats, egging on Bozo to get back up. Bozo finally snapped to his feet and went back at Biddle, who again went down.

Rawbone, still in the middle of the floor, stood over Biddle and shook him. "You ain't out, Biddle. Get the fuck up."

Nearly defeated, Biddle got back up and wildly flailed his arms, his fists hitting nothing and not at all intimidating Bozo. Before Rawbone could stop him, Bozo leaned toward Biddle and smashed his fist into Biddle's skull; it sounded like a shattered gourd, and Biddle collapsed to the floor, out cold. Bozo flopped on top of him, yelling obscenities, punching Biddle's lifeless face until it was bloody red.

"Get up, Biddle," commanded Rawbone, again returning to the center of the room. Bozo moved to stand a foot away, his fists still up and ready to go.

Standing over Biddle, Rawbone began laughing his guts out. "I think this mothafucka's finished."

The room erupted with noise; some were laughing, others yelling and jeering, all finally squealing animal-like cackles and croaks.

One of the boys yelled, "Get the fire hose!"

"That's it," another shouted. "That'll wake Biddle up!"

"Yeah," grumbled another, whose hanging hernia flopped about in his pants like the lazy privates of an old man. "Somebody kick that son of a bitch!"

Yet another urged, "Get up, Biddle. Wake the fuck up!"

Incredibly, Biddle began coming out of his stupor. He slowly leaned on his elbows for some leverage, but while struggling to rise, Bozo bent down and smashed his fists again into Biddle's blood-ied face. Before Rawbone could contain him, Bozo flopped on top of Biddle, opened his mouth, and chomped down on Biddle's ear, tearing it from his skull along with temple skin and a glob of sideburn hair.[1]

Biddle, holding the side of his head, did little to compress the wound, and blood spurted between his fingers. "My ear!" he screamed.

On his haunches, with hair and skin dangling from his lips, Bozo wiggled the fleshy morsel in his mouth, formed his lips into an "O," leaned back, and spat as he threw his body forward. The bloody ear smacked into the concrete wall and bounced off, landing on the toe of a boy's shoe. I gasped in horror, heaving my lunch into my lap.

ENDNOTES FOR CHAPTER FOURTEEN

1. See Appendix A.3.1/Resident Beaten to Death by Roommate/2001. A New Lisbon resident was accused of beating his roommate to death.

   Also see Appendix A.3.2/Resident Strangled in His Bed/2001. A mentally impaired New Lisbon resident was accused of strangling to death a fellow resident.

Part Four

Sacred family! . . . the supposed home of all the virtues where innocent children are tortured into their first falsehoods, where wills are broken by parental tyranny, and self-respect smothered by crowded, jostling egos.

Johan August Strindberg
The Son of a Servant
1886

CHAPTER FIFTEEN
Mr. Wheeler

THE BASEMENT'S HELL continued to assault my senses. I was less inclined to trust, and depression began taking hold. As for the nights, when I wasn't being raped, they were sleepless. All too often, slumber was interrupted by relentless nightmares. I sometimes dreamed that I'd become like the others and would often awaken in sweaty despair, my nightgown soaked and clinging to my trembling body. At other times, I was awakened by my own frightened screams.

I was frustrated over having heard nothing from Dr. Alprin in several months. On top of that, Mr. Wheeler hadn't pulled duty at Birch in a while, and I missed him.

Mr. Wheeler had been continually sharing the Sunday papers with me. Those offerings fueled my intellectual growth. I found that the more I learned, the thirstier I became for more knowledge. The newspaper was the catalyst that eventually allowed me to read well enough to make sense out of life and see the substantial contrast between the outside world and my surroundings. I read everything: the articles, the advertisements, the want ads, and the funnies. Mr. Wheeler, realizing what these contributions meant to me, made sure I got the papers one way or another. Mr. Fein often passed them on to me when Mr. Wheeler had to work other cottages. At first, I stashed the papers beneath Birch, but someone caught on that a kid was getting under the building and they screened shut all the openings. Eventually, that contraband became the playground's graveyard of hidden wisdom; that's where I began digging holes in the sand and burying my loot.

I was determined to see Mr. Wheeler, so I went to Bobby with my plan. But to do this meant "breaking perimeters"—a serious offense.

"Bobby, I need your help."

"Fuck, yeah. I'll help ya, Chuckie. What do ya want me to do?"

"I think I know which room's Mr. Wheeler's."

"How'd ya find out?"

"Remember when you asked me why I was always at the window when everybody else was watchin' TV?"

"Yeah, what about it?"

"That's how I found out where Mr. Wheeler lives. He drove by our cottage last night and I watched him park his car. After he climbed the steps to the second floor, I saw the light come on in one of the windows. It's his room, I'm sure of it."

"You better be. When are ya gonna sneak over there?"

"Tonight."

"But it's snowin' out."

"I don't care. I'm goin'."

"And how are you supposed to do that? You won't have no shoes. You know they lock 'em in the lockers at night so we can't go nowhere."

"Don't worry. I've got that one figured out too."

"You're crazy!"

"Crazy or not, I'm doin' it."

That night, I quietly snuck up behind Bobby while he was watching television and whispered in his ear, "Bobby, I'm goin' now."

Startled, he looked up at me. "Where?"

"Sh-hh," I warned, putting my finger to my lips. "To see Mr. Wheeler. Come on and watch for me. I'll wait for you in the bathroom."

"Okay, I'm comin'."

Once in the bathroom, I explained, "I'm gonna go into to the basement. Just sit at the top step like you want to be by yourself or somethin' like that, and then wait for me to come back. Take this." I handed him a marble.

"What's this for?"

"When I get back, I'll knock at the door . . . not loud, so you'll have to listen for me. When you hear me, drop the marble down the steps. That'll let me know it's okay to open the door and come up. Got that?"

"I'm scared."

"Don't be. I'm the one who should be scared, but I'm not."

"You should be, Chuckie. If they catch you, you know what might happen to you?"

"I can guess."

"If you get caught, maybe they'll kill you."

"I don't give a shit anymore."

"You ain't really goin' over there in all that snow, are ya?"

"Hell, yeah."

"But it's freezin' out there."

"I know, I know."

"Okay, then, I'm with ya, Chuckie."

Once Bobby got over the fear of my getting caught, his eyes lit up with intrigue. For Bobby, it was more of a game, like beating the system and getting away with something. He was daring that way. But my reasons were different. My love-starved soul needed Mr. Wheeler.

"Okay, let's go, Bobby."

Our eyes met in silence. Like so many times in the past, we were locked into our mutual thoughts.

Bobby broke the stare. "Okay, Chuckie, let's do it."

"Thanks, Bobby. I love you for this."

"Sh-hh, not so loud, Chuckie. Want somebody to think somethin' bad?"

"Fuck all that, Bobby. Christ, I'm your brother!"

"I know, but—"

"Ah, forget it. Check to see if anybody's comin', okay?"

My brother stuck his head out the open door of the bathroom and checked both ways. "Nobody's comin'. Let's go, Chuckie."

At the top of the staircase leading to the basement, Bobby's eyes suddenly began to pool.

"Don't worry, I'll be all right."

"Come back soon."

"I will. See ya."

I tiptoed down the steps, opened the door, and walked on.

Upon entering the darkened basement, I instantly felt the bristles of a harsh brushstroke of black-and-blue memories. The ice-cold hallway shouted sinister vulgarisms. I made my way down the dank, concrete tunnel, passing the huge boiler, its flickering glow revealing a wide-open mouth of burning embers. Above it were spiders that crept and crawled up and down translucent strands of sticky spittle.

I turned away and continued through lazy puddles of water from the constantly leaking pipe joints, each step splashing my bare feet, ankles, and shins. Overhead were the all-too-familiar clanging pipes, once again playing an eerie percussion from their heated breaths, vocalizing an off-key jingle as the steam trickled into old-fashioned radiators that hiccupped and belched their dance of warmth.

I stopped at the threshold of the basement room, trying to shake off reminders of chronic boredom and years of blood, turmoil, and tears.

I dressed quickly. Since I couldn't get to my shoes, I grabbed a number of shirts from other boys' boxes and wrapped my feet, tying the arms of each shirt around my ankles. I made my way to the outside door and opened it. Snow flurries and cold air blanketed me as I stepped over the threshold. I climbed the dozen or so steps that led to ground level, and there I crouched and looked both ways.

Confident no one was around, I plowed through the snow and made my way to a tree that stood guard over the front door of the

Diagnostics Building. I hid. Looking in all directions, I headed for the trash cans beside the building. Just as I reached them, the corner of my eye caught the flashing glow of headlights in the distance; it was the patrol guards making their rounds. I ducked behind the rubbish cans and laid flat on my stomach. By the time the guards made it to the building, my back was covered with snow. As they parked, their high beams cut a hollow tube of light through the flurries in my direction. Then a patrolman got out of the passenger side of the car, while his partner remained at the wheel, and whipped his eight-cell flashlight as he headed for the key station on the wall in front of me. I remained motionless.

CLICK! CLICK!

With the time clock punched, the man meandered down the walkway to the waiting car and got in. When they took off, I stood for a moment, watching the back end of the car's lights finally diminish into a blurred haze. I continued across the grounds toward the staff housing where Mr. Wheeler lived. Almost there, I headed straight for a huge oak tree, dormant for the winter; it looked like a chiseled snow sculpture, its limbs layered with rippling ice. With only a few yards to go, I hightailed it to the base of the apartment building and eased my way below the second-floor window that I believed was Mr. Wheeler's.

The temperatures were in the low twenties, and I was shivering so hard that it became painful. My feet were freezing from the wet snow. I clumsily rolled up a snowball, took aim, and heaved it at the window. It missed, hitting the brick wall with a splat. Painfully, I balled up another one and again missed. But on the third try, I finally struck my target, penetrating the rusted-out screen. Watching the broken snowball slide down the windowpane, I saw a blurred silhouette come to the window and raise the shade.

The shadowy figure opened the window and looked out, shouting, "Hey, you! What are you doing throwing snowballs at my window! Who are you, anyway?"

Unsure it was Mr. Wheeler, I ducked under the nearby steps

that led to the building's entrance.

The man had now come down to the door and stood at the top of the steps. "Okay, you boys, I know you're there. Come on out." Recognizing Mr. Wheeler's voice, I stepped out from underneath the stairway and showed myself.

"Who are you, boy?"

I stared up at him from the dark, snowflakes falling into my eyes.

"Come up here, young fella. Come on. It's okay, I won't hurt ya."

I broke my stare and started making my way up the steps.

Pulling his collar up around his neck, he asked, "What's the big idea? You could've broken my window. Hey, wait a minute. Is that you, Charley?"

"It's me, Mr. Wheeler, it's me. Please don't be mad."

"Never you mind about that," he said, laughing. "You're quite a comic. I never had a snowman come visit me before. Christ, Charley!" His voice became serious. "What're you trying to do, catch your death of cold? And what in the heck are those?" He roared with laughter, pointing down at my feet. "By golly, you're something. Come on, I better get you inside. You need to get warmed up."

Once inside, he brushed snow from my head. "So what brings you to these parts, kiddo?"

"I wanted to see you."

"I got ya, son, but I'm a bit concerned. You snuck over here, didn't you?"

"Nobody saw me."

"I sure hope not. And how do you propose to explain being gone?"

"They won't know. There's a new man on, and he doesn't know who's who yet. Plus, I got my brother watching for me."

"Christ, you're shivering. Come here beside the radiator. It's nice and hot. You really took a chance coming here, you know that?"

CHARLES A. CARROLL

"I know, but you won't tell on me, will you?"

"Of course not. I'll think of a way to get you back, but meanwhile, you're not leaving until you get properly warmed up. I got an idea. Come over here and sit down." He pointed to the edge of the bed. "Let's get those things off your feet. I bet they're cold."

"I'm freezing."

"I can see that. Here, let me help you with those," he said, dropping to his knees.

As Mr. Wheeler unknotted the shirts from my feet, I looked around. The room was simply furnished—a bed, a nightstand, a lamp with a water-stained shade, and a small, oval, hooked carpet that covered the floor beside the bed. There were no knickknacks or creative touches, and certainly no frills.

"Mr. Wheeler, are you mad at me?"

"Me? No. Look at you with your rosy cheeks and frosty red nose. Why don't you go back over there and warm your hands while I fill a basin with some warm water. I've got one under my bed. You just stay put."

"Golly, Mr. Wheeler, I missed you a lot."

"And I missed you too." He retrieved the basin from under the bed and turned to me. "My God, boy, you could've frozen to death out there! But I gotta hand it to you. You've got guts."

"Mr. Wheeler, what kind of music is that you have on the radio?"

"If it bothers you, I'll shut it off."

"No, no, don't do that. I like it."

"You do?"

"What kind of music is it, Mr. Wheeler?"

"It's classical music. That's Rachmaninoff's Symphony no. 2. They're playing the third movement, the Adagio. This is one of his most captivating parts of the entire piece. It's really calm, like it's constantly searching for light."

"Gosh, Mr. Wheeler, it is?"

"Yep. Does it fill you with a sense of joy? Does it enrapture you?"

"You say a lotta funny words, Mr. Wheeler."

"You think so, do you? You know, it's rare for a boy your age to like that kind of music. How's it make you feel?"

"Good."

"Does it talk to you?"

"That's it, that's it! That's what it does! It talks to me. Gosh, listen to that part . . . that's really something."

"That's where it's searching for light. Pretty, isn't it?"

"It is! It touches me here," I said, pointing both hands at my heart.

"That's because music's the language of the heart. It carries messages and embraces the soul. It has a unique way of plucking heartstrings."

"Gosh, the way you say words."

"They come from the heart too, son."

"I'd like to talk that way someday."

"I have a hunch you will. There's something special about you, son," he said, setting the basin on the bed. "Let's get a blanket around you." He reached for the army blanket covering the bed and placed it around my shoulders. "This'll help warm you up. There, is that better?"

"Thanks. I'm still freezing."

"You'll warm up soon. You just stand there, get warm, and enjoy the music while I fill the washbasin with hot water."

After filling the basin halfway, he returned to the end of the bed and placed it on the floor.

"There now, come over here and put your feet into that, son."

I placed my feet into the warm water.

"Mr. Wheeler?"

"What is it, son?"

I smiled. "I like it when you call me son."

He sat beside me and put a comforting arm around my shoulders. "Tell me, Charley, what were your foster parents like?"

My smile quickly faded. "I don't know." I turned away from him. "My foster mother hated Bobby."

"Did she, now? Why was that?"

RUBY WAS A simple woman requiring few creature comforts, but also a woman who was highly principled, much of her morality based on her mother's interpretation of the Catholic Church's idea of virtue. She was thrifty, pulling the economic strings of the household, a result of living through the economic hardships brought on by the 1929 stock market crash.

As a means of holding expenditures down, she kept a flock of chickens in the backyard. The chickens provided meat and an ample supply of eggs, and she turned the pretty-patterned chicken feedbags into a wardrobe of dresses and blouses. She stitched the bright-colored cotton fabrics on a treadle sewing machine after carefully cutting from paper patterns. When she finished an article of clothing—be it a blouse, dress, or skirt—she would slip into it minutes before her husband came home to show it off, never forgetting a dab or two of her favorite perfume, which she obtained from the neighborhood Fuller Brush man.

Ruby was industrious and liked working in the backyard garden. She had a small area of ground that she tilled to perfection. She could often be seen weeding between crops, pruning her garden delights, and, every so often, turning the mulch bed.

The garden provided the most delectable homegrown vegetables throughout the summer months. What she prided most were her blueberries. She would carefully cultivate them until they were nearly as large as a dime and bursting with succulent flavor, often adding them to our breakfast cereal. In addition, she was an avid canner and stocked the pantry shelves for the winter months.

Ruby was domestically proficient, but shared few of her activities with my brother and me. Everything was out of bounds: the garden, the chicken coop, and any other projects that fancied her interest. We were to be seen and not heard.

Ruby was a homebody, and her privacy was of foremost importance. We were warned to never discuss the goings-on in the home with outsiders. If she found out that we told a soul anything whatsoever, we were assured a belt whipping by Dustin, which was always at the behest of Ruby.

Dustin was different. He could be found tinkering in the backyard shed, forever adjusting, aligning, restoring, and improving an iron, lawnmower, or any other broken treasure for people who couldn't do it for themselves. He never charged for his labor, but gladly accepted monetary appreciation when offered. Dustin was the "fix-it" man of the neighborhood, and his unselfish nobility and willingness to help attracted the neighbors to him like a magnet. He was considered by all to be the friendliest guy around.

Ruby and Dustin, however, had something uniquely in common: neither wanted us to join their homespun interests, which pushed us further into the playground of our minds. We often watched, wishing we could be a part of the projects, wanting their respect and hoping we would one day feel a camaraderie. But their world and ours were two hemispheres, set apart; familial companionship only existed in our wishful dreams and inner yearnings. Thus, our psyche of displacement was assured.

During our second year with the Whipples, Bobby was enrolled in parochial school, and Ruby brought me along on his first day. Bobby reacted violently when he saw a nun standing at the top of the school steps with extended arms to welcome him. For Bobby, it was like being led into hell. He wanted nothing to do with the rosary-bead coddlers.

"No, Mommy, I ain't goin'!"

"Let's go!" Ruby said, grabbing him by the seat of the pants and lifting him up the steps the rest of the way.

Throughout Bobby's time at St. Christopher, Ruby would get periodic calls from the school that he was misbehaving and interrupting the teaching process. Bobby's ill-suited placement, however well meaning, caused him to become more defiant and withdrawn, driving him deeper into our mutual world of isolation. He began finding that negative attention was better than no attention at all, his defiance a means of groping his way out of the darkness of parental abandonment. It was also a means of eluding the ghostly figures haunting him from the Catholic orphanage and escaping the stale, starchy, and cold academic air of parochial school. Bobby may have incited cheers from his classmates, but it turned the nuns against him.

To further exacerbate the problem, he would stick frogs in teachers' desks, break points off freshly sharpened pencils, or bring garter snakes to school hidden in his Flash Gordon lunch pail, letting them out in either the auditorium or the girl's bathroom. He also pulled thumbtack stunts and went on spitballing sprees. On a number of occasions, he even managed to Scotch tape bad words on the backs of some of the nuns. And he only seemed to get worse as time went on.

One day during Bobby's second year at St. Christopher, the school called Ruby yet again. The principal, Sister Mary Rose, needed a word with her, and this time it sounded more serious than usual. Ruby stopped at Dustin's work to bring him along. When they arrived, Bobby was in the principal's office, sitting in a chair facing the corner. By that time, I was also enrolled and had been brought to the office and ordered to take a seat next to Sister Christina, Bobby's homeroom teacher. Bobby turned his head and looked at me. He had the expression of a shameful kid; tears were dribbling down his cheeks.

Sister Christina, annoyed with Bobby's sobbing, went over to him and scolded, "Turn around and get your nose back in that corner."

Ruby greeted the principal. "Hello, Sister. Remember me?"

"Of course I do, Mrs. Whipple," said Sister Mary Rose. "How could I forget your wonderful spoon bread?"

"Look, here's some more. I just happened to make some before

Sister Christina called me this morning."

"How thoughtful. I'm sure I'll enjoy it. Please have a seat, Mr. and Mrs. Whipple."

"No, thank you. I prefer standing," Dustin retorted.

"Suit yourself," she replied, and then turned to Ruby.

"So what's this all about?" asked Ruby, forcing a smile through her anger.

"It's your son, again, Mrs. Whipple." She nodded at Bobby.

Bobby turned and looked at Ruby.

"You keep your head in that corner!" barked Sister Christina.

"Mrs. Whipple, I think Robert's homeroom teacher should tell you what happened. Sister Christina, tell them."

Ruby turned to Sister Christina.

"Do forgive me for not telling you all about it over the phone. I thought it fitting that you come here. What your son did was most despicable. I'm sorry to tell you this, but he took down his pants and, with his free hand, shook his . . . you know what."

"He didn't!"

"He did!"

Dustin laughed, slapping his knee and flashing a bright smile at Bobby.

Sister Christina snapped around and looked at the man, her features twisted into a maddening sneer. The principal's face went bloodless. On the wall behind her, a crucifix all but turned upside down.

Ruby jumped up out of her chair, grabbed Bobby by the wrist, and pulled him out of his seat. "Honey, gimmie your belt."

"Ruby!" protested Dustin.

Red faced and puffed with anger, Ruby pulled down Bobby's pants, threw him over her knee, and whacked his hide with her bare hand.

Bobby screamed and repeated the words, "I won't do it no more! I won't do it! I promise!"

Finished with him, Ruby scolded, "That'll teach ya. Now pull up your pants and don't ever, *ever* do somethin' like that again!"

Bobby, sliding his red bottom into his pants, said, "That didn't hurt."

"Oh, no, but it will when you get home, and if I have anything to do with it, you'll be goin' back to the orphanage for good! Now sit down."

"Orphanage?" cried Sister Mary Rose. She stood, her rosary beads rattling against the desk, her eyebrows raised, her lips sucked into a rosette.

All eyes landed on Ruby. Squirming, as if collecting her thoughts, she responded, "Can we have a private moment? Perhaps we could have Robert and Charles go into the other room."

"The hall. They can go out there."

As I stood, Bobby shoved his chair out of the corner and joined me. Ruby, pointing to the door, sternly warned, "And the two of you better behave out there."

Once outside the office, I checked to be sure no one was roaming the halls. Then I pulled out my Superman comic book and laid on my stomach, pretending to read as I kept my ear to the door's threshold.

"Now then, what's this orphanage business all about, Mrs. Whipple? I thought they were your children."

"Sister, it's true, they were in an orphanage. We're not their real parents. They're wards of the state and we're just fostering them. We got 'em a couple years ago."

"Both of them?"

"Yes."

"Then you mean to adopt them?"

"No, not as long as there's still a chance for a child of my own."

"I see. How are the prospects?"

"'Better' is what the doctor said."

"God will give you one in good time. Now tell me, what about the orphanage? It was Catholic, I hope."

"Yes. They were at St. Walburga."

"St. Walburga! They're in this diocese."

"The thing is, I'm not sure about Robert. I never dreamed he'd be such a problem."

"Why didn't you tell us about St. Walburga when you enrolled the boys?"

"We do have a right to our privacy, don't we?"

"Mrs. Whipple, you weren't protecting the children's privacy. We should've been informed. That information shines a whole different light on Robert. What about Charles? Has he been a problem at home?"

"Yes."

"Ruby, stop it!" interrupted Dustin. "I think he's been a good kid."

"Okay, okay, I'll put it another way. He's better behaved than his brother."

"Let me tell you something, Mrs. Whipple," the principal continued. "Kids under similar circumstances, who don't have their own parents, usually suffer some emotional harm. They require a bit more patience at home. Had we known all this before, much of this could've been prevented. That information would've given us a better perspective on Robert. You weren't being fair to him by not telling us everything. Mrs. Whipple, have you ever heard of Johan August Strindberg?"

"No, I don't think so. Who's he?"

"A fine writer who wrote something back in the 1800s called *The Son of a Servant*."[1]

"That long ago? What did he say?"

"He said that children can have difficulties when they don't have good parents, and that bad parenting causes misbehavior."

"So, what's that have to do with me?"

"Think about it, Mrs. Whipple. Think about how you treat Robert and Charles. A little thought on the subject might improve the behavior of your foster children. Meanwhile," she continued, letting out a tired breath, "knowing what I've learned today about your reluctance to tell me pertinent details pretty much explains why Robert is the way he is. May I ask you, when Robert was at St. Walburga, did his current behavior surface then?"

"No, not that I know of."

"That's what I thought. Mrs. Whipple, that boy's been hurt!"

"Hurt? But Sister, we've been model foster parents to both those boys."

"A certain kind of behavior just doesn't appear out of nowhere. It's caused by something."

"Well, it's got nothing to do with our handling of him. Frankly, I suspect something's mentally wrong with him."

"Mental?" countered Sister Mary Rose. "Not on your life. It's an emotional thing."

"The principal's right, Ruby," asserted Dustin.

"I agree," said Sister Christina. "Robert's emotionally deficient and a bit of a trickster . . . but surely not mentally deficient. I've checked his grades and they're fine. He's had no trouble keeping up with the others."

"Sadly, though," remarked Sister Mary Rose, "—and I'm sorry to tell you this—but I'm inclined to say that the boy doesn't belong here. He's too unruly. He might be best suited in a more controlled environment, where they have staff equipped to deal with such behavioral problems."

"Sister," said Ruby, "I think he needs to be tested. Maybe I should have a word with one of the state social workers to see what they have to say about it. Meanwhile, what do we do with him until then? Surely he can't just stay home all day."

"But if we keep him, it wouldn't be fair to the other children."

"Please, Sister, perhaps you could—"

"Stop it right there, Mrs. Whipple. We're not equipped to handle your kind of boy."

"Yes, but—"

"I'll tell you what. If you think you can talk some sense into him, you know, get him to behave in a manner that's acceptable to

PLATE TEN
ROBERT L. CARROLL
c. 1948
POMPTON LAKES, NEW JERSEY

the principles of this fine Catholic school, I'd be willing to give him another crack at it. But if you're unable to do that, you'll leave me no alternative but to—"

"I know I can, Sister. I'll straighten out his britches for good."

"Okay, then, let's do this. We'll keep him on, but you must come through with your end of the bargain or out he goes. And one more thing, I think I'll take you up on the testing idea."

"What do you mean?"

"I'll have our psychologist, Sister Agatha, take a look at him. She's a fine sort and very qualified. Incidentally, she was just sent over to us from St. Walburga. She was there long before Robert ever got there, and I'll bet she remembers the boy. Would that satisfy your curiosity as to his mental capacity?"

"Oh, yes, yes, Sister. Thank you."

"Okay, I think that does it."

I abruptly stopped listening at the door and turned to my brother. "Bobby, quick, they're comin'! Sister Bluebeard's here!"

"Sister Agatha?" asked Bobby, like he couldn't believe his ears.

"Yep. I heard 'em. Sh-hh! Here they come."

Shortly after the visit to the principal's office, Bobby was sent to Sister Agatha, who tested him and promptly labeled him retarded. The principal informed Ruby, who, in turn, wasted no time reporting the school's findings to the State Board of Child Welfare.

From then on, Ruby watched my brother with a wary eye, peeking between curtains, sometimes rubbernecking around corners of the house, and she often scolded him without reason. Ruby's behavior convinced Bobby that adults were unfair and could not be trusted.

Because she felt disgraced, Ruby straitjacketed Bobby into a state of constant fear, locking him into perpetual distrust. It seemed as though she were punishing him for forcing her to keep a "retarded" boy under her thumb.

One day I was sitting on the toilet, listening to Ruby in the kitchen as she talked with someone on the phone.

"I see . . . okay . . . no problem . . . no, I won't pack his things until Friday afternoon . . . you'll take him then? Good. Thank you, Mrs. Johnson. Goodbye."

My heart sank. I all but slithered into the toilet like an injured snake. The following Friday—January 27, 1950—came quickly. I acted as if it were just another regular day, never telling Bobby what I had heard—using my duffel bag of tricks, not to put on a false front for the big people this time, but for Bobby.

We were in the backyard playing with Wiggie when a car turned into our driveway. I pretended to be as surprised as Bobby.

"Who is it, Chuckie?"

"I don't know."

We hid and watched.

A black lady got out of the car and went into the house. A short time later, Bobby was called from the back window to come inside.

"Mommy wants me, Chuckie. I'll be right back."

I jetted into the woods and hid in a pile of dead leaves. A short time later, I heard a car start up and two doors slam. I ran to the edge of the hill. The car pulled away, and Bobby was in it. I dropped to the ground and buried my face in my hands, kicking leaves about and punching the ground with my fists, screaming, "I'm sorry, Bobby, I'm sorry! I should've told you what I heard!"

I lifted my head and looked down the road as far as I could see. It was empty. All that was left was a trail of dust. My only friend was gone.

"CHARLEY, IT SOUNDS like you've never forgiven yourself for that, have you?" questioned Mr. Wheeler.

"No, I guess not."

The water in the basin had cooled off considerably. I pulled my feet out and Mr. Wheeler rose from the bed to get a towel. He returned, handed me the towel, and sat down beside me.

"What a shame, Charley," he began. "You've been through so

much. Are you warmed up yet?"

"Yes, sir."

"What about those feet?"

"The warm water did it. They ain't cold no more. You're nice, Mr. Wheeler."

"You think so?"

"Heck, yeah—the best!"

"I got ya! Look, son, maybe we should be heading back to Birch. We can't press our luck too much, you know."

"Can I ask you a question, Mr. Wheeler?"

"Sure, son, what is it?"

"Why haven't you been working over at Birch? I miss you a lot."

"The thing is, son, it's not that I didn't want to see you. It's just that they don't like employees getting too close to patients, so I have to be very careful. But I'll drop over now and then when I know Mr. Fein's on duty. Would you like that?"

"You will?"

"I promise. By the way, what've you been doing with those newspapers that I've been giving Mr. Fein for you? Have you been reading them?"

"Every chance I get. I've already read 'em all. I used to read 'em under Birch."

"What do you mean 'under' it?" he asked, reaching for the basin and taking it to the bathroom.

"I crawled under Birch and read there, by a screen where the sun shines in. Nobody knew, not even my brother. I got dusty all the time, but I didn't care. If they asked me how I got so dirty, I'll just told 'em I was playing in the backyard. They didn't know nothin' about me."

"But now?"

"They closed up the spot where I crawled in. So now I hide the papers in the yard."

"I see. Would you like me to send over more, son?" He settled back on the bed beside me.

"Gosh, Mr. Wheeler, you mean it?"

"Sure, if you want me to." He smiled. "What about a dictionary? Could you use one of those?"

"A dictionary!" I exclaimed. "A real dictionary? Gosh, Mr. Wheeler, that would . . . that would do it! Then I could really learn a whole lot."

"Well, the next time I'm in town I'll pick one up for you. I'll send it over with Mr. Fein. How would that be?"

"Perfect! Gosh, you're the best man in the whole wide world. Thanks!" I turned to the man and hugged him.

"You're welcome, son . . . you're so, so welcome," he said affectionately as we broke our embrace. "Come on, let's get these shirts back on your feet."

"Okay." I began wrapping my feet, but Mr. Wheeler stopped me.

"No, no," he interrupted, getting on bent knees. "Let me do that for you . . . There." He tied the last knot to my ankles.

Once he was up on his feet, he leaned over and hugged me. Then he released my shoulders and looked down at me. "Charley, I'm very fond of you."

I suddenly felt very angry. "I hate this place, Mr. Wheeler. It ain't fair . . . it just ain't fair. It's an awful place, and what goes on at Birch is . . . is . . . it's just all bad, that's all. I've gotta get outta here or I'll go crazy."

"Now, now, now, enough of that. Let's see, since you're all warmed up, do you feel at least a little better?"

I nodded.

"Good. Then come on. I better get you back before they find you missing."

"They won't. The new guy doesn't know our names yet."

"I know, you said that. That's what gets me about you. You've got a lot on the ball. Dammit, what's a kid like you doing in a place like this? It pisses me off, Charley. Really makes me angry." He paused a moment. "You know, Charley, Dr. Alprin and I have talked about you."

"You have?"

"A couple of times. In fact, I heard from him just last week. He's really taken to you, Charley."

"What do you mean by that?"

"He likes you. He's concerned for your welfare. I think you found a friend in him."

"You do?"

"He speaks highly of you and he's convinced there's nothing wrong with you, even though he hasn't given you that IQ test yet. Now he's trying to find out why the hell they ever put you in this place. He's a good buddy to have on your side, Charley."

"I'm glad he likes me. And I like his secretary too. Do you know Lady Ann?"

"Yeah, I met her once. She sure is a pistol, isn't she?"

"A pistol. That's what she is—a pistol. She's a funny lady. Did she say anything about me?"

"She told me she thought well of you too. They both enjoy you over there."

I smiled. "Hey, what time is it, Mr. Wheeler?"

He reached into his pants pocket, pulled out a Westclock pocket watch, and flipped open the cover. "It's eight twenty."

"Wow, that's a nice watch."

"It was my father's."

"He gave it to you?"

"No, he left it to me. He passed away some time ago."

"You mean he died?"

"Yes, Charley, he did."

"I'd sure like to have one like it someday."

"You just continue be a good boy and, who knows, you might just get your wish."

"You mean it?"

"We'll see, son. We'll see. Ready to go?"

"Yes, sir."

"Okay, before we go, let me take a look out the window to make sure nobody's there. We don't want to meet up with the patrol guards. They're the last people we want to see."

"I know. They're bad people."

Mr. Wheeler drew the drape and looked both ways. "Looks quiet out there. Come on, let's see if we can pull this off without being seen. Ready?"

"Yes, sir."

I followed Mr. Wheeler as he went down to the front door and slowly opened it. He stuck out his head, snow instantly blowing in.

"I don't see a soul. Come on, just stay behind me."

We made it to the 1940 Ford deluxe wagon and got in. Mr. Wheeler attempted to start up the vehicle, but it wouldn't turn over.

"Maybe I flooded it. Let's just sit here a minute until it dries out." A few moments later, he tried starting the car again. "Damn this thing, it won't start!"

"Try it again, Mr. Wheeler."

He turned the key. The engine hesitated, then roared to a high pitch.

"You did it! You did it!"

"Finally. These freezing temperatures make engines sluggish. Let's give it a chance to warm up. The wipers should clear that window. Let's try them."

"Hey, they work, Mr. Wheeler! We can see, we can see!"

"I got ya, boy. They do work good, don't they? Now listen, son, once we get over to Birch, slip out of the car and get your butt back into that building. I'll leave you off between Birch and Pine. Nobody'll spot you from there. Is it a deal?"

"Sure."

He turned on the radio, adjusted the tuner, then smiled as he found a station he liked.

"Mr. Wheeler, what's that on the radio?"

"That fine music is Tchaikovsky's Piano Concerto no. 1."

"Why does that guy have such a long, funny name?"

"Because he's Russian."

"You know a lot about that stuff, huh?"

"When you love something enough, you learn all about it."

"Gee, that guy can really play, can't he?"

"He sure can. Okay, here we go."

We started around the drive and listened to the music.

"Oh, Christ!" Mr. Wheeler said, hitting the brakes. "There's the patrol car, and I think they're heading our way."

"What should we do? Maybe I should get out now. I don't wanna get you into—"

"Quick, get all the way down on the floor," Mr. Wheeler commanded. "I'll handle it."

Mr. Wheeler rolled down the window.

"What the hell brings you out tonight, Wheeler?" asked the patrolman.

"I'm going out for milk and bread."

"In this crazy weather? Hell, man, you've gotta be out of your cotton-freakin' mind. I'll tell ya what, instead of goin' into town by yourself, I'll go with you. We can stop and have a couple of beers. Whatta ya say?"

Oh, shit, I thought. That's all I need.

"No, not tonight."

"It's no problem. I can turn the car over to my new partner here, and then ride with you."

"But what about Supervisor Reynolds? He not gonna go for that."

"Screw him! He's out sick. So what the hell, let's go out and have a little fun. My new man will cover for us. Plus, my throat's dry for a nice cold beer—and maybe, just maybe, we can land a sweetie for both of us at good old Johnny's Grill. C'mon, you're a ladies man. Whatta ya say?"

"I'd love to, but—"

"Mr. Wheeler," I whispered, "don't let him in the car."

He lowered his hand to calm me. I remained motionless.

"Hey, I got an idea, Wheeler."

"Yeah, like what?"

"Let's go over the pantry. Why go all the way to hell and back? Heck, I can get everything you need over there."[2]

"Nah, that's okay. I need to get some other things too."

"Okay, have it your way. Hey, do you have chains on those tires?"

"No. Why?"

"Hell, man, look at all this snow. By the looks of it, it ain't gonna let up anytime soon. Cripes, for all I know, if it keeps up like this, before long we may all be up to our asses in it."

"Well, I think I can make it there and back with no problem. Like I said, Jack, I've got a couple of other matters to take care of tonight. Sorry, buddy."

"Okay, then, how about after our shift? I can pick you up in the snowplow. Come on, Wheeler. Oh, and Johnny's Grill has a raffle tonight. And the pretty girls—let's not forget them."

"Jesus, Jack, you don't take no for an answer, do you? Okay, then," sighed Mr. Wheeler, no doubt accepting the invitation just to get rid of him. "You win this time. Where do you want to meet after work?"

"Atta boy! I knew I could count on you, Wheeler. I'll pick you up at your apartment. I'll just honk, okay?"

"Sure, see you then." Mr. Wheeler finally rolled up the window and took off. "Okay, son, you can come up out of there now."

"I don't know why, but there's something about that man I don't like. He gives me the willies. Who is he, anyway?"

"That's Jack Ballanger. He's all right. He's just got a cop mentality and likes to throw his weight around."

"No, no. It's not that. That guy gives me the creeps."

"Forget him. He's gone now."

"Gosh, if they knew I was hiding and all, you would really get in trouble."

"Never mind me. What about you?"

"I know. I'll be okay."

"Damn, look at it snow. It could turn into a blizzard."

"I was scared, Mr. Wheeler, when they came."

"You had good reason to be."

We rounded the circle that led to the Diagnostics Building, then pulled over to the side of the road.

"Okay, Charley, are you ready to hightail it over there?"

"I'm ready, Mr. Wheeler." I grabbed the door handle.

Mr. Wheeler looked around to see if all was clear. "Okay, Charley. Now!"

I opened the door and ran. A minute or two later, I made it to the basement door. Unable to remember which shirt belonged where, I frantically stuffed them all into boxes and quickly slipped into my nightgown. I headed down the hall to the door leading up to the day room, knocked softly, and waited for the marble to roll down the steps. Nothing. I knocked again, this time a little louder, and placed my ear against the door. I still heard nothing but the blare of the television set.

Shit! Shit! I thought. What's he doing? Is he deaf?

I knocked again, listened, waited a minute, and still nothing.

I carefully opened the door and peeked through the opening. My brother wasn't there. I crept almost to the top of the staircase until I could peek into the first-floor level. Seeing no one, I ran up the rest of the way and went into the day room. There I found Bobby. I gingerly walked over and tapped him on the shoulder. He swung around and looked up at me.

"Hi, Chuckie. Let's go to the bathroom."

"Yeah, let's go."

When we reached the bathroom, he swung around and said, "Did you really do it, Chuckie?"

"Yeah, I did it. Look, my hair's still wet from the snow, and I'm cold as hell. What happened to you?"

"I forgot."

"Forgot? Christ, Bobby, how do you forget something like that?"

"I'm sorry, Chuckie. I wanted to watch *The Lone Ranger*. Are you mad at me?"

I sighed. "I should be, but I'm not. Forget it."

"So what happened?"

"Let's go to the back, next to the radiator. I'm still cold."

We squatted on the floor, our legs crossed. Bobby rested his chin on the heel of his hand, anxious to hear the details.

THE NEXT DAY, Rawbone called me to his desk.

"Me?" I asked, my heartbeat thumping out of rhythm.

"No, fuckin' *me*, asshole. Get up here."

When I reached him, I could feel everyone's eyes on my back, especially Bobby's. Rawbone reached out and grabbed a handful of shirt, pulling me into his open legs.

"Today," he said, "you're gonna be my sweet thing."

"Rawbone, please don't."

"Don't get lippy with me, goddamn it." He unbuckled my belt, his eyes void of a soul.

I looked down at his hands. "What're ya doin'?"

"Drop 'em!"

"Drop what?"

"Your pants, stupid!"

"No!"

"Oh, no?" Rawbone leaned back and shoved his foot into my chest. I went sprawling across the floor. Rawbone jumped from the desk, came over to me, grabbed my pant legs, and yanked. "Now roll the fuck over, mothafucka!" he yelled, his fists balled up in front of me.

"No!" I said, trying to cover my privates. "Beat me up. I don't give a damn anymore!"

"Don't fuckin' '*No*' me," he said, kicking me in the ribs.

I let out a sharp, piercing cry.

"Now roll over!"

"No!"

"The hell you ain't, mothafucka." He bent over, grabbed a handful of flesh with both hands, and flipped me over onto my stomach like a side of beef. "Now stay there," he demanded, placing his foot on my back. I turned my head to one side and looked up at him.

He sneered down at me. "You got a pretty ass. See this big mothafucka I got?" He waved his hard penis over me. "This'll do the job," he bragged. He dropped to the floor and straddled me between his knees. "And don't turn around and look at me again."

"Okay, I won't, but not in front of my brother, please."

"Fuck him and you too! Don't move!"

Rawbone leaned back, spread the cheeks of my buttocks, collected a wad of saliva, and spat. "Hm-mm, you got a good-smellin' ass."

"No, no, no!" I pleaded. "Not that way. Do it between my legs like you always do."

"Shut the fuck up and take it like a man." Without another word, he flopped on top of me, gripped my mouth with his open hands, and rammed his large penis into me. I yelled—not the scream of a child, but a guttural cry.

Just then, the stiffened postures of the others came to life: eyes rolled in delight; many unzipped their flies, spat on their dicks, and started jerking off; still others looked on, moaning and flittering their tongues.

I felt helpless, angry, and afraid, wanting to block my senses, but I could not. Again, I was chained to my normalcy, my heightened consciousness, and my awareness of just how terrible my dismal surroundings were.

Everybody joined in. I felt like a broken piston as the basement filled with the cackles and gibberish of pent-up, horny boys. The kids in that basement resided in an emotional wasteland, as if a thousand devolutions had rolled back their human nature to its most basic primal needs.

When Rawbone finished, he snapped to his feet, zipped up, and ordered, "Okay, you morons, roll up them stinkin' dicks. The fun's over."

But was it really over? Far from it. Each act of rape seemed timeless and endless, as though it would keep on until it ripped out my heart and, finally, run its course to its coup de grâce, leaving my soul forever changed.

That night, full of despair, I consulted Bobby.

"We should run away," he suggested.

"Run away?" I asked.

"Yeah! Why not?"

"You mean now?"

"Not now, dummy. When it gets warmer, you know, like when it's spring."

"But where? Nobody wants us."

"Fuck that. I ran away from this place before and I'll do it again. I know all the places to hide."

"Hide where?"

"The woods. I know the woods like I know this place. And if we get caught, so what? We'll go to Cedar. It's better than here. Want to?"

I hesitated for a moment.

"Don't think about it. Do you or don't you?"

"But . . . I mean . . . ah, fuck it. You're right. Okay, this spring."

THE BONE BREAKING continued, as did the assaults and rapes, while Mrs. Steele chalked up the evidence as the results of anything from spastic clumsiness to "hard kid's play."

How much did anyone know about such occurrences? How many of these incidents were deliberately suppressed? I'll never know. But one thing was certain: there was no indication that any member of the bureaucracy or its do-gooders ever set foot in either of those basements or investigated what was going on in the dormitories after the lights went out. It seemed no one was aware of the

CHARLES A. CARROLL

predatory aspects of our existence. This, coupled with New Lisbon's infatuation with the appearance of total order at any cost, created a script wherein stronger boys brutalized weaker ones and widespread back turning converted monitors into monsters and transformed employees into dictators. That combination subjected all of us to the Stone Age of Insanity—and, worse, it was far from over.

ENDNOTES FOR CHAPTER FIFTEEN

1. See Part Four epigraph preceding this chapter. Johan August Strindberg, *The Son of a Servant* (1886), *Scholar Island*, "Parents," http://www.scholarisland.org/parenthood.htm (accessed June 10, 2005).

2. See Appendix A.2.5/Theft; Falsification; Conduct Unbecoming a Public Employee/1997. An employee was accused of stealing expensive equipment from New Lisbon and using it for his private business.

   Also see Appendix B.2/Employee Theft of State Property/1996. A Trenton Psychiatric Hospital maintenance engineer was accused of stealing supplies from the institution.

CHAPTER SIXTEEN

ChapStick

WITH CHRISTMAS APPROACHING, my emotional discomfort grew, as did that of so many other children around me. Holidays were like that for most of us. Christmas was a time of year when you were reminded who cared and who did not—a holiday that either confirmed one's value or tragically denied it. It was a duel between feeling whole or destitute. Most wanted Christmas to just go away and never come back, as if it were an intrusion of a stark reality, particularly when we received Christmas cards from unknown people. I personally found the cards offensive. An unknown name on a card did little to connect with the heart, especially for those with no real human contact at all. These cards were tragic teasers; they took so many of us to the edge of "normal" human kindness, only to be disappointed because the senders of the cards were phantoms—no one was there.

One morning, Mrs. Steele yelled from the staircase, "CARROLL! Get up here on the double!"

When I reached the upstairs landing, rays from the bright morning sun caused me to squint, destroying my focus and then making it all too clear. One look at Mrs. Steele's face told me she was pissed. Her large frame swelled in and out as she looked down at me from the top step.

"What took you so long?"

"I . . . I came as fast as I could, Mrs. Steele."

Just as I was about to say something else, my eyes were diverted by the flush of a toilet in the bathroom behind her. To my surprise, Mr. Wheeler appeared at the open doorway, holding a newspaper under one arm and clumsily fiddling with the buttons of his fly.

I swallowed hard, thinking she had learned that I'd snuck over to see Mr. Wheeler or that he was feeding me newspapers. Mr. Wheeler was quick to relieve me of that guilt.

"Hi, son," he greeted.

"Hello, Mr. Wheeler. I'm glad to—"

"Never mind him!" rumbled Mrs. Steele. "What took you so long?" she repeated, looking back at me.

"I came right away, Mrs. Steele."

"Don't give me those lyin' eyes."

"But it's true, Mrs. Steele . . . when I . . . when I heard you, I—"

"Shut up! I've heard enough outta you."

At that moment, I saw her as a babbling anti-Christ in drag wearing she-devil's clothing, her blood red fingernails the pitch-fork tip of her terror and her portly rear end the natural blowhole for all of hell's fire. I was terrified of her.

Mr. Wheeler intervened. "Please, Betty. He's only a boy. And he didn't take that long. Plus, I told you what Dr. Alprin said about him. He was very impressed with this young man, and—"

"Stop it, Melvin. Haven't we been through this before with this boy? As far as I'm concerned, those snot-nosed kids over at Diagnostics who are just out of school think they know it all. They don't know nothin'. I see these kids every day. They don't! They give 'em funny tests and, before you know it, a rumor gets around that one of 'em is normal. I ain't buyin' it. And you, Mr. Normal, come with me."

"But . . . I *am*—"

"Hush! Don't you dare talk back to me. I'm about to put your hiney through the wringer. Let's go."

As we all headed for the sewing room, Mrs. Steele continued to rant without looking back at either of us.

"These kids are all loony, you know, off-and-on normal. When are you gonna learn that, Melvin? And as for this one," she flipped her thumb over her shoulder, "if he's normal, then I'm a chitchat nut too. And if ya wanna know the truth, I wouldn't give ya a plug nickel for him or for his bratty brother. They never wanna listen. I'm sick of it."

"Now, now, Betty, be nice."

"Nice?" snapped Mrs. Steele, turning around. "I *am* nice! I just don't wanna hear anymore about that *normal* crap. You just don't get it, Melvin. They don't put kids in places like these unless there's somethin' screwy with 'em."

"Calm down, Betty. You're gonna make yourself sick."

"Maybe you're right."

When we reached the middle of the dormitory, she stopped again and turned to Mr. Wheeler.

"Ain't this room pretty? Smell that nice clean air. And look how nice those beds are made up."

"It's cold as hell in here, Betty," asserted Mr. Wheeler. The flapping curtains waved a wintry chill throughout the elongated room. "If I had my way, I'd slam those windows shut, heat up the room, fill it with kids, and let them romp about. I can just see them now, bouncing on the beds like trampolines, reaching the ceiling with their fingertips, and having pillow fights." He cleared his throat.

"Don't be cute. I couldn't have that. What would the visitors think? And what about Superintendent Yepsen? He'd have a fit. Let's go," she snapped, grumbling all the way to the sewing room.

Once there, Mrs. Steele turned to me and pointed to the chair next to her sewing machine. "Okay, Mr. Normal, sit there and don't move. Melvin, if you don't mind, see that pile of clothes over there?" She pointed to the shelf. "Would you bring them over to me? Oh, and see that box under the ironing board? Bring me that too. I'll use it to pack his things."

"Sure, Betty."

Mr. Wheeler retrieved the clothes, turning to look at me from between two shelves and sending me a smile and a wink. I returned a secretive smile.

As Mrs. Steele began packing away the clothes, my mind drifted into many possibilities. I wondered if it could be my aunt again. And if it was, where was Bobby? Maybe it was Ruby and Dustin. Maybe they changed their minds.

"Stop daydreaming, Carroll. Put these on," ordered Mrs. Steele, tossing a pair of pants in my face. "Snap out of it. We can't keep Dr. Alprin waiting. And, Melvin—"

"Dr. Alprin, Mrs. Steele?"

"Don't you dare interrupt me, boy! Children should be seen and not heard. When are you gonna learn that? Now get those pants on before I lose my temper."

"But where, Mrs. Steele?"

"Use my bathroom. Melvin, fetch Rawbone for me, will you please?"

"Sure, Betty."

A few minutes later, Mr. Wheeler returned with Rawbone.

"Rawbone," ordered Mrs. Steele, "take this box and him over to Diagnostics. He's goin' home with Dr. Alprin for Christmas."

"I'm going to Dr. Alprin's house?" I exclaimed.

"Yes, and shut up! You and your questions. You have a hard head, mister. Not another word, ya hear? And you behave yourself on this outing. If I hear one bad thing about your behavior, I'll tan your hide with a sturdy piece of that willow outside."

"I'll behave, Mrs. Steele. I promise."

"You better. Now get out."

"Bye, Mr. Wheeler. Are you on tonight?"

"Never mind all that!" Mrs. Steele retorted. "You wanna know too much. Get him outta here, Rawbone."

"Yes, ma'am."

"See ya, kid. Keep that chin up," said Mr. Wheeler.

"I will." I smiled back at him.

"Oh, stop it, Melvin. Must you pamper him?"

When we got about halfway to the Diagnostics Building, Rawbone suddenly stopped and turned to me.

"Ya think you're fuckin' smart, don't ya, white-ass?"

"What did I do?"

"I should kick your mothafuckin' ass!"

"But I ain't done nothin'."

"Don't gimmie that shit. You know what I'm talkin' about. Think I don't know what's goin' on with you and that doctor guy? How do you rate, mothafucka? I deserve it, not you. And why's he think you're so goddamn special, anyway? He's fuckin' your ass. Ain't he?"

"Heck no!"

"Listen, mothafucka! I'm the one they found in a fuckin' trash can when I was a baby. And I'm the one who went through a hundred foster homes and got my ass kicked all the time, not you! But who does he pick? You! You're suckin' his dick, ain't ya?"

"I ain't that way, and he ain't either."

"You pet mothafucka! Keep it up, sucka, or you'll be suckin' dick when you get back!"

"But I didn't know Dr. Alprin was takin' me to his house."

"Fuck you!" he grimaced, his face taking on the look of a black-pitted rock. "Don't gimmie that shit."

"But I didn't. Honest, Rawbone. I didn't, I didn't! Honest to God."

"Fuck all that. Bring me back somethin'."

"Like what?"

"Damn you, Rawbone," shouted Mrs. Steele from one of Birch's windows. "This ain't no time to be talkin'. Get him over there! Dr. Alprin's waitin'!"

Rawbone waved at her blindly and immediately headed for the Diagnostics Building. When we reached the steps, Rawbone stopped and turned to me.

"Bring me somethin' back, mothafucka."

"Like what?"

"Gold."

"Gold?"

"You heard me. Gold, mothafucka!" He rubbed his fist into my nose. "Now let's go."

We entered the building. When we reached Lady Ann, she rose and flaunted her unusual charm. I was glad to see her.

"Hi, young man." She turned to Rawbone. "I've been meaning to ask you, what's your first name? We like addressing everyone by their first names."

"Kenneth, ma'am."

"Well, thank you, Kenneth. Just put the box down and go back to your cottage."

"Yes, ma'am."

Before leaving, Rawbone leaned over, putting his hand to the side of my ear, and whispered, "Gold, mothafucka. Don't forget." He turned and made his way down the hall.

"What did he just whisper to you, Charles?"

"He just told me to have a good time."

"That was nice of him. So, how's my sweetie today?"

"Fine, Lady Ann."

"You know, Charles," she said, her eyebrows rising a trifle, "I'm always happy to see you and your lovely dimples."

I blushed. "Is it really true, Lady Ann?"

"What's that, handsome?"

"Is Dr. Alprin really taking me to his house?"

"Of course he is. Isn't that wonderful?"

Lady Ann's cartoonlike personality inadvertently pulled me out of my sullen state to a lighter side I'd almost forgotten existed. She hadn't changed a bit; her face was overloaded with flaking eye makeup and bright lipstick. About all she was missing was a red, glued-on nose, an oversized pair of clown shoes, and a zany, polka-dot umbrella.

"You look troubled, Charles. Live it up. This is a big day for you. Come on over here and let me cheer you up." She directed me to the chair next to her desk. "What's wrong, honey?"

"Nothing, Lady Ann."

"Well, you just looked so solemn, that's all. Are you sure?"

"Yes, ma'am."

She leaned over the desk and whispered, "Dr. Alprin's going to test you today before you guys leave."

"Right now?"

"In a few minutes."

"Is it easy?"

"That depends on which one he gives you, but they all do the same thing. It'll tell him how smart you are. Dr. Alprin's a wonderful person. He's not normally on today, but he came all the way from home just to get you. He has a generous nature. He's kind, always looking out for the underdog."

"What's that 'dog' word mean?"

"Someone who could use some help. Who knows, you might've found a friend for life. He's that kind of guy."

"Like how?"

"He has a kind of record-breaking loyalty, that's what."

"Gee, I don't know what all that means, but I guess it's good, huh?"

"He's a rare find, Charles. Cherish every moment with him, okay?"

"Yes, ma'am."

"Stay there a minute." She rose to her feet. "I'll go back and let him know you're here."

A few moments later, from the far end of the hall, Lady Ann called out, "Charles, come on back here with us."

As I went skipping down the hall to Dr. Alprin's office, thrilling waves of excitement—feelings that were strangers to me—suddenly entered my damaged system, a hint that there was still some "child" left in me. Perhaps I wasn't emotionally ruined yet.

"Hello, Charles," said Dr. Alprin, smiling. "It's good to see you again. Thank you, Lady Ann. Did he bring clothes?"

"Yes, Doctor. They're on the floor in front of my desk."

"Fine. I'll get them on my way out. Have a seat, Charles. I'm just finishing up on some work. Would you mind if I give you that IQ test I talked about last summer before we go?"

"No."

"Good. After the test we can get going."

Motionless, I sat in my seat studying the man. Dr. Alprin's face was heavily shadowed from not having shaved, and he wasn't wearing a suit or tie this time. His casual shirt was open, revealing a thick bed of hair. When he turned his head, I noticed that the tufts of hair protruding from his ears were unclipped.

A minute or two later, he looked up from his papers. "There," he said, "I finished it." He inserted a pen into his shirt pocket. "Ready for the test, Charles?"

"Yes, sir."

"Then let's get started. Come on. Let's go over to this table."

Once we took our seats, Dr. Alprin leaned forward and looked at me over the rim of his glasses.

"I've been meaning to tell you that Mr. Wheeler came to see me a few weeks ago. He mentioned your concern about returning here. I gather he cares about you."

"He does like me, huh?" I answered with the pride of a wide-eyed kid. "He's been helping me a lot. Dr. Alprin, is this test really going to tell you how smart I am, like if I'm retarded or not?"

"You've asked me that question before. Thinking you're retarded is foolish. Why do you think you are?"

"This place treats me like I am."

"Well, Charles, I don't think you're retarded. In fact, I was convinced of that fact when I first met you. What else do you think about yourself?"

"I don't know. I'm nobody special."

"Everybody is somebody."

"Not in this place."

He hesitated a moment. "Let's discuss that issue another time. For now, we'll get started, okay?"

"Okay."

"I'm going to ask you some questions. Since I now know a bit about your background, I'm asking some as a mere formality. Charles, have you ever taken an intelligence test?"

"No, I don't think so."

"What about other kinds of tests?"

"What do you mean?"

"Just any other kinds of tests?"

"Only in school."

"You mean in the classroom?"

"Yes."

"Never in a special room with just another man or woman?"

"No, never."

"Charles, did anyone ever tell you why you were brought to New Lisbon?"

"No."

"Any idea why they might've sent you here?"

"Because Ruby just didn't want me no more."

"Do you think there might be any other reasons?"

I looked away from him. "I don't know."

He paused again. "How are your writing skills, Charles?"

"I know my printing and I know how to do handwriting."

Dr. Alprin looked down at my folder. After fingering through it, he looked up at me and said, "Next, I'm going to ask you quite a few questions. Just answer them as best as you can. Here's the first. Why does oil float?"[1]

"Because it's light."

"What do you mean by light?"

"I don't know . . . because it's light."

"Can you tell me what you mean by light, Charles?"

"It floats on water, so it's light, right?"

"That's a good answer."

CHARLES A. CARROLL

After about half an hour of questions, Dr. Alprin slid a piece of paper in front of me that had a large square with the pattern of a maze on the inside. He marked an "X" at the upper left and lower right corners, then handed me a pencil and pointed at the square.

"Charles, I want you to imagine you need to walk through here. This is the beginning, and this is the end." He pointed to one "X" and then the other. "Show me how you would walk from here to here."

I spent a few minutes drawing lines through the maze. When I finished, I looked up at him and told him I was through. He took the paper, looked it over, and tucked it into a folder along with my other answers.

"That's good. You did very well today. I've no idea why they sent you to this place, but I'm going to try to get to the bottom of these things. Meanwhile, stop thinking there's anything wrong with you. Is it a deal?"

"Then it means I'm not retarded?"

"Let's not get into that again. Tell me something, do you know who wrote the story of *Romeo and Juliet*?"

Self-conscious about not knowing the correct answer, I replied with my eyes lowered to the floor, "I don't know."

"Don't be disappointed, Charles. With only three grades of school before you came here, it stands to reason you might not know the answer. William Shakespeare wrote it. Maybe someday you'll read a little of his work. He'll expand your soul, broaden your mind. He may even sweep you off your intellectual feet. One thing is for sure, reading stuff like that will deepen your wisdom and strengthen your character. Well, Charles, that's it for today. Ready to go?"

"Are you really taking me to your house?"

"Didn't they tell you?"

"Yeah, but I just wanted to make sure, that's all. I'm ready."

"Good. Come on. Marilyn and I decided to share our holiday with you. She likes to celebrate Hanukkah, so we thought it'd be nice to have you join us with our families. They'll all be there . . . my mother and father and, of course, Marilyn's side of the family. Listen, forgive me for not letting you know sooner. I didn't want to tell you about my plans until I received full clearance from Administration. I only learned of their decision yesterday."

I smiled. "Can I ask you a question?"

"Sure, Charles. What is it?"

"What's 'Hanukkah' mean?"

"It's like Christmas. Come on. Let's get going."

As we stepped into the hall, something by the doorjamb caught my eye. "What's that, Dr. Alprin?"

"That's a mezuzah. It's Dr. Kahn's."

"Who's Dr. Kahn?"

"One of my colleagues. He's Jewish."

"Jewish? What's that mean?"

"It's a religion."

"A religion? I don't get it. If there's only one God, why are there so many religions?"

"That's a long story," he chuckled. "No time to explain that one, but let's go back to your original question about the mezuzah. It's a small scroll of parchment, or paper, with biblical verses written on it. That paper's usually enclosed in some kind of case, like you see here. And they hang them on doorposts, at the entrance to a house—or an office—to bless and protect people. Now, are we ready to go?"

"Are you Jewish too, Dr. Alprin?"

"Yes, but I don't practice it. You might say I'm nothing. Anything else?"

"Jewish. A new word. Thanks."

"You're welcome, Charles. Let's go."

As we walked down the hall, waves of happiness rolled through me again. Everything in me smiled at the mere thought of leaving New Lisbon.

"Hi, Lady Ann. Where did you tell me his things were?"

"They're right here by my desk. Don't forget, Dr. Kahn still wants to talk to Charles."

"Christ, that's right! He mentioned it to me yesterday."

"Hold on. I'll tell him you're out here."

"Well, Charles," said Dr. Alprin. "Now you'll get a chance to meet Dr. Kahn. He's interested in what you have to say too. Here he comes now."

Dr. Kahn's horn-rimmed glasses gave him an intellectual look. He was a small man whose lower lip turned to one side when he talked.

"Hi, Charles. I'm Dr. Kahn." He extended his hand. "How are you today?"

Shaking the man's limp hand, I answered, "I'm happy."

"Happy because you're going on an outing?"

"Yes, sir."

"I'm glad. Charles, I wanted to ask you something. Just answer me the best you can."

Oh, God, I thought, what if he doesn't believe I'm normal? I felt that if I couldn't convince him, then all this with Dr. Alprin would have been for nothing. I sensed Dr. Kahn's authority and knew I had to muster everything within me to win his approval. But I wondered, do I act as if I'm smart or just be myself? Nevertheless, I felt an ice-cold nervousness come over me when the brows of the man lifted for the first question.

"Charles, I want you to think back, like before you came here. Do you recall ever getting a test like the one Dr. Alprin gave you today?"

"No."

"Never one like it from any other agency or institution, or when you were at school in Pompton Lakes?"

"No, sir."

"Are you absolutely sure?"

"Yes, sir."

He paused for a moment of thought. His expression seemed

wounded, and he sighed deeply as he absorbed my answer.

"That'll do it, Charles." Dr. Kahn patted me on the back. "You're a fine boy. Dr. Alprin, he's all yours."

"Come with me, Charles." Dr. Alprin picked up the box of clothing. "Have a nice Christmas, Lady Ann."

"Thank you, doctor. Goodbye, Charles. Have a wonderful holiday."

"Thanks, Lady Ann."

As we walked down the long corridor, I asked Dr. Alprin, "Do you live far away?"

He answered, "It's a pretty good distance from here. Hopefully, we'll beat some of the heavy holiday traffic. It's still early."

While Dr. Alprin put the box in his trunk, I looked around before getting into the car, and the reality of New Lisbon pounced on me like a rabid dog. Right then and there, I wanted to tell Dr. Alprin everything. But the chains of silence and the slap of fear immediately hushed me; I figured that if I uttered a word of any of it, and it got back to the residents at Birch, I would pay the price in the basement of terror.

I turned my eyes away from Birch.

"The door's unlocked, Charles. Get in."

As soon as we got into the car, an enormous weight lifted from my shoulders, as if the ghosts of New Lisbon were ready to leave me alone. I let out a deep sigh and turned to Dr. Alprin, giggling, "I'm happy, I'm happy, I'm so happy. Thank you, Dr. Alprin . . . I can't believe it."

"Believe it. And I'm delighted you're happy."

"Do we have to go to the Administration Building first?"

"No, Charles," he replied, turning the engine over and taking off. "I've already signed you out."

"There's a nice lady over there."

"You mean at the Administration Building?"

"Yep. Her name's Millie."

"Millie? You must mean Mildred Page, the receptionist over

there."

"Yeah, that's the one."

"She's a nice lady, Charles."

"Dr. Alprin, what about my brother?"

"What about him?"

"Can't he go with us?"

"I tried arranging it, but Mrs. Steele told me he was on restriction."

"He's not on restriction. She's a liar."

"But that's what she told me, Charles."

"She's a liar. I hate her."

"It's okay to dislike people, Charles, but never hate them. Hate pays you first."

"What do you mean?"

"Hate has a way of eating out a good heart and making it rot."

"Gosh, hate does that?"

"You bet. Maybe we can bring your brother along next time. For now, try to put him in the back of your mind, okay?"

"I can't. He's all I have and . . . and he's my best friend."

"He'll be all right. Let's call this day yours."

Feeling sad for my brother, I lowered my head. I was riddled with guilt, as though I were cheating him out of something good and had no right to this trip without him. Finally, we approached the main drive leading out of New Lisbon.

Dr. Alprin slowed the car, rolled down his window, and began waving. "Hi, Mr. Biddlemier. How're you today?"

"For what's it worth, fine, Dr. Alprin. It's my back . . . lumbago . . . this cold weather, I guess."

"I'm sorry to hear that, Mr. Biddlemier. Try to have a good Christmas."

"I will."

"Goodbye!" Dr. Alprin rolled the window back up and increased his speed.

"What's 'lumbago' mean, Dr. Alprin?"

"Back pain."

"Only old people get that?"

"Sometimes."

We turned onto the public highway, leaving New Lisbon behind us. I felt like I'd been cooped up in a box and the lid was suddenly opened. Each mile untied one more layer of the mummy wraps that had bound me for so long. After more than two years, I felt alive again—breathing in deeply, taking in the cold sunshine, and exhaling a good dose of good riddance.

As we rode those miles, I soaked up every inch of scenery. I was enraptured by a freedom I never understood before; it was glorious. The outside world was heaven, and everything behind me was hell.

"Charles, would you mind telling me about your school before you came to New Lisbon?"

"I don't mind."

"How did you do in school?"

"I liked it."

"Really? What was school like?"

WHEN RUBY ENROLLED me in St. Christopher, I wasn't any happier about it than Bobby had been when he started school. At first the nuns were suspicious of me, figuring that if Bobby was ornery, then I would be too. Over time, however, because of worthy grades and consistently good behavior, they eventually changed their minds about me. As it turned out, I had a natural respect for learning and diligently applied myself.

As for the religious goings-on at parochial school, I was unimpressed. I found conventional dogma questionable and the nuns' handling offensive. St. Christopher's internal arteries and quiet hallways held a papal aura that actually soured my senses more than appeased them.

I was averse to the nuns' religious notions because their piety was predicated on a fear of God, and of themselves, more than any internal reverence or spirituality. I witnessed kids being stuffed into dark closets, often hearing their frightened shouts throughout the hollow-sounding hallways, their screams posing a threat that any one of us could be next. And, to further torment the trapped child, the nuns would kick the closet door with the backs of their hardened heels or slap the door with their hands. I couldn't capture any respect for them.

In all their piety, the nuns walked amongst themselves like stuffed penguins, shuffling about as if a low-trickle battery powered their legs, their black-and-white habits flowing as if by some special divine force. I cringed at their uppity chins aimed at God. They were all packing hip-slung rosaries like holy gunslingers. They were a prayerful, beady bunch, with glistening crosses bouncing from their knees as if to defy the unbelievers, always portraying a kind of religious nobility characteristic only of their holy orders, projecting an attitude that they had been sanctified by God and privileged above "ordinary" people.

In all, their sanctimonious air was an insult to anything heavenly or genuinely pious—a bastardization of Catholicism, the Holy Trinity, and the meaning of divinity. It was religious lunacy, pure and simple.

And so, the nuns' crude representations of God tattooed an indelible ink of fear into my system. Though these servants of the Lord professed to teach love, tenderness, and kindness, they had a way of shoving Catholicism down my throat without a spiritual lozenge and, in the end, suffocating every last breath of devotion within me.

But I acted the part, parading with prayerful hands and displaying appropriate affectations, while all along hating every minute of it.

It was education, not nuns, that improved my confidence. Working out problems and accomplishing results eased the negative effects setting in from the lack of human warmth and stimulation at

PLATE ELEVEN
CHARLES A. CARROLL
C. 1949
FIRST HOLY COMMUNION OUTFIT
POMPTON LAKES, NEW JERSEY

home. Academia attracted me like the opposite poles of a magnet; I was at one with it.

By the time I was eight, I could read better than most kids in higher grades, not because I was smarter, but because I was willing to work a little harder at it.

"I KEEP LEARNING more and more about you, Charles. Hey, look. See that sign? We're almost there."

"I can read that."

"You can?"

"Yeah. It says 'Welcome to Somerville.'"

"That was very good."

"That's an easy one."

"Good for you. You never cease to amaze me. We'll turn off at the next exit."

"Yeah!" I shouted, caught by another surge of excitement.

My main concern now was not New Lisbon but whether I could measure up to this wonderful opportunity and just be a regular kid. I wanted to be perfect in every way, relieved of the constraints of my past.

Dr. Alprin left the main road and, within a few minutes, turned into the driveway of a modest, two-bedroom home at the end of a cul-de-sac. His wife, apparently having heard us pull up, opened a window and stuck out her head as we stepped out of the car.

"Hi, honey. Hi, Charles! Welcome, welcome, welcome!" The wind blew the woman's black hair into silky tangles. "I'll see you two inside. Brrr, it's cold—too cold to be at this window."

"It sure is, Marilyn. We'll be right in. I've got to get his things from the trunk."

"Okay, honey," she said, quickly closing the window.

His wife's affectionate greeting touched off something inside me. I realize now that I was ill at ease, uncomfortable about how to receive her affection. The ongoing abuse had simply eaten away at me like a nasty worm, drilling holes in and out of my confidence until it resembled Swiss cheese.

Nevertheless, I was determined to mask these symptoms, committed to make this visit work, to appear as an untroubled kid—even if it meant making believe all over again as I had done at the foster home. I struggled with what I felt and what was expected of me, secretly fighting an inner duel to beat the syndrome of child abuse at its own game—and win.

When we walked into the house, I was nearly overcome by tears—not of sadness, but of delight from it all. The house was warm, cozy, and simply furnished. It was a world unto itself; the decorative trimmings, the soft colors, the rich smells of food cooking, and an opera playing in the background all combined to give me a feeling of coming home.

Dr. Alprin's wife greeted me heartily. "Charles, I'm Marilyn. How are you?"

"Fine, ma'am," I replied. Mrs. Alprin looked like the sort of pampered matron commonly displayed in society magazines.

"I've heard so much about you. Stan, let's take that box right into the bedroom. Come with me, Charles. We've got something to show you." She led me to the spare bedroom. "This is going to be your room, Charles."

"This is *my* room?"

"Do you like it?"

"Heck, yeah!" I said, but secretly I felt more like an intruder than a truly welcome guest.

"And look at those." She pointed to the velvet drapes. "I made them especially for you. Purple is for royalty. You're our royal guest. And look over there. A television! Now you can watch TV all you want when you go to bed."

"Honest? You mean you wouldn't mind?"

"Not at all."

I felt tears coming on, but fought them back, feeling something like a busted toy not yet fixed.

"And look over there on the bed."

"What is it?"

"Come over and we'll open it." She picked up a cellophane package and tore it open. "Look," she said, shaking out the articles of clothing and holding them up like on a clothesline. "Pajamas! Aren't they cute?"

"They're . . . they're really nice," I answered. "Better than what we wear at New Lisbon."

"What kind of pajamas do you normally wear?"

"Ghost clothes."

"What kind of pajamas are those?"

"They wear nightgowns, Marilyn," explained her husband.

"We only wear pajamas when Mrs. Steele knows there's gonna be visitors. I hate those white nightgowns. I feel like Casper the Friendly Ghost."

"Nightgowns at your age? Why nightgowns?"

"Who knows?" interjected Dr. Alprin. "That's the way Mrs. Steele does things over there, I guess."

"And who's Mrs. Steele?"

"His cottage mother, Marilyn."

"Well, that's nonsense. As long as you're here, it's gonna be pajamas, period. And look at the darling prints. An elephant . . . a lion . . . oh, look, a cute giraffe too. Do you like them, Charles?"

Again, the voice of abuse inwardly whispered: You don't deserve it.

"Well, Charles?" prompted Marilyn.

I wanted to feel joy, but only now was I beginning to realize that New Lisbon had made me permanently unhappy. My boyhood was gone. And worse, I felt apart from everything. I was a serious thinker in a little boy's frame. So to get around that, I once again took out those manipulative tools stored deep within me, dusted them off, and, with well-rehearsed precision, began playing family. What I didn't know then was that, by pretending to be someone else, these kind people could well have ended up loving the wrong boy.

With moist eyes, I looked up at Marilyn and answered, "They're just what I wanted."

"I knew it, I knew it!" she said with relief. "I knew you'd adore them."

I changed the subject. "I like that music."

"You mean that opera I have on? You like it?"

"I can't understand it, but it makes me feel . . . it makes me feel good."

"Honey," she said, turning to her husband, "he likes 'Rondine al Nido'! I can't get over it. I think we have a sensitive child here."

"I *am* sensitive, Mrs. Alprin."

"Are you now? That's a pretty strong statement coming from a little boy."

I lowered my eyes and mumbled, "And I'm not a little boy anymore."

She drew back in silence, as if trying to read into what I had said. "Okay then, you're a big boy now. How's that?"

"It's okay, ma'am," I murmured softly under my breath, "but that's not how I meant it."

"I'm sorry, Charles, I didn't get that."

"I said, that's okay, ma'am."

"Call me Marilyn, Charles."

"Yes, ma'am."

"Honey," she said, turning back to her husband, "I can't get over him liking opera. Oh, that reminds me, Stan. If you're taking Charles swimming and to that football game over at Rutgers University, maybe you guys should get going."

"Jesus, you're right." Dr. Alprin looked at his watch.

"Gosh, swimming too?" I exclaimed. "But . . . but it's cold out."

"My husband's taking you to the Y, Charles."

"What's the Y?"

"The YMCA."

"What kind of place is that?"

"A fun place, Charles. A place for recreation, swimming, and—"

"A swimming pool? You mean an inside one?"

"Yep."

"Oh, boy! I'm ready!"

"Good. Get your jacket back on," said Dr. Alprin, reaching for his own and putting it on. "I already have a pair of trunks in the car that'll fit you."

At the Y, Dr. Alprin walked from his locker, with his swim trunks tucked under his arm, to my locker, where I was undressing. He was naked. It was the first time I saw a grown man completely unclothed. His hairy body struck me as rather odd. He had hair on his back, on top of his shoulders, and up and down his arms and legs. Overall, he had a formidable physique; he was fit, muscular, and very lean.

I slipped into my trunks and we headed for the pool. I swam the entire length twice. During the third lap, just as I was passing Dr. Alprin, a man jumped off the diving board above us, belly-flopping. Startled, I grabbed onto Dr. Alprin in a desperate attempt to be rescued.

"Get off me! I don't like anybody hanging on me," he growled, wiggling out of my hold.

I was stunned by his reaction, having no idea why he recoiled that way. The room went into a roar of absolute silence. I felt alone and unconnected, as if stranded from the man's warmth, his behavior imprinting me with a painful strain of rejection and mistrust. I was hurt.

At the football game, I carried on in a manner expected of me. I did what others did: rooted and cheered, stood up on the bleachers, and yelled, picking up enough football jargon to fit in. I was again making believe, because I was not of that world. All of it was too sudden. I felt different—and, over and over again, I hated discovering that difference within me. So, to not reveal my charade, I put myself back on the adoption display rack, acting like a free-wheeling kid, behaving like everybody else for the sake of approval and feeling loved, if only a little, by somebody.

PLATE TWELVE
HANUKKAH DINNER
C. DECEMBER 1953
ELEVEN-YEAR-OLD CHARLES A. CARROLL SEATED BETWEEN DR. ALPRIN AND HIS WIFE, MARILYN

Dr. Alprin and his wife had invited their families over for Hanukkah. When dinner was served, I excused myself and went to the bathroom, passing the master bedroom where I saw purses, coats, hats, and scarves sprawled over the king-size bed. I went into the bathroom and peed. As I was standing over the toilet, Rawbone's orders drenched me with fear.

When I exited the bathroom, I tiptoed into the bedroom and rifled through some jacket pockets. Then, when I spotted an open purse, I leaned over and looked inside. On top of a billfold was a lady's gold watch. I snatched it, stuffed it into my pocket, and returned to the dinner table—feeling freed from Rawbone's bondage, but never hating myself more.

The second and final day of my visit, Marilyn fixed a spaghetti dinner. I ate what she put in front of me, but didn't enjoy it because I was guilt ridden over stealing the watch. The fact that I had done such a terrible thing kept needling at me, but so did Rawbone's threats. The thought of returning to New Lisbon re-dressed me into my mummy wraps and placed me back into that dark box—with the lid, once again, about to slam shut.

After dinner, I helped Marilyn dry the dishes.

While holding a plate, she said, "Give me your hand a minute, Charles." She placed the flat of my hand against her belly. "Feel that?"

"Gosh, what's that?"

"That's my little baby. It kicks sometimes."

"It does?"

"Sometimes."

I turned and resumed drying the dishes.

"Oops! There it goes again." She again took my hand and held it to her stomach. "Yikes, did you feel that?"

I pulled my hand away and fell silent, reaching for a dish.

"Charles, is something wrong?"

Grimacing, I turned to her. "Are you really gonna have a baby?"

"Yes, and God did it."

"And then what's gonna happen to me?"

"What do you mean, Charles?"

"I don't know . . . I . . . I . . . uh, nothin'."

"Here, look."

She took my wrist again, but I pulled it from her hand.

"No, I don't want to," I said, reaching for a carving knife to dry.

"Charles, what's gotten into you? You look pale."

I looked at her stomach from the side. The baby was wagging its finger at me, and from a sinister smile filled with rotting teeth, it whispered a warning: "There ain't room for one more."

Shaken, I turned away, wanting nothing to do with that unborn child as a flashback of Ruby reminded me of a long-ago rejection. I snapped around and looked up at Marilyn.

"Do you like me?" I asked.

"Why, of course I do. Why wouldn't I, honey?"

As I looked into her eyes, a sickening feeling came over me. My grip on the carving knife tightened.

"Charles, you're shaking."

My internal tools melted away. All my manipulative defenses were gone.

"What is it, Charles? What's wrong?"

"You remind me of Ruby."

"Who's Ruby, honey?"

"My foster mother."

"I didn't know you had one. Tell me about her."

"She stopped wanting me because she . . . she . . . oh, never mind."

"No, no. Go ahead, Charles."

"Ah, nothin'," I said, still holding the carving knife in a fierce grip—my heart racing, my forehead beading sweat, my mind going blank, and all logic dissolving—when suddenly, a force beyond my own raised the knife up to her face, not to harm, but to question.

I muttered, "This could kill a baby, huh?"

Marilyn's eyes opened wide. The saucepan she was holding went crashing to the floor as she ran into the other room to her husband.

"It's time you took Charles home."

"But . . . but what happened?"

"Never mind. Just get him out of here."

On our way back to New Lisbon, feeling horribly troubled over what I'd done, I turned to Dr. Alprin.

"Dr. Alprin," I asked, "why did I do that?"

"You mean what you said to my wife?"

"Yes, that's it . . . I . . . I did a terrible thing, didn't I?"

"You frightened her. You don't blame her, do you, Charles?"

"No," I answered. "But I don't know why I did it, I swear I don't. It was like . . . like somebody else in me did it. Why did I do that, Dr. Alprin? Why did I say that?"

"Well, Charles, you might have homicidal tendencies."

"What's that mean?"

"Maybe that you want to kill someone or something or—"

"Kill? Me? Never! I don't wanna kill nobody. I swear I don't."

"Then maybe it's something else—not a person at all, but a thing, like something deep inside you."

"Like what?"

"A hurt feeling, maybe."

"Yeah, maybe that's it."

"Charles, sometimes when we're not loved enough, that's what happens. We need to be *first*, you know, the only one—number one, so to speak. Understand?"

"I . . . I think so."

"I wouldn't worry about it, Charles. You didn't act on it. You just asked her a question. Granted, it wasn't the most appropriate way to go about it, but that's how you chose to vent your frustrations. I'd forget it if I were you."

"But . . . but I didn't choose it. It wasn't me. I don't know what made me say something like that."

"Impulses can be like that sometimes. Many of us say or do things we regret later on. Let it go. Forget it, Charles. Did you get enough to eat?"

"I guess. I mean, I ate, but I wasn't hungry."

"But I thought you liked spaghetti."

"I do, but knowing I had to go back to New Lisbon . . . you know, that kind of stuff. I hate going back to that place. I hate it. I hate it."

"I can't blame you much for that."

Now I was concerned whether Dr. Alprin was going to shut me out of his life forever, as he was my only hope of ever getting out of that institution. And while I needed him more than anything in the world, I was sure that I'd blown it, that I had completely destroyed his friendship beyond repair. And I knew, in my heart, that I couldn't blame him.

I threw my hands up to my face and began sobbing, repeating through my hands, "I hate it. I hate it. I hate that place. I don't like nothin' about it. I don't belong with a bunch of nuts."

"I know it must be hard, Charles. Try to calm yourself. I'm going to stop to get some chewing gum. Would you like some?"

"No, but can I come in with you?"

"If you want to." He reached into the glove box and handed me a tissue. "Here, blow your nose and dry your eyes."

Dr. Alprin pulled into a small market. Inside, at the counter, he pointed to a ChapStick. "You could use one of those."

"What is it?"

"You have chapped lips. Try it."

"Okay."

The heavyset, balding man behind the counter said, "Mister, that'll be another dime."

Dr. Alprin paid for the ChapStick and handed it to me. As I shoved it into my pocket, I felt the watch, and a sudden stab of sin smacked me in the face. Consumed with guilt, I ran out of the store crying and got into the car, leaving Dr. Alprin behind.

When he returned to the car, he asked, "What the hell was that all about?"

"I . . . I don't know. New Lisbon, I guess."

"Try to relax, Charles. I know it can't be easy for you." He turned over the engine.

"But, Dr. Alprin, I'm worried." I was thinking about the knife again. "It was like somebody else said that to Marilyn."

"Your subconscious, perhaps?"

"What's that?"

"Sometimes it's mixed-up stuff deep down inside you, like things we never talk about. But now you're doing the right thing. You're talking about it."

Still crying, I said, "But I don't feel funny inside."

"Sometimes it's not recognizable—that is, until something like this happens. Try to pull yourself together."

"But I hate me for that. I hate me!"

"Maybe you need to talk more about it. Want to?"

"I don't even know where to start."

"Wherever you like."

IT HAD BEEN more than a year since Bobby had been taken from the Whipples, and I was continually filled with deep-rooted resentment and serious degrees of loneliness. Still lingering was an unanswered question: what role did Ruby play in his removal?

I was in the living room one day, my knees sunk deep into the sofa. I was daydreaming, looking out the window, when it occurred to me to finally confront her. She was in the kitchen, listening to *The Arthur Godfrey Show* while ironing one of Dustin's work shirts.

I turned and called out to her, "Mommy, can I ask you a question?"

"Sure, honey," she said. "Give me a minute to finish Daddy's shirt." A few moments later, she came into the living room. "C'mon in the kitchen, Charles. We'll talk in there."

I squirmed off the couch and headed for the kitchen, my heart beating fast. I took my usual seat, watching her every move as she hung the last of Dustin's freshly ironed shirts on a wire hanger.

Without looking back at me, she asked, "What's up?" She unplugged the iron, draped the electrical cord over the ironing board, and took a seat at the opposite end of the kitchen table. Readjusting my posture in the vinyl chair, I looked into her eyes, seeking clues as to how to begin. The look on her face instantly clammed me up.

"Well, don't just sit there. What is it?"

I swallowed hard.

"Something got your tongue? Come on, get on with it. I've got things to do."

Silence fell between us.

"Forget it, then. Now I've got somethin' to tell you."

"Me?" I said, pointing to myself.

"Yes, you! Are ya ready for your surprise?"

"A surprise for me?"

"Yes. How'd you like to have a brand new brother?"

"But I got one."

"No, I don't mean that. I mean a new stepbrother. In fact, it could even be a stepsister."

"Stepsister? I don't play with girls."

"But, Charles, I'm gonna have a baby."

"Where are you gonna get it?"

"Right here," she said, pointing to her well-advanced belly.

"In there? What's it doin' in there?"

"God put it there."

"But you told me storks bring babies home."

"God decided to do it this way."

"How do you get it out?"

"The hospital does it."

Upset, I said, "I don't want a new brother or sister. I want my own brother. And Mommy, you never call me Chuckie like Daddy? How come?"

"There you go again asking questions. And stop raising your voice. Daddy does what he wants, and I do what I want. Now you listen." She leaned over and waved a finger at me. "Get your mind off your brother. He's gone. You have to accept that. You're always bothering me about him."

I stuffed my fingers into my ears, squeezed my eyes shut, and blurted, "No! I want my brother!"

"Stop that!" she scolded. "Do you want your fingers to get stuck that way? Just think a minute. A brand new brother, Charles."

"No!" I shouted, brushing her hand aside and snapping to my feet. I ran into the bathroom and locked the door.

Ruby pounded on the door. "You locked me out again, you brat! Open it!"

"No!"

"Now you listen!"

"What?"

"God gave Mommy's tummy a baby, and you better face it."

"No, no, no!"

"Open this door."

"No!"

"Dammit! I said open it!"

"No, no, no!"

A moment later, I heard her footsteps on the hardwood floor and the sound of the front door slamming. I stepped up on the toilet seat and peered out the window. Unable to see her, I cautiously opened the bathroom door and tiptoed to the back window. She was in the garden, weeding on her knees. That's when I decided to run away.

"So that's what's behind it all. Now I see everything more clearly. Did you run away that day, Charles?"

"I don't wanna talk anymore. Is that okay?"

"Of course it is." Dr. Alprin slowed the car and pulled over to the shoulder of the road. "Here." He reached into the glove box and handed me another tissue, giving me a moment to wipe my face.

"You see, Charles, you have some deep-seated resentment, and what happened with my wife was your way of venting that frustration. I think that's all there is to it. Like I said earlier, that wasn't the best way to go about it, but that's behind us now. Forget it. Try some of that ChapStick."

"Okay." I pulled the cap off the ChapStick and rubbed the waxy vanilla against my lips.

"Feel better?"

"This stuff works good."

"See, I told you."

"I like it. Thanks."

"Good. I'm glad."

Dr. Alprin sped off. About twenty minutes later, he alerted, "There's New Lisbon up ahead now."

I sank deep into my seat, squeezing my eyes shut.

We drove up to the Administration Building and parked. After he signed me in, my whole heart wanted to cry, but I held back. I wanted to be that perfect boy again, but inside, I knew it was too late. What I had done at his house was despicable, and I realized it too well. I felt as if I'd lost the only good thing in my life, the only chance to be freed from that place once and for all. Something inside me ruined it. Whatever it was, I deeply hated that "thing."

When Dr. Alprin wished me goodbye, I watched his back disappear out the door. Uncontrollably, I doubled over and cried harder than I had ever cried before, clutching the ChapStick like a holy relic. I was sure I'd never see him again.

When I returned to Birch, Mrs. Steele said, "Lady Ann told me that Dr. Alprin gave you an IQ test. What happened?"

"He said there was nothing wrong with me."

"And what's that supposed to mean?"

"He said I wasn't retarded."

"Yeah, and I'm a trinket in a Cracker Jack box."

"No, no, it's true. I'm not like the rest of them."

"You're not?"

"No. They look funny and I don't. They act different too."

"Look, buster," warned Mrs. Steele with her usual finger in my face. "Let's get somethin' straight. I don't like kids who wear glasses with crooked eyes or stupid, silly boys that are tall, short, skinny, fat, or smart-alecky. I hate cripples and I can't stand harebrained kids—or kids that walk funny, talk funny, bounce balls, chew gum—or spoiled, bratty kids that fart quietly and blame others. And as for you," she continued, placing her finger at the end of my nose, "I hate liars! Especially snotty-nosed kids who think they can put one over on me."

"But I ain't lyin', Mrs. Steele, honest!" I pleaded, making an "X" over my heart.

"Oh, stop that cross-my-heart crap! I want the truth, boy, the truth!"

"But I'm tellin' you the truth. Honest, Mrs. Steele."

"I'm about to slap the snot outta you, boy! Cut it out!"

"But, I—"

"I know, I know, '*but I'm tellin' you the truth*,'" she mimicked. "No buts! You're gettin' me mad, boy! They don't put people in these places who're fixed right in the head.[2] Don't you get it?"

"But I ain't lyin', Mrs.—"

"Shut up!"

"But Mrs. Steele, I've been tellin' you the truth. Please believe me."

"I said shut up!"

An insidious silence fell between us. I felt trapped at the doorway between right and wrong, between telling the truth and not being believed. Feeling overwhelmed by Mrs. Steele's injustice, I lowered my head and began crying, my tears falling to the hardwood floor at my feet.

Mrs. Steele sighed with impatience. "Oh, for Christ's sake," she scolded. "Stop your whinin' . . . and look at me when I'm talkin' to ya."

I looked up at her cold stare.

"That's what I thought. You've been lyin' to me all along. And don't give me those alligator tears. Get out! Get outta my sight before I take my belt to ya."

I bolted out of the sewing room. About midway down the hall, I felt a sudden rage come over me. I stopped and leaned my forehead against the wall. Unable to contain myself, I shouted tearfully, pounding the wall with my fists, "I hate her! I hate her! I hate her! Goddamn it, I hate her!"

The jingle of Mrs. Steele's keys snapped me around. Down the hall, just outside the sewing room, there she was, fists on her hips and staring straight at me, her heavy breathing ballooning her fleshy frame. She was red faced and flinty mad, finally breaking her cardboard posture and bellowing, "You brat! I heard all that! Get your ass back here." She pointed at the floor in front of her.

I turned the other way and ran to the basement. As I headed for my place on the backless bench, Rawbone stopped me.

"No, no, no," he said. "I want you over here with me." He pointed between his legs dangling over the side of the desk. "Where's my shit you promised?"

"I got it right here," I said. "Look, I didn't forget." I reached into my pocket, pulled out the watch, and held it up to his face. I was sure he'd approve.

"You dope!" he screamed, grabbing the watch and throwing it against the concrete wall. "What the fuck am I supposed to do with a lady's watch?"

"But . . . but . . . you said gold."

"You asshole. You mean that's all you brought me back?"

"But I . . . I . . ."

"Go over there and pick up that watch, you stupid mothafucka!"

After returning the watch to Rawbone, he took a closer look at it and, reading the back, mumbled, "Fourteen-karat gold . . . To Mother, Love Stan, 1950 . . . Fuck it. I'll keep it." He leaned back and shoved the watch into his pocket.

"You like it then?"

"Fuck you! Go back to your seat."

That night, and for nearly a year thereafter, the ChapStick became my only solace. I slept with it, grasping it tightly as I cried myself to sleep. It was like taking a little love to bed with me; it nurtured me and reminded me of Dr. Alprin's goodness, helping me, at times, to forget my dismal surroundings. As for what I had said to Dr. Alprin's wife, I couldn't forgive myself. It tormented me for months.

The saber rattling of New Lisbon's transgressions went beyond my reason, slicing my better sense into pieces. I had not escaped the abuse; it had become a part of me. My highly buffed veneer was penetrable. Underneath, I was learning of its decay and, unknowingly, smelling the bad breath of a Pavlovian conditioning that ruled my existence. I began to doubt my ability to survive the emotional consequences and, particularly, maintain my sanity.

ENDNOTES FOR CHAPTER SIXTEEN

1. In 1905, Alfred Binet and Theodore Simon developed the first modern intelligence test. This was modified in 1916 by Lewis Terman of Stanford University and has since been known as the Stanford-Binet Intelligence Scale. David Weschler developed his first scale in the 1930s; I was probably given a version of the Weschler test at New Lisbon.

In recent years, IQ (intelligence quotient) tests have been criticized for being designed according to middle-class ideals and/or standards. Some critics call for them to be tailored, in language and cultural references, to the socioeconomic class to whom they are given; if not, the tests may be responsible for some inaccurate results and the misplacement of "normal" or typically developing children. Changes are now being made to address this issue. It should also be stressed that IQ tests should never be the sole criteria in diagnosing mental retardation.

And while it was originally thought that a person's IQ was stagnant, it has been shown that IQ scores may sometimes be improved, up to the age of about ten or eleven, if a child is given the opportunity to learn. With many children entering institutions at a young age, this possibility only adds to the injustice of leaving them to languish in those facilities without benefit of any substantive education or mental stimulation. Low, or often nonexistent, expectations may reinforce diagnoses that might have been inaccurate in the first place.

Wikipedia, "Alfred Binet," http://en.wikipedia.org/wiki/Alfred_Binet (accessed June 11, 2005). *Psychologie Online*, "The Intelligence Quotient (IQ)," http://www.psyonline.nl/en-iq.htm (accessed June 11, 2005).

2. In *The State Boys Rebellion* (New York: Simon & Shuster, 2004), author Michael D'Antonio tells the story of Fred Boyce. In 1949, at the age of eight, Boyce was committed to the Walter E. Fernald School for the Feebleminded in Waltham, Massachusetts. Even though IQ tests showed Boyce was normal, he was labeled a "moron" and remained institutionalized for eleven years. Aside from receiving little education and suffering physical and sexual abuse, Boyce and others were, without their knowledge, given radioactive oatmeal as part of an experiment conducted by MIT and Quaker Oats.

CHAPTER SEVENTEEN
A Stately Affair

AGAIN, THEY WERE all singing that song, the one normally sung to a girl, but with my name filled in. The unmelodious gibberish spilled from clumsy, swollen lips, from stilts of fear and damaged minds, from bodies bearing the usual evidence of the basement's brutalities—broken limbs in casts, splints, and slings, and eyes blackened and swollen shut. Any God-given humanity had been punched right out of them.

Shortly after breakfast on September 18, 1954, Mrs. Steele yelled from the day room landing, "RAWBONE! Get Carroll up here immediately!"

I started a mad dash out of the room, but was halted when I tripped over somebody's feet. The basement roared with laughter. I grabbed onto the handles of my self-respect, got up, and ran the rest of the way to the basement steps that led up to the day room, leaving behind the final verse of that hideous song.

As I took the first step up the stairs, I heard Mrs. Steele cussing to herself.

"Damn that kid! Where's that bratty kid?"

"Here I am, Mrs. Steele."

Blinded by the daylight, I looked at the black-red image of Mrs. Steele's outline. When my vision cleared, I couldn't believe my eyes. Mrs. Steele was smiling, her beefy belly slumped over the railing and her closed hand extended to me with something in it.

Nervously, I pointed to myself and asked, "For me?"

"No, I just act this way. Yes, it's for you. Take it," she said with an air of untouchable glory. "Cripes, you'd think I gave ya somethin' to be afraid of!"

I inched my open hand out to hers. She released her grip, spilling a treasure trove of Christmas hard candy.

"Gee, thanks, Mrs. Steele!" I knew I could use the candy later to appease Rawbone.

"Don't give me that 'what a nice lady' look. I don't go for that sentimental crap. Just eat it, shut up, and come with me."

Once in the sewing room, Mrs. Steele ordered me to take a seat. She lowered a crooked finger to my face. "You've been doin' good these days. I like that. Maybe you're startin' to learn somethin' I've been learnin' ya. You're a lucky boy today."

"I am?"

"Just button your lip. You ain't yet earned the privilege to ask questions around here, mister."

"Y-y-yes, ma'am."

"That's better. Now listen . . ."

As Mrs. Steele babbled on, I couldn't help but reflect on the foul odors of the basement and wonder how she could permit us to stay down there like that. Biddle's ear came to mind, as well as the rapes, the beatings, the broken bones, the years of sheer boredom. My thoughts were interrupted by approaching footsteps.

"Hi, Mrs. Steele. You wanted me?"

"Yes, Jackson," she said, pulling the waist of her dress up over her midriff bulge. "Dress him in those clothes over there." She pointed to a shelf at the far end of wall. "I'll be back down at twelve thirty. My Henry's sick today. If I don't get up there and sit with him, he'll be pissin' a bitch at me, and I can't have that. Got it?"

"Yes, ma'am."

As she turned to leave, Jackson looked over at me with an expression I'd seen all too often. A familiar dread ran through me and the room became uncomfortably quiet. Jackson looked down at me and smiled, two decaying teeth protruding from his grinning mouth and a hard-on revealed through the crotch of his pants.

"About time I got ya alone," he sneered. "I don't see ya no more since Mrs. Steele sent ya to the other side. Rawbone is stickin' it to ya, ain't he?"

I didn't answer.

"I've been waitin' for your ass."

"But Jackson, I don't wanna."

"Get up!" he hissed, grabbing my wrist and pulling me out of my chair.

"Please, Jackson."

He led me to the back of the room, unbuckled my belt, and pulled down my pants.

"No, don't make me."

"Shut up! I can hear when Mrs. Steele comes downstairs from her apartment. Lay down," he ordered, unzipping his fly.

"You'll just put it between my legs, right?"

"Yeah, yeah, sh-hh. Lay down."

I obeyed him.

"Promise you won't put it inside?"

"I won't, I promise. What's in your hand?"

"Candy."

"Gimmie it."

"No, no, no. It's for Rawbone."

"Just gimmie it. I ain't gonna take it."

He placed the candy at arm's length in a little pile on the floor and straddled me. On bent knees, he inched himself down, spread my cheeks, and spat.

"No, no, no, not there! You said you weren't gonna put it there."

He leaned forward, threw his hands around my mouth, and shoved his penis in all the way. I yelled. Snot and slobber spurted through his fingers. I thrashed, wiggled, and squirmed, trying to throw him off me. But he was too powerful and able to complete the deed, though never more brutally than this time; I was certain he'd injured me internally.

Jackson jumped to his feet and zipped up, as if it had been nothing more than a casual get-together. He bent over and picked up the candy, tossed one piece into the air, caught it in his mouth, and then walked over to the pile of clothes Mrs. Steele had left for me.

"I gotta go to the bathroom. You fuckin' broke your promise, Jackson. That hurt!"

"You liked it," he said arrogantly.

I picked myself up and went into the bathroom, where I evacuated the sin, but not the memory. When I went to flush the toilet, I noticed the water was red. Frightened by it, I recoiled and began crying. The sight of the blood shoved me back against the wall of a moral firing squad; I felt their bullets go through my heart. While my sanity bled, I flushed the toilet. One thing was clear to me at that moment: this had to stop.

A few moments later, Jackson was at the door.

"Did you fall in?"

"I'm comin'," I said, finally opening the door.

"It's about time. What were you doin', jackin' off?"

I didn't say anything, but walked by him to the clothes, remaining silent.

At twelve thirty, Mrs. Steele returned, her face revealing traces of sleep.

"You look nice," she said in approval. "Jackson, I'm so proud of you. Those clothes fit him good. He's beautiful. I know how to pick out the right clothes, don't I, Jackson?"

"Yes, ma'am."

"Okay, you go ahead and shut up those bratty kids down there. Listen to them. Leave 'em alone for a minute, and . . . go shut 'em up. I can't handle it today. I've got one of those damn headaches again. I'll call ya when I'm ready to have you take him to the Administration Building."

"Yes, ma'am," said Jackson, slipping out of the room with

Rawbone's candy.

Mrs. Steele left me sitting there. After about twenty minutes, she returned with Jackson again and announced, "Well, guess it's time you knew what's goin' on. You've been picked to go to Perth Amboy. And don't ask me what it's all about. You always wanna know too much. You'll learn about it soon enough. I'll say one thing, though." Her face bubbled with pride. "Today's your lucky day. Okay, Jackson, get 'im over to Administration. They're expecting him."

When we reached the Administration Building, a number of newspapermen were hanging around with big, fancy flashbulb cameras strapped to their shoulders. A trail of escort vehicles, with American flags on both sides of their front fenders, was lined up along the curb in front of the building. In and around the vehicles were very official-looking men in dark suits, whom I soon learned were government security agents. Upon reaching the line of parked cars, we were met by two boys from other cottages, accompanied by Millie and a man who acted like he was in charge.

"Jackson," said Millie, "you can go back to your cottage. You're not needed now. I'll take over from here."

We were led to a limousine. Two security agents sat in front, and as soon as we got in, we were whisked away. The agent on the passenger side instructed us to keep our mouths shut and say as little as possible at all times, that we were nothing more than observers. About an hour later, a sign by the road read:

WELCOME TO
PERTH AMBOY

Ten minutes later, we entered a tennis complex. Another sign read:

PERTH AMBOY TENNIS CLUB
BRIGHTON AVENUE COURTS

The number of reporters in front of New Lisbon's Administration Building was minuscule compared to the swarm of newsmen at Perth Amboy; they were everywhere. As we drove across the gated boundaries, reporters and camera crews followed on foot. Flashbulbs clicked. A strange bureaucratic jargon filtered through the open car windows; I was surrounded by sound-bite slogans and government men giving orders. The air was charged with excitement and mystery, even secrecy, as some of the men seemed to talk out of the sides of their mouths. Everybody except us was on foot, being checked for proper identification or patted down as they entered the restricted area we were approaching. Some underwent a more thorough search, the guards apparently looking for weapons or anything else that might otherwise put the day's dignitaries at risk.

The other boys acted like starstruck fans, while I sat quietly, watching and listening to the spectacle, not so much from curiosity but as a victim who had become weary, suspicious, and cautious of anything to do with such people. By then, I had lost all respect for members of the bureaucracy. I was mystified, but about all I could do was wonder what was next and why we had been picked for what appeared to be an important occasion.

Cartwright and Mead, the other two boys next to me, were, as far as I could tell, the least retarded of New Lisbon's population. I suspected they were the institution's "model" patients; physically, they appeared completely normal and, like me, were beautifully dressed in suits. But there was one telling clue that all wasn't right. Still dangling from the button of Cartwright's jacket was an inventory tag. Not only did no one remove it when he was issued the suit, but even more revealing, Cartwright never gave it a second thought.

Our limousine and the one in front of us drove onto the tarmac, while others behind us detoured to an area set aside for official state cars. In the center of the tennis court, we were instructed to get out of the car and sit on bleachers designated for us. Flashbulbs clicked from every direction as we took our places.

While sitting there, one of my feet suddenly felt wet. I looked down, picked up my pant leg, and noticed that lines of blood had seeped into my left shoe. Startled, I got up and spoke to the security agent standing at the far corner of the bleachers, indicating I had to go to the bathroom.

"Sure," he said, pointing the way. I was permitted to go, unattended, just as the tennis players were gathering in the middle of the main court.

In the bathroom, I went into a stall, dropped my pants, and tried to squeeze out the bloody fluid. When I spread my legs and looked into the toilet bowel, a bright red horror stared back at me. Blood coated the inside of the entire toilet. I slipped off my left shoe and discovered that I'd been bleeding more than I realized. I flushed the toilet—and when the water cleared, I dunked my shoe and thrashed it, clearing it of any obvious blood, and slipped it back on. Distraught, I sat back down on the seat, buried my face in my naked knees, and wept. A few moments later, someone walked in to use one of the urinals. I withheld my sobs, watching the man pee through the gap in the door. After he left, I quickly got up, pulled off my underpants, and dunked them. After wringing them out, I got dressed again and stepped out of the stall just as two men entered the bathroom.

"Are you Charles Carroll?"

"Yes, sir."

"Come with us."

They led me to the middle of the tennis court where I was joined by Cartwright and Mead.

"Ladies and gentlemen," spoke a heavy-set man on a megaphone. "Let's give these fine-looking boys from New Lisbon a big hand. Fine lads, aren't they?" Everybody applauded. It was the 12th Annual Invitation Tennis Tournament. I stood next to the nation's top-ranking tennis players: Hal Burrows from Charlottesville, George Stewart from Newark, Sid Schwartz of Brooklyn, and Irv

Dorfman of New York City. All were seeking the title.

Finally, the big moment came with the arrival of the governor of New Jersey, Robert B. Meyner. We stood and posed for pictures. And though I felt a deep sense of disgust, I smiled.

The governor, a formidable tennis player himself, came over and stood next to me. Cartwright and Mead were told to return to their seats. Someone gave me a tennis racket and told me to hand it to the governor. Just as I turned to the governor and extended the racket to him, an order rang out.

"Hold it right there," said a photographer as the governor grasped the racket. *Snap. Flash. Blink.* Dozens of flashbulbs went off. The picture taken at that moment appeared in many newspapers across New Jersey—most notably, Newark's *Star-Ledger*, published statewide.

The fans in the bleachers wore American apple-pie smiles, while none of them knew that the ceremony was as crooked as a jagged saw, a first-class snow job, one that allotted additional funds to New Lisbon but did little to improve conditions. I'd been hustled, and I deeply resented it. I took exception to the whole spectacle; they were filling their coffers at the horrible cost of our abuse and educational neglect.

When the "show" was over, we each received a handful of hard candy, sent along by Mrs. Steele.

On our way back, the small American flags on both front fenders waved in righteous glory, while the two officials up front spouted on about the success of the event.

When I saw the massive Administration Building, I was again sickened by its promise of staunch integrity; its declaration of safety and security wracked my nerves. From the moment we passed over New Lisbon's threshold, I knew I could no longer tolerate the prospect of continually having my ass kicked—or fucked.

I WAS ELEVEN years old, and for the past three years I had hung onto

CHARLES A. CARROLL

my manhood as if masculinity were more important than injury or death. However, I now saw that I was torn between two evils: rape without protection and rape with protection. This immoral equation was clearly misanthropic and antisocial, though I reasoned it was one that worked. But I had to ask myself whether I was willing to endure the assaults to maintain my honor—or trade them off for "dishonorable" security. Could I use that avenue to stop Rawbone and Jackson from continually hurting me? I knew that once I crossed over that line, I would be thought of as a punk. And from that stigma, there would be no turning back. It was a decision that meant converting my "good looks" into a lethal weapon. No longer could I ignore the lack of prospects for any legitimate sources to take action. And though I considered my only alternative utterly despicable, I was now finding that option more and more palatable.

Plate Thirteen
12th Annual Invitation Tennis Tournament in Perth Amboy, New Jersey
September 18, 1954
Charles A. Carroll, eleven years old, handing tennis racket to Governor Robert B. Meyner

CHAPTER EIGHTEEN
Refined Madness at Its Best

A FEW SHORT months passed and the holidays were quickly approaching. Bobby and I were sitting in the day room, surrounded by Christmas decorations. Bobby glanced at Mrs. Steele to see if she was looking, then stuck his hand under the table.

"Take this. Hurry up, before somebody sees it."

I leaned back and looked down at his hand.

"What is it, Bobby?"

"A note. Just take it and put it in your pocket."

"Who's it from?"

"From Desarino. He slipped it to me this morning in the dining room."

I took it and quickly shoved it into the watch pocket of my pants.

"Hey, Chuckie," began Bobby, "Desarino's the baddest motherfucker here. You're fuckin' lucky . . . I mean, *really* lucky. Nobody'll fuck with you no more if *he* likes ya."

I had only spoken with Desarino a few times since that first night he'd brought me raisins, but his unmistakable feelings toward me had always hung in the air.

"I don't know if I want a Kid."

"You're nuts. You don't see Rawbone fuckin' with *me*, do ya?"

"No."

"What the fuck are ya waitin' for? Hey," he whispered, "he even has some stuff for ya."

"Like what?"

"How should I know? Maybe it's some good food. Sometimes he works over in the employees' dining room, you know—not just ours. And their food is a lot better than that shit they serve us. Why're ya lookin' at me like that?"

"I don't know."

"Get a Kid, Chuckie."

"I don't know. It's just that . . . I don't know."

"Hey, Chuckie, stop thinkin' about it. You need Desarino. He's nice. Hey, are we still gonna run away?"

"Maybe."

"Maybe, what?"

"Maybe . . . maybe in the spring," I said.

"You said we'd run away *last* spring, then you chickened out. I know one thing, if you don't get a Kid, you're gonna wind up in a pine box like some of the others around this place. We gotta run away. I don't want a dead brother."

"Oh, cut it out, Bobby."

"At least Desarino won't bust your ass wide open like that fuckin' Jackson and Rawbone."

"Sh-hh, Bobby, not too loud!"

"He'll only put it between your legs, Chuckie," whispered Bobby.

"How do you know that?"

"Don't worry, I know. You don't believe me, huh, Chuckie?"

"It isn't that, it's just that . . . it's just . . ."

"It's just what?"

"I don't know. It's just that . . ."

"Ah, forget it. You'll do it once you're dead. Hey, did you hear about Mosely?"

"You mean that guy that looks at me funny in the dining room like he wants to do it to me too?"

"That's the one. Anyway, Desarino saw him lookin' at you the other day and kicked his fuckin' ass behind the dining room where they keep all the slop for the pigs. Desarino don't like nobody lookin' at you fuckin' funny, Chuckie."

"God, Bobby, you're swearing a lot."

"Ah, fuck that shit! There ain't no God in this place. You mad at me now?"

"No, why?"

"For sayin' that about God."

"No, not really. You're probably right."

"I know I'm right. Anyway, Chuckie, somebody's killin' people around here. Heck, you could be next."

"How's that?"

"Remember that rat in Spruce Cottage?"

"I heard about it. What about 'im?"

"When they found 'im missing, they thought he ran away. But he didn't run away," Bobby explained.

"I know. They found him behind his cottage."

"Yeah, buried alive. The nuts did it because of that show on television, *You Asked For It*."

"Yeah, that's what I heard . . . that they saw somebody on television getting buried alive. The guy on TV lived, so the stupid nuts tried it."

"That's what they *say*, but that's not what happened," Bobby corrected.

"So what really happened?"

"Somebody did it because he was a rat. Maybe an attendant? Look what happened to Clarence Shepherd. All they found were his bones."[1]

"Because the buzzards got 'im, that's why."

"That's right. And you could be next, Chuckie. Wanna be dead? Wanna be in that stupid graveyard near the cornfield?"

"No."

"Then get a Kid. It's the only way in this place. You look like everybody else here when you take your clothes off."

"Whatta ya mean?" I asked.

"Your black-and-blue marks, that's what I mean. You have 'em all over ya."

"I do have a lotta black-and-blue marks, huh?"

"You know you do. Remember that guy that ate a whole potato? He wasn't eatin' it. Somebody shoved it down his throat. And now he's dead too. Want that?"

"Oh, stop it, Bobby."

"Okay, don't get a Kid and see if I care."

I turned away, thinking about the day of the tennis tournament, and finding it more and more difficult to argue with him.

That night, I slipped out of the dormitory, clutching Desarino's still unread note, and headed for the bathroom to look at it. But just as I was about to enter, I caught a glimpse of the inflated Santa Claus, an annual Christmas fixture, among the quiet shadows of the day room. An ill-boding chill came over me. It was staring at me as though jacking off, the black hole of its mouth twisting into a lascivious grin. Disturbed by its presence, I crept over to the blown-up object, hurled back my fists, and began beating the shit out of it—jabbing its face until it crinkled like tinfoil. Then, hearing the sound of hissing air, I stepped back and watched as it expelled Christmas from its bloated frame. When it dropped to its knees, I gave one swift kick to its robust belly, and, like a blown tire, it went *pop*, shrinking into an unrecognizable pile at my feet. But I wasn't through with it yet—not yet. Over and over again, I stomped on it, my ears thumping to the beat of my heart, my body dripping with sweat, until all evidence of its perverse meaning vanished. Out of breath, I cautiously leaned over the son of a bitch, looking for any signs of life. There were none. Santa Claus was dead.

I went into the bathroom and read Desarino's note:

Deer Carol,

Just a few lines to let you no I love you verry much. You're so cute, and I dream about you everey night. I see you everey day in the kichen. I have all ways wanted to talk to you again but I thoght it woud make you mad. Do you like me? I hope so. Ill be serving cake tomorrow and I'll save you some. Dont get mad, okay? May be you can be my Kid. I love you with all my hart and sole and dream about you all the time. If you need any thing let me know and if anybody bothers you let me know and Ill kick their asses in. be my Kid, okay? I love you. Throw this note away so I dont get in trobble.

Love and kissis with all my hart and sole,

Desarino

I ripped up the note, threw the love pieces into the toilet, and flushed. I watched the whirling fragments disappear into the dark viscera of that alternate world of Kids and protection, but not without sensing the enormous power a "yes" answer would provide. However, like any proposition of that magnitude, there was always a question of price. Was I willing to pay it?

I went to bed that night knowing that the next day would bring another round of torment and abuse—and a major decision. As I laid there, I was overwhelmed by the loud snores and pathetic mutterings of disturbed children in their sleep, crippled by their awful dreams. I knew I was trapped, hog-tied to New Lisbon's complete sociological failure, and it was time to do something about it. I'd had enough. I was fed up with serving as Rawbone's private livestock, appeasing Jackson's predatory hard-ons, and hoping for an end to Mrs. Steele's outright denial of reality. When I awakened the next morning, my decision was made. I was ready to be a player.

WHEN I ENTERED the dining room for breakfast the next morning, like so many times before, I was hit by a barrage of sounds from rattling, pressed-out trays and hundreds of residents of various cottages talking amongst themselves, bringing the noise level to an unintelligible hum.

If the hoards of flies didn't ruin appetites, the food did. However bad looking and tasting, though, many patients ate with the fervor of hungry pigs, slurping their meals and scraping the last remaining bits of food on their trays, ending the banquet with one final lick of their spoons.

I spotted Desarino at the front of the dining room. He was serving cinnamon cake at one of the steam tables, just as he had said in his note.

Committed to my decision, I had entered the mess hall that morning feeling like a traitor to myself. I was dry-mouthed and frightened, but in an effort to look good and follow through with the choice I'd made, I began primping every chance I got, catching a glimpse of myself in windowpanes as the line neared the steam tables. At times, I patted my hair, fixing a curl here and there to fit the part.

While I waited my turn in the chow line, I kept wondering: Am I cute enough? Has Desarino changed his mind? Did he mean all the things he said in the note? I was filled with many mixed emotions. One part of me said it was all about getting protection, while another said it was homosexuality. One part was half-charmed by the prospect, another part unsure and perplexed. And, at times, I felt dirty about the whole thing. As I neared the serving tables, my troublesome thoughts converted into physical responses. I began to notice my heart palpitating, much like a kid approaching his first date.

When I looked at Desarino, I didn't see him as a predator. I felt drawn to him. This change of perception signaled that maybe I was more assimilated than I'd given myself credit for, and that maybe, just maybe, I had been in denial of my own feelings. Surprised by these thoughts and emotions, I remember asking myself, What is

Charles A. Carroll

happening to me? Why am I feeling such things? I again took a closer look at Desarino. His hair was coal black, just as I remembered. And, like before, he was wearing an Elvis Presley ducktail. Desarino's forehead was covered with rolling natural curls. He was muscular and obviously took great pride in his overall appearance. His jeans were starched and hand creased, and he wore a tight-fitting T-shirt that showed off his washboard stomach. Atop one shoulder was a pack of Lucky Strikes, neatly tucked into his rolled-up sleeves that clearly exposed his firm biceps.

Desarino caught me staring at him and smiled. I turned my eyes away and blushed. When he turned away, I stared again. I could hardly keep my eyes off him. Each time he caught me looking, his eyes whispered, "It's okay." He appeared flattered by my glances. Nevertheless, I turned away in a deliberate attempt to appear coy, at times withering into myself like the fawn in Tchaikovsky's Swan Lake ballet. The next time he caught me looking at him, I didn't shy away; I smiled.

When I finally reached him, he said, "Hi." Instead of plopping one piece of cake onto my tray, he gave me three.

"No! No! No!" I protested. "I'll get in trouble," I explained, pushing the cake back onto the table.

"Take it, Carroll," insisted someone from the line. "Nobody's gonna say nothin'."

Desarino slid the two pieces of cake back onto my tray. "He's right. Nobody's gonna say shit."

When I attempted to push the cake back again, his hand stopped mine.

"It's good to see you again. Did you get my note?"

"Yeah. I threw it down the toilet."

"Are you mad at me?" he asked.

"No."

He gently removed his hand from mine, leaned over, and softly asked, "Then you'll be my Kid?"

I hesitated.

"Please? Don't say no. I . . . I love you."

"Hey!" yelled someone. "You're holdin' everybody up!"

Desarino's eyes locked on the complainer. "Fuck you!" he threatened, his jagged, dark eyebrows turning inward toward the bridge of his nose. "Wanna do somethin' about it?" He raised the spatula over his head as if about to use it on the man.

The complaining patient fell silent.

Desarino's eyes turned back to me and he leaned closer. "You wanna be my Kid?"

"I, uh . . ."

"Please?"

"Okay," I said without any further hesitation.

Desarino's face sparkled with a smile.

"Bye," I said softly, giving him a smile in return.

I headed for a table, shooing flies off my tray every step of the way, and took a seat.

One boy noticed I had three pieces of cake and called over to Rawbone, "Hey, look at Carroll's tray!"

I shrank in fear. Rawbone rose to his feet, rubbernecking over the heads of the others.

"Where?" he asked.

"Right there," said the boy, pointing to where I was sitting.

"Hey, Carroll," grumbled Rawbone. "Where'd you get all the fuckin' cake?"

Heads from four or five tables looked over at me. I was red faced—embarrassed over the implications of the extra dessert.

Rawbone hurried over, swiped all three pieces of cake from my tray, and returned to his seat. Bobby, three tables away, heard the ruckus and looked over at Rawbone. Bobby then stood up and mouthed some words to me, something to the effect that he'd be right back. He went to Desarino. Desarino eyed Rawbone.

Rawbone, with one look at Desarino, realized the significance of what he'd done and ran back to me with the cake. "Are you Desarino's Kid?" he asked.

Boldly, I stood up and answered, "Yes, I am."

Desarino stared from the steam table.

"Shit!" complained Rawbone. "You should've told me. I asked you where you got the cake. Here, take 'em. I don't like cake anyway. I'm sorry, okay?" He affectionately patted me on the back.

Though hardly believing my ears, I looked up. For the first time, I realized Rawbone was just a gutless, two-bit punk. I felt a surge of victory. I looked over at my brother. There he was, signaling an okay sign and smiling, while patients at nearby tables mumbled, "Carroll's got a Kid."

Only then did I begin to finally grasp Bobby's brand of protection. Although I was still torn between right and wrong and the discomfiture of being someone's Kid, I couldn't help but appreciate the novelty of feeling I would never be hurt again.

Now, with the lid up on my metaphorical coffin, a whole new world of sunshine cradled me with warmth and affection. I could breathe again. I felt renewed.

Three days later, after returning from an errand for Mrs. Steele, Rawbone showed up at Birch Cottage with two blistering black eyes. It was official. I had crossed over to the other side.

DURING THE DAYS and months that followed, each time I went to the dining room, Desarino all but genuflected at the sight of me. It was impossible not to be flattered by his attention and, as time passed, I became less self-conscious about it. His appreciation pumped life into the empty vessel that was my self-esteem.

Desarino, as I discovered, was also a tragic victim who didn't belong at New Lisbon any more than I did. We had arrived at the institution much in the same manner: it was a court thing. Sending Desarino to New Lisbon was simply a decision to clear another matter from the courts' bulging caseloads. Like me, he was a ward of the state.

Our bond continued to grow stronger and stronger at the far

window of Birch's dormitory. There we kissed and hugged, professing our love for each other.

As it turned out, our periodic get-togethers evolved into a relationship that was anything but sexual. From Desarino, I learned about many of the Colony's unconventional alliances and how they worked; indeed, some were sexual, but many were not. Ironically, sex tended to be an incidental, rather than primary, motivation sustaining these unions. Love and belonging were the driving forces. Protection was more an extension of that shared love, and sex a mere bodily release rather than an act of homosexuality.

What was antisocial to the real world was socially acceptable and full of grace in our self-made subculture; it was the real world that became the intruder. So New Lisbon was filled with lonely and forgotten people sharing fondness for each other in exchange for being attached to *someone*, rather than detached from *everyone*—and sharing expressions of love, because the "civilized" mainstream had left them behind in the Colony's Stone Age of Insanity. The residents themselves had found a way to close the "human gap" left by the bureaucracy's failure.

One must understand that, while many of these relationships were, in the eyes of the public, oddballs of sorts, they worked, and were as necessary to the human spirit as food is essential to the body. They filled lifeless souls with dignity; many had codes of conduct as virtuous as, if not nobler than, their conventional counterparts. The level of commitment sometimes grew to the point of defending that commitment to the death.[2]

Desarino and I began pulling in the lost pieces of our self-worth, gathering the fragments of our self-esteem, until we could finally feel whole again. We sensed that to be without love was the worst human disgrace; but to be *of* it, in whatever manner, was sublime. Desarino sang words of "love, not hate," of "caring, not force," of "kindness, not rape," and of "compromise, not homosexuality." What we had *looked* queer, but it was not. Yes, our "love" was between men, but among men who needed what New Lisbon failed to provide us—respect for our own humanity.

And so, finally, Desarino and I took our metaphorical vows hand in hand and were married without rice or fanfare at the side road of an oddball socialization on the outskirts of a refined madness at its best.

ENDNOTES FOR CHAPTER EIGHTEEN

1. Clarence Shepherd, a fourteen-year-old New Lisbon resident, was diabetic and required injectable insulin daily. Missing for three months, he was eventually found by hunters, his bones bleached by the sun and picked clean by buzzards. His death was highly suspicious because he did not fit the profile of a runaway. He was a passive kid—never aggressive to others or toward the system. Though very young at the time, we were all shocked by the incident, never believing the runaway theory. Perhaps, with today's forensics, the manner of his death could be cleared up. It is time to open the state's graveyards and investigate all questionable deaths.

   See Appendix A.2.6/Neglect of Duty; Resident Freezes to Death/1996. A New Lisbon employee was charged with failing to monitor a resident and allowing him to leave Yucca Cottage unnoticed. The resident was later found frozen to death.

2. In the 1950s, while working on New Lisbon's farm, a resident allegedly murdered another resident in a scuffle over the first resident's Kid. It was purported that the victim's head was bashed in with a tractor crank. Note: The state later stepped in and closed down the farm due to chronic violations of fair labor practices.

PLATE FOURTEEN
OUTSIDE BIRCH TWO
C. 1953
BOYS ON THEIR WAY TO THE DINING ROOM

Part Five

Without memory, our existence would be barren and opaque, like a prison cell into which no light penetrates; like a tomb which rejects the living . . . If anything can, it is memory that will save humanity. For me, hope without memory is like memory without hope.

Elie Wiesel
Nobel Peace Prize Lecture
1986

CHAPTER NINETEEN

Homicidal Tendencies

ONE NIGHT SEVERAL months later, two burly institutional cops caught Desarino kissing me from the dormitory window. It was Mr. Ballanger and his partner, Jimmie, both of whom were the men who stopped Mr. Wheeler on that night when I snuck over to see him. Mr. Ballanger yanked Desarino from the ledge and, with billy club raised, ordered him to the front of the cottage. It was almost summer, but nighttime temperatures had dipped to the thirties. Though barefooted and in nightgowns, Mr. and Mrs. Steele ordered all of us outside and made us face the road where Mr. Ballanger and Jimmie were waiting. As we stood there shivering from the cold, the high beams of the squad car were switched on. Only then did we see Desarino lying in front of the car, spread-eagled in the middle of the road, his head covered in blood, barely conscious.[1]

Mr. Ballanger ordered Desarino to get up on his feet. "Okay, Jimmie," he said to his partner. "You drive. I'll escort this son of a bitch to jail. Follow me."

Mr. Ballanger began shoving the butt end of the billy club into Desarino's back, forcing him forward. Desarino stumbled and floundered like a drunken man. I pitied him.

As we stood watching the gruesome procession move at a snail's pace, Jimmie aimed the side-door spotlight on Desarino as Mr.

Ballanger beat Desarino about the arms, legs, and back,[2] shouting, "You homosexual son of a bitch! Keep your fuckin' ass moving!"

We all watched in horror until the squad car's backlights vanished into the black arms of the night.

It was claimed that Desarino was sent to the New Jersey State Hospital at Trenton[3], although that was never confirmed. But if it were true, we knew they would administer electroshock treatments as a means of putting him in his place; threats of such disciplinary measures were commonplace at New Lisbon.

Knowing I had lost Desarino's protection, Dr. Alprin's remarks about "homicidal tendencies" suddenly rang true. Now murder was necessary. After half a year of security, the umbilical cord was severed. I felt lost, alone, and frightened all over again, and I knew I could not survive a return to Rawbone's abuse. Further, I was convinced that Rawbone would retaliate for having had to restrain himself for so long.

While in the backyard the following day, I found a heavy rock and stored it close to the back of Birch—for retrieval when and if Rawbone bothered me again.

A short time later, Rawbone paid me a visit in the middle of the night. He shoved a sock in my mouth and proceeded to beat me up. As he did, I curled into a ball and took the beating in silence.

Rawbone whispered, "That's for the two black eyes Desarino gave me 'cause of you, mothafucka!"

After the beating, I tossed and turned, thinking what it would be like to kill Rawbone. Murdering him was my only option, and there was no turning back. Not anymore.

When Rawbone fell back to sleep, I slipped out of Birch in my nightgown to retrieve the rock, which I carefully hid it in my bed. Before long, I heard Mr. Westly's time clock click at the key station and knew he'd soon be asleep in the hall. I waited. About an hour later, after I heard Mr. Westly's snores, I slipped quietly out of bed, taking the rock with me.

In the shadows of the night, I eased myself over to the bed where

Rawbone was sleeping soundly, the full moon highlighting the outline of his body. One look at him and the devil ran through my veins. I pictured his head smashed in like a watermelon. I also imagined him gone from Birch and what that would mean, not only to me, but to the other pathetic souls suffering under his reign.

I slowly raised the rock over my head, determined to crush his skull. My stomach knotted. Beads of sweat rolled down my face as I held the rock high over him. My arms shivered. My breathing stopped. My heart thumped against my rib cage, begging for redemption. My eyes widened like those of a madman, and just as I was about to deliver the fatal blow, there was a whisper more frightening than the idea of murder. It was Bobby.

"No, Chuckie," my brother whispered, grabbing both arms. "Not that way." He pulled me from between the beds. "C'mon," he coached. "I've got an idea."

"Let me do it," I begged.

Bobby whispered, "No, c'mon."

As he led me away, I told him that Rawbone had beaten me up again.

"I know," he said. "I saw him. And gimmie that." He took the rock from my hands.

Bobby took me to my bed. There, he opened the window, tossed the rock out, and quickly closed it. Sitting beside me, we again discussed running away as an alternative to any repeat of what I had almost done that night. Before he went back to bed, we decided to run away that summer, when the Steeles went on vacation—and this time I was committed to following through with that decision.

ENDNOTES FOR CHAPTER NINETEEN

1. See Appendix C.1.3/Staff and Youth Violence; Unsafe "Lock and Drop" Restraint/2004. A U.S. Department of Justice investigation of two Maryland youth facilities revealed dangerous restraint methods, often resulting in injuries and serious harm.

2. See Appendix A.2.7/Duty Neglect and Striking Resident/1999. A New Lisbon employee was accused of failing to monitor a Birch Cottage resident and hitting him after he wandered off.

3. The first of New Jersey's public mental hospitals, the New Jersey State Lunatic Asylum was founded in 1848. Its name was changed in 1893 to New Jersey State Hospital at Trenton, then changed again in 1971 to its current name, Trenton Psychiatric Hospital.

CHAPTER TWENTY

Uttered Odes under
Leafy Sonnets

ONE DAY LATER that summer, as we had so carefully planned, I awoke before dawn. Using the rungs under each bed, I pulled myself across the floor on my back, from bunk to bunk, until I reached Bobby's bed.

I shook him, whispering, "Wake up, Bobby, wake up. It's me."

He didn't budge. I shook him again.

"Bobby, Bobby," I insisted. "Wake up. Wake up. It's me."

He mumbled, "Leave me alone."

I shook him again. "Bobby, come on. Get up. It's time."

Bobby rolled over and looked at me between the two beds. "Already?" he asked, sleepy eyed and yawning. "What time is it?"

"I don't know, but it's almost daytime."

"Is everybody still asleep?"

"Yeah. C'mon. We gotta hurry."

"Okay, get outta the way."

I ducked under the bunk again and gave Bobby enough room to join me. We pulled ourselves on our backs, through the tunnel of beds, collecting dust like mops.

When we got to the end of the room, I whispered, "See if you can see Mr. Westly."

Bobby stuck his head out and looked into the hall. "He's still sleeping, Chuckie. C'mon."

We slipped out from under the beds. As we crossed over the center aisle, I looked into the hall. Mr. Westly was leaning his chair back against the wall, his toes barely touching the floor, his two fingers clinging to one edge of the newspaper while the rest of it sprawled on the floor at his feet. We made it to the bathroom, the cold tile under our feet immediately clearing the cobwebs from our sleepy heads. We emptied our swollen bladders and tiptoed down the steps that led into the basement. Like smelling salts, the odors instantly sobered us.

The basement windows near the ceiling revealed the onslaught of daybreak. The birds were giving us a throaty warning: we had better get moving. Like brave soldiers, we went straight for our boxes and began dressing.

"Ah, shit, Chuckie. Our shoes!"

"That's right. They're upstairs in the bathroom lockers. Now what do we do? It's startin' to get light out."

"We got time. Come on. I got an idea."

We snuck back upstairs into the bathroom, the steps creaking along the way. Bobby went into one of the cubicles and began forcing the bar that went across the roll of toilet paper to prevent anyone from removing the entire roll from its housing.

"Sh-hh, Bobby. You're makin' too much noise."

"Hold on, Chuckie. I think . . . I think I . . ." His fingers were turning white under the bar as he strained to rip it loose.

CRA-A-A-CK!

"Shit, Bobby, that was too loud!"

Bobby ran for the door and looked both ways. "Nobody's comin'. C'mon. Those little locks ain't shit."

"What're ya gonna do?"

"Watch," he answered, sticking the bar into the loop of the lock.

One twist and the lock gave way. Bobby went over to my locker and repeated the process; again, it worked. We took out our shoes, tiptoed back into the basement, and slipped them on.

"The bread, Chuckie. The bread I hid. It's up there." He pointed to a four-inch pipe that went through the wall where I first began hiding my newspapers.

I stood on the bench and began stuffing what amounted to be about three loaves of bread into my clothing. I jumped off the bench and told Bobby, "C'mon. The sun's comin' up. We gotta go before it's too late."

We went to the outside door and snuck up the steps, hunched low. When our eyes reached the top, we looked both ways.

"I don't see nobody. Do you, Chuckie?"

"Nope, I don't see nobody."

"Then let's go."

I followed my brother along the edge of the building, staying close to the bushes that lined the outer wall. Once we made it to the first corner, we paused, looked in all directions, and then made our way to the back of the cottage.

It was a long distance from Birch to the woods. The corn stalks were high enough to afford some refuge from being seen; from there, we had to cross over the back road and scale the fence that divided New Lisbon from the forest. With the Steeles gone, there'd be no chance of them seeing us from their apartment window.

"Ready, Chuckie?"

"Yeah, I think so. You?"

"Fuck, yeah. Let's go." He grabbed me by the wrist and pulled me along.

We ran across the sandy terrain of the backyard with the speed of Olympians, finally reaching the cornfield. We made our way through the high stalks and then, finally, to the back road that bordered the institution. Crouching down, we looked both ways and crossed it, running for the fence. Once there, we dug our toes into the wire mesh and scaled it, dropping to the other side. Then we scrambled for the woods and hid under a bed of golden leaves, our imaginations dancing in a circle of utter ecstasy. We slipped out from under the leaves and looked back at New Lisbon; one glance from that distance was enough to sober us.

When I looked over at Birch, the morning sun's orange glow colored the gables. The shale roof was drying of its morning dew, leaving spots of ashen grey. The multiple tubular smokestacks jutting from the laundry building appeared like ready erections, spewing New Lisbon's disgrace. We turned and looked at each other, our hearts bursting with excitement and mystery as to what laid ahead. It was time to move on.

"Ready, Chuckie?"

"Yeah, fuck it. Let's do it."

The forest was dense. As we went deeper, we were bombarded with prickly twigs, castor bean plants, and poison oak and ivy. But once we passed through the woods, the going became a bit easier.

As an early breakfast, we ate wild berries that not only helped quench our thirst but filled our empty bellies. We finished off the meal with our bread, which had flattened when we dropped from the fence. We moved on, no longer running *to* anything but, rather, running *from* everything.

"Chuckie, we've gotta get to the swamp. There's water there, but it's a long way from here. Maybe we can make it before it gets dark. And there's quicksand."

"Quicksand?"

"Hell, yeah! There's lotsa quicksand out here. Don't worry, I know all the bad spots."

We pushed onward for the rest of the day and finally reached a clearing.

"Hold it, Chuckie. I'm thirsty. Are you?"

"God, yes. What are we gonna do?"

"When me and my Kid ran away the last time, they caught us before I could get our canteen. I know where it is, and I think there's some water left in it. If there ain't, there's a spring at the swamp. C'mon."

"Are you sure, Bobby?"

"Yeah. And if the spring's dried up, we can drink swamp water."

"Swamp water?"

"Shit, yeah. But we gotta boil it first."

"Oh, yeah, and where are we gonna get matches?"

"I got some. Look, a whole book."

"Holy cow! Where'd you get those?"

"I stole them from Mr. Westly's pocket when he was asleep a couple nights ago. See? I think of everything. I've gotten a lotta shit from his pockets—even money once."

"You're lyin'."

"You think I'm lyin', again? You never believe me, Chuckie . . . C'mon, I'll show ya where we hid the canteen before we got caught."

About a mile later, Bobby stopped me. "See over there? That's the place."

"What place?"

"Where we left the canteen. C'mon."

He led me to a tree. "There." He pointed up into the branches. "I told ya."

"What's it doin' up there?"

"So the animals don't take it. Hold on. I'll get it." He scaled the tree. "Hey, Chuckie," he hollered. "It still has water in it. Here, catch."

After quenching our thirst, our fears began to elevate with the day quickly fading.

"We'll stay here tonight," instructed Bobby. "Help me dig."

"Dig?"

"Yeah, c'mon."

Using our hands, we dug a hole the size of both of us. Then we filled it with leaves, laid down, covered ourselves with more leaves, and bedded down for the night. As we stared at the stars high above us through the trees, listening to hooting owls and fighting off punishing mosquitoes, we began trading dreams. We were young, hearty, and filled with imagination, certain the darkened woods were brimming with spooks, wolves, coyotes, and mean grizzly bears. Nearby, croaking frogs sang a throaty serenade, sending off-key messages that we converted into sonnets and songs. Before long, we fell off to sleep, safe in each other's arms.

Upon awakening the next morning, we were hungry and dehydrated, but never happier. We rose from our leaf beds and played house, romping about our living room of the woods, using downed trees as our furniture. The sun, pushing through the glittering leaves, was our crystal chandelier. We never felt more at home or more at one with each other than at that very moment.

With no berry patches in sight, we ate more bread and drank what was left in the canteen. Then we headed for the swamp, knowing we'd need to replenish our water supply.

Along the way, we shared jokes that weren't funny and vulgarisms that no longer seemed sinful, flinging about profanity as if there were no God, sin, or morality. We created our own reality, and it was good. We remained loyal to our idealistic foolishness and the prospect of never being found, though what awaited us was, of course, a mystery. Although we never said as much, we both sensed death would be sweeter than being caught and returned to New Lisbon.

By noon, we had discovered a deer path to follow.

"Hey, Bobby," I asked. "Is there really a swamp?"

"How come you never believe me?"

"Bobby, it ain't that. It's just that you told me yesterday we'd reach the swamp by nighttime, and we're still not there, that's all."

"Okay, okay, so I was wrong. Forget it. It's not far now, and I'm thirsty too. Hey, Chuckie, did Mr. Stone ever mess with you?"

"You mean you know about the music teacher?"

"Everybody thinks he's so special. He messes with me every time I'm in his class. He likes playin' with dicks. Once he showed me pictures of nasty ladies doin' shit to each other. Do ladies do that too?"

"I don't know," I replied.

"They're ugly pictures. Did he mess with you too?"

"The first day I was in his class."

"What did he do?"

"He was at a table playin' Chinese checkers with some other kids and asked me to sit next to him. Before I knew it, he was playin' with my dick."

"What, in front of everybody?" Bobby seemed surprised.

"No, he snuck his hand under the table while I was sittin' next to him. When I looked under the table to see what it was, he was unzippin' my fly and jackin' off the boy sittin' next to him on the other side."

"Did he stop when he saw you lookin' at his hand?"

"No. He just kept doin' it with the both of us. I didn't know what to do, so I just let 'im. And another time he showed me some dirty pictures from a deck of cards like he did with you. Did the ones he showed you look like Old Maid cards?"

"That's them. Did he make you jerk him off?" Bobby asked.

"Yeah, but he didn't take it out. I did it through his pants."

"Me too. The same thing. And he's married too. I seen his wife before. I don't get it. Why's he doin' shit like that if he's married?"

"I don't know, Bobby."

"He likes baby dicks, Chuckie . . . little boys who don't shoot. I know somebody else like him, but he likes bigger dicks."

"Who's that?"

"You won't believe me if I tell you."

"No, no. Tell me. I'll believe you. Tell me, Bobby."

"That fuckin' Mr. Powers. He likes suckin' on it."

"Mr. Powers? He was on duty a couple times at Birch. He never messed with me."

"He will if he gets his hands on you. Can you shoot, Chuckie?"

"Yeah, a lot sometimes."

"That's all Mr. Powers needs to know. When he finds out, you'll be next."

"I wouldn't mind that."

"You're sick," Bobby said, laughing.

"Does he really do that, Bobby?"

"He did it to me more than once."

"Did ya like it?"

"It was okay. That asshole likes it when you shoot in his mouth. I don't know how anybody can do that, and swallow it too. God, I wonder what that shit tastes like. How can somebody like that shit? He even takes his teeth out when he does it."

"Takes out his teeth? Does he really take his teeth out?"

"I ain't shittin' ya. He's got false teeth. Didn't ya know that?"

"They look like regular teeth to me."

"Can I ask you somethin'?"

"Like what?"

"Did Desarino ever put it between your legs?"

"No. He doesn't do that shit."

"He never tried to do it to ya?"

"Honest to God, no. But he liked to kiss me a lot."

"Does he kiss nice?"

"In a way." I paused a moment. "I wonder what girls are like, Bobby."

"Me too. Hey, Chuckie, look! There's the swamp. C'mon!" He tugged at my arm.

When we reached the water's edge, the swamp looked dead. The water was covered with green slime and wasn't moving. The only signs of life were above the surface. There were millions of swarming fleas and dancing water spiders creating small ripple trails behind them. The swamp held a distinct odor of its own; it stank. Not far away, near the middle, were dry mounds with overgrown brush and trees.

I turned to Bobby and asked, "Where'd you say the spring was?"

"C'mon, I'll show ya," he said, abruptly pulling me along.

Bobby was right. There was a spring and it was active. We laid on our bellies and drank, after which Bobby filled the canteen.

The rest of the day, we ate whatever berries we could find.

"Hey, Chuckie, it's getting dark. If we stay around here, the swamp bugs'll eat us alive. There's a spot where me and my Kid slept the last time we were here."

"How long before they caught you the last time Bobby?"

"Not long enough . . . four days, but they didn't catch us here. We made it to Browns Mills. We were sleepin' under a house. A stupid dog gave us away."

We left the clearing and headed into the woods.

"Hey, at least this time we won't have to dig like yesterday."

"Holy shit, Bobby. Look! A snake!"

"That's just a garter snake," Bobby explained. "It won't do shit to ya. It's the water moccasins ya wanna watch out for. If they bite ya, you'll be dead in a minute, 'cause they're poisonous, and there's a lotta them in this old swamp. But if we don't bother them, they ain't gonna bother us."

"One bite, and you're dead in a minute?" I asked.

"That's what my Kid said. Follow me. We're almost there."

Bobby led me deeper into the forest and then abruptly stopped. "Hear that?" he alerted. There were rustling sounds coming from the thicket deeper into the forest. "It's comin' from over there. Sh-hh. Let's go see what's up."

We crept the rest of the way, then spread the leaves of a bush and saw a deer giving birth to her fawn. I was in awe over the maternal spectacle, feeling emotions I hadn't felt since leaving Ruby. I was in a kind of trance as the doe completed the birth process. We watched her nibble at the afterbirth and then lick her fawn, displaying maternal instincts that warmed my heart. The fawn began making earnest attempts to stand on its spindly legs. It stood for a moment, then flopped to the ground. The doe nudged it. Attempting to get back up, the fawn wobbled, trying to steady itself, its legs quivering and unsure. But once the little animal got its footing, it began galloping about almost immediately, its back legs kicking as it ran around its mother. My heart quietly applauded the event.

Then, without warning, Bobby gave out one loud clap, sending the critters scampering deeper into the thicket where they quickly disappeared. Bobby roared a belly laugh.

Angered, I turned to Bobby. "Shit! Why'd you do that?"

Bobby didn't answer. He laid on his back, holding his stomach from so much laughter.

"Dammit, Bobby, that wasn't nice. Don't you like deer?"

"So I clapped. So what? They're only animals."

"Bobby, you're an asshole!"

"You mad at me?"

"You didn't have to scare them off. That shit's beautiful."

"Punch me in the jaw, if you want to. I deserve it."

"I ain't gonna do that 'cause I love you. Plus, you're my brother."

"Shit! Want somebody to hear us?"

"Who? The fuckin' birds? God, Bobby. We're not at New Lisbon, ya know."

"I know that, but only queers talk like that."

"That ain't got shit to do with it . . . ah, fuck it! You make me mad sometimes. And another thing. We're the intruders, not the animals. So shut your face up before I . . . ah, fuck you."

"Don't get mad. Let's find that spot where me and my Kid slept," Bobby suggested.

"I can't stay mad at you. You know that."

We found the spot and replaced the old leaves with fresh ones. Night was almost upon us, and we took our places in the dugout and covered ourselves with more leaves. As we both stared into the darkening sky and watched the stars begin to flicker high above, the swamp's nocturnal lullabies once again soothed our troubled minds; that was all we needed to drop off to sleep.

The next morning, we awoke hungry and wasted no time eating the rest of the bread and whatever berries we could find.

"Hey, Chuckie, what do ya think they'll do if they catch us?"

"You told me once we'd go to Cedar. I hope you're right about that. I've had enough of Birch."

"Me too. I've been tryin' to tell ya that Cedar's a playhouse. I got friends there. There's Smithy, Shaw . . . Leggett . . . and, uh . . . Garigiola, Izzy, and—"

"Do I have to hear about that place? This is our home now."

"But nobody'll fuck with us there. You just wait and see."

"Let's just pretend there's no place like that. It'd be better. And I don't wanna wait and see what it's like."

"The attendants are nice there. They don't beat us up like the monitors at Birch because they ain't got monitors. Hey, Chuckie, wanna go to the swamp?"

"Heck, yeah. Let's do it."

When we reached the swamp, we took off our shoes and waded in the murky water, slime clinging to our ankles. I looked down, the sun brightening clear spots in the water.

Pointing, I asked, "Bobby, what're those wiggly things?"

Bobby leaned over and looked. "They're gonna be mosquitoes. They like water that's stuck."

"Stuck?"

"You know, water that doesn't move."

"Stuck water? That's a good one."

"Let's go over there." He pointed to one of the dry mounds in the middle of the swamp.

"Way out there? Why?"

"So the smellin' dogs can't smell us. My Kid taught me that."

"Do those things bite?" I asked, pointing at the mosquito larvae.

"They ain't got no teeth," Bobby laughed. "Look, I'll show ya." He stuck his hand in the water. "See? They ain't shit. Let's go."

"You mean swim? What about our shoes?" I asked, scratching my arms from pesky mosquito bites and a breakout of poison ivy.

"Oh, shit. I think you got poison ivy, Chuckie."

"I know. It itches a lot. Look at my arms."

"Looks like either poison ivy or poison oak. Don't scratch it, or it'll make it worse. C'mon. At least we're happy. Let's take our shit off so it won't get wet."

We proceeded to strip down to our shorts, and before I knew it, Bobby dove in. I dove after him into the murky water.

"C'mon, Chuckie, keep up."

"Hey, Bobby, look. Is that a rat over there?"

"It's a muskrat. C'mon! They can be mean. Keep the fuck up!"

Something began biting my feet. I screamed. "Ouch! Shit! Bobby! Something bit my foot!"

"Swamp rats! Keep swimmin'. No, no, no! Not that way! This way!"

"Ouch! They're bitin' me, Bobby."

"I know. One just bit me too. Shit! They hurt. They're nasty motherfuckers! We're almost there. Keep up! Don't stop!"

"I'm turnin' back, Bobby!"

"No, no, Chuckie. Look, we're almost there. Stay with me! Keep swimmin'! Don't stop! We'll make it!"

I began slowing down.

Bobby turned back, grabbed hold of me, and began pushing me forward while the rats bit our legs and feet.

"I think I'm bleeding, Bobby."

"I think I am too. Fuck it! We can't stop now!"

We made it to the small island midway to the other side of the swamp.

Bobby sat up and looked at his legs. "Look, Chuckie. Look at my legs."

I could tell he was trying to hold back his tears, but the pain overwhelmed him.

"Don't cry, Bobby. I'm bleeding too. You know I hate it when you cry. At least we're outta the water now."

"Damn rats!" complained Bobby. "They ain't never done that shit before. Me and my Kid swam this thing a couple times. They must've been hungry or somethin'."

The poison ivy burned more than it itched. Out of breath, we laid there, looking up at the sky, both of us smacking mosquitoes as they drilled their hypodermic needles into our flesh.

"Chuckie, we can't stay here. We gotta get outta here or these mosquitoes'll eat us alive. We gotta keep goin'. If we swim to the other side, it's not as far. Let's do it now and get it over with."

"Yeah, we better."

"Then let's do it."

Like brave warriors, we dove in and swam like hell, finally reaching dry land, this time unmolested by the rats. We ran into the woods to get as far away from the mosquitoes as we could and sat on a fallen tree to nurse our wounds. The bleeding stopped. Covered in slime and goo, we dried ourselves out.

"Bobby, did you hear that?" I alerted. "Sounds like somebody's—"

"It's just those deer again. It ain't nothin' to worry about."

A few moments later, we heard a commotion behind us.

"Bobby, Bobby," I again warned. "Maybe somebody else ran away and—"

"Don't move!"

Bobby was suddenly tackled to the ground. It was Mr. Ballanger. He had Bobby in a headlock, shouting, "If you try anything, I'll use my billy club on ya."

"Bobby!" I pleaded. "Do what he says! Don't hurt my brother. Please, Mr. Ballanger!"

Mr. Ballanger's partner, Jimmie, put the handcuffs on me and started to escort me to a path that led to their state vehicle.

"I don't get it," said Jimmie. "I've heard a lot of good things about you, Carroll. What's gotten into you? Your ass is in deep shit. You know that, don't you?"

"Yes, sir." Trenton, I thought. Now they'll want to fry my brain into submission, or worse.

Mr. Ballanger asked my brother, "When are you gonna learn never to go back to the same place twice? I caught you before in this same spot." He cuffed my brother.

"So I guess you caught me again, Mr. Ballanger."

"You're damn right. And it better be the last time. God, you got a hard head. You never learn, do ya? Maybe they'll send you to Trenton this time and shock some brains into that stupid skull of yours. Where are your shoes? And where in the hell are your clothes?"

"They're on the other side of the swamp," I answered. "Way over there in that direction."

"That's great. That's just great. You must think I'm Christopher Colombo! And I sure as hell ain't gonna swim it," snarled Mr. Ballanger.

Jimmie laughed. "Christopher Colombo . . . now, that's a good one."

"What the hell are you laughin' at, Jimmie?"

"Ahhh, forget it. Hey, Jack, why don't we just take them back as they are," suggested Jimmie. "We've got a couple of blankets in the jeep. They can wrap themselves in those. Whatta ya say?"

"Sure, why not? That'll work. We'll get 'em both fixed up as soon as we get back to New Lisbon."

"I'm sorry," pleaded Bobby. "Mr. Ballanger, I—"

"Save your breath, Carroll. I've had enough outta you. You'd lie through your own mother's teeth if you had a chance. I'm tired of your broken promises. And why in hell did you have to pull your brother into this?"

"It's not my brother's fault," I said. "I wanted to run away. Tell 'im, Bobby."

"No need to defend your brother. I know him like a book."

"But it's not Bobby's fault. It's mine," I pleaded. "Honest, Mr. Ballanger, honest to God."

"Sure, kid, sure. And look at you two. What happened?"

"Poison ivy, I think."

"Not your arms, dummy. Your legs and feet. You're both bleeding. What the hell did—"

"The swamp rats did it," interrupted Bobby.

"You both need medical attention or you'll get an infection. Let's go."

They led us to the waiting four-wheel-drive Jeep, carefully hidden about twenty yards from where we got caught. We climbed into the backseat.

Mr. Ballanger got in and turned to both of us. "Look under your seat, boys, and wrap yourselves up in those blankets. There's two or three of them under there."

As we pulled out the blankets, Mr. Ballanger looked at me. "What gives with you, Carroll? You disappointed a lotta people back there, and that goes for me too. This isn't like you."

"I just had to, that's all."

"And what's that supposed to mean?"

"Because."

"Because what?"

"Oh, nothing."

"Goddamn it, answer me. Why?"

"I can't. Just don't blame it on my brother. It's not his fault. It's mine. *I* wanted to run away."

"So you can't tell me why?"

"No, sir, I can't."

Mr. Ballanger turned around in his seat, started the engine, and sped off.

Once at New Lisbon, still hugging our blankets with crossed arms, we were directed to the superintendent's office.

"Well, well, well," said Dr. Yepsen. "You two really did it to yourselves this time, didn't you? Never had a runaway brought to me in the shape you two are in, but then again, nothing surprises me around here anymore. And look at you two, no clothes, wrapped in dirty blankets . . . and you, Carroll." He looked hard eyed at me. "Besides running away, I hear you haven't been cooperative in school. What's up with that?"

I answered, "Because they don't teach me anything there. It's like . . . like kindergarten, sir. And I don't like Mr. Stone."

"Mr. Stone? Why, he's one of our best—a fine music teacher."

"It's because he likes to—"

"No excuses. Betty Steele warned me about you and your made-up stories. And young man, you're beginning to give me the impression that you're never satisfied no matter how much we do for you. Don't try my patience! Understand?"

"I . . . but . . . I mean, nobody wants to listen to anything I have—"

"Dammit! What's it going to take to get you to settle down and fit in, young man?"

"Me? Fit in? In this place? I don't see how, sir."

"Dammit. There you go again. I've been good to you. In the last two days, we went through considerable expense to find you two boys. Had Mr. Ballanger not found you, I dread the thought. Remember the Shepherd boy?"

"Yes, sir."

"That could've happened to you. You two don't know how lucky you are. Jesus, son, we've had kids die out there. What's the matter with you?"

I lowered my eyes to the floor and said nothing, disgusted that he wouldn't hear me out about Mr. Stone's molestations.

"A sudden tight-lip, I see, huh?"

I continued to stare at the floor, realizing that any further dialogue with the man would be futile.

"Today you're lucky . . . Charles, isn't it?"

"Yes, sir."

"Because Mr. Ballanger speaks well of you, I'll go easy on you. I should send both of you to Trenton . . . that's what you both deserve. What about you, Carroll?" He directed his attention to my brother.

"What about me, Dr. Yepsen?" Bobby asked, pointing to himself.

"This is your fourth escape. It's not going to be tolerated anymore. And what's worse, you pulled your brother along this time."

I interrupted, "But, Dr. Yepsen, he didn't talk me into it. I wanted to go."

"But why? We're good to you here."

"I just couldn't help myself, that's all."

"Well, you're going to have to from now on." He looked at my

CHARLES A. CARROLL

brother. "So, Carroll, what should we do with you this time?"

"How would I know, Dr. Yepsen?"

"You can start knowing by answering to these serious charges, that's what. Well?"

Bobby shrugged his shoulders.

"There's no excuse for you. What do you think we should do with you?"

"That's up to you, Dr. Yepsen."

The superintendent leaned over and began reading Bobby's progress report. Without looking up, he said, "Mr. Mitchell says here that you were well behaved at Cedar. Maybe that's where you need to stay . . . where they can keep you under wraps and where you can be closely monitored. Since Mr. Ballanger is now going to be supervising Cedar along with Mr. Mitchell, I think they can handle you. Therefore, I'm going to recommend that you return there—with your brother, this time. As for Birch, forget about it. Poor Mrs. Steele has enough on her hands without keeping tabs on the likes of you. But I'm warning you, if your name comes across my desk again—and I mean just one more time—and I mean just one more mess-up—there'll be no more breaks and no more warnings. Next time, it's Trenton. Good luck, boys."

I was excited about going to Cedar. The thought of being rid of Birch and its monitors delighted me. Though I wondered if Cedar was the carnival-like atmosphere that Bobby so often claimed. Was it really absent of monitor repression? But something else troubled me even more: Bobby. I knew if he screwed up one more time, they would send him to the State Hospital at Trenton and administer electroshock treatments in an effort to "tame" him. That thought overwhelmed me with utter dread.

CHAPTER TWENTY-ONE
Britches, Pitchforks, and Haystacks

WE WERE TREATED at the hospital and released into Mr. Ballanger's care. On the way to Cedar, I couldn't help but be reminded of his brutality toward Desarino. Knowing the extent of his viciousness scared me, while Bobby, on the other hand, appeared to take him in stride. It was Bobby's carefree attitude that deeply troubled me, particularly with the threat of Trenton looming before him.

We pulled up to Cedar Cottage and I noticed shadowy faces looking at us from behind heavy-gauged mesh windows. When we entered, everyone mingled in the day room because, unlike Birch, there was no basement. The room was noisy, resonating with sense-less muttering and shouting as some residents faced walls and corners and talked to themselves or simply wandered about. Most were unshaven and dirty looking, wearing scruffy and ill-fitting clothes. Their feet bore raggedy shoes with flapping soles that had practically disintegrated. Most residents were older men, one as old as eighty, but they were like the boys of Birch in bigger bodies. There were some teenagers too, but none as young as Bobby and me.

While walking through the room, Bobby was greeted warmly by several of his friends—Smithy, Leggett, and others. We were finally led into what was the equivalent of Birch's sewing room, an office of sorts where most of the winter clothing was stored over the summer months. The room gave off the odor of mothballs, immediately reminding me of Bobby's inappropriate remark to our aunt.

Unlike Birch with its two sides, Cedar was a stand-alone cottage, one of the houses of detention. It was for the Colony's unruly but manageable residents, while Fern Cottage was installed with two tiers of jail cells and several isolation rooms for New Lisbon's incorrigibles and most dangerous. Cedar housed around fifty, but it had been designed to hold about half that; they squeezed everybody in by simply putting the beds closer together.

In the office, Mr. Ballanger warned, "We don't take any shit here. See this?" He extended his foot and displayed his steel-toed shoe. "I'll shove this right up your asses if either of you get outta line. There's no more hiding behind Mrs. Steele's apron. This is *my* cottage, and you'll do as I say. Understood?"

Before I could answer, Bobby blurted, "You know I'll be good, Mr. Ballanger. I ain't never gave you no trouble."

"Bullshit, Carroll. Your promises aren't worth a damn. I guess you call running away not giving me a bad time? I'm sick of you tryin' to hand me a line. And don't think I don't know about you forcing open that crawl-hole in the ceiling to sneak over to Birch last time you were here. It got back to me. And you're lucky I wasn't running Cedar then. Mr. Mitchell should've locked your ass up in Fern and thrown away the key. So I don't think you've learned a goddamn thing."

Mr. Ballanger shook his finger at Bobby. "I'm gonna give you one more warning. Don't make me regret giving you another chance. The bullshit stops right here. Now go over to that pile and pick out a pair of shoes, and you'll find somethin' that fits you in that closet over there. Yes, you too, honey-buns." He looked at me with undressing eyes and a half-broken smile portraying a hint of lust. "And get those shorts off too."

"Can you turn around, Mr. Ballanger?"

"Don't try my patience, boy. Get with it or—"[1]

"Okay, okay," I said, turning from the man and removing my underwear. I quickly clutched my privates and went over to the clothes closet to put something on.

Mr. Ballanger barked, "I said find a pair of shoes first. Dammit, boy! I'm not gonna tell you again—hell, I ain't got time to be pussyfootin' with you all day. I've got other things to do."

One week into our arrival at Cedar, we, along with twenty others, were assigned to work the stump fields. They handed us grubbing hoes, which were stored in a shed along the way. Once in the backwoods, we used them to chop down trees and clear overgrown brush. The work was grueling. Our young hands took on the look of hardworking men.

Besides clearing the Colony's backwoods, we had to work the piggery. We scrubbed the concrete slabs on which the pigs ate our leftover food, dumped there by tractors three times a day—after every meal. The piggery was, in effect, New Lisbon's garbage disposal.

When we weren't working at the piggery or in the backwoods, we picked crops in the fields. After loading the trucks, we were ordered to follow the bounty to the cannery, where we peeled onions, diced carrots, and stewed tomatoes. We canned these products and readied them for shipping to other mental institutions throughout the state.

While Mr. Mitchell was strict but fair when supervising us, Mr. Ballanger was mean and unforgiving. Being in charge of Cedar simply gave him the necessary clout to indulge his ruthlessness among the Colony's most helpless residents, hoisting his "no mercy" strategies on a pedestal of machismo. He was the most loathed supervisor, not only by the residents, but also by its other personnel. He enjoyed the prestige of having once been a Colony cop, often flaunting his badge-wearing authority and finding ways to discredit others who didn't agree with his brutal tactics or got in the way of his potential promotion.

Mr. Ballanger was particularly hard during the winter months.

When Mr. Mitchell was in charge, he allowed us to warm ourselves over the fire barrel now and then, but Mr. Ballanger would not. All too often, from a distance, we'd see him warming himself over a fire and laughing at us while sucking on a wet cigar, most of it hidden in one cheek, the lit end protruding from his thick lips. We all had colds, many of us on the edge of pneumonia—and, because there were no handkerchiefs, we wiped our runny noses on our coat sleeves. The fabric of the sleeves became caked with mucus and slobber, and it stiffened over time to an ash white color. During especially cold weather, the mucus would crystallize on our chins and fall to the ground in shattered, icy bits.

The nights at Cedar were sleepless, with bad dreams and sweat-beaded foreheads, howling with the all-too-familiar moans and guttural screams of so many fighting off the monster of abuse.

Cedar's residents were the embodiment of the Colony's ultimate failures. Most were renegades who had been bold enough to stand up to New Lisbon's wrongs—pleading for basic decency, more rights, and a democratic way of life—but they did so with fewer and simpler words. Residents who spoke the loudest and became a nuisance to those in charge were either sent to Fern Cottage or shipped to Trenton where their minds would be "fixed" once and for all. Many who went to Trenton were never the same after they returned—they would come back just the way New Lisbon wanted them: docile, obedient, and unassuming.

Cedar reflected a lot of the Colony's indignities. The place was filled with skeletal heartbreak. Residents' souls were robbed by the ravages of abuse—abuse that took the human soul and wrung it out of the shape of its "civilized" essence. And worse, these love-starved people were treated as if they had no right to feel indignant at their abandonment, as if feeling anything were a crime.

In the end, it took a horrible toll on them. By the time patients made their way to Cedar, their eyes were empty of any hint of innocence, the depths of their stares resembling unoccupied, open graves, their mannerisms listless like a week-old snowman left out in the sun. Over time, I saw them not as "dopes" but people with feelings, forgotten by the world. As with the boys at Birch, their personal struggles often seemed to make me more sensitive to *their* plight than my own. And their shabby existence gave me a purpose: to make it through, to survive, to outlast the experience so that I could one day tell their story, as if somehow sensing early on that I could be their only voice.

One night during that cold winter, I was awakened from my sleep. Someone stood over me, his pants dropped to his ankles, his breathing labored. The faint moonlight shining through the window at the foot of my bed did little to reveal the identity of the perpetrator. The darkened image waved his penis over me, its lazy foreskin splashing preseminal fluid in my face.

"Kiss it," the man whispered, pulling back the foreskin.

I froze.

"Come on, you know you like it. Kiss it."

I stared at him, suddenly recognizing his voice. So disturbed by the revelation, I bellowed, "It was *you*, Mr. Ballanger, the one jacking off while Jackson raped me that night at Birch, huh? It was you, wasn't it?"

Mr. Ballanger leaned over and picked up my head. "Come on, now." He pulled my face closer to his penis, panting like a dog. "Kiss it."

I pulled my head out of his hand. "I don't wanna."

"Don't gimmie that shit. I know you like it."

"No. It smells."

"That's pussy juice. You'll get used to it. Your nose will eventually crave it. I saved it for you. Come on." He again reached for my head. "Give it a little kiss."

"Please don't, Mr. Ballanger," I pleaded, turning my face away.

"You sucked Wheeler's dick. Why not mine?"

"I did not. He ain't like that. He's a nice man."

"Don't gimmie me that. I see the way he looks at you."

"It ain't true, Mr. Ballanger."

"Shut up! I'll be nice to you if you kiss it."

"Please don't, Mr. Ballanger, ple-e-ase."

"You little shit!" He socked me in the face, still holding my head.[2] "Everybody knows you're a fruit."

"I'm not that way, Mr. Ballanger. I only did shit like that when somebody made me. Honest. Cross my heart and hope to die."

"Come on. I've been onto you a long time. One little kiss, that's all, and then I'll go."

I pulled my head out of his hand.

"Oh, that's it. Okay, then, we'll do it your way. Roll over."

"Roll over?"

"Just do as I say, goddamn it, or I'll beltchya again."

Paralyzed by my deathly fear of the man, I obeyed.

Mr. Ballanger shoved me over and crawled into my bed, his thick knees sinking deep into the mattress, the bed springs snapping like rubber bands. He began showering the back of my neck with slobbering kisses. His foul cigar breath disgusted me and the weight of his body crushed my small frame. He rose up with a grunt, tucking me into the folds of his bulging legs. I pleaded into my pillow and screamed aloud.

Mr. Ballanger slapped the back of my head. "I didn't give you another chance for nothin'. Now it's time to pay up."[3]

I screamed again into my pillow, begging the son of a bitch to stop.

Bobby, whose bed was across the aisle from mine, awoke and sat up. When he realized what was happening, Bobby began rocking back and forth, uttering words of despair. "Stop it . . . stop it . . . please, God, stop 'im!"

Startled, and as if coming to his senses, Mr. Ballanger quickly rose up and looked over at Bobby. He sprang out of bed, pulled up his pants, and warned both of us to keep our mouths shut or he'd have us sent to Fern Cottage. Then he hurriedly left the room. Just as he exited the dormitory, the night attendant, apparently awakened by the ruckus, came running.

"Bobby, Bobby," I whispered. "Pretend you're sleeping. The night man's comin'."

After the attendant exited the dormitory, I sat up sobbing. "I love you, Bobby. Thanks."

"Shut up, Chuckie," he defended, "before somebody thinks somethin' nasty. You okay?"

"He beat me up, Bobby."

"I know, Chuckie, I know. Go back to sleep."

The next morning I awoke with a swollen eye. I ran to the bathroom to see what I looked like. With one glance at my face, all my suffering seemed to rise from inside me, and it was as though God left my soul. Now I wanted nothing more to do with Him. I wanted to disappear into the cracks of time. I wanted to exist no more.

As soon as we gathered in the day room after breakfast, I slipped from the crowd and hid in a large, walk-in clothes closet. I snapped off the light, curled up under some clothing, and privately cried to myself, never feeling more helpless and alone.

An hour or so later, I heard Mr. Mitchell yelling for me from the other side of the locked door.

"Which one?" asked someone on the other side of the door.

"The new one. Where is he?"

"He's in the closet and won't come out. He's been in there since we came back from breakfast."

Mr. Mitchell banged on the door. "Carroll, come out of there!" He tried the doorknob. "Open up, Carroll! This door's not supposed to be locked."

"No!" I shouted through the door. "You can't come in. I've got a chair under the doorknob and I ain't movin' it! Stay away!"

"Move that chair out of the way or I'll . . . goddamn it, don't make me break the door down. I will if you don't move it!"

"But I need to be alone."

"I don't care. Now open it!"

"Ah, shit." I finally resigned myself to Mr. Mitchell's demands and slid out from under the old clothes, pulled the chair from under the doorknob, and opened the door, pleading, "Please don't be mad at me, Mr. Mitchell."

"What the hell were you doing in there?"

"Nothin'."

"Nothing? What the hell happened to your face? Who did that to you?"

"It's nothin'," I answered, remembering Mr. Ballanger's warning.

"Come with me."

I followed Mr. Mitchell into the office.

Looking into my eyes, he said, "Now listen, Carroll. I want to know who did that to you."

"I did it. I got mad."

"You hit yourself?"

"Yes, sir."

"Why?"

"I don't know."

"You don't know? Christ, boy, you deserve better than that. Don't you like yourself?"

"Not anymore."

"But why? You're one of the better-behaved kids around here. And why would you want to beat up a nice face like that? You're a good-looking boy. Don't do that to yourself again. Listen to me, son." He placed a comforting hand on my shoulder. "I know you're not like everybody else. You're different. What would possess you to do something like that to yourself?"

"I hate being handsome."

"You do? I'm beginning to think there's more to this than meets the eye. What is it? Come on, spit it out."

"I just . . . I can't . . . it ain't nothin', honest."

He sighed in frustration. "I won't press it. Now listen up. Somebody's coming over to have a word with you. And young man, do me a favor. Please keep this visit to yourself, 'cause I'm not supposed to do it. I broke the rules for you. Okay?"

"But who is it?"

"You'll see soon enough."

"I won't say nothin', Mr. Mitchell. I promise. And thanks."

"Don't mention it, son." He left the room.

A minute or two later, I heard footsteps approaching from down the hall. Then the door opened.

"Hello, son."

Surprised, I jumped up. "It's you, Mr. Wheeler!"

"Wait a minute, son." He held me out in front of him. "What in the hell happened to you? Who . . . who did this to you?"

"I . . . I did it."

"You did that? That's not you. Come on, Charley, I know you better than that."

"I got the newspapers, Mr. Wheeler."

"Don't try and change the subject. Level with me."

"I . . . I can't tell ya."

"And why not? Since when did you stop trusting me?"

"I trust you, but . . . I just can't, Mr. Wheeler. I just can't. That's all."

"Sit down. We're going to get to the bottom of this. I think it's time you leveled with me, so let's have it. Since when can't we trust each other?"

I lowered my eyes to the floor and began sobbing.

"Charley?"

Tearfully, I looked up at the man. "Will you . . . I mean, if I tell you, will you promise not to tell anybody? It'll only get me in trouble."

"If that's what you want, it's a deal." He lifted one hand and tenderly brushed away my tears. "You know you can trust me, son."

Sobbing, I told him the whole story from beginning to end. He listened with shock written all over his face.

"So, it was that son of a bitch Ballanger, huh?"

"Yes, sir."

"Does Mr. Mitchell know anything about this?"

"He asked me about it, Mr. Wheeler, but I didn't tell him the truth."

"Well, look. The reason I stopped by was because I don't see you much now that you're here at Cedar. I'm still not happy that you ran away last summer, but that's behind us now. Charley, tell me, has anything like this ever happened to you before?"

"You mean by a man?"

He nodded.

I pictured all those times with the music teacher, Mr. Stone, but somehow I couldn't bring myself to talk any more about the New Lisbon staff. Then I thought back to another time.

"Yes," I replied.

"When was that?" Mr. Wheeler asked.

"When I decided to run away at Ruby and Dustin's. But I didn't really. I kind of ran away."

"What happened?"

I WENT TO the hall closet and got a pillowcase. In the bedroom, I stuffed Bobby's picture in the pillowcase and then went to the kitchen and pulled canned food items from the cupboards. I quickly left the house and headed straight for the old bridge at the bottom of Sunfair Road, a tranquil setting where I often visited the privacy of my inner world. As soon as I slipped under the bridge, I heard a car approaching. I stepped out to look. It was Dustin. I ducked back under the bridge, looking up through the cracks between the old, weather-beaten boards. The planks thundered and clapped as Dustin crossed over, a fine summer dust falling from them.

I came out from under the bridge, hurried up the embankment, and watched Dustin make his way up the driveway. Returning to the water's edge, I noticed a man fishing upstream, but his fishing hat hid his identity. I crept up behind the man and greeted him. He all but jumped out of his hip-high waders.

Looking down at me, he exclaimed with a loud and hearty voice,

"Well, I'll be a bowlegged jellybean!" The man's hat was dotted with feathered fly-hooks of all colors and sizes.

"It's you, Father!"

"Chuckie, my boy. It's been a long time. What brings you to the stream this afternoon?"

Before I had a chance to answer, he boasted, "Watch this," flinging his fly rod with the finesse of a professional fisherman.

"Gosh," I said. "You fish good!"

The priest was our neighbor and had befriended Bobby and me some time ago. He was always genial and was someone in whom I could confide my troubles. He often talked to us about fly-fishing, but this was the first time I'd seen him display the art. I learned quickly there was more to fishing than just dropping a line in the water.

"Watch this." He whipped another cast over the surface of the water several times and reeled it in.

"You don't have to be a priest today?"

"I'm retired, Chuckie. That's why you haven't seen me in so long. I like to travel now. And when I'm home, I take it easy, so I do what I like best: fly-fishing. How's my favorite boy been?"

"Okay, I guess." I lowered my eyes to his waterproof boots.

"That was a very weak answer. You want to talk about that?"

I looked out at the water, then asked him, "You like fishing a lot, huh?"

"Chuckie," he said, turning to me, "when I get a chance to do some fishin', well, I'm like a kid all over again. Now, you look a bit sad today. Is anything wrong?"

"Nah. It ain't nothin'."

"So tell me, how's everything at home?"

I lowered my eyes, kicking the gravel at my feet.

"I see," he said. "Still having problems over there, huh? So, tell me, where's your brother?"

I looked up at him, my eyes pooling.

He was suddenly sympathetic. "What is it, boy?"

"Oh, nothin'." I put the pillowcase down at my feet. "Father, can you show me how to fish like you?"

"For you, anything! Come on."

We walked upstream a bit to the old priest's favorite spot.

"Watch this." His line was doing a magic dance over the surface of the water.

"Is it hard?"

"Wanna try it?"

"Do ya mean it?"

"Better put your stuff over there where it's dry."

Excited, I ran with my things to a drier spot and quickly ran back, reaching for his fly rod.

"Not so fast. First, let me show you." He straddled me from behind and placed the butt of the rod in my belly. He put his hands over mine and guided them onto the rod, then pulled me backwards with him and flung the fly rod forward.

"Hey, look at that! Not bad, if I must say so. Okay, now you try it." He handed me the rod.

"Really?"

"You bet."

I mimicked his lesson and cast out the line.

"What a cast! That was terrific! Did you say you never did this before?"

I was smiling. "Not with a fishing rod like this one."

"Keep your line moving . . . that's the trick . . . that's it, just keep it coming. After you reel it all the way in, you do it all over again."

"But if the hook ain't in the water, how can the fish bite it?"

"That's the art of trout fishing. You must fool them into thinking that the colorful little feather is the real thing."

"Really?"

"You bet! When one of those critters hits the line, they'll give you the time of your life."

"They will?"

"Watch me again." He took the fly rod from my hands and began whipping "S's" over the surface of the water. I watched him reel it in. Then he turned to me and asked, "Chuckie, were you running away?"

"How'd ya know?"

"I've lived a bit longer than you. Am I right?"

"Y-yes, sir. But you won't tell my mommy and daddy, will you?"

"Why were you running away, Chuckie?"

"I hate them!"

"Now, now, now. That's no way to talk."

"But I do, I do . . ."

He turned to me with kind eyes and asked, "Where's your brother, son?"

"I don't know."

"How come you don't know?"

"Nobody wants to tell me. I don't know why."

"Chuckie," he said, crouching down to my level and raising my chin. "Look at me. I see you're very troubled. You need to talk about this. What happened?"

"She took 'im, Father. She . . . she just took 'im away."

"Who?"

"A lady."

"A lady? When?"

"A long time ago."

"I know I haven't seen you boys in a while, but your brother was with you the last time you were at my house."

The thought of Bobby gone tormented me. I began to cry.

He pulled me to his chest and said, "Go ahead, boy. It's okay. I understand." Then he held me at arm's length. "Tell me what you know."

I told him everything, even about overhearing Ruby on the phone and how she kept her secret from us and how, since then, I was never able to trust her.

"Tell you what. I'll have a talk with your folks, then we'll see what this is all about."

"No, no, no! They'll get mad."

"Why?"

"Because Mommy told me never to tell anybody anything."

"Never mind that."

"But if they find out, I'll get in trouble."

"Don't worry, Chuckie, I'll take care of that. You've got my word on it. Do you trust me?"

"A priest? Sure. But, Father, don't say nothin'. She'll make my daddy whip me."

"I wouldn't worry yourself about that."

"But I—"

"Never mind. I know your daddy very well. Is he home?"

"Yeah, he just came home."

"Come on, we'll go there."

"But . . . but . . . they'll get mad!"

"I'll make sure they don't. You come with me, boy."

When we approached the bridge, the priest turned to me and said, "I get out of breath easily. Let's go under the bridge. There's a nice rock over there we can sit on. It's a good place to rest my old, weary bones."

Sitting, he expelled a tired breath of relief. "There, that's better." He took me by the wrist and pulled me closer to him, breathing hard through his nose. "You're a fine-looking boy. You don't mind that, do you?"

Perplexed, I looked down at my lap. The priest was fondling my privates.[4]

"Now we've got a secret."

"We do?"

He looked down at his intruding hand, squeezing me.

"This is our secret," he said. "And you know never to tell a secret, right?"

I looked at his hand, then looked back up at him, wondering why he was doing that. But because I was so drawn by his tenderness and companionship, I attached little significance to his actions.

I finally answered, "My mommy said the same thing, that I should never tell a secret."[5]

"She's right. The devil swallows up little boys who tell secrets. And you know where they go, don't you?" He tousled my hair with his fingers.

"Hell?"

"That's right. Come on. I'm rested now."

"And you promise they won't get mad at me?"

"I promise."

I picked up the pillowcase and slung it over my shoulder. As we headed toward the embankment, the gravel beneath our feet crackled.

"You're my favorite boy. I'm not going to do anything that'll hurt you. Trust me?"

"Yes, Father."

"Look at what I got." He reached into his pocket and pulled out three different-colored lollipops. Bending over, he said, "Here."

"For me?"

"Yep!"

"All of 'em?"

"You bet!"

I tore the cellophane off one of them and pocketed the other two, shoving the open one into my mouth.

"Ah, you like the red ones, huh?"

"They're my favorites."

When we reached the top of the embankment, he instructed, "Put that pillowcase down a minute."

I obeyed.

Before I knew what was happening, he raised me into the air high over his head and straddled my legs around his leathery neck. Once firmly in place, he bent his knees, picked up my pillowcase, and handed it to me. With his fly rod straight out in front of him, we began the journey home, singing, "Over the river and through the woods, to grandmother's house we go . . ."

When we reached the front door, he raised his arms and lowered me to the ground. Then he pulled out a lollipop, unwrapped it, and stuck it into his mouth, shoving the sweet morsel to one side of his cheek.

"You stay here," he said, the lollipop stick protruding from his lips. "While I'm inside, keep a keen eye on my fishing gear, okay?"

I whispered, "You won't make 'em mad at me, will you?"

"No, Chuckie. Didn't I promise you that I'd take care of everything?"

"Y-yes, Father."

"And I'll take this in with me." He grabbed the stuffed pillowcase and knocked on the door.

Dustin opened it.

"Well, look who it is, honey, it's the good Father!"

"Who'd you say it was?" asked Ruby from somewhere inside the house.

"It's the good Father. When did ya get back from Florida, Father?"

"Some days ago. May I come in?"

"By all means." Dustin opened the door wider. "Are you comin' in, Chuckie?"

Forcing a smile through my guilt, I said, "I gotta—"

"He's gonna watch my fishing gear," interrupted the priest. "That's all right, isn't it?"

"Oh, sure, Father. Come in."

After Dustin closed the door, I sat down on the steps and waited. About twenty minutes later, the priest appeared, closing the door behind him.

I looked up at him. "They're mad, ain't they, Father?"

"Not at all, son! Come on, we'll go to the side of the house and talk."

Once there, he lowered his deep-set, blue eyes to mine and said, "You know, Chuckie, life isn't always fair. Your brother's not going to be coming home anymore. I wish I could tell you otherwise.

PLATE FIFTEEN
CHARLES A. CARROLL WITH WIGGIE
C. 1948
POMPTON LAKES, NEW JERSEY

Although, if it's any comfort to you, they said he's with some nice people who love him very much. Chuckie, you're gonna have to be a big boy about this."

"But . . . but it hurts, Father," I said, looking down.

"I know, and it'll hurt for a while, but eventually you'll come to blame no one. Oh, how I wish I could fix this one for you, but I can't." He took my chin and guided my eyes toward his. "You do believe me, don't you?"

"I . . . I can't ever forget him . . . and . . . and it's all her fault . . . but, Father, can you be *my* friend forever and ever, anyway?"

"It's a deal! Now listen. You'll have to be strong . . . stronger than ever before. Kneel down, my child. Let's pray." He placed his hand on the crown of my bowed head. "Oh, Heavenly Father . . ."

When he finished praying over me, he said, "You can get up now, son." Once I was back on my feet, he affectionately patted me on the cheek. "And may God be with you, my son."

The priest picked up his fishing gear, turned, stepped over the concrete tire stop, and disappeared down the driveway.

"CHARLEY," SAID MR. Wheeler, with a comforting hand on my shoulder, "I'm sorry you had that terrible experience. Anything like that can't be easy on any kid. As for that asshole, Jack Ballanger, don't worry yourself about him. I have my ways of taking care of people like that."

"But . . . but how, Mr. Wheeler? If he finds out I told you anything, he'll—"

"Never you mind about that. Son, I've got some good news for you."

"For me? Like what?"

"I talked to a couple on your behalf . . . the Hendersons. They're lovely people and would like to meet you."

"But they don't know me."

"They know all about you. And the best part is that they'd like to adopt a boy just like you."

"They would? But I want *you* for my daddy."

"I looked into that too."

"You did? You mean you would adopt me if you could?"

"Yes. The thing is, single people don't have a chance with today's system and the way it's set up. They prefer couples—you know, a husband and wife. I thought the Hendersons would be an ideal placement for you."

"But what about my brother?"

"Charley, I don't think they're considering *two* boys."

"But . . . but . . ."

"But what, son?"

"My brother, Mr. Wheeler. I want my brother with me."

"Charley, I understand how much you love your brother, but you must understand that this opportunity with the Hendersons could very well be your only ticket out of here."

"I know, but . . . but Bobby . . . he needs me, and I need him. Nobody loves us but us."

"*I* love you."

"I know, but that's different."

"Look. I'll tell you what. I'll have a talk with the Hendersons, and we'll take it from there. What do you say?"

"Okay," I said, suddenly turning and hugging the man. "I hate it here, and so does Bobby. I love my brother, Mr. Wheeler. I love him."

"I know, son."

I was silent for a moment, then asked, "Is Mr. Henderson like you? I want him to be just like you."

"I know, Charley. Boy, you say the nicest things. But keep this in mind . . . people are different. Nobody's the same. You'll like Mr. and Mrs. Henderson. And I'll promise you this: whatever I can do to get you out of this place, I will. And Charley, remember that you're not alone anymore. You've got me, and now you have the Hendersons."

"You forgot somebody."

"I did?"

"My brother. I've got *him* . . . and he's my best friend."

"Of course, Bobby too. Now one more thing. I've already spoken to the superintendent about the Hendersons, and it's all been arranged. But you must understand, it won't be for a little while yet, because Mr. Henderson's in the hospital at the moment. He's due to be out soon, and when that happens, they'll arrange for you to meet them, okay?"

Mr. Wheeler tenderly placed a hand on the side of my face and smiled. "Hey, do you know Lady Ann?"

"Sure. I remember her."

"Well, here." He removed his hand from my face and leaned over to take something from the paper bag at his feet. "She wanted me to give you this."

It was a book, the one titled *Somebody Up There Likes Me*.

"Gosh, she remembered."

"Lady Ann told me that you were looking through it once, and she thought you might like to have it. Oh," he said, reaching into the bag again. "Here's the Sunday paper too."

"Thanks, Mr. Wheeler. Now I can learn more new words again." Delighted with the offerings, I reached over and hugged the man again, whispering, "You're the best man I know in the whole wide world."

Chuckling and flattered, he put me out in front of him and said softly, "My boy, if you need to see me, just let Mr. Mitchell know and he'll contact me. How's that sound, son?"

"But he might tell and—"

"No, no, no, he's okay. You can trust Mr. Mitchell."

"Gee, thanks, Mr. Wheeler. I wish you were my father. I really do."

"Oh, Charley, you say the nicest things." He pulled me close and gave me a hug. "Just hang in there. Someday you're going to turn out to be a fine young man."

I pulled myself from his arms. "You mean it, Mr. Wheeler? Do you really mean it?"

"I do, son. Just always trust me. You do trust me, don't you?"

"Heck, yes."

"I have to go, son. But I won't be far away. I'll come and see you now and then, okay?"

"You will? Promise, Mr. Wheeler?"

"Yes. Yes, I will, my boy." He got up from his chair.

"You make me so happy, Mr. Wheeler." I gripped his coattail.

"I'll be back soon, I promise."

"Cross your heart."

As he crossed his heart, I began to cry. "Don't go, Mr. Wheeler." Tears were streaming down my face.

"I have to."

"I'll miss you, Mr. Wheeler. Do you . . . do you think you can bring me more reading stuff? I want to learn things."

"I'll do what I can. You can count on it. Read that book. I read it. It's good. Gotta go, kid. Stay here. I'll let Mr. Mitchell know I'm finished with you."

Later, I told Bobby about my conversation with Mr. Wheeler, except the part about the Hendersons. I couldn't bring myself to tell him that, at least not yet.

Days later, Bobby came running to me. "Chuckie, did you hear about Mr. Ballanger?"

"No, why?"

"He had a heart attack."

"Good! I hope he croaks!" I exclaimed, hoping inside that he'd die and rot in one of the worst cesspools of hell for all eternity.

SEVERAL WEEKS LATER, I was called to the Administration Building where Millie commented, "Charles, I heard you're doing very well at Cedar."

"It's better there than Birch."

"Good. Then perhaps it's better suited for you. You've turned out to be a fine, handsome boy. How old are you now?"

"Thirteen."

"Really? I guess you know that this is a special day for you and may well be one you'll never forget. Come on, follow me." Millie led me to a waiting area outside the superintendent's office. "Have a seat, Charles. Dr. Yepsen will be out to see you shortly. If you need anything, I'll be at my desk, okay?"

"Thanks, Miss Millie."

"Not at all, cutie."

A short time later, Dr. Yepsen opened the double oak doors of his office. "Well, hi there. So we meet again. I hear you're doing very well at Cedar. I'm glad you didn't disappoint me. Mind coming in here with me?"

When I entered his office, my feet sank into posh carpeting that gave me the feeling I'd stepped into another world. Like the last time I was there, I was struck by the richness of the room: the dark paneling on the walls, the deep sofa, the broad desk polished to a high sheen, the photographs of smiling family members and posing bureaucrats.

"Have a seat," offered Dr. Yepsen, directing me to a chair beside his oversized desk. He left for a moment, and then returned with two other people.

"This is the Carroll boy I've been telling you about. Mr. Carroll, I'd like to introduce you to the Hendersons. They came to meet you."

"I'm Mr. Henderson, Charles," said the man in a hearty voice.

I rose to my feet and faced them, immediately extending my hand. "Nice to meet you, sir," I said, a bit shyly. My God, I thought, Mr. Wheeler had promised me this day would come, but I hadn't really believed it. I was surprised and delighted.

"We've heard so many nice things about you from Mr. Wheeler. He speaks well of you."

"I really like him."

"Yes, he's a good person." Mr. Henderson turned to the woman next to him. "This is my lovely wife."

I held out my hand to her, forgetting what Ruby had said about never extending your hand to a lady unless it's offered first. Mrs. Henderson had a newborn infant in her arms, swaddled in a pink blanket. Only the bottle of milk stuck out of the blanket. She released one hand from the child and extended it to me.

"Nice to meet you, Charles."

"And nice to meet you too, ma'am."

She turned to her husband. "What a beautiful boy he is, isn't he, honey?"

"Yes he is, dear."

"Please have a seat." Dr. Yepsen directed the Hendersons to the sofa. "And Carroll, turn your chair around so we're all facing each other." The superintendent took his own seat behind the desk.

Mr. Henderson wore bib overalls, a beat-up baseball cap, and a loosely knotted bandanna around his neck. His hands were callused, his fingernails chipped, broken, and dirty; his neck and forehead were toughened from working outdoors; and his wire-rimmed glasses rested on a sunburned, peeling nose.

His wife wore dusty jeans and black-and-white sneakers with thick, red shoelaces. Like her husband, her hands were callused from hard work.

We got acquainted through small talk. Dr. Yepsen pretty much allowed our conversation to take its course, now and then leaning all the way back in his leather executive chair, the heavy springs squeaking whenever he moved.

"I understand you're quite an intelligent young man," said Mr. Henderson, who displayed fidgety mannerisms, like fiddling with the buckles of his overalls and periodically flicking something imaginary from his left thumb. "How'd you like coming home with us?"

"Can my brother come too?"

The Hendersons looked at the superintendent.

"Well, Carroll," interrupted Dr. Yepsen. "We were thinking of your welfare. We want what's best for you."

"That's right, Charles," agreed Mr. Henderson. "We both do." He nodded toward his wife.

The baby began to cry. After calming the infant, Mrs. Henderson said to me, "Melvin told us how much you like school." Her eyes were wide and showed genuine interest.

"I love school and miss it a lot."

"Well, we have a wonderful school in our community that you could attend," she explained. "And you'll love where we live. There's lots of nature, lots of trees and animals and . . . well, we live a farm life. We even have a tractor you can drive."

"A tractor? And I can drive it?"

She nodded. "And if you don't know how to drive it, I'll teach you. There'll be lots of chores. You'll have to do things like turn the haystacks so they won't sour. Have you ever used a pitchfork?"

"No, ma'am."

"You'll get the hang of it. Have you ever worn farmin' britches?"

"I don't think so, ma'am."

"There'll be crops to pick and stalls to be cleaned. You wouldn't mind any of that, would you?"

Again, my brother came to mind.

"It's just that—"

"Charles?" interrupted Mr. Henderson. "You wouldn't mind earning your keep, would you?"

"It isn't that, sir. It's . . . I mean, what about my brother?"

"Carroll," interjected Dr. Yepsen. "The Hendersons have a lovely little farm in the Poconos and—"

"But my brother, I mean, he can't—"

"Carroll, your brother will be fine right where he is. Maybe we could arrange something at a later time. It'd—"

"But why not now? He doesn't like this place either."

The Hendersons and Dr. Yepsen looked at each other. Then Dr. Yepsen looked at me.

"They have lots of animals too, Carroll . . . oh, and a new baby."

"Yes, Charles, I have her right here. Come over and look. Her name's Jennifer." Mrs. Henderson unwrapped the baby and held her up. "She'll be your new sister. Would you like that?"

The sight of the baby made me crumble inside. Ruby's baby came to mind, as did Marilyn's baby, whom I could still see wagging its finger at me. I felt a cold, familiar chill.

"Is something wrong, Charles?" asked Mrs. Henderson.

I fell silent. The baby began to cry.

Calming the baby, Mrs. Henderson reiterated her offer. "Wouldn't you like a new stepsister, Charles?"

"Ma'am, I don't want a stepsister. I just want my brother, that's all."

Mr. Henderson cut in, clearing his throat. "Charles, you don't have to give us an answer right away. We can give you time to think about it."

I said nothing, dropping my eyes to my lap. The room hushed to a somber silence.

Dr. Yepsen rose to his feet. "Maybe we all need to give this further thought. Charles, please come with me."

Outside the door, Dr. Yepsen stopped me. "Mr. Ballanger thinks the world of you. He'll be back in a few days, so I'll have a word with him. Maybe he can talk some sense into your head. Meanwhile, continue to behave yourself. Goodbye, son."

ENDNOTES FOR CHAPTER TWENTY-ONE

1. See Appendix A.2.8/Physical Abuse of Residents; Denial of Privacy/2001. A New Lisbon employee was accused of striking two residents when they refused to get dressed without benefit of privacy.

2. See Appendix B.3/Verbal Abuse and Punching Patient in Face/1991. A Trenton Psychiatric Hospital employee was charged with cursing at and threatening a patient, then grabbing the patient, pushing him down, and punching him in the face.

3. See Appendix B.4/Soliciting Sexual Favors from Patient/1999. A Trenton

Psychiatric Hospital employee was charged with coercing sexual favors from a patient in exchange for bringing her prohibited items.

4. In January 2004, twenty-one men sued the Diocese of Paterson, New Jersey, and Bishop Frank Rodimer. Most of the men said they were sexually abused as children (including "forced masturbation and oral rape") by the Rev. James T. Hanley. Among the parishes Hanley served from 1968 to 1982 were Our Lady of Good Counsel in Pompton Plains and St. Christopher's in Parsippany, exactly where I spent those years with Ruby and Dustin. When announcing the lawsuit, Mark Serrano, a leader of the Survivors Network of Those Abused by Priests (SNAP), said: "Today is a day to recall the suffering that happens to children and continues as they grow into adulthood." Wayne Parry, Associated Press, "Bishop and Diocese of Paterson sued in sex-abuse case," *The Philadelphia Inquirer,* January 13, 2004, http://www.philly.com/mld/inquirer/news/local/7697034.htm (accessed June 10, 2005).

5. I recommend *The Trouble with Secrets* by Karen Johnsen (Seattle: Parenting Press, 1986). This book helps children understand the difference between when they should keep a secret and when they should not.

CHAPTER TWENTY-TWO

An Angel with a Dirty Face

"Bobby! Bobby! I've gotta see Mr. Wheeler," I pleaded, after returning from Dr. Yepsen's office.

"What did the Administration Building want you for?"

"Dr. Yepsen wanted to talk to me."

"What for?" asked Bobby suspiciously.

"He just said he was glad I didn't disappoint him."

"Just for that?"

"That was it."

"And why do ya have to see Mr. Wheeler?"

"Because Mr. Ballanger's comin' back, that's why. If he gets his hands on me, he'll . . . he'll . . . ."

"But how're we gonna get you over to Mr. Wheeler?"

"I don't know. I thought you might know."

"They padlocked that crawl-hole in the ceiling I used to use to get out. They welded that fuckin' thing shut and—"

"We have to think of somethin' else."

"Hey, I got an idea! Follow me, Chuckie."

I followed Bobby to the far end of the dormitory where he motioned to a window.

"There. See that?" He pointed to the heavy-gauged screen.

"I don't see anythin'."

"Watch this." Bobby hopped on the sill and pressed his foot against one corner of the screen.

"Holy shit," I said. "It's loose."

"Yeah, but not enough." Bobby jumped down and pressed the side of his face against the screen. "See those bolts?"

I pressed my forehead against the screen to have a look. "Yeah, I see them. So?"

"They're loose, dummy."

I took a better look. "You're right. They're stickin' out a little bit. So what's that mean?"

"You still don't get it. The wood's rotten, that's why."

"Rotten? How do you know that?"

"Those bolts wouldn't be like that if they wasn't. Think, Chuckie, think. God, you're dumb sometimes. I'll bet if we tried kicking out this screen real hard, those bolts would bust loose."

"Do ya think so?"

"I know so. Wanna bet?"

"You mean right now?"

"Not now, Chuckie. Wanna tonight?"

"I'm scared."

"There you go actin' like a scaredy cat. Wanna bet me a penny?"

"I ain't got no penny."

"Make believe you do."

"Okay, I'll bet ya."

"Come on. Let's go back in the day room. We'll do it tonight."

After showers that night, Bobby pulled me aside. "Hey, Chuckie, when everybody starts watchin' television, we'll do it, okay?"

"Let's wait until the night man comes on—you know, after he does the count—'cause after that he'll be in the day room watchin' TV with everyone else. Plus, by then it'll be dark so it's harder to see me from the street."

"Good idea, Chuckie. You're startin' to use your noggin."

That night, around seven, Bobby and I left the day room and headed for the dormitory. I quickly stopped by my locker to retrieve my coat, making sure no one was looking.

"Bobby, I don't wanna get you in trouble. Remember what Dr. Yepsen said?"

"He don't scare me. Come on. If I can get you out, don't forget, you gotta be back by fifteen minutes to nine—no later—or they'll catch ya."

"I'll be back by the nine o'clock count. Just be here to help me back in the window. I can't do it alone."

"I know that, silly. I'll throw down a sheet."

As soon as we reached the targeted window, Bobby hopped onto the sill and began pressing on the screen with his foot. The screen made a cracking sound.

"Bobby, Bobby, you're makin' too much noise."

"I think I got it." He was shaking from the strain and his face was beet red.

"Stop it, Bobby. Sh-hh, you're makin' too much noise. I better check to see if anybody heard it."

"Go ahead. I'll wait."

"No, no. Get off the windowsill first, just in case somebody did."

"Okay," he said, jumping down to the floor. "Hurry up. Come right back."

I ran down the dormitory and peeked around the doorway that led to the day room. Apparently, nobody had heard anything, so I ran back to Bobby.

"It's okay, Bobby."

"See? I told ya." He hopped back up on the windowsill. "Chuckie, are you sure you wanna do it tonight?"

"Heck, yeah! I've *gotta*. Mr. Ballanger's comin' back. Plus, I have to talk to Mr. Wheeler about somethin' else."

"Like what?"

"I'll tell ya when I come back," I answered, intentionally not saying anything about the Hendersons.

"You better. Let's try again."

This time, pushing harder, the veins of his forehead looked like they were about to burst.

"Bobby, Bobby." I tapped him on the shoulder. "I think we need help."

"You're right." He let out a frustrated breath. "I got it. Get Goony."

"Goony? Why him?"

"Because I know he can do it."

"Think he'll tell on us?"

"That stupid motherfucker can't even talk, much less rat, on somebody. I'll give 'im some of the candy my Kid gave me yesterday. He'll do anything for candy. Go get 'im, Chuckie."

"There he is now."

"Hey, Goony," called out Bobby. "Come down here." Bobby looked at me. "Chuckie, look under my pillow and get two bars of candy. Just two, okay?"

"Okay, Bobby. I'll be right back."

Goony weighed about two hundred pounds. He was unusually strong, his arms thick with muscle. I returned with the candy bars at the same time Goony joined Bobby.

"Goony, we need you to help us," said Bobby.

"Got cany?"

"Show him the candy, Chuckie."

I held up the two Milky Way bars. Goony reached out for them.

"No, no. Not yet. After you do it," promised Bobby.

"I do what?"

"Hold it a minute, Goony. Hey, Chuckie, move that bed under the window."

"Okay, Bobby." I pushed the bed into place.

"That's perfect. Hey, Goony, do this." Bobby hopped up on the bed, laid on his back, and pressed his two feet against the screen. "Come on. You try it."

"I do it. I do it."

"Chuckie, help me get 'im up."

We got on either side of Goony to hold him in place.

"Goony, put your feet against the screen like I showed ya . . . yeah, yeah, like that." Bobby positioned Goony's hands on the side jambs of the windowsill. "Perfect. That's it. Now push as hard as you can."

Goony began pushing. The window frame cracked, but Goony was struggling. We decided to give him a hand and propped ourselves behind him, pushing on his back as his oversized feet pressed against the screen.

"Harder, Goony, harder!"

Goony's muscular legs began shaking, his face filling with wrinkles and blood.

"Don't give up, Goony. That's it . . . harder, harder. Want some candy, don'tcha?"

Goony suddenly stopped and reached for the candy. Bobby withdrew his hand.

"No, no, Goony. Not until you do it."

Once more, Goony positioned himself and began pushing.

"That's it, Goony. Keep it up. Don't stop."

"Cany. Cany for me?"

"Yeah, yeah, keep it up."

CRA-A-A-CK!

"Holy shit!" exclaimed Bobby. "He busted the whole fuckin' thing out!"

The screen tumbled to the ground. We snickered and laughed our hearts out, praising Goony for a job well done.

After we finally collected ourselves, afraid of catching somebody's attention from the day room, I warned, "Quick, Bobby, go see if anybody heard us."

"Nah, they got the television blastin' and—"

"No, no, you better go check, just in case. Quick, go look."

"God, Chuckie, you worry about every little thing. Okay, wait here. Be right back."

Goony was still sitting and gripping the windowsill. I watched Bobby down at the other end of the dormitory, peeking around the door. He came running back.

"It's okay, it's okay," he repeated in a loud whisper. "Nobody heard shit. Help me get Goony down."

As we helped Goony off the bed, he kept mumbling, "Me cany. Me cany. Me cany."

"Okay, Chuckie, you can give 'im the candy now."

"Here, Goony." I handed the chocolate bars to him.

"Satisfied now, Goony?" asked Bobby.

Goony tore open one bar and began eating it.

"Go back to the day room, Goony," ordered Bobby.

We watched Goony make his way down the dormitory, shoving the second bar into his mouth by the time he reached the door. Once he rounded the corner, we turned to each other.

"Chuckie, you ready?"

"Heck, yeah." I threw on my coat, jumped up on the sill, and slipped through the window.

"Hey, Chuckie, watch out for the cops."

"I will."

I turned and slipped away into the night. I ran all the way to the old oak tree in front of Mr. Wheeler's building, then stopped and checked for his car. It was parked along with others about halfway up the block. I looked up at his window and it was lit. Wasting no time, I ran inside and up the steps that led to his apartment. Just as I raised my hand to knock, a man opened the door and stepped out. I looked at him from head to foot. He was a slim man, wearing a pair of tight, white pants that outlined his penis. He reeked of cologne.

"Who are you, darlin'?" he asked in an effeminate voice.

"I'm, uh . . . is Mr. Wheeler here?"

"Melvin, it's for you."

"I'll take care of it, Phil. I know the boy. I'll call you tomorrow."

As the man left, he looked back at me two or three times before disappearing down the steps.

"I had to see you, Mr. Wheeler."

"This is quite a surprise. How'd you get here? Did they transfer you out of Cedar?"

"No, I snuck out."

Realizing the seriousness of what I'd done, he checked the hall again to see if I'd been spotted by anyone. Then he looked at me and said, "You're a gutsy little rascal, aren't ya? Come on in and have a seat over there." He pointed to the edge of the bed. "So, Charley, what's this all about?"

"Mr. Ballanger's comin' back and—"

"Jack Ballanger?"

"Yes, sir. He's better from his heart attack. Now he's comin' back."

"Hold it." Mr. Wheeler pulled out his pocket watch. "It's twenty to eight. What time is count over there at Cedar?"

"At nine, but if I can get back there by a quarter to, I won't get caught."

"Okay, I'll make sure you're out of here in plenty of time. How'd you hear Jack Ballanger was coming back?"

"That's what Dr. Yepsen said."

Mr. Wheeler smiled. "You're quite an amazing boy. You know what this could mean if they catch you? It could mean Fern or worse."

"I know, but I had to see you. Don't let Mr. Ballanger do anything to me again."

"I already took care of that, son."

"What do ya mean?"

"I'll get back to Ballanger in a minute. Stop fretting. First, I want you to see something." He reached for a mirror on the nightstand. "Look at yourself in the mirror. What do you see?"

"Me."

"I know that. What else?"

"I don't know."

"See those freckles?"

"Yes."

"Did you know each one of those is a kiss from God?"

"They are? I didn't know that. Mr. Wheeler, who was that man? He looked at me funny, and he smelled funny too."

"Funny? How?"

I shrugged my shoulders.

"He's a friend. Now about those freckles."

"I didn't know God kissed boys. He's a man. You're kidding, right?"

"I kid you not. It's true, Charley. See how blessed you are?"

"I am?"

"Of course you are. By the way, I heard what happened with the Hendersons."

"They told you?"

"No, Dr. Yepsen did."

"What did he say?"

"That he didn't think they were right for you."

"He said that?"

"Yes, he did. Is there anything you'd like to add?"

"He lied to you."

"How's that?"

"I don't know. Do we . . . do we really have to talk about it?"

"Not if you don't want to. Look, Charley, I don't care what you did or what you said to the Hendersons. I know you love your brother, but I must tell you, you fouled up a good chance of getting out of this hellhole. You know that, don't you?"

"I . . . I know."

"Well, look, the Hendersons are behind us now and—"

"Oh, and Mr. Wheeler, I read that book you gave me."

"You mean the one by Rocky Graziano?"

"That's the one. He was a prizefighter and he got in some trouble. They sent him to Riker's Island in New York. Somebody tried to rape him too, like me, but he took care of it himself. That man went through a lotta bad stuff. He was honest about everything in that book. I never read a book like that before. That's the kind of book I want to write one day."

"I have a feeling you will, Charley."

"I know I will. I'd write it now, but I don't know enough big words yet."

"What do you think it'll be about?"

"About this place."

"Then you should do it."

"I will, when I get smart enough."

"Maybe you can tell your story to somebody and get them to write it for you."

"Nope. I wanna do it myself. But I can tell you one thing. If I ever get outta this place, I'll get smart enough. This place don't teach ya nothin' except bad things. It's a sad place."

"In that case, I'll bet it won't be a Dick and Jane book."

Laughing, I said, "No, it won't be about Dick and Jane, or Spot, or Puff the cat. It'll be about bad people. There's a lotta bad people in this place. Why's it like that, Mr. Wheeler? You and Dr. Alprin are the only good ones. I miss Dr. Alprin. Have you seen him?"

"No, Charley, because he's not working here anymore. I believe he took a teaching job somewhere."

"You mean he's gone?"

"Yes, Charley. I'm afraid so."

"I didn't know that. He was a really nice man."

"Well, he sure thought a lot of you too. You know, Charley, I'm proud of you, because you . . . you have noble ideals, and I think one day you'll follow through with them. I really do."

"You do? You always say good things like that. Nobody else does."

"Let me tell you something, Charley. It's not the *big* words that count, but the words that come from your heart. Those are the only ones that have any real meaning. Perhaps, when you get older and a bit wiser, you'll understand what I mean. In fact, I have no doubt that you will. You're a fine, fine boy, son."

"You really think so?"

"Yes, I do. Now let's talk about Mr. Ballanger. Remember when

I asked you if anybody ever did anything like that to you before him?"

"Yes."

"And you said, 'You mean by a man?' Remember saying that?"

"Yes."

"What did you mean by that?"

"I don't know." My eyes avoided his.

"Okay, let me put it to you this way. Has any *boy* ever done anything like that to you, before Mr. Ballanger?"

"You won't tell nobody if I tell you?"

"Certainly not."

"It happened before I came to New Lisbon, and since I've been here too."

"Who?"

"Just don't tell nobody, 'cause if they find out I told, when they get me alone, they'll beat me up."

"Beat you up? Tell me who's been strong-arming you and I'll take—"

I looked away again and shook my head. "I can't."

"Don't worry, son, I'll—"

"No, no, forget I said anything, Mr. Wheeler. Please. I'm just too afraid."

"Okay, but if anything like that happens again, you be sure to let me know, okay?"

"Okay, I will. Mr. Wheeler, can I ask you something?"

"Sure, kid."

"Why do people like to do that stuff with boys—I mean, boys with boys?"

"It's not uncommon, Charley, for people to do those things in a place like this. Tell me, son, besides the priest, you said there was somebody else before you came here?"

"Yeah, there was a boy . . . oh, and there was a girl too, but we were all messin' around together—her and Bobby and me. It was fun."

"Want to talk about it?"

"Okay."

I DECIDED TO do a little fishing. I took the flagstone pathway, jumped the concrete divider, and headed down the driveway, getting mud all over my galoshes from a recent rain. I headed down Sunfair Road to the bridge, worked my way down the embankment, and retrieved a shovel that I kept hidden in the brush. I began digging for nightcrawlers. After gathering a few, I went to my favorite fishing spot and threw out my first cast.

PLUNK!

The sinker landed in the middle of the stream. Then, I heard footsteps approaching behind me. I scooted up the embankment and leveled my eyes over the ridge. Two teenage boys were coming down Sunfair Road, each of them jumping from dry spot to dry spot to avoid getting mud on their bare feet; their shoes were tied by the laces and slung over their shoulders.

I scurried back down the embankment, quickly grabbed my rod, and returned to fishing. A moment or two later, I heard their feet kicking pebbles on the old bridge, their broken shadows flickering through the cracks.

One boy was wearing a straw hat and sucking on a sliver of grass, the cuffs of his tight jeans rolled up to his shins. His friend, an overweight kid, was wearing coveralls and limped when he walked.

When they reached the middle of the bridge, they stopped, stretched over the railing, and looked down at me.

"Hi, kid!" one of them greeted.

I waved and then whipped another cast, attempting to show off my skills, my sinker breaking their shadows into dozens of ripples. As I reeled it in, my test line snagged the rocks, but I managed to work it loose. I threw out another cast, but this time it landed on the embankment on the other side of the waterway.

CHARLES A. CARROLL

The two boys laughed and one of them shouted, "Where'd ya learn to fish, kid?"

Feeling self-conscious, I didn't answer. I worked the line loose, reeled it in, and quickly recast. This time, my sinker landed in the middle of the stream.

The two boys clapped and laughed, hollering, "It's about time."

I looked up, their eyes meeting mine.

"Any luck, yet?" one yelled.

"Nah," I answered. "Nothin' yet."

As I reeled it in, my line snagged again.

"Hey, kid, is that what you call fishin'?"

I looked up, blocking the sun with my free hand, then turned away, trying to work my line loose. They continued to mock me, both of them laughing and snickering. I looked up again and gave them a self-conscious smile.

After I finally freed my line, they applauded. I reeled it in and, with a mighty thrust, sent it back out.

"Hey, you!"

"What?"

"I'm comin' down to show ya how to fish, kid." The thinner boy slid down the hill on his rear end, his butt collecting mud along the way. Once he made it to the bottom, he came running over to me. At that moment, I felt a misty spray hit my face. I looked up. His friend was urinating between the railings of the bridge and laughing. I ducked out of the way and joined in the laughter.

"Hey, look, ya got one, kid," shouted the boy next to me, pointing to my fishing rod secured between my feet.

I grabbed my pole and began reeling in, exclaiming, "I caught one! I caught one!" Every inch of me swelled with pride.

"Hey, Richard," shouted his friend up on the bridge, "don't let 'im lose it!"

"I won't, Porky!"

"Porky?" I asked. "Is that your friend's name?"

"It's his nickname. Watch it! Don't let 'im get under the rocks."

Struggling with the trout, it flipped out of the water and dove deep, making a run for the log not more than ten feet from the shoreline.

"Ah, shit! Ya let 'im get under that damn log!"

"What do I do now?"

"Gimmie that thing. I'll show ya how to do it!" He took the rod from me. "Let's see if I can get 'im loose for ya. Follow me."

Staying with him, I said, "Bet ya he's a humdinger!"

"It could be." He struggled to work the line free. "What's your name, kid?" he asked as we walked along the water's edge under the bridge.

"Chuckie."

"Okay, Chuckie, there ya go. I got 'im loose for ya. Here." He handed back the fishing rod. "Now you bring 'im in."

I took the rod and began reeling in the thrashing critter, but the fight wasn't over yet. The fish lashed and tugged, surfaced, then dove deep, bending my pole in half.

"Stay with it, kid!"

"How ya guys doin' down there?"

I shouted through the spaces of the planks, "I got it now!" I finally reeled in the exhausted brown-speckled trout to the water's edge.

"That's some fuckin' fish ya caught, kid!"

The fish laid at our feet, its tail fin smacking the ground.

I turned to Richard. "Could you take 'im off the hook for me?"

"Sure, kid, but instead of takin' the hook out, just cut the line. That way you can just carry it home and remove it there."

"Good idea."

"Got a knife?"

"No."

"Hang on a minute." He looked up at the bridge. "Hey, Porky, throw down your knife!"

"Okay," yelled the hefty kid from the bridge, unsnapping the sheath on his hip and quickly tossing the knife at our feet.

"This'll do it, kid. Where do ya live?"

"In the green house up the road."

"You mean that one behind us on Sunfair Road?"

"That's the one."

"Follow me."

He picked up the line, carried it to the pilings under the bridge, dropped the near-dead critter between two rocks, and then sat down on a large boulder.

"There, now it ain't goin' nowhere. Sit down here." He patted the boulder next to him. "I wanna show ya somethin'."

I complied and said excitedly, "Boy, that sure was a big one I got, huh, Richard?"

"Yeah, and I gotta a big one too." He suddenly stood, unbuttoned his tight jeans, pulled his pants and underwear down to his knees, and proudly displayed his hard penis inches from my face.

"Why's it like that?" I asked innocently, pointing to his penis.

Holding it at the base, he said, "Suck on it like a lollipop, kid."

"That ain't no lollipop!"

"See this?"

I looked up at his white-knuckled fist.

"Open your mouth, I said." He grabbed the back of my head and pushed my face against his penis.

"No!" I pushed him away with the side of my arm.

"Goddamn it, Richard, we gotta go! If you don't come up, I'm comin' down and draggin' your ass outta there. I hope you're not doin' what I think you're doin'."

"Ah, shit!" Richard pulled up his trousers and zipped up. "I'm comin'!" He turned and climbed the embankment without ever looking back, as if getting away clean from a taboo event.

Once on the bridge, I watched them through the open spaces of the weather-beaten planks. Richard said to Porky, "Ya sure know how to fuck up a wet dream, don't ya?"

"What's that supposed to mean?"

"Ah, fuck it!" he said, throwing his arm around his friend's shoul-

PLATE SIXTEEN
CHARLES A. CARROLL (LEFT) AND ROBERT L. CARROLL
C. 1949
POMPTON LAKES, NEW JERSEY

der. "Let's go. This place ain't no fun anyway."

I watched their images flickering through the cracks between the boards until they were finally gone. Shaken by the experience, I laid back on the rocks, trying to make some sense of it. I watched the clouds pass by through the slats of the bridge, the trickling water soothing me, taking me back to an incident a couple of years earlier.

Bobby and I were playing one day, but we weren't alone. We had invited a little girl from the neighborhood to join us, for fun and curiosity. The girl's name was Autumn, and her innocence dazzled like rhinestones. She was frilly, every bit as feminine, virtuous, and sinless as the Virgin Mary. I think I cherished Autumn as much as Jack did Jill, suspecting all along that Jack and Jill were not just fetching a pail of water.

Autumn was wearing a plaid skirt, her waist trimmed by a shimmering patent-leather belt. She wore a light blue blouse with three-quarter sleeves that ended with delicate, white-laced ruffles. Her Buster Brown shoes and checkerboard socks neatly clung to her tiny ankles.

Dangling about her shoulders were two neatly tied braids, each end finished with a dainty red bow. She was pretty, with cute features: a tip-tilt nose perfectly placed, a face framed by blond bangs that swept across her alabaster forehead, eyes rich and sky blue. Little Autumn looked like a living doll, as if she had just stepped through the cellophane window of a polka-dot box. She was the first of my childhood infatuations.

We all climbed into Wiggie's doghouse. It was there that Bobby and I had originally made our Indian blood-brother pact, vowing to remain true to it for the rest of our lives. As the three of us huddled in the small quarters, Wiggie begged to enter. We allowed her to come in, but when she began slapping her plumelike tail against the dusty floor, we kicked her out. She obediently curled herself into a ball outside the opening and waited for us to emerge.

We wanted this event to be private, so I nailed a brown burlap bag over the entrance. The darkened atmosphere inside not only added spooks and goblins to our imaginations, but also ignited an enormous sense of curiosity. We virtually kicked out the rest of the world and proceeded on our innocent quest.

Autumn faced us, with her back to the opening. Her natural scent awakened my prepubescent curiosity.

While tickling one another and giggling, I stopped and said to her, "Hey, Autumn, we'll show you ours if you show us yours."

The moment was as pure as Kingdom Come and as unsullied as the Mother of God. We viewed our private parts with interest, totally submerged in the process of childhood exploration and the earliest stages of physical discovery. We were free spirited and guileless, and never further from any thoughts of societal or religious condemnation—that is, until Ruby overheard our goings-on.

"Pigs! Pigs! Pigs!" she shouted, ripping the burlap sack from the opening. She pulled out Autumn first, shouting hysterically, "Go home, you little pig! I'm tellin' your mother!"

Reaching in, she grabbed our little legs and proceeded to drag us out. Holding the burlap up to our faces, she scolded, "I never wanna see this thing over Wiggie's door again!"

Ruby pulled down our pants and smacked our fannies. That was the first time she ever gave us a licking.

After she ordered us to pull up our pants, she grabbed us by our collars and headed for the house, shouting every step of the way, "You pigs!"

The words "You pigs!" snapped me out of my daydream. I sat up, slid off the rocks, and immediately headed home. Because of my fear and lack of trust in Ruby, I never mentioned one word of the bridge incident; I was all alone with it.

"THAT'S QUITE A story, Charley. Thanks for sharing it with me. Now tell me, what about boys in this place? Have you had any problems with them?"

I turned away from Mr. Wheeler to avoid eye contact. "Can I tell you about that another time?"

"Sure. That'll be fine." He paused a moment. "Oh, and before I forget, Mr. Ballanger's never coming back."

"Never?"

"Never."

"But Dr. Yepsen said—"

"Don't worry yourself about him, okay? Just trust what I'm telling you."

"Gosh, thanks, Mr. Wheeler. I feel better now." I hesitated. "Mr. Wheeler, there's one other man here that did shit with me."

"And who's that?"

"Mr. Stone."

"Stone? The music teacher?"

"Yes."

"Are you sure?"

"I'm sure. He did shit with my brother, and other kids too, but nobody wants to believe me. Can I have a hug, Mr. Wheeler?"

"Only one hug? How about two of them?"

"Okay."

He leaned over and gave me a hug, but instead of releasing me, he slipped his hands under my arms and began tickling me.

Mr. Wheeler had me laughing and giggling, pulling me onto the bed. Suddenly, he flopped on top of me, tickling me all over. At that very moment, I don't think I ever loved another human being more, except for my brother.

"You're a funny man, Mr. Wheeler. You make me laugh. I wanna be like you someday. I wanna be just as smart as you too."

Mr. Wheeler got off me and rolled over on his back. We just laid there quietly, looking up at the ceiling. I broke the silence, rolling on my side and looking at him.

"Mr. Wheeler, I'm glad you're my friend."

"You mean that, Charley?"

"Yes, sir."

"Then take this," he said, tickling me again.

"I'm gonna get you for that." Laughing, I slipped out from under his hands and began to wrestle with him. Before long, our hair was a mess, my clothes were ruffled, and his shirttail was sticking out of his pants.

Then the room went black.

"Hey, what happened?"

"It's that light again. I've been having trouble with it. Every time I stick a bulb in that socket, it burns out. I think it has a short."

"It's really dark in here, Mr. Wheeler."

"It's spooky, isn't it, son?"

"Yeah, but it's fun."

I felt surrounded by his genuine affection. With him, the pitch dark didn't trouble me. All that could be seen in that room were the glowing numbers on the clock beside his bed. I was actually hoping the light would never come back on. I wanted that moment to never go away. For the first time since arriving at New Lisbon, I felt safe in the dark.

"Let's see if we can get that light back on."

"No, no. It's fun like this."

"But it's getting late, Charley. Let's get up and find a new bulb."

We climbed off the bed. Mr. Wheeler felt for my arm and led me to the closet where he kept the light bulbs. I went in first.

"Feel around for them, Charley. Bet you can't find them."

On my tiptoes, I felt for the bulbs on the top shelf.

"They're up there somewhere, Charley. Did you find them, yet?"

As I searched, Mr. Wheeler leaned forward, his body against my back.

"No luck yet, Mr. Wheeler."

"Keep trying, son. They're there."

"Ha-ha-ha. I can't find them, but this is fun."

"You're having fun?"

"Heck, yeah!"

"It's a blown bulb, Charley. Let's forget about the bulb."

"No, no, I'll find it."

Then, still from behind, Mr. Wheeler wrapped one arm around me, pulling me closer. He began rubbing against me again, but this time harder. My grin froze in place. My insides collapsed, and my heart fell into a heap of shattered pieces. I didn't move. I heard him unzip his pants. He reached for my hand and lowered it, sliding his hard penis into it.

I dropped to the floor, curled up, and began crying, "Not you too, Mr. Wheeler . . . oh, God, not you too."

That moment instantly destroyed our alliance, taking our father-and-son union and hurling it into the blinking archives of my rapes and assaults, and he was now its newest entry.

Mr. Wheeler tucked his penis into his pants and pulled up his zipper. Then he leaned over and began stroking my hair, all the while apologizing. Repelled by the angel with a dirty face, I removed his hand and rose to my feet, edging my way out of the darkened room. Mr. Wheeler followed. Standing at the open door, he continued to profess apologies. For a moment, I wanted to believe him, to cherish what we'd had, but I couldn't ignore my deep sense of disappointment and my stubborn moral pride.

For the first time, I saw Mr. Wheeler not as a pillar of strength but as a false front of morality.

As I turned away from him, he feebly mumbled, "I . . . I don't know what came over me, Charley. I'm . . . I'm sorry . . . I'm so, so—"

Crying, I interrupted, "Desarino was right. And Mr. Ballanger was right too. He said shit about you, but I didn't believe it. I hated him, but he was right. He knew you better than I did."

"But I . . . I didn't mean it, Charley . . . please don't let this—"

"Stop it! You're one of them!" I shouted, recoiling from the man as if he were a salivating, long-toothed vampire and the epitome of all New Lisbon's sins.

I ran into the night, never feeling more hurt, alone, or betrayed.

PLATE SEVENTEEN
MELVIN WHEELER
DRAWING BY CHARLES A. CARROLL

CHAPTER TWENTY-THREE
Bobby

THAT NIGHT, WHEN I returned to Cedar from Mr. Wheeler's room, an ambulance was parked in front. Its red and yellow lights were blinking, its back doors wide open. I actually gave it little thought, thinking that somebody probably had a grand mal seizure, since such episodes were common. I hurried to the window where Bobby was supposed to be waiting for me; he wasn't there. I wondered if he had pulled the same stunt as the last time I returned from seeing Mr. Wheeler, when I found Bobby entertaining himself in front of the television. I stepped back to see if I could eye anyone in the dormitory. Goony was lingering at the window.

"Goony!" I called out. "It's me. Come here."

Goony opened the window and peered out. "Cany . . . cany . . . cany," he kept saying, his hands cupped in front of him.

"I'll give you some after you help me up. Where's my brother?"

"Cany . . . cany." He poked his finger into his open mouth.

"I said I'd give you some, but you gotta get my brother first. Hurry and get 'im."

"Me cany?"

"Jesus Christ, Goony! I said I would. Now hurry up and get my brother."

Goony disappeared from the window. I turned and looked at the ambulance. Two men were escorting someone from the cottage toward the back of the vehicle. Goony appeared in the window.

"Well, what happened? Did you find Bobby?"

He shrugged his shoulders.

"What's that mean, Goony?"

He shrugged his shoulders again.

"Goony, help me inside. Throw me the sheet. It's on the floor. Hurry up and help me."

"Me cany?" He again pointed to his mouth.

"Yes! I've got some inside under my brother's pillow. Get the sheet."

"No."

"No? Why not? I'm gonna give you some candy."

"No!"

"You stupid fucker! Get me that sheet or I'll kick your ass." I was bluffing, of course, knowing that if he ever socked me, just one punch would probably turn my face inside out. Yet, to my surprise, he complied, throwing down a sheet. It landed in a pile at my feet.

"No, no, Goony. Not that way." I tossed the sheet back into the window. "Hold one end and drop the other end down."

"Me cany?"

"Yes, yes! Just help me up! Please?"

"Okay. I drop."

"Good! That's it. Now hold it tight. Don't let it go. Here I come. That's it. Don't let go!" I crawled inside the window.

"Me cany?"

"Not now. I'll be right back."

Pushing him aside, I ran down the dormitory into the day room. Everybody was looking out the windows.

"Where's Bobby?" I asked one man.

He pointed out the window.

"Outside? You mean that's my brother?"

The mute man nodded.

I opened the window and shouted, "Bobby! Bobby! Hey, Bobby! Is that you?"

There was no response.

I turned to the same man. "Are you sure it's him?"

His tongue tripping over his teeth, he nodded again. I went to the next window, shoving two patients aside as I opened it.

"Bobby! Say it ain't you! Bobby! Bobby! It's me!"

I listened for my brother's voice, but with all the gibbering going on in the room, I couldn't hear a damn thing. I turned to everybody.

"Shut the fuck up! All of you! I can't hear 'im!"

The tone of the room softened.

I turned back to the window. "Bobby! I'm here! It's me! Tell me it's not you!"

"They got me, Chuckie!"

"But why? What did you do? Where're they takin' you?"

"They got me, Chuckie! They fuckin' got me!"

I felt someone behind me. It was Goony.

"Gimmie cany . . . gimmie cany."

"Shit, Goony. Not now, goddamn it!"

I ran to the window closest to the ambulance and heard Bobby yelling.

"Chuckie, they're takin' me away!"

"Leave 'im alone! Don't hurt 'im! It's my fault!" I yelled.

Bobby's friends—Smithy, Shaw, Leggett, and Garigiola—shouted over each other, "He's goin' to Trenton. He cut his wrists again!"

"Not again! Hey, hey, hey! You out there!" I screamed, pounding on the heavy screen. "He only does that shit to get attention! He doesn't really wanna kill himself. Please believe me . . . please, please, please!"

The streetlight illuminated what they were doing to him. I watched them snap buckles in place up and down his straitjacket until he was completely secured, then they lifted him into the back of the ambulance.[1] When I saw the two back doors slam shut, I slid to my knees, pounding the floor with my fists and cussing at God.

Goony was behind me with his hands cupped to his mouth. "Me cany . . . me cany . . . me cany."

I rose to my feet, shoved his arms aside, and looked back out the window, tears dribbling down my face. I was suddenly interrupted by a tap on the shoulder and a whisper in my ear.

"They oughta fry his brain, mothafucka."

I whipped around with a balled-up fist, stopping it inches from the perpetrator's jaw. My eyes widened. Blood drained from my face.

"It's you!"

"Fuck you. Thought ya got rid of my ass . . . huh, mothafucka?" He rubbed his black-knotted fist in my face. "I hate your cryin' ass."

"Shut up, Rawbone!" boomed Mr. Pring from across the room. Mr. Pring was a new man, assigned to Cedar from another cottage. "You're not in Birch anymore," he scolded. "Your bullying won't be tolerated here."

"I never did shit to nobody. Ask Mrs. Steele. Carroll can tell you. Tell 'im, Carroll. Tell 'im I didn't do shit to nobody."

I turned away, muttering under my breath, "Goddamn it. I should've killed the son of a—"

"What was that? You're mumbling. Speak up," ordered Mr. Pring.

"Nothin'," I said, turning back to him. "I was just talkin' to myself, that's all."

"Tell 'im the truth, Carroll. Tell 'im I ain't done shit to nobody."

"Shut your mouth, Blacky," Mr. Pring snapped. "As far as I'm concerned, you're a yellow-livered skunk. Get to bed. Lights out in five minutes. Carroll, come over here. Dammit, Rawbone! I said to get your ass moving. What I have to say to Carroll ain't your business."

"Ah, fuck it. I'm goin'." Rawbone retreated into the dormitory.

"Now what was that I think I heard you say?" Mr. Pring asked.

"Nothin'. I was just shootin' my mouth off about nothin'. Mr.

Pring, can I ask you a question?"

"Sure. What is it?"

"Was Mr. Ballanger behind my brother being sent to Trenton?"

"Yes. He ordered it several weeks ago, before he got sick. Here's the scoop. The state now says that if someone is a danger to himself or others, he goes to Trenton. Why did your brother cut himself up like that?"

"I asked him why he does that shit sometimes, and he told me he does it 'cause that's when people pay attention to him. He just has some problems, that's all. But does he wanna die? Hell no! And did he really cut his wrist tonight?"

"No, he's going because he has a history of doing that to himself."

"And Mr. Ballanger was the one behind it?"

"Yes, that's what happened."

"That son of a bitch!"

"Watch your tongue, young fella."

"Sorry, sir."

"So attention is behind it, then?"

"Yes, sir."

"That's what I figured, but he's got himself into a fix this time."

"What do you mean?"

"The thing is, he's done this before, and now New Lisbon doesn't want to take a chance with him anymore."

"Why not?"

"Because if he—"

I interrupted, "Look, Mr. Pring. If my brother really wanted to kill himself, he would've cut himself deeper than that little bullshit. It's for attention, I'm tellin' ya—just for attention."

"I believe you. Like I said, the state says that if someone is a danger to himself, he goes to Trenton. State policies have changed, and that's the way it is now. They made it into a law, so they have no choice, however minor the cuts may be. Trenton will figure all this out. You just watch and see if I'm not right. They're experts up there. They won't hurt him. They'll help him. Mark my words."

"They screwed up a lotta people over at Trenton with this electricity stuff they're usin' on the brain. I've seen guys come back from there worse off than before they went. Haven't you noticed?"

"I'm . . . I'm not a shrink. What would I know about things like that? I just work here. Then again, now that you mention it, you may have a point there."

"I know I do."

"But you may be reading more into it than is warranted. He'll be okay, you'll see. And don't think I don't know what he means to you. I do. I really do."

"Yeah, I guess so."

"Go to bed, son. Try to get some sleep."

"Thanks, Mr. Pring."

"Good night, son."

Willie Pring was a guard at Fern Cottage for a number of years, but he had become Mr. Ballanger's replacement at Cedar. He was a large man, like Mr. Ballanger, and very much a woodsman type; he wore bleached-out Levi's, his waist adorned with a large, silver belt buckle, his head usually topped with a sweat-stained cowboy hat. He liked plaid lumberjack shirts, accented by Bull Durham tags that dangled from the pockets, and he often rolled his own cigarettes with one hand.

Mr. Pring was a southerner at heart; he was a redneck, a racist, and freely admitted it, often spieling off racial slurs as fast as he could roll a cigarette, lick it, light it, and deeply inhale it—all with the quick stroke of one hand. But although Mr. Pring was vulgar and tasteless, I liked him. He was a straight-up man. You didn't have to guess what he was thinking. And if he liked you, you could count on his support.

Once in the dormitory, Rawbone began picking on me; he immediately told me that he saw me outside, climbing into the dormitory window, and threatened to tell on me.

I responded with disbelief, "You mean you'd rat on me? After all those times when I never said shit about you?"

"A smart-ass too, huh, dick weed?"

"Leave me alone, Rawbone." I started to walk away.

"Don't ignore my ass, mothafucka."

I turned and looked at him. "Look, Rawbone. I ain't done shit to you. Lay off."

Mr. Pring entered the dormitory.

"Bedtime! Let's go. That goes for you, Blacky. Back away from Carroll and get your ass into bed."

"But Carroll's startin' shit with me."

"Oh, bullshit! Come on, everybody. No more standing around."

"Mr. Pring, I'll get them all to bed," Rawbone offered. "I'm a good monitor. Ask Mrs. Steele."

"You? Let's get something straight, Rawbone. I don't need a monitor to do my bidding. As far as I'm concerned, Mrs. Steele's been on the wrong track for a long time with boys like you. Beat it. And I ain't tellin' you again. In bed! Carroll, come with me. I want another talk with you."

In the day room, Mr. Pring rested a comforting hand on my shoulder.

"Just what is this thing between you and Rawbone?"

"I don't know, Mr. Pring. He's always had it in for me. I hate 'im. I . . . I just hate 'im."

"Well, he's not gonna throw his weight around here like he did at Birch. Stay away from that colored boy. Don't let him talk you into a private fight with him. You need more meat on your bones, son. You're a small thirteen-year-old and he's a big nineteen. Avoid him, and do what's good for ya. Okay?"

"I guess so, sir."

"Go to bed and try to get some sleep."

"Yes, sir."

When we returned to the dormitory, Rawbone was in the same spot, as if waiting for my return.

Mr. Pring shouted, "What in the hell are you doing still standing there? I don't think you understand English. Move it. I'm not tellin' you again."

"Okay, okay, I'm goin'. Goddamn it, Mr. Pring. Why're you ridin' my black ass?"

"Just shut up and hit the pillow, smart-ass."

I went to bed that night with an angry heart over Mr. Wheeler and an aching heart for Bobby. I was especially wrought with fear that they would turn Bobby into something he was not, destroy his spirit—or worse, produce a brain-dead kid, breaking him into submission like a wild horse, finally leading him in any direction with the slightest tug of New Lisbon's bureaucratic reins.

A few nights later, with thoughts of Bobby running through my head, I tossed and turned, unable to sleep for more than an hour at a time. Around two in the morning, awake and restless, I opened my eyes when I heard footsteps coming in my direction. It was the night attendant making his routine count. I watched him pass me and go to the far end of the dormitory where he punched his clock at the key station. Then, on his way back, his flashlight stopped when he approached my bed. I closed my eyes and pretended to be asleep. He stepped forward and slipped something beneath my pillow.

Once he was gone, I reached under the pillow and pulled out the object he had left there, holding it in the moonlight over my head. It was a pocket watch. I turned it over and read the inscription:

For Charley
A friend forever
Melvin
1956

For a moment, I was lost in sentimentality. I threw my face into the pillow and wept bitterly, clutching the watch as I had once done with the ChapStick, holding it close to my heart and mourning the warmth and trust, now gone, that it represented. Images of Mr. Wheeler morphed into those of Bobby in a straitjacket, and I cried even harder, sobbing as I had years before when I watched my brother disappear down dusty Sunfair Road.

Then thoughts of Mr. Wheeler's advances suddenly slapped me across the face with a good, sobering dose of realty. I kicked off the sheets, stood up, drew my hand back as far as it would go, and hurled that pocket watch back into the face of the boogeyman. After it smashed into the wall and fell in pieces, I crawled back into bed, wiped away my tears, and swore never to trust anyone again.

The next morning, Mr. Mitchell entered the day room and announced, "Okay, everybody, listen up. Smithy, Shaw, Leggett, Garigiola, and Carroll—I want all of you in my office to get ready for transfer. Rawbone, you're going back to Birch."

ENDNOTES FOR CHAPTER TWENTY-THREE

1. See Appendix A.1/U.S. Department of Justice Investigation of New Lisbon/ 2003 and 2004. During a fifteen-month period, the Justice Department found over one thousand documented instances of restraining residents by wrists and ankles and, sometimes, chest belts.

CHAPTER TWENTY-FOUR
Requiems of Fear

IT WAS MARCH 16, 1956. Twenty-eight other boys and I made our way to the Administration Building, carrying with us our meager belongings. Three buses were parked in front, along the same curb where the social worker, Mrs. Johnson, had parked more than four years earlier to deliver me into the hands of New Lisbon.

Two of the small buses were already loaded with kids from other mental institutions across the state who were judged "suitable" for the next phase of their confinement. They were considered borderline cases of retardation and well-behaved, educable boys fit for transfer. Rumors and speculations were already circulating among us about where we were being sent.

We approached the lead bus. There to greet us were Mr. Powers, the man who had molested Bobby, and Mr. Stone, who had for years gotten away with staining the souls of hundreds of prepubescent little boys. Both pedophiles were being transferred with us.

"Okay, boys," said Mr. Powers. "Everybody in the bus. Put your clothes under the seat."

Just as we began to board, Mr. Mitchell came up from the rear of the line, waving his arms. "Hold it, Mr. Powers. Everybody's not here yet!"

"Who's missing?"

"Rawbone and Jackson."

"Rawbone and Jackson? Where in the hell are they, then? And wasn't Rawbone sent back to Birch?"

"He was, but he just had to get the rest of his clothes there. Mrs. Steele didn't have time to pack them when he was first sent to Cedar last night. He'll be here soon, along with Jackson."

"Hell, Mr. Mitchell," barked Mr. Powers. "Why didn't somebody tell me?"

"It was a last-minute thing. Here, take this." He handed Mr. Powers the roster sheet. "Be sure to check off each name as they board. And don't forget, they can't just sit wherever they want. See this?" He pointed to a line on the sheet.

"Okay, fine. I don't see what the big deal is. Let's go, the rest of you. All aboard."

Before it was my turn to board the bus, I noticed a new sign etched over the Administration Building entrance that read:

WE ARE HERE TO
STRENGTHEN THE BODY
BROADEN THE MIND
NURTURE THE SPIRIT

Rawbone and Jackson finally arrived, clinging to their boxes.

As they stepped onto the bus, Mr. Powers ordered, "Jackson, you sit in that seat and slide your box under it." Jackson shuffled to his seat. "You, Rawbone, come with me." He took the lead to the back of the bus. "You sit there."

"Where we goin', Mr. Powers?" Rawbone asked.

"Never mind. You'll find out soon enough. What in the hell took you two so long?"

"Mrs. Steele was cryin'. She didn't want me and Jackson to leave."

"She'll get over it. Plus, she doesn't need scumbags like you two around anymore. As far as I'm concerned, they should've let you rot in Cedar."

"But Mr. Powers, I—"

"Shut up. I don't wanna hear any more outta ya."

Mr. Powers went to the front of the bus and sat in the driver's seat. He started the engine, which rumbled a bit unevenly, then settled down. Mr. Stone took a seat behind him.

"Everybody ready?" asked Mr. Powers, glancing in the rearview mirror.

"Yeah, were ready!"

"Let's go!"

"Come on!"

"Get us outta here!"

Rawbone and Jackson remained quiet, sitting in their seats like virtual outcasts. And no wonder—they no longer had the support of Mrs. Steele, plus the bus was filled with their victims of many years. Meanwhile I sat quietly, looking at both of them, thinking how each had tormented so many residents for so long. And now they were alone with themselves, their power gone, their special liberties defunct.

"Well, boys, that's it!" shouted Mr. Powers, shoving the vehicle into first gear with a grind.

The older-model bus started to creep along, and the other two buses followed. Everybody cheered except me. I sat quietly, watching and listening, saying nothing, but inwardly asking: Is New Lisbon really over? And if so, what additional horrors were ahead of me still?

As we approached the entrance, I looked back at the Administration Building in its majestic splendor. The bus backfired a sooty farewell from its dirty rear end as if mimicking how I felt about the place, eerily reminding me of a similar send-off from St. Walburga a lifetime ago. As we passed old man Biddlemier, who still hadn't retired, the gentle man choked on the foul exhaust, feebly waving to all of us with one last goodbye.

I turned in my seat. Everybody began laughing and lollygagging, their faces awash with a kind of childlike wonder I had never before seen in them. Their expressions mirrored a transformation from damaged spirits to groping hope.

I wanted to believe that, finally, some of us had gotten away—that maybe, just maybe, we had escaped the mighty grip of abuse. But as I glanced at Mr. Stone and Mr. Powers, I realized that, with the transfer of the pedophiles along with us, I had my doubts.

"Hey, you guys," a boy shouted above the voices of the others. "They got a fuckin' swimmin' pool, and a basketball court, and—"

"A swimmin' pool?" someone hollered.

"You're dreamin'!" another boy called out.

"I heard they got movies . . . and good ones too!" the boy behind me submitted.

I turned around and replied to him, "Sure they do. Just keep dreamin'."

"It's true, Carroll," the boy insisted. "They got color movies, not the black-and-white, junky ones."

"Hey, kids," shouted Mr. Powers over the mix of voices, "watch your language, 'cause I have my wife's picture in my wallet!"

Everybody roared with laughter.

Rochester, a boy who had also been brutalized by Jackson and Rawbone, stood up, his previously broken arm limp and crooked due to shoddy medical attention. "I heard they're nice in that place. I heard they don't beat ya up there."

"Shut the fuck up, Rochester, you toothless nut," someone bellowed. "It's all bullshit! Just sit down and shut the fuck up."

Rochester slumped in his seat.

"Oh, yeah," defended another kid. "I heard it's a nice place."

"That's not what I heard," interjected another. "I heard they beat ya up in that place . . . that it's worse than the Colony."

"That's not true," disagreed the first kid. "I heard it's nicer there."

It was clear the boy wanted to believe only in good things; it wasn't hard to understand. I wanted to believe the good things too, but I found it difficult to have faith in anything. I saw these boys as pathetic dreamers, hanging onto a fabricated thread of imaginary hope.

Mr. Powers pulled the bus to the side of the highway, pulled on the emergency brake, and left the engine nervously idling as he got out of his seat and faced us.

The two other buses parked behind us. One of the drivers got out and walked over to Mr. Powers's side window. "What's going on?"

"Nothing, Sam. No problem. I'll be getting along in a minute. Just wanted to have a word with these kids."

He turned to address us. "Okay, boys, now listen up. The bad language has to go. And that means *you*." He pointed to one of the boys still snickering. "The profanity's gotta stop. Is that clear?"

The boy, trying to hide his smile, asked through his fingers, "Is there a picture of a dog in your wallet too, Mr. Powers? Maybe it's barking."

"Yeah, your dog ain't gonna mind, even if your wife does," another shouted.

Everybody laughed.

"Seriously, you guys," pleaded Mr. Powers. "Try to pipe down a little. It's not funny anymore. Now just be quiet a minute."

The boys quieted down.

"Let's make a deal. I don't want to see anybody getting up out of their seats while the bus is moving. And try to cut back on the bad language. Do we have a deal, boys?"

"Yes, sir," most answered.

One boy stood up. "Mr. Powers, where are we goin'?"

"To Bordentown. We'll be there in about half an hour."

Everybody turned to one another as if to ask, Where's that?

"Don't ask me any more questions. I wasn't even supposed to tell you that much. Okay, boys, try to behave—and remember, stay put in your seats." Mr. Powers returned to the front, and we began the next leg of our journey.

"Yahoo!" yelled a few. The air bristled with roaring and clapping approval. A few minutes later, we passed a sign that read:

CHARLES A. CARROLL

BORDENTOWN
15 MILES

The laughter in the bus was starting to affect me in a positive way. Though the trail of misery was long and hard to forget, the miracle of the others' transformation began seeping through the pores of my bad memories. Yes, I worried that whatever was ahead might be worse than anything experienced before, but I wanted to believe that we were being returned to civilization or, better yet, back into the arms of caring people who would restore our humanity.

Mr. Powers shouted at the top of his voice, "Laugh on, young people, laugh on!"

I watched Mr. Powers. Only now was I getting a true glimpse of the apparent allure of his outgoing personality. On the surface, he was a delightful character. Children gravitated to his charm while, in fact, it was nothing more than a magical ploy to seduce. His penchant for giving blowjobs didn't bother me a bit. But I was beginning to learn that, no matter how friendly, warm, or gentle the come-on, what appears to be "tender molestation" is, in reality, sexual abuse.

About twenty minutes later, we came to a steep grade in the road. When we reached the top of the hill, the sun was high in the sky, blazing in the windows of the bus.

"See that sign, boys?" alerted Mr. Powers. "We're here."

We all stretched over one another to see as the bus turned into the institution.

The sign read:

EDWARD R. JOHNSTONE
TRAINING AND
RESEARCH CENTER

There was a front gate, but it was never closed. There were no

PLATE EIGHTEEN
EDWARD R. JOHNSTONE TRAINING AND RESEARCH CENTER SIGN

barriers, no guards, and no fences. As we followed the two-lane asphalt road, I could see the Administration Building a few hundred yards ahead.

"Girls!" someone shouted.

"Girls? Where?" everybody asked, followed by the banging sounds of windows snapping open.

"Right there, look!"

Every face was instantly glued to the windows. They exploded with cheer, some brandishing hard-ons and howling with erotic catcalls. Girls stood in small huddles, some pointing, some laughing, some talking amongst themselves, others waving gallantly at the busloads of boys gawking and mentally fucking every female they laid eyes on.

"Get your tongues in, boys!" ordered Mr. Powers.

Everybody laughed.

"Look over there! More girls!"

Ahead of us, girls were crossing the road, some walking backwards at the side of the bus so as not to miss any of the new faces entering Johnstone. When we passed them, all the kids on the left side of the bus ran to the right side in an effort to not miss a moment.

As we passed the girls' cottage, all three buses blew their horns. Hands blew kisses from windowsills as some of the girls yelled "Be my boyfriend" and "I've got something good for you," holding up their breasts—and one girl mooned us from a window, her upper thighs revealing powder blue garters. When the boys saw her, their eyes popped out of their heads like sprung springs.

The moment was mystical: dead spirits came alive for the first time in years. Many secretly pulled out their dicks and beat them off; others crushed lips against windows and flicked their tongues. The scenario was worse than that of sailors coming into port. Until that day, these boys had been locked into puberty and masturbation and forced to contend with the sins of others. They had existed in an alternate sexual universe, but they snapped back almost as quickly as rubber bands—coming to their sexual senses at the sight of the sweet-looking girls, as though they'd been injected with sexual adrenaline. Most every boy hopped onto a plateau of imagined copulation, mesmerized by the thought of "normal" sexuality.

Even Jackson and Rawbone came alive, no longer lost in their feelings of helplessness. In a way, I could hardly blame them for mourning their lost power; after all, they were also victims—of the state, of people like the Steeles, and of their own families who had abandoned them.

I wanted to feel like all the others, but at the same time wanted no part of it. The Colony had long ago killed something within me, something that made me feel not excited, but threatened. The past had worn away at my sexuality, leaving me entirely confused. Inside, I was cold and unresponsive as we passed the girls, groping for the reasons behind my emotions.

And then the now-simple explanation occurred to me: *I* wanted to be admired and cheered, still the cutest kid in the institution. I wanted to be adored in the same way the boys were looking at those girls, but I had lost my celebrity status and resented it. I realized I didn't know where I fit in, and I suspected there were others like me.

Thoughts of pussy and perfume gave me the feeling I'd been psychologically asphyxiated, then suddenly set free to explore my own inner passions. But my subconscious couldn't let go; it was oddly reaching out for the same people who had tormented me, seeing them for the first time not as predators, but perhaps as sexual foils to appease my discolored yearnings. Inwardly, I still wanted to be treated as if I were not worth a damn.

Externally, however, I had to maintain an image, so I began laughing and projecting a pseudomasculinity—and feeling no guilt. I had to pretend in an effort to thwart anyone from discovering that something was wrong with me. Yes, the side effects were right on target. The lingering damage emerged in me like a needling monster, reminding me that I had not escaped from the ravages of the past.

CHARLES A. CARROLL

How many others had serious issues with gender confusion? I don't know. But one thing I do know for sure is that we had all been pushed to the edge of homosexuality—and yes, there were those who preferred that way of life.

So I went through the motions and acted out what was expected of me—acted as though I were unaffected by the years of trauma and abuse, hiding my true feelings and my fears of psychosexual dysfunction that were caused by that abuse. I had to fit into this whole new world, even if it meant losing myself in it.

We passed a sign in front of a building that read:

CREATIVE PSYCHIATRY

It left me stunned. Was Johnstone the center of New Jersey's psychiatric experimentation? Was this where the state would close the gaps of its previous psychiatric screwups and the courts' misguided handling of overflowing caseloads? Knowing where I came from and what had happened to others and to me—and what they were now about to do to Bobby—I sensed there was no time to dismiss any of the sign's ambiguous implications.

Shaken, I sat up in my seat and looked at the dreaded sign again. Its dubious prospects filled me all over again with requiems of fear that maybe, just maybe, Johnstone represented the ultimate psychiatric "solution" that would seal my good mind's fate into the mindlessness and stupor of a long-term insanity from which there would be no escape. Now all I could do was hope I was wrong.

Part Six

I was no longer subjected to a draconian environment where God dumped His dirty tricks, where bellies grinned from crooked smiles and crazy children cried from slobbering jaws, where acts of violence were applauded and hushed. Now I would be victimized by another world—the outside world—whose very soul was knitted from contrivances of "civilized" ideals.

Charles A. Carroll

CHAPTER TWENTY-FIVE

Thrown Back into the Twentieth Century

BEFORE GOING TO our cottages, we were led into Johnstone's auditorium, where the superintendent was already speaking. I looked around the large room and noticed two black men leaning against a side wall with their hands in their pockets under soiled aprons, their black skin a glaring contrast to the white chef's uniforms.

Next to the two cooks were four electricians, standing shoulder to shoulder, with tester-leads hanging from their back pockets. Along the same wall were several plumbers dressed in soiled bib coveralls, hands blackened from the pipe gunk typical of decaying cast-iron elbow traps and rusted joints. Also lined up against the wall was the administrative staff of Johnstone, in suits and ties, with nametags on their jackets.

Dr. Stevenson was a short, balding, rotund man. He sounded angry, his voice carrying a no-nonsense tone, but his message held an air of fairness. I listened more closely.

". . . and humanitarian values. That's what Johnstone's all about! Our values here at Johnstone are about standards. It all starts with respecting children, not abusing them."

Dr. Stevenson extended both hands straight out over the podium. "Listen!" He directed his comments to us. "I know that, until now, most of you have lost any sense of having been cared about.

But not here. Here, you'll be cared for like you're somebody. There's no such thing as a *nobody* here at Johnstone. *Everybody* counts. Here, we encourage you to play and discover your humanity. We'll be patient with you until you gain some measure of yourself. We know of your suffering and where you came from, but that's all behind you now. The past is over. It's time for a fresh start. Am I making myself clear?"

The applause was thunderous. Feet stomped and hands clapped. I was not yet convinced.

Dr. Stevenson pointed at the employees standing along the wall. "Proper handling will repair the damage done, and if it's the last thing I do, I'll see to it."

Suddenly, a mockingbird introduced itself at one of the open windows.

"See!" said Dr. Stevenson. "Even the birds agree."

A round of laughter and applause followed.

Dr. Stevenson's eyes panned us. "There isn't one of you who's not deserving of my prescription for a better well-being. All of you deserve it. And let me tell you new boys this: if I have my way, you'll get everything you deserve." He cleared his throat. "That's my job. I don't mean just the good boys, but the bad ones too. You'll be treated fairly. I guarantee it."

The room filled with howls of approval.

"Okay, pipe down. I'm not through yet. Yes, I said bad boys too. That doesn't mean, however, that you'll be allowed to get away with anything. What it means is that should you break the rules, you'll be treated with respect and dignity. We don't abuse you here. Why? Because abuse is like a ladder, but with all the rungs removed. You look up and there's nowhere to climb. We don't tolerate that. We, here at Johnstone, repair you. We groom you. We teach lessons. We don't instill fear. Now then, is there anyone among you who doesn't find what I've said a decent way of handling matters?"

Before I knew what I'd done, I was on my feet.

"Yes, young man," pointed Dr. Stevenson. "What's on your mind, son?"

The room got as quiet as a graveyard. Weak-kneed, I leaned forward, grasping the back of the chair in front of me, hanging onto it as if I were about to go down with the Titanic. I looked around. Turned heads were staring at me.

"Go ahead, son," instructed Dr. Stevenson. "Your question, please?"

With a feeble, cracking voice, I said, "You mean . . . I mean, sir . . . you mean you know about New Lisbon and what's been going—"

"Speak up son! We can't hear you!" interrupted Dr. Stevenson.

So devoid of self-confidence, I crapped out and said, instead, "Sir, I . . . I have to go to the bathroom."

"Sure son, there's one at the back of the room."

Now I knew they knew, and nothing could've angered me more, and nothing could've drawn me closer to one day writing this book. As I headed for the bathroom, Dr. Stevenson resumed.

"Anybody else?" he asked.

No one said a word.

Through the door of the bathroom, and over the sounds of my urinating, I could hear Dr. Stevenson's every word throughout the hollow-sounding room.

"Now here's why I brought all of you together today. This morning, one boy, who's now in the infirmary, received an unnecessary beating by one of my newer employees. As some of you already know, Mr. Cartridge is no longer with us. I fired him on the spot. I did this because I will not tolerate any kind of abuse, and this applies to all of you standing along the walls. If I catch any one of you ever laying a hand on any of these boys and girls, I'll fire you too."

In the middle of Dr. Stevenson's monologue, I returned from the bathroom and took my seat.

"We don't hit kids around here. We build their spirits and respect their bodies. If you people don't remember anything else, remember this: there's no legitimate reason to ever hit a kid. Period! And as for you new boys today, welcome to Johnstone."

I wanted to believe it all. I tried inhaling a whiff of that humanitarian air, but found myself coughing up particles of suspicion and doubt. I wasn't ready to trust anyone or anything.

As I soon discovered, Dr. Stevenson lived in a small, unassuming house that stood between one of the male cottages and the gymnasium; he basically lived alongside Johnstone's inhabitants. But this was only the beginning of the kind of civilized world I was about to encounter. Dr. Stevenson not only lived among us, he was friendly as well—not a stuffy, stiff-collared bureaucrat like Dr. Yepsen at New Lisbon. Dr. Stevenson acted like a friend, a man who had not lost touch with our needs, even going so far as to refer to us as "students" rather than "patients"—an approach that was intended to instill in us some degree of self-esteem.

Upon arrival at my assigned cottage, I quickly learned that New Lisbon-style dormitory life was over. I was assigned to a bedroom with one other roommate whose name was Erickson. It turned out that Erickson's biggest complaints were my nightmares, which invariably interrupted his sleep. While some may contend that bad dreams help liberate the sufferer, my nightmares continued to enslave me.

Tommy Erickson was a bright kid who had no business being in a place like Johnstone any more than I did. He was normal too—only in his case, he had made it to the eighth grade of the public school system before being institutionalized. I never did learn why he'd been turned over to the state—maybe because he was quiet, reserved, and, for the most part, stayed much to himself and revealed little about his personal life. We got along fine.

Unlike New Lisbon, the employees and patients all ate in the same dining room and ate the same food. The chefs were *our* cooks too, not just the cooks for the attendants. The dining room floor was spotless, buffed to a high shine. There were tablecloths and folded napkins, upon which were laid knives, spoons, and forks. The supper that first night consisted of delicious roast chicken, a pad of real butter sunk into mashed potatoes, and sides of gravy, giblets, and cranberry sauce. The corn on the cob came with its own cob dishes and holders. On each end of every table were sweating pitchers of ice-cold water and milk, and the table centers offered freshly baked cornbread with honey.

My first meal at Johnstone left me in shock. A little light of hope permeated some blackened piece of my heart. The days of the fly-covered walls and foul-tasting stews had truly come to an end. And later, even more surprising, it was common to see state inspectors dipping thermometers into meat at the steam tables to make sure everything was served at the right temperature.

Johnstone had begun its life a century earlier as the Bordentown Manual Training School, a vocational school for African Americans. We were among the first groups to be admitted since its recent rebirth and renaming.

About the only thing similar to New Lisbon was Johnstone's landscaping: manicured lawns and circular garden beds bordered by jagged bricks and neatly trimmed shrubs. There were eight buildings in all on the large campus overlooking the Delaware River: the Administration Building with large, white pillars; the Stevenson house; three cottages, two for boys and one for girls; a first-class gymnasium, complete with tongue-and-groove flooring, an electronic basketball hoop, and bleachers that moved with the push of a button; a school building still under renovation; and a garage housing a tractor and state vehicles to be serviced.

When the school was completed a year later, concerned teachers banded together, wanting to help those who had been academically held back, as if fully realizing the gross misconduct of the bureaucracies from which we had come. Johnstone's teachers wasted no time in improving our skills in reading, writing, and basic arithmetic. None of this was adequate, but it was a far cry from New Lisbon's feeble attempts to school its residents. In other words, the days of rug and potholder classes were in the past. Gone was the making of women's handbags from Camel, Domino, Fatima, and

Lucky Strike cigarette wrappers—handbags like those proudly displayed behind a glass case in New Lisbon's Administration Building to emphasize to its visitors the proficiency of its educational programs. The days of the "nut souvenirs" were over.

It had been more than four years since my mind had been stimulated. Unlike New Lisbon, I was being encouraged, rather than discouraged. But despite the improvement in my lot, the memory of my brother never waned. I had to see him. I had to know how he was doing and what was left of him after Trenton had finished "fixing" him. So plagued was I by the thought of Bobby's condition that I pleaded to see him over and over again at the Administration Building, only to have my requests denied.

However, the new times were relatively good to me. And, by such handling, I began recapturing some sense of my boyhood—a boyhood not continually harmed by the sins of others. But like any major bureaucratic system on its maiden voyage, there were, now and then, episodes that needed addressing, as there was a dark side to Johnstone. It had flaws—serious flaws. It was riddled with pedophiles—and not just those sent over by New Lisbon.

CHAPTER TWENTY-SIX

The Explorer Scoutmaster

THE FALL OF my second year at Johnstone, the institution took on a whole new look. Several acres of the lawn in front of the Administration Building had been transformed into a campsite for Explorer Scout Week—a festive jubilee that included not only the Explorer Scouts, but also New Jersey Governor Robert B. Meyner, the same man to whom I had handed the tennis racquet at the 12th Annual Invitation Tennis Tournament three years earlier.

The Explorer Scouts' Volunteer Services frequently helped the state and local police or fire departments during victim searches, natural disasters such as fires and floods, and anything else requiring extra manpower. One might say that the Explorer Scouts were the voluntary custodians of the community, wherever and whenever needed.

It was an occasion for awards, where city officials would pin medals, stripes, or badges on those who had done an exceptional job over and above the call of duty—heroic lifesaving rescues and the like. A thousand people were expected to arrive, including hundreds of state officials and a number of private philanthropists.

To assist the Explorers, six of Johnstone's students were chosen to help—and I was one of them. The older boys parked cars, and we all served food and assisted wherever needed.

PLATE NINETEEN
JOHNSTONE ADMINISTRATION BUILDING
EXPLORER SCOUT WEEK TOOK PLACE ON THE FRONT LAWN

I was glad to be part of the event, but also scared to death of it. My "peers" from the outside world left me intimidated and feeling disadvantaged, uneducated. I didn't think I was good enough or normal enough. I felt shy and embarrassed all the time, less than—and never a part of—anything. I had this deeply rooted fear that maybe "they" were right about me, that I *was* retarded, and that what they saw in me was, perhaps, something beyond my own ability to comprehend. But my natural-born instincts and reason secretly doubted them—a suspicion I deliberately hid so I wouldn't stand out, so I wouldn't be subjected to unreasonable punishment or, worse, sent to Trenton for "fixing" because I was too outspoken. I wasn't yet completely trusting that Johnstone wouldn't do to me what New Lisbon had done to so many of its patients.

As a result, I wanted to appear like everyone else; I was always determined to hide that continuous inner battle—a war that never ceased. So I reverted to my old habit of make believe, pretending to be the kid I so longed to be, appearing untroubled and carrying on as though I were better off than I really was. I felt it was my duty to be academically resourceful by "acting" smart, spouting clever philosophical slogans from memory and astute recapitulations of scholarly brilliance from books I'd read. I became an expert at pulling off this charade.

All this bluffing was done in an effort to reverse the intimidation process. When people asked, "What's a smart guy like you doing in a place like this?" I knew I had pulled it off without a hitch.

After three days of serving food, I was asked to help the Explorer Scoutmaster. When I finally caught up with the man late that morning, I couldn't help but be impressed with the regalia attached to his uniform—ribbons, pins, stripes, and a gold-braided shoulder cord that looped under one arm. He wore fatigues, Magnum knee-high SWAT boots, and, on one hip, an intimidating USMC combat knife. Dangling from the other hip was a World War II metal canteen fastened to his fatigue belt. He had all the trappings of "importance."

"Sir," I said, all but snapping to attention. "I was told you needed me."

"Hi, son. Yes, I do. So you're a student here too, huh?"

"Yes, sir."

"You can be my assistant today. How's that sound?"

"Okay, sir. What do we do?"

"Let's inspect the tents to make sure they're all put up the right way. Come with me. We'll do a spot check, okay?"

"You're the boss, huh?"

He stopped, turned, and lifted his aviator glasses. "That's right! These young men need discipline. I weed out the wise guys real fast. You're not a wise guy, are you?"

"No, sir."

"Just kidding." He dropped his sunglasses to the bridge of his nose. "I didn't get your name."

"Carroll, sir."

"How do you spell that?"

"C-a-r-r-o-l-l."

"Heck, I already know about you."

"You do?" I asked with surprise.

"That's right. But don't ask me what I heard," he replied, lifting his glasses and winking. "If I told ya what I know, then you'd know what I know. See what I mean?"

"I guess so, sir."

"I'm really only kidding. Actually, I heard some very nice things about you. I hear you're one of the brighter ones in this place."

"You heard that about me?"

"I'm Mr. Maybrook." He held out his hand.

"Pleased to meet you, sir," I replied, shaking his hand.

"That's a good handshake you have there, son. Where'd ya learn it?"

"From Dr. Alprin. He told me a weak handshake leaves a bad impression."

"Hey, he's got something there. Who's Dr. Alprin?"

"The doctor who tested me. He found out I was normal."

"Wait a minute. Give me that one again."

"He's the doctor that found out I'm normal."

"If that's true, then why are you here?"

"Because I'm too old to be adopted anymore."

"How old are you, boy?"

"I'm gonna be fifteen in November."

"I see. What's your first name?"

"Charles."

"How did you get yourself into a place like this?"

"By mistake."

"By mistake? You mean they thought there was something wrong with you when there wasn't?"

"Yes, sir."

"What about your mother and father? Where are they?"

"I don't know."

"Well, I never heard a story like that. You're not kidding me, are you?"

"No, sir. It's really true. Honest."

"You mean to tell me that you don't know anything about your own people?"

"That's right, sir. Never met them."

"But how did you get into a place like this?"

"My foster parents did it."

"Your foster parents? Why, son?"

I hesitated. "Do you really want to know?"

"You bet I do. Let's take a seat over there on that bench. I'd like to hear about this."

THE SMALL MEDICAL world of Pompton Lakes marveled over Ruby beating the odds and conceiving a child. But now that she had conceived, there was a question as to whether the child might be still-born. Nonetheless, as the pregnancy progressed beyond the early, uncertain days, she became more outgoing. She smiled more, and the mood of the entire household became congenial.

As she dished out her good humor, I gulped down every loving morsel until that void from not being loved enough all but vanished. The home's eggshell floor had disappeared and, for the first time, my emotional footing seemed on solid ground.

Dustin changed too. He started playing with me like a pal, throwing a football to me now and then. He even began sharing his shed projects, without the usual rebuttals, and encouraged my hands-on participation in his chores. In one instance, he allowed me to help him slaughter the chickens, permitting me to pull off the feathers after he had dunked a bird into a pail of scalding water. We became a team. After a month or two of Dustin's positive reinforcements, I began looking forward to him coming home from work, often running up to the car and greeting him. Never before had I felt such a sense of belonging.

But this wonderful home life soon began to fade. The closer Ruby came to full term, the more indifferent she was toward me. And Dustin slowly started his retreat as well. Once again, I found the need to listen from behind doors and sneak up to open windows to try to gain some insight into what was being kept from me. My lack of trust in the family unit, as well as my experiences with the priest and Richard under the bridge, planted a seed deep inside me—a seed that soon sprouted weeds that cluttered the garden of my emotional well-being.

Ruby delivered a healthy, nine-pound baby girl she named Destiny. Several days later, Dustin brought Ruby home. As soon as I saw them, I ran outside.

Standing on my tiptoes, I said excitedly, "Let me see the baby, Mommy! Please let me see it!"

Ruby pulled the child away from my reach. "Don't touch her, Charles."

"Why not?"

"Because your hands are filthy! You wanna give her a disease?"

"But Mommy—"

"Get away. I don't want ya even breathing on her. Go on! I've got things to do."

Hurt over being rejected, I backed off, now climbing ever deeper into myself.

Things returned to "normal" after that, with Dustin and, particularly, Ruby keeping me at a distance. One day, sometime after the baby's arrival, I was fishing in the middle of the stream below the house when a rainbow trout took my line and zigzagged under a rocky crevice. I fought with the fish until I finally worked it loose, and then immediately ran home, barging through the door. The doorknob smacked the wall.

"Mommy, Mommy! Look what I got!" The helpless fish was dangling in front of me from the test line.

Ruby snapped, "Sh-hh! Do ya wanna wake up the baby? And since when do we come in the house without knocking? How many times do I have to . . . oh, forget it. Just get that thing outta here before it stinks up the house."

"But I—"

"Now what?"

"I want Daddy to see it."

"What am I supposed to do about that?"

"Can I keep it in the tub until Daddy comes home?"

"The tub? Forget it. Where're your shoes? It's cold out. Why'd you take your shoes off?"

I looked down at my feet.

"Well, where are they?"

"Under the bridge."

"Under the bridge? You get right down there and get those shoes before somebody steals 'em."

"But my fish'll die by then!"

"Sh-hh! Destiny's asleep."

"Mommy, ple-e-ase?"

"Okay, gimmie that thing. You're so hardheaded. I'll put it in the sink. Now go get your shoes."

"The sink? No, it needs to swim. Can you put it in the bathtub?"

"You asked me that already. I said no. When will you learn to listen?"

"Oh, please, ple-e-ase?"

"Good, Lord, it has to be alive too? Go outside and rinse your feet. I'll be in the bathroom."

"You're the best mommy in the whole wide world!"

"Don't give me that again. Go on, get."

When I returned, Ruby had already removed the hook from the trout's lip and released it into the bathtub, water gushing from the faucet.

"Look, I drew this."

"Not now, I'm busy. And keep your voice down. You're determined to wake Destiny, aren't ya?"

"No, I just—"

"There. That should be enough water."

"Here, look at the—"

"Not now. I gotta get Daddy's lunch ready. He'll be here any minute."

"He's comin' home? Now?"

"Isn't that what I just said?"

"How come?"

I folded the drawing and stuck it into my back pocket. As I was about to get my shoes, I heard a car coming up the driveway and ran to the side living room window, shouting to Ruby, "I think that's Daddy."

"I said go get your shoes, young man."

"Look, Mommy, it's not Daddy."

"What?"

"It's not Daddy. Look! It's a lady."

"A lady? Oh cripes, already? Quick, go out in the backyard. And don't come back inside until I tell ya to."

"But who is it?"

"I said get goin'."

I jetted out the back door and scaled the embankment. I un-leashed Wiggie and headed for the edge of the woods, watching the lady get out of her car.

"Hi, Mrs. Whipple," shouted the woman, waving to Ruby, who was still looking out the window.

"Hi, Mrs. Johnson. You're early."

"I know! I decided to beat the traffic."

"Good. Come on in. My husband's not here yet, but he's on his way."

"That's good."

I watched the large lady adjust a bundle of papers on the passenger seat of the car. When she finally straightened up, she shoved the papers under her arm and walked to the flagstone path. She was wearing a breezy, loose dress, with bold ruffles clear down the front, and a hat with a plume stuck into it. When she rounded the front corner of the house, I took Wiggie back to her doghouse, leashed her, then proceeded to the open window from which Ruby had greeted the mystery lady. As I was about to peek in, I heard a car coming up the driveway; it was Dustin. I scooted to hide behind two drums of lantern oil. As soon as Dustin disappeared around the front of the house, I resumed my position under the window—only this time, I sat with my back to the wall and listened.

"That was nice, Ruby. Where's Chuckie?" asked Dustin.

"I told him to stay outside until I called for him."

"What about Chuckie's things? Are they packed?"

"They're in the closet, honey. Want me to drag them out of there?"

"If you think the time's right," answered Dustin.

"I don't think that's a good idea right now," said the strange lady. "Why don't we wait until after the paperwork's out of the way. Then we'll take care of his clothes. I want to do this quickly once he gets back in here."

"I think she's right, Ruby."

I buried my face in my hands, feeling fate's toe kicking me in the gut. Assuming what was about to come, I unleashed Wiggie again and ran into the woods to the rocky hideaway where Bobby and I often played and made believe. After crawling into the rocks, I pulled the drawing from my pocket and looked at it. The picture flooded me with memories of the past five years—memories of the people I had tried so hard to love and trust. Soon I heard leaves crunching under footsteps. I turned to the opening in the rocks. Dustin's face filled it.

"You've got to come out, Chuckie."

"No, Daddy!"

"Want the rats to eat ya?"

"No."

"Then you better come out, or they will."

"No, Daddy, no! That lady wants to take me away. She's the one who took Bobby away, ain't she?"

"Yes, that's Mrs. Johnson. You were at the window again, huh, son?"

"Yes. Don't be mad."

"I'm not, son. Come on out. It's time to be a big boy."

"But I don't wanna be a big boy. It hurts too much."

"Come on. Mommy wants you inside."

"No, Daddy, no!"

"If you don't come out, Mommy'll make me put a strap to ya. Do ya want that?"

"No."

"Then come on out."

"No!"

"Not even for me?"

I didn't reply.

"Didn't we put the plane together?"

"Yes."

"And the train set?"

"Yes."

"And what about the snowman? I helped you with that, didn't I?"

"No, you only did it with Bobby."

"Oh, that's right. Come on, son."

"Oh . . . oh, okay. I'm comin'."

As soon as I emerged from the rocks, Dustin picked me up and hugged me.

"And you're not gonna give me a lickin' this time?"

"No, no, no, son. I'm sorry about this, boy . . . I'm really sorry."

"Do I really have to go, Daddy?"

"I'm afraid so, son. I'm so sorry."

"But why?" I asked, burying my face into his leathery, sunburned neck. "I don't wanna go, Daddy."

"I know, Chuckie, I know. This isn't easy for me, either."

"You mean you don't want me to go?"

"Let's put it this way. I was afraid this was gonna happen one day."

"What do you mean?"

"Chuckie, I stopped doing things with you because I knew this day would come."

"Then why are you letting Mommy do this to me?"

"I'm sorry, Chuckie."

Crying, I threw my face back into his neck, exclaiming, "Daddy! I didn't do nothin' wrong!"

"I know, son. Life just isn't fair all the time."

"I hate Mommy!"

Comforting me, he said, "Don't hate, son. Hate'll tear your heart apart. Come on and try to pull yourself together."

"But it hurts, Daddy, it hurts!"

"I know, son. Come on. We gotta go." He lowered me to the ground and we walked toward the house, Wiggie following behind.

When we entered the kitchen, Ruby and Mrs. Johnson were

sipping hot coffee, steam curling about their noses. Mrs. Johnson was puffing on an unlit cigarette in a rhinestone cigarette holder.

"Where'd you find him?"

"In the boulders. Honey, he was at one of the windows again."

"He never learns, does he?" Ruby reached under the table. "Here, Charles, put these on."

"But those are his Sunday shoes, honey. Where's his regular ones?"

"Under the bridge."

"What are they doing there?"

"Oh, that reminds me, he went fishing and caught a trout. It's in the bathtub."

"What's it doing in there?"

"He wanted you to see it."

"Maybe I better go and get his shoes first."

"No need. Mrs. Johnson just told me that where he's going he won't need 'em . . . they'll provide him with new ones. So just leave 'em there. They're pretty beat-up anyway."

"Okay, whatever you say. I'll go look at his fish."

When Dustin returned, he said, "That's a nice rainbow you caught today."

"I don't care about that fish no more."

"That's enough, Charles," ordered Ruby.

"Honey, are you sure you don't want me to get his shoes?"

"She's right, Mr. Whipple," Mrs. Johnson interceded. "He won't need them anymore. Why don't you have a seat with us for a minute, because I need to get this show on the road. We have several hours of driving ahead of us." She removed papers from her briefcase, spread them over the kitchen table, and handed a pen to Ruby. "I need these signed."

"Where?" Ruby asked.

Mrs. Johnson pointed out the appropriate spots. "Where I marked an 'X' on each one."

"Oh, there, okay." Ruby signed each one without hesitation,

then handed the pen back.

Mrs. Johnson extended the pen to Dustin. "You need to sign them too, all four, under your wife's signature."

"Sure, no problem," said Dustin, showing no indecision.

"Isn't that your child I hear, Mrs. Whipple?" asked Mrs. Johnson.

"Yes, that's my sweetie. Excuse me a minute. She needs her bottle. I'll be right back."

Dustin turned to Mrs. Johnson. "How's his brother doing?"

"I'm sorry, Mr. Whipple. I can't divulge that information. But you needn't worry. He's fine. He's adjusted well."

"Where is he?"

"I'm not at liberty to tell you that, either. I'm sorry."

"Will I be with my brother, Mrs. Johnson?"

"Oh, yes, indeed."

"Oh, goody."

"Oh, you like that idea, do you?"

"I miss him."

"Well, you'll be seeing him before long. Mr. Whipple, I think it's time to get his things."

"Where do you want them?"

"Would you mind putting them in the trunk of my car?"

"Not at all. Do you have the key?"

"Oh, sure." She reached into her purse. "This is the one for the trunk." Dustin took it and headed out to the car.

After quieting the baby, Ruby returned.

Mrs. Johnson looked at her. "I guess you know that your allotment for Charles will end today, right?"

"Oh, yes. You mentioned that to me on the phone, remember?"

The lady nodded.

"Where's my husband?"

"He just took Charles's things from the closet and is putting them in the trunk. I was wondering, did you ever read the original court order on the boys?"

"Court order?"

"Yes, the one Miss Bea left with you when our agency placed the boys."

"Oh, that court order. Actually I did, but not completely. Why?"

"Well, when I took Robert, that would've been the time to take Charles too."

"How's that?"

"Had you read the court order, we wouldn't be talking about it right now. Read it sometime. It said that the boys were not to be separated."

"It said that?"

"Yes, it did. Don't blame yourself. It was our oversight. Come on, Charles." Mrs. Johnson took me by the hand. "We've got a long ride ahead of us. Are you coming to see Charles off, Mrs. Whipple?"

Just as Ruby was about to answer, Dustin returned.

"Here's your keys, Mrs. Johnson. I put his things in the trunk. Will there be anything else?"

"No, I guess that's it. Are you two going to see Charles off?"

Ruby answered, "It's best we don't."

"And what about you?" Mrs. Johnson eyed Dustin. "Want to see the boy off?"

"Like my wife said, I think it's better we stay behind. It'll be less harmful to the boy. We've gotta tend to Destiny."

"I see," said Mrs. Johnson, leading me to the door with a look of disapproval. Before stepping outside, she turned to both of them. "Don't forget, Mr. and Mrs. Whipple," her voice was tinged with sarcasm, "if you ever decide to use our agency again, come see us. We're always looking for good state parents who wish their foster children off. Let's go, Charles."

Mrs. Johnson led me along the flagstone pathway. We stepped over the concrete divider and headed for the state car. I stopped and looked back at the house. No one was there. I turned and looked up at Wiggie on the hill by her doghouse. She was staring down at me, yelping, barking, and no doubt sensing she would never see me again. She whined and whimpered her goodbyes as I tearfully shared my sorrow with her.

"Stop that. Get in the car. You're making the dog bark."

Wiping my tears, I got into the car. Mrs. Johnson backed out of the driveway onto Sunfair Road. Before stepping on the gas, she looked over at me.

"What's that paper you got in your hand?" she asked, snatching it from me.

"That's mine." I snatched it back.

"How dare you, you little brat. I should give you the back of my—"

"But it's mine! I drew it at school. Look." I unfolded it for her to see.

"Who are they?"

"It's me, and my mommy and daddy."

"Get over it." She pushed the drawing aside.

As Mrs. Johnson sped off, I stuck the drawing out the window. The wind took it away as I released my fingers. The car screeched to a halt.

"What did you just do?"

"Nothin'."

"I saw what you did."

"I don't want it no more, 'cause they ain't my mommy and daddy no more."

"Don't get impudent with me! I'll give you the back of my hand. And you better hope there's no policeman around, because we could get into trouble for that. Don't you ever do that again."

Three hours later, Mrs. Johnson rounded Four Mile Circle, headed east on Route 72, and pulled into the driveway of New Lisbon.

"So, because they had their own child, they dumped you?" questioned Mr. Maybrook.

"That's right."

"Jesus Christ. And you were with them how many years? Five?"

"Yes, sir."

"Well I'll be damned. Let's put all that behind you for now. Let me see you hold yourself at attention."

"Like this, sir?"

"Not bad. I think you're a natural-born Explorer Scout. You're gonna pan out just fine. Come on, let's check some of these tents."

As Mr. Maybrook went to each tent, he tested loops and straps, inspecting fraying eyeholes and snaps to make sure everything was tight and properly secured. The Explorers who passed by clicked their heels and saluted. He continued strutting down the aisles of the bivouac, tugging the support cables of one tent and pulling the cord of another.

"Hey, son," he said, suddenly standing on tiptoes with binoculars raised to his eyes. "That's my boy there." His was voice filled with parental pride. "Can you see him?"

"I don't see nobody, sir."

"Here, take these." He offered me the binoculars. "He's the one coming this way, the one in his scout uniform."

I peered through the binoculars. "I don't . . . is he the . . . oh yeah, I see who you mean. He's the one walking by himself, right?"

"That's him. That's my Billy," he said proudly. "Come on, we'll meet him halfway. My son's a little younger than you, but only by a couple years. He could use a friend like you."

"How old is he, sir?"

"He'll be twelve soon. Maybe you can teach him how lucky he is to have folks. I think you'd be good for that."

We finally met up with his son.

"Hi, Dad."

"Hi, son. This is Charles. He's a student here. Charles, this is my son Billy. Billy, meet Charles."

"Hi, Charles."

"Hi, Billy." We shook hands.

"You live here?" asked the boy.

"Yes, for about a year and a half."

"That's a long time."

"Why don't you two get acquainted. I gotta go. Catch up to you later."

Billy turned to me. "Are your parents here today?"

"I don't have any."

"You don't? Gosh, that's sad. What's it like not having a mother and father?"

I shrugged my shoulders. "I really don't know."

"Isn't this a place for, you know, people funny in the head?"

"Yeah, but I'm not the only one here that's normal."

"I didn't know that. I thought everybody here was screwy in the—"

"Hey, boys!" yelled Billy's father from one of the other tent rows. "Come over here."

"I like you already, kid. Come on. Let's see what my dad wants."

I was taken by the boy's cordial remark. We hung around together every minute we could, and when it came time for me to return to my cottage, a childlike sadness came over both of us. I was deeply touched that a "normal" kid could like me to that extent and found that his camaraderie helped validate my own sense of worth.

As the days rolled by, each time I walked out of the cottage, Billy was waiting for me. We became inseparable. For the first time since Mr. Wheeler, I found I could trust someone and realized that I still had it in me to give of myself. It was a wonderful revelation, and I relished it.

On the final day of the fundraising festivities, Billy turned to me and said, "Maybe I can get Mom and Dad to let you come over to the house some weekend."

"I don't think this place will let me."

"My dad can do it. And he likes you. I'll ask him about it. He knows everybody important here."

CHAPTER TWENTY-SEVEN
Mt. Holly Jail

IT WAS SEVERAL months after Explorer Scout Week. I had been assigned to the observatory tower, which, at that time, was the most prestigious job a kid could land at Johnstone. After learning all the different types of American airplanes, I was sent to the tower to watch for enemy aircraft that might have slipped through our radar nets. Should I spot an unidentified aircraft, I was to report it via a single-frequency radio that tied directly to nearby McGuire Air Force Base and mark the sighting in a logbook.

While on duty one day, Rudolph Stranard, a tall, lanky sixteen-year-old and one of my closest friends, came running up the steps.

"Hey, Carroll, the new superintendent that replaced Dr. Stevenson wants to see you."

"Dr. Parnicky wants to see me. What for?"

"Gimmie those binoculars. I'm takin' your place. Did ya hear about Stanford Remington? He drowned in the Delaware River last night."[1]

"Him? There's no way. He's the best athlete here. You're kiddin', right?"

"Fuck, no. They just announced it in our cottage. Go on, you better get goin'. Hey, Carroll, I think . . . I think you're gettin' out."

"Me? Yeah, sure."

"No, no. I think it's true, Carroll. I swear it."

"I'll believe it when I see it."

I ran all the way to the Administration Building and up the steps to the superintendent's office.

"Hello, Carroll," greeted Dr. Parnicky. "You know Mr. Maybrook, right?"

"Sure, he's that Explorer Scoutmaster. He's a nice man. He comes to visit me sometimes with his son."

"Well, he thinks quite favorably of you and wants you to join his family."

"You mean for good?"

"Let me put it this way. They're considering adopting you."

"Me?"

"That's right. How do you feel about that prospect?"

"I can't believe it, sir."

"Well, it's true."

"You mean I'm really getting out?"

"Perhaps eventually. We'll start off with a few weekend visits. Mrs. Maybrook and her four children will be here to pick you up tomorrow afternoon. The adoption decision will come later, after they've gotten to know you better. Let's try it out for a few weekends, and then we'll see how it goes. Mr. Maybrook's civic background is quite impressive. No one, it seems, has a negative thing to say about the man. In fact, I even spoke personally with several members of the Mt. Holly police and fire departments. Everybody speaks well of him. In my opinion, and my colleagues', this'll be a fine placement for you. And Carroll—"

"But, sir—"

"Let me finish. They're a fine family, and Mr. Maybrook will be a good male role model for you. It's just what you need. Now then, what were you going to say, Carroll?"

"Will I be able to go to school and all?"

"I don't see why not. I did contact your teacher, Mrs. Shepherd[2], about that prospect, and she tells me you're seriously behind for regular school. Although public schools now hold special classes for boys like you—children who are behind—and also for those who have difficulty learning at a normal pace."

"But, Dr. Parnicky, I learn fast."

"It's nothing to be ashamed of, son."

"But I don't have any trouble learning. I love to learn."

"Mrs. Shepherd told me that you're at about a third-grade level, but that your reading skills far exceed that. She's quite impressed with you."

"I know. I learned how to read some when I was at school in Pompton Lakes. I didn't know a lot of big words then, but now I've learned a lot of them and I can read real good. I'm not perfect, but I'm good enough to know what I'm reading."

"And you did most of that yourself?"

"Yes, sir."

"Interesting. I think you'll do fine on the outside. You've grown into a fine-looking boy. I think you're ready for this family. Any other questions?"

"Yes, Dr. Parnicky. Could you help me see my brother?"

"Where is he?"

"At the State Hospital at Trenton. He was sent there from New Lisbon."

"I'll look into it. Anything else?"

"Yes, sir." I hesitated. "Is there a chance I could be a little retarded?"

"Not according to Dr. Alprin's report. He says your only problem is that you've been held back. I tend to agree with him."

"He was a nice man. I wish he'd come and see me."

"Who knows, he might. He thought a lot of you."

"I know."

"Let's get back to the Maybrooks. How do you feel about all this?"

"I'm a little scared."

"That's understandable. You've been here what . . . almost two years, isn't it?"

"Yes, sir. And four years or so at New Lisbon."

"And you're how old now?"

"I turned fifteen in November."

"I see. In any case, Carroll, for as long as you've been in these places, I guess I'd be a little scared too. Enjoy the good news—plus, you have the right people interested in your welfare now. That's important, because when outsiders are interested in you, that tells us we're on the right track. You've been exemplary and, from what I hear, you've made it this far in pretty good shape. I've little doubt that you can and will make it out of here before long. You've got what it takes, son."

"Honest, sir?"

"There's something special about you. I think you're a real survivor. You'll adjust well. I'll tell you what. Go back to the observatory and finish your shift. Stranard's waiting for you to relieve him. Keep that chin up, okay?"

"Thank you, sir."

Dr. Parnicky rose to his feet and extended his hand. "Now go and be a good boy. Good luck, Carroll."

I left Dr. Parnicky's office excited, though still feeling as if I didn't deserve any of it. The next day I was ready, having packed enough things to take me through the weekend. And while I still carried the damage from the past, now, for the first time, I was looking ahead to the future. But I also knew that the prospects for being adopted hinged on gaining approval, that I had to be what they wanted me to be; if I were not, I could be risking everything. The idea of being free was more than I could absorb.

Everyone arrived except Mr. Maybrook. As soon as I stepped into their car, I went on stage, my duffle bag of survival tools oiled, honed, and ready to rise to the occasion.

Billy's father was a truck driver who often made cross-country trips for companies in the canned-food trades. He was on a delivery run that weekend. One look at Billy's face and I knew he was happy to see me. Skippy, his youngest brother, came for the ride. He was seven years old and not as talkative as Billy, but nevertheless curious and friendly. And there was Jeff, Billy's older brother. He was sixteen and said little. Isabella, their sister, was five years old. As for Billy's mother, she was a short, plain lady who wore no makeup and displayed few feminine frills. Her greeting was warm and friendly, but still held a bit of distance, as if she were locked into a world of her own. It was like she was there, but not there.

When we reached their house, to my amazement, Mr. Powers was waiting in the driveway.

"Hi, Carroll," he greeted. "I thought I'd surprise you with a visit."

"Who are you?" asked Mrs. Maybrook.

"Forgive me, ma'am," he said warmly. "My name is Tom Powers. I'm an attendant at Johnstone and I've been working with this boy for years. He's a fine young man. I thought I'd drop by to see how he's taking everything. You see, oftentimes when children go on the *outside*, it can be upsetting to them."

"What a nice thing to do, Mr. Powers. I must tell you, my children are having a ball with Charles. We all seem to be getting along beautifully. Please come in."

When we approached the house, I was taken aback by the Maybrooks' apparent level of poverty. It was an old frame structure with a near "shanty" look. The outside hadn't been painted in years, and the old coat of paint was peeling. The windows were crooked and did not open easily. The front screen door swung open on loose hinges, the screening torn and frayed. When Mrs. Maybrook opened the storm door, it scraped the linoleum flooring. And though I was surprised by the condition the house was in, none of it really mattered. I wanted only one thing out of this: to be loved, finally, by somebody. After a little while, Mr. Powers left—wishing me, and the family, good luck—and leaving Mrs. Maybrook highly impressed with his "show" of goodwill and duty-bound commitment.

Over the course of the four weekends I spent with them, I learned that the icebox was off bounds, much as it had been at St. Walburga—only there was no padlocked chain around it, but rather, a psychological chain. Nothing could be taken from the icebox without permission from Mrs. Maybrook—and for good reason, because most of the time, all that was in it were the needed ingredients for the next meal. They lived from hand to mouth and from day to day. At one point, I remember wondering: why was I added to their burden? I felt alone with my impressions, the only one who seemed to see such things.

During visits, Billy's mother was always detached, as if she weren't a part of the "adoption integration process"; nor did she demonstrate any maternal connection with her children. She acted more as a custodian of the household, staying to herself and speaking little. Yet she was never unkind to any of us. Sometimes I would look at her and wonder if she was unhappy, not necessarily with me, but somehow troubled.

But irrespective of all that, those weekends were like a magical elixir to me. It was not the adults of the family to whom I gravitated, but the children, especially Billy. They would shower me with affection and laughter and a kind of fun that gave me the feeling I was wanted and loved—in effect, welcoming me as if I were a member of their own family. Before long, I looked forward to joining them each weekend.

After four trial weekends, I was told I would leave Johnstone permanently to be with the Maybrooks. The institution wasted no time setting up financial aid to assist the family in supporting me, as the state had done with the Whipples when I was with them. This support included medical vouchers and government-provided clothing. The clothing was to be delivered every three months for a year, but this support could be extended for another year if the Maybrooks pled hardship; hence, Johnstone made the process as economically painless as possible.

So on the Friday of the fifth weekend, I was officially released to the Maybrooks with the idea that, sometime in the near future, they would sign the necessary documents to finalize the adoption. The past was over. I was now headed into the future to eventually make my way.

While with the family that first weekend of full release, there was a knock at the front door. I ran and opened it. It was Mr. Powers, who offered to take me for a ride to talk and see how I was getting along. Mrs. Maybrook happily obliged the man, wholly impressed and completely trusting of his intentions. After a few short minutes of small talk, I left with Mr. Powers, who drove me into town, treated to me to a banana split, and then wasted no time taking me to a secluded area on the outskirts of Mt. Holly where, hidden from view in a heavily wooded glen, he leaned over from the driver's seat and blew me.[3] He then returned me to the family, bade us goodbye, and quickly left, having successfully sold himself to Mrs. Maybrook as an ambassador of altruism and skillfully mesmerized her with his "do-gooder" ploy—while, in fact, he was a salivating, coy fox who had just captured and seduced his prey.

About a month later, when Mr. Maybrook came home from a week on the road, he decided to take us all to the Poconos for the weekend. He had a friend who owned a cabin up there and allowed us to use it.

The trip was a virtual gala to me. There were the usual scoldings now and then as we horsed around in the station wagon all the way up there, but the trip helped break up everyone's stay-at-home boredom. I made sure not to reveal any of the emotional burden collected over the years. I needed to portray myself as a perfect, happy boy to ensure they would never change their minds. I'd learned from Ruby and Dustin that being myself only held me back. This time, I wouldn't let that happen.

When we reached the mountain cabin, I was enchanted by the stream that ran by the cabin and the scenic calm of the wooded surroundings. I couldn't have felt more at home with the majesty of the picturesque setting. The tranquility immediately took me back to my days with the Whipples, where I'd spent many hours enjoying the gentle fondness of nature's hand with Wiggie, our dog, and, particularly, with my brother.

I did some swimming and hiking with the other children, after which we had a barbecue on the front lawn and ate to our heart's content. After the meal, we played games and laughed a lot, finally capping the day with a little wrestling—only to end in a match between Mr. Maybrook and me. His reserved wife watched from the cabin porch, sitting in a rocking chair, with her youngest daughter in her arms. Billy and Skip were off to one side watching our every move, happily egging us on.

It was the first time in my life when I didn't feel like a spectator of my own play, but a participant, snatching morsels of a newfound freedom. I got outside of myself and became just a plain kid, dumping my old seriousness like unwanted baggage, its usefulness finally spent.

During the wrestling match between Mr. Maybrook and me, the others started to join in. One of the boys grabbed his father's leg while another held a grip on Mr. Maybrook's arm, finally taking him to the ground. I got the man into a headlock. It was a joyous moment, and we all shared in the laughter. Then, all at once, we let go, running in all directions, taunting him, sometimes only inches away from his grasp. While reaching out for me, he missed and landed flat on his face. We all laughed at how silly he looked.

I stood over him chuckling. "Hey, Mr. Maybrook, I got ya that time, didn't I?"

"Why you little piss-ant," he responded with sudden anger. "I'll bust your back, you little snot-nosed kid!"

I turned red, astonished by the man's reaction. A smile was frozen on my face. "But I was only playing, Mr. Maybrook."

I looked over at Billy. His finger was to his lips, motioning me to shut up. I looked at Skip. He had lost his smile. I looked over at the porch where, moments before, his wife had stood, laughing and kidding along with the rest of us. She'd gone inside the cabin. It became eerily quiet, so quiet that it seemed even the birds were no longer chirping and the trees no longer rustling as the breeze had hushed to a ghostly calm.

As Mr. Maybrook clumsily rose to his feet, Billy beckoned, "Come on, follow me!"

I turned and ran after Billy into the woods. He consoled me and explained that his father had a bad temper and a short fuse. About half an hour later, we returned to the cabin, acting as if nothing had happened. But my belly couldn't forget the incident. I was too sensitive to let something like that go without giving it meaning. I knew I could never let my guard down around Mr. Maybrook, never trust his temperament again. Once inside, nothing was said. I assumed the whole thing had been forgiven and forgotten and there'd be no more to it.

At the end of the weekend, we headed back home. In the kitchen that evening, we all ate grilled cheese sandwiches with Kool-Aid.

Just as I took the final bite of my sandwich, Mr. Maybrook ordered, "Okay, boys, that's it. I want you all in bed."

One by one, each kid went upstairs, except me.

"Mr. Maybrook," I asked. "Could I have another sandwich? I'm still hungry."

"When I tell you go up to your room, that's what I mean," he retorted, abruptly leaning back and smashing his foot into my chest. I went sprawling to the floor, a chair falling on top of me.

Mr. Maybrook reached down, grabbed me by the wrist, and began dragging me out of the kitchen and up the steps.

I screamed, "I only wanted a sandwich! I'm sorry! I'm sorry!"

He dragged me into the bedroom, threw me on my bed, and began throwing fists at me. Billy and his brother helplessly watched, crying and begging their father to stop. But Mr. Maybrook continued to punch me, pummeling my face, arms, legs, and stomach.

"Stop it, Dad, stop it!" Billy pleaded. "Leave him alone!"

"Yeah, Dad!" insisted Skippy. "Pick on somebody your own size!"

"Hey, Paul!" shouted the next-door neighbor from the sidewalk below. "If you don't stop hitting those kids, I'm calling the cops!

I've warned you before!"

Mr. Maybrook stopped. I slid out from under him, ran down the steps, and crashed through the side screen door into the black night. I kept running, bumping into shrubs and falling into bushes. After several blocks, I sat on a curb with my face buried in my arms, crying and shouting, "Why me, God? I didn't do nothin'! Why?" I just sat there for a while, in a near state of shock, unable to move.

The police found me and took me to the local Mt. Holly jail. The next morning, I awoke in my cell, realizing my future with the Maybrooks was over.

I laid on my steel bunk, feeling once again lost, abandoned, thrown away. Just like that awful, fateful day nearly seven years earlier when I left the Whipples, I was reminded that nobody wanted me—and, again, not a soul waved me goodbye.

I was suddenly pulled from my thoughts by the clicking sounds of jailor's keys dragging down the long row of iron bars. He stopped at my cell.

"Carroll, roll it up. The people from Johnstone are here. Let's go."

ENDNOTES FOR CHAPTER TWENTY-SEVEN

1. See Appendix A.2.9/Employee and Institutional Neglect in Resident's Drowning/1993. A resident of Fern Cottage drowned during an outing at a nearby park, resulting in a review of New Lisbon's inadequate policies and past practices regarding supervision.

2. Please note that Mrs. Shepherd, my teacher at Johnstone, was no relation to Clarence Shepherd, the fourteen-year-old New Lisbon resident who was found dead after he was missing for three months. See Chapter Eighteen Endnotes.

3. See Appendix F.1/Websites about Male Sexual Abuse. It's a myth that "if a boy experiences sexual arousal or orgasm from abuse, this means he was a willing participant or enjoyed it. In reality, males can respond physically to stimulation (get an erection) even in traumatic or painful sexual situations." *MaleSurvivor*, "Myths About Male Sexual Victimization," http://www.malesurvivor.org/myths.htm (accessed June 21, 2005).

CHAPTER TWENTY-EIGHT
Radio City
Music Hall

MRS. SHEPHERD, ONE of my schoolteachers at Johnstone, was a kind lady who took a special interest in me when she discovered I was bright and anxious to excel. She was tall, young, attractive, and pregnant with her first child.

One afternoon a few months later, she came to my cottage with dress clothes for me to wear. After I changed into the new outfit, she took me to the Administration Building and signed me out.

Once we were in the car, she asked, "Have you ever been to New York City?"

I told her no.

"Then you're in for a treat, because that's where we're going."

We made it to the city after dark. The bright glitter and twinkling neon signs reminded me of the camera flashbulbs when I was at Perth Amboy with the governor, and I sensed that I was again being paraded out as an unwilling ambassador for the state's misguided system. I was Johnstone's shining example of borderline retardation, a prop, the quintessential handsome freak with underlying mental maladies.

While Johnstone may have been more humane than New Lisbon, I nevertheless resented representing a "nut place." I was a mistake, the state's mistake, and I paid heavily for it.

When we arrived at Rockefeller Center, I stared up at the marquis for Radio City Music Hall, remembering all the times I'd read about the famous theater in Mr. Wheeler's newspapers. But all I saw was the uncrossable chasm that existed between my world and the real world. Fed up, I turned away from the glamorous lights with out-and-out disgust.

We entered the office building and took the elevator up to NBC Studios, where we were warmly welcomed by a middle-aged lady who resembled an old-fashioned librarian straight out of a turn-of-the-century periodical. She went into another room to let someone know we had arrived, and then returned and went back to her typing. Even though it was evening, the place was bustling as though it were the middle of the workday. After about fifteen minutes, a large, burly man entered the waiting room with the confidence and attitude of a "boss."

Removing from his mouth an unlit cigar and flashing a pinky ring full of diamonds, the man looked over at us and, in a deep baritone voice, said, "You must be Mrs. Shepherd."

"I am," she replied, rising to her feet.

"I appreciated our lovely chat over the phone last week. Why don't you both come into my office. Jan," he addressed the librarian-looking woman, "please hold all calls."

"Okay, Bill, but what about Mr. Thompson? He's still on hold."

"Tell him . . . just tell him I'll call him back."

"Yes, sir."

We entered the office.

"Is this the boy you were telling me about?"

"Yes, it is. This is Charles."

"Hello, Charles." He extended his hand.

"Pleased to meet you, sir," I said.

The man closed the door behind us. "Please have a seat."

He pointed to several high-backed cane chairs in front of his wide, oval desk. The wall behind him was covered with fancy golden plaques and awards. Plopping his big frame into a cushioned executive chair, he stuck the cigar back between his lips and lit it, his cheeks folding around it like a sandwich. When he removed the soggy cigar from his mouth, saliva clung to it like a long, stretched-out rubber band, breaking just as he reached the ashtray.

"Now then, Mrs. Shepherd," he said, licking saliva from his pudgy lips. "We're all set to broadcast your fundraising appeal later tonight. Perhaps we can go over our last talk, just to make sure I understand what Johnstone needs. That way I can tighten up the message before we go on the air."

"Sure thing, Mr. Ballini. We at Johnstone feel we have a duty to each and every one of our boys and girls. Our aim is to rebuild their lives, to instill dignity. You might recall my telling you that all of them came from other institutions, many from conditions not con-ducive to healthy emotional development. And while government funding is improving, it has a long way to go before being adequate to meet our ideals for these children. We have a financial short-age."

"Yes, yes. I recall your mentioning that to me last week." He stuffed the cigar back into his mouth.

"Now we're seeking private funding."

"I understand," Mr. Ballini replied, dropping ash all over him-self and the desk. "Excuse me." He brushed himself off and then leaned forward, pressing the side of his face on the surface of the desk, and blew the rest of the ash onto the deep carpeting. "As you might well know, time is money in our business. Advertising expo-sure is expensive."

"We're aware of that, and I've brought you a check for the first broadcast," said Mrs. Shepherd.

"How much total time do you want to buy?"

"Whatever it would take to establish the funds we need."

"I'd suggest an hour over a period of one month. We have a large audience tuning into our station."

"Yes, I believe you mentioned that to me when we spoke. You did a wonderful job raising money for The Training School at

Vineland. Now our school would like to give it a try."

He shoved the knuckle of a bent finger deep into his left eye, as if to remove the irritation from the cigar smoke that curled up into it. "Well, if it'll help kids like this handsome young man, we'll do our best."

"He is good looking, isn't he?" Mrs. Shepherd smiled at me. "Let me put it to you this way. The boys and girls at Johnstone are a good bunch of kids, and many of them show few traits of mental deficiencies."

"I hear they're beginning to use a lot of new drugs in these places."

"Yes, that's true in some institutions. Thorazine and reserpine have been used pretty widely in the mental health system for about four or five years now.[1] They're both antipsychotic agents—tranquilizing drugs. I think that once they get a handle on it, they'll start releasing more patients and we'll begin to see a great exodus from these places."

"Is that a fact? And how soon do you think that will be?"

"It's hard to say. These drugs might be helpful, but I don't think they should just release people into the community without adequate aftercare. That's a bad idea. The thing is, Mr. Ballini, you can't take totally dependent people and expect them to suddenly function as if they've been independent all their lives."

"That makes sense," remarked the man, with raised brows and approval filling his face. "Do you use these drugs at Johnstone too?"

"No, we're not too keen on the pharmacological revolution taking place in so many of the other state institutions. Thorazine may minimize aggressive behavior, but we're inclined to forego the drugs. We prefer to work with the students to develop their personalities rather than subdue them."

"What about getting them back into the community?"

"Johnstone believes in a gradual reentry process," continued Mrs. Shepherd. "We slowly incorporate into their lives a sense of responsibility so that, down the line, there isn't a problem with cultural shock."

Mr. Ballini interjected, "Yes, I agree. It sounds like you've thought of everything."

"Well, we think we're on the right track. For example, our outings program helps in this process."

"Yes, please go on, Mrs. Shepherd."

"Many institutions don't take their kids anywhere. But we at Johnstone like to encourage them to experience the outside world. It's good exposure. We make a point to take our students to places like the Bronx Zoo, the state fair, and the seashore. And when we do, you should see their faces. No drug can ever put expressions like that on faces."

"So what you're saying—"

"What I'm saying is that we want to seek out those missing pieces in their lives . . . you know, pick up the pieces and put them back together again, if you will."

"I see."

"And if we begin now, those pieces won't fall apart later when society demands these children take responsibility for themselves. Of course, I'm bucking the trend, but that's how I see it, and it seems that the officials at Johnstone agree with that contention. I've always been a firm believer in a well-balanced childhood."

"I think you're right," Mr. Ballini said, nodding. "Well, I think I've got the information I need. I'll have a script for you to review in an hour, and then I'll go over funding formats. We'll broadcast tonight at midnight. How's all that sound?"

"Excellent."

"Meanwhile, there's lots to eat at our buffet counter. We have wonderful caterers here in New York City. After that, just have a seat in our waiting room outside my door, and as soon as I can put all this together, we'll get started."

"You're so kind, Mr. Ballini. Thank you."

At midnight, we attended a ten-minute radio broadcast. The station had a listening range of five neighboring states, reaching thousands of people. We left the city a short time later, finally making it back to Johnstone in the middle of the night. When I got to my room, I slammed the door behind me in disgust. I had been used once again.

ENDNOTES FOR CHAPTER TWENTY-EIGHT

1. Reserpine, often sold as Serpasil, first received U.S. FDA clearance in 1953. *P-I-E-N-O*, "The P-I-E-N-O Parkinson's List Drug Database: reserpine," http://www.parkinsons-information-exchange-network-online.com/drugdb/117.html (accessed June 11, 2005).

   Thorazine, the trade name for chlorpromazine, was first approved in the U.S. for psychiatric treatment in 1954. *Wikipedia*, "Chlorpromazine," http://en.wikipedia.org/wiki/Chlorpromazine (accessed May 28, 2005).

CHAPTER TWENTY-NINE

The Conduct
Machines

ABOUT A YEAR later, shortly before my seventeenth birthday, Dr. Parnicky consented to allow me to see my brother. Patients visiting patients in other institutions had never been permitted.

Perhaps I should have felt privileged, but I did not. Actually, I dreaded learning what they might have done to Bobby, fearing little would be left of his mind after their infamous electroshock treatments. I'd known long before then that such devices were being employed by less-than-scrupulous psychiatric "professionals" who were doing more harm than good to their patients; I'd seen the results in people returning to New Lisbon from Trenton. These electrical devices were conduct machines, notorious for their use in "quieting" the patient, destroying bothersome and overt behavior. The institutions soft-pedaled the idea to the public that the machines were anything but negative, that they restored balance to the mind and instilled some semblance of normalcy in the individual. Instead, these devices would slam a mind shut and then call it a cure.

Ronald Cook, an aging sociologist who was my caseworker at Johnstone, drove me to Trenton. Mr. Cook had a chronic dry-mouth condition. To alleviate the dryness, he sucked on sourballs, one cheek bulging as if swollen from a punch to the jaw. He would juggle two or three of the candies over his dentures, his conversations often amounting to slurping variations on a theme. He was an odd man of sorts: a nerd, soft spoken, prone to reciting heady monologues of Shakespeare's breezier poetry. I found his chatter boring—not the words, but his incessant monotone that held so few highs and lows. We made it to the hospital in about half an hour.

The State Hospital at Trenton was set back from the road about a hundred yards. The main building was a large, brick conglomerate with many wings, set off by emerald green lawns. The grounds held an aura of competence, concern, and calm. This psychiatric hospital also did surgery for patients from state institutions; it was the place where they sent Fleming with his compound-fractured arm. However, the hospital was primarily devoted to psychiatry. It took referrals from the courts, patients from state institutions who were considered unmanageable, and those people in the community with "out of the ordinary" behavior who were brought to officials' attention by law enforcement agencies.

Mr. Cook introduced himself to a receptionist who wore a corsage made of cheap crepe paper on her uniform.

"Can you arrange to have Mr. Carroll escorted to his brother?" he asked her.

She smiled at him. "That's no problem. I'll take care of everything."

Mr. Cook turned to me with his sourball breath. "I'll be waiting in the cafeteria."

I watched him disappear into one of the many side doors at the far end of the hall. The receptionist leaned over the counter and tapped me on the shoulder.

"Young man, I don't want you standing there. You're in my way. Go sit down over there," she ordered, pointing to a row of chairs around an island of plastic plants. "I'll see if I can get an orderly down here so you can go upstairs and see your brother."

"Thank you, ma'am."

Her voice sounded over the intercom. "Mr. Kenneday, James

Kenneday . . . please report to the front desk immediately. Visitor waiting."

About five minutes later, a black man approached the desk.

"Yes, Mrs. Virginia? You called?"

"See that boy over there? Take him to Wing Seven. He's here to see his brother, Robert Carroll. They'll be ready with him in about a half hour. Take him to the snack bar. I'll let them know you're there waiting."

"Hi, kid," said the man, turning to me. "I'm James, but everybody calls me Blackjack."

"Blackjack? That's a funny name," I replied.

"That's my name. Come on. I'll take ya upstairs."

I immediately rose to my feet and followed the man.

"Ya look a little like him, but I'll bet you're not as feisty as he is, are ya?"

"Yeah, but only in my mind."

"That's the kind of thinkin' that keeps people like you outta these places. I already like ya, kid. I'll tell ya one thing—and I don't mean to hurt your feelings—but that brother of yours sure can be a bugger at times. He's not easy to settle down."

"Blackjack, can I ask you a question?"

"Sure, kid."

"What did that lady mean about getting my brother ready? What's there to get ready?"

"He's in treatment right now, but they'll be finished with him in a few minutes. He's tough." Blackjack stopped walking and looked up. "This is our elevator."

We took the elevator to the second floor. As soon as we emerged, I was struck by sights, smells, and sounds similar to those at New Lisbon's hospital: antiseptics and strong detergents, high-backed wooden wheelchairs and gurneys on squeaky wheels going in all directions, and overflowing laundry carts being pushed up and down halls by people in hospital whites.

"The snack bar's at the other end of the hall. Come on. Just stay with me and don't pay these people no mind. I know they look kind of funny, but don't let any of that bother ya. Most of them are harmless. It's the ones ya can't see that are dangerous. They keep *them* in special rooms and padded cells. There's the snack bar. Want somethin'?"

"I don't have any money."

"No problem. What would ya like?"

"Could I have a soda?"

"You got it, kid. Let's sit over there." He pointed to two chairs against the far wall of the snack bar. "What kind of soda do ya want?"

"Can I have a Coke?"

"One Coke comin' up. I'll be right back."

When he returned from the vending machines, he took a seat next to me.

"Here's your Coke. And I have somethin' else for ya." He reached into his breast pocket. "A Baby Ruth bar. Like 'em?"

"They're good, but they look like, you know—"

"Don't bother with the details. I know what ya mean, kid. Here," he said, handing it to me.

I guessed Blackjack to be in his late forties. He was a handsome man with copper skin. His hair was processed, combed straight back, revealing a receding hairline. A salt-and-pepper mustache framed his full lips above a chiseled, squared-off jaw.

"When will they let us know my brother's ready?"

Sipping his coffee, he said, "See that buzzer over there?" He pointed to the far wall. "It'll ring when they're ready for us."

"You know that lady downstairs?"

"Yeah, what about 'er?"

"I didn't like her."

"You too? Don't pay her no mind. She's just the bossy type. Nobody likes her 'cause she told the truth about another employee abusin' one of the patients. Now nobody wants to talk to her."

"But it sounds like she did the right thing."

"She did!" snapped Blackjack. "It's just that, in these places, when an employee snitches on another employee, they get the silent treatment . . . it ain't nothin' new around here, kid. That's just the way it is."[1]

"Hey, Blackjack, why do they call you that?"

"You mean Blackjack?"

"Yeah."

"I like playin' the game. Cards. Blackjack's my name and that's my game . . . and I'm not bad at it either. People been callin' me that more than twenty years."

"Gosh, that's older than me. Have you been here that long?"

"Heck no, man. I'd be nuts by now if I worked here that long. I've been here three years, and believe me, that's long enough. I won't be stayin' much longer. Hey, kid." He looked at me inquisitively. "Do ya always ask people a lotta questions?"

"Sometimes. That's what Dr. Alprin asked me once."

"Who's Dr. Alprin?"

"A friend I had once, and I miss him."

"So what did ya tell this doctor guy about all your questions and stuff?"

"That if I didn't ask questions, I couldn't learn anything."

"That was a good answer." He took another sip from his coffee, steam clinging to his full mustache each time he removed the cup from his lips.

"I'll bet everybody likes you here, huh?" I asked him.

"Don't count your chickens before they hatch, kid. Not everybody does, and I don't mean just here, either. Ya can't get everybody to like ya, no matter who ya are or how nice ya are. That's life, kid. And as for the people in this place—and I'm talkin' about the patients—most of 'em are just plain pissed off. Take a look around ya. Look at their faces. They all look dull and tired out. This is a depressin' place. It's from places like this that they came up with the name 'mad house.' Everybody's mad as hell!"

"But my brother isn't."

"Don't you believe it. He's pissed. And I agree with him. He shouldn't be in this shitty-ass place. I like your brother. His only problem is his spunk. This place knows how to ruin somebody's natural-born spunk."

"So why's everybody mad, Blackjack?"

"Think about it, kid. Most of 'em were angry before they came here, but they got even madder after the folks got through with 'em in this hellhole." He exhaled a frustrated breath. "That's how it is, kid. It's a fact. Most of 'em aren't here 'cause they're crazy, but 'cause they *act out* bein' crazy. Your brother is one of 'em. He ain't crazy, but he acted like he was. Got it, kid?"

"Got it, Blackjack. I thought the same thing, but didn't have the right words for it." I paused and took a sip of my Coke. "Hey, Blackjack, do you know anything about those electric shock treatments they give people? I've seen lots of guys comin' back from this place a lot worse than before they were sent here. And I've heard lots of bad things about it, like you can die and—"

"For some, it seems to do a lotta good. But for others, it just ruins 'em. None of that shit is foolproof. Understand?"

"Yeah. Did they do them on my brother?"

"They sure did. A lotta times. They got him on drugs too. The drugs are takin' over everything. Therapy in a pill—that's what it's come to."

"Why?"

Blackjack leaned in closer to me, conspiratorially. "To reprogram 'em, what else? They call it erasin'—erasin' the information that makes 'em do the things they do. Some of 'em are dyin' and—"[2]

"Dying?"

"You heard me. They give 'em drug cocktails—a bunch of drugs mixed together—and sometimes it kills 'em. I've read articles in the paper 'bout how they use drugs in some of these hospitals, and the way I understand it, it's not gonna get any better. Shock treatments can kill too." He paused for a moment, maybe waiting for those facts to sink in. "It's like this, kid. They think shockin' 'em destroys the problem, but it don't. In the long run, it makes 'em worse. Some ain't got no memory no more, and some just have heart attacks and die. That shockin' shit is evil."[3]

"Gee whiz! Could my brother lose his memory?"

"Probably not for good. Some get it back after a few weeks, but other folks—well, they're never the same. But still, some spring right back. And some get better. But if ya ask me, it's scary stuff. Hey, did ya know your brother tried committin' suicide after he got here?"

"I didn't know that. But he just cuts up his arms like that to get attention. New Lisbon got fed up with him. It was easier to send him here than put up with him."

"I think he did it for attention too, kid. Poor boy, he has scars up and down his arms from doin' that shit. He's done it so many times that his arms look like railroad tracks. I think I know 'im pretty good. He's a nice kid. A lotta these doctors are outta their minds. And what's bad, they think *he's* outta *his* mind—ya know, sayin' he's a danger to himself. But don't get me wrong, some of these patients try to kill themselves and succeed. Of course, sometimes the employees goof up. I hear a lot, and not just about this place."[4]

"Blackjack, why can't the doctors here see that those cuts on my brother's arms aren't deep and all? They'd have to be blind not to see that. My brother wants to *live*, not die. He does that shit because of what he feels inside. It's got nothin' to do with wanting to die and all."

"You got a good point there, kid. Do ya know why doctors act the way they do here?"

"No, why?"

"It's the screwed-up education they give 'em. Blind. That's a good way to put it, kid. Their education does that to 'em. The only thing that bothers me about your brother is that maybe one day he'll cut himself too deep and do himself in. He could kill the wrong person. Listen, kid, don't tell nobody I've been talkin' to ya. We got a deal?"

"I ain't no rat. I like you, Blackjack. You're a nice man."

"Where're you from, boy?"

"Johnstone."

"What's that?"

"A place for nuts."

"You?"

"Yep."

"But why?"

"A mistake. It's a long story."

"There ain't shit wrong with you that I can see."

"I know." Mulling over our conversation, I couldn't get my mind off the shock treatments. "Can I ask you something else, Blackjack?"

"I'm all ears."

"How many volts are there in those shock machines?"

"Plenty."

"What's that mean?"

"A lot—sometimes hundreds of volts, dependin' on how bad they think the person is.[5] And they keep that power on for three, four seconds.[6] Those things make some people have seizures."

"Seizures?"

"Yeah, have a fit. They aim those things right here." He pointed to his temples. "It's enough electricity to fire up a whole room. House plugs only have a hundred and ten volts, you know."

"Honest?"

"No kiddin', kid."

"How do I know my brother won't die from those shocks. Why doesn't everybody die when they get that much electricity?"

"Nobody knows. Anyway, that's what the doctors say. As far as I'm concerned, too many of them things are dehumanizin' and degradin'. But I must admit, like I told ya earlier, I've seen 'em do miracles on people, especially the depressed ones."

I was silent a moment. "Hey, Blackjack, why do they have such a big name for a fit?"

"You mean 'seizure'? You writin' a book or somethin'?"

"Someday."

"Yeah, right. And I'm the Virgin Mary."

"No, no, it's really true. Someday I will."

"Hey, there's the buzzer now. Remember, I didn't say nothin' to ya 'bout any of this, okay?"

"I ain't gonna say nothin'. Cross my heart."

"Come on, let's go."

Blackjack led me to the second-floor receptionist's desk where a nurse instructed, "Mr. Kenneday, you can take the young man upstairs to the third floor. His brother's ready now."

"Thank you." He turned to me. "Come on, kid."

As we got in the elevator again, I turned to Blackjack. "How do you think my brother's doing, really?"

"He seems to be comin' along."

"Are you sure you don't think my brother's . . . you know, *nuts*?"

"I already told ya I didn't. Your brother just talks too much. That's his problem."

"I love my brother. I just hope they don't fuck him up."

"He's got a hard head, and he's gutsy. He just has to understand that he can't act that way in a place like this. They take his shit too seriously. That's what gets 'im in trouble. I try to tell 'im to tone it down, but he don't listen. Like I said, he's got a hard head. He'll tell ya to go screw yourself in a hot minute. That's the kind of kid he is." He looked up. "This is where we get off. Just follow me."

I thought we would never come to the end of the long corridor. The walls amplified our conversation, but only in between screams heard along the way. We had to shout now and then to hear our own voices.

"What's in that room? And . . . and why are they screaming like that?" I asked.

"I'm not supposed to let ya see what's in that room."

"How come?"

"There's a rule against it, that's why."

"I can't just peek?"

"Not in that room."

"What's going on in there?"

"It's the Ice Room. Let's just keep walkin'."

"What do they do in there?"

"They strap patients down in bathtubs filled with ice water, slap down the wooden lids⁷—wait a minute, I'm talkin' too much. If they find out that—"

"Ice water?"

"Forget it, kid. You don't wanna know the rest. Forget I said anythin'."

We kept walking, passing open day rooms filled with maniacs, schizoids, combatants, and screamers. I witnessed an encyclopedia of lunacy, a menagerie of human freaks—most drugged and slobbering onto themselves, many waltzing a Thorazine shuffle. Thorazine was a notorious "zonk-out" pill, the equivalent of a chemical lobotomy, transforming aggressive behavior into a slow-motion ballet.

"Are ya scared, kid?"

"A little. Those people we passed . . . it just seems like a shame. What's the purpose keeping them all like that—I mean, in that condition? Is that the way they always are around here?"

"I'm afraid so, kid. It's complicated. Ya know, after a while ya get used to it. Hell, man, I don't even hear the screams anymore."

"But they're human beings."

Blackjack didn't respond. Instead, he offered, "Your brother's in that wing up ahead . . . that's Wing Seven."

"Oh, good. I've seen enough, anyway."

As we reached the far end of the hallway, Blackjack pulled out a ring of keys and inserted one into the heavy steel door.

We entered Wing Seven, and I peeked into the first doorway on my right. "What's that concrete thing in the middle of the room?"

"This is the shower room. It's so the water won't drain into the hallway."

"Where's the shower heads?"

"There ain't none. At night, we hose 'em down over there." He pointed to the side of the room, then gave a nod upward. "See those?"

I looked up. "Yeah, I see 'em."

"They're air towels. Hot blow-dryers. That's how we dry the patients after we wash 'em and rinse 'em down with the hoses."

"No towels?"

"They aren't allowed to have towels 'cause they could hang 'emselves with 'em."

"Jesus," I mumbled. "Hey, where's my brother?"

"This is it. He's inside that door. Now look, when you see 'im, don't act like anything's wrong."

"What do you mean?"

"You'll see what I mean when we go in."

Blackjack led me to the door and unlocked it. We entered a stark green room. He snapped on the light and said to me, "Just cool it and have a seat in that chair."

He locked the door behind us, then went to a side door and tapped on it. A man opened it and entered; he was wearing a police-type uniform.

"Is that Robert Carroll's brother?"

"That's him," answered Blackjack.

"Mr. Carroll, your brother will appear on the other side of the glass. Just stay in your seat, and I'll be right back. Blackjack, wait outside, and be sure to lock the door. When the visit is over, I'll call for you to come back in."

"Yes, sir," said Blackjack, exiting the room.

"I'm going to leave the room and bring your brother to you. Just be patient, okay, Mr. Carroll?"

"Yes, sir."

The windowless room had an air vent in one corner. In the middle of the ceiling was a white porcelain basement fixture, a frostless lightbulb glaring from its socket. After five minutes of waiting, an orderly entered from the side door and lifted the accordion-type door that revealed a glass partition the thickness of a bank teller's window. There was a cutout hole at the bottom, covered by a screen.

"Bring your chair over and have a seat here," he directed. "You'll be seeing your brother on the other side in a few minutes."

The man left the room.

Another few minutes passed when, suddenly, two men in guard uniforms entered on the other side of the glass partition, bringing Bobby with them. He was listless and wobbly, as if unable to stand on his own two feet. They led him to the chair and seated him, then left us to ourselves.

One look at my brother and I started to cry. "Bobby! What've they done to you?"

Slumped over, he partly lifted his lazy eyelids and looked at me, but said nothing.

"Bobby, it's me, it's me! It's Chuckie!" I couldn't stop the tears cascading down my face. "For God's sake, say something!"

Bobby remained motionless, like a zombie. Pale and green, dark circles were under his eyes as if he hadn't slept in many days. He looked emaciated and malnourished. Anger boiled within me.

The orderly entered the room on Bobby's side of the glass.

"Sit up!" he ordered Bobby, straightening him in his chair. "Talk to your brother. Look, that's your brother on the other side. Lift your head. Say something. I ain't got all day to be messin' with you, Carroll."

"Please don't yell at him," I pleaded through my tears. "Give him time."

The man left the room.

Bobby's eyes were still barely open, the whites of his eyes streaked with red veins.

Beside myself, I shouted, "What the hell have they done to you? Goddamn it, Bobby! Please talk to me!"

He didn't respond.

I dropped my mouth to the hole. "Come closer and talk to me," I begged. "Please, Bobby."

Slowly he raised his head. Half-open, his eyelids rested lazily over his eyeballs.

The same man stepped back into the room, but this time on my side of the barrier. He brought a chair, placed it beside me, and sat down.

"Mr. Carroll," he said, "we can't force your brother to talk to you. He's on a special medication, one that'll bring him around from the sedation."

"What's that mean, sir?"

"We gave him some medicine earlier because he was out of control, but for your visit, we needed to reverse his condition. The only thing is, this drug that we gave him, it takes longer to react with some patients. Some come out of it faster than others. In other words, it's possible that he may not come around soon enough to really visit with you."

"But why in the heck would you even—"

"Let me finish. What I'm saying is that he may not come through it before you have to go. We can only allow so much time for a visit. Rules are strict about that. And like I said a minute ago, with some people it takes longer to work. Try to be patient, and let's see how it goes. Okay, Mr. Carroll?"

Instead of leaving, the man remained sitting beside me.

I pressed my face against the glass. "Bobby!" I tried again. "Please wake up! It's me, your brother, Chuckie. Come on, Bobby, it's me." I backed off the glass partition and turned to the man. "Can't you let me on the other side with him?"

"Sorry, kid, that's against the rules. It's for your own protection."

"Protection? From him? He'd never hurt me."

"Sorry, Mr. Carroll. That's the rules. Rules are rules. They're not made to break—not in this place."

I turned back to my brother. "Bobby, I'm sorry I can't come

around there and be with you. They won't let me. You know I love you, don't you?"

Then, to my surprise, Bobby began showing signs of coming out of his stupor. Ever so slowly, he lifted his eyelids a little more and began inching his head closer to the glass, finally directing his mouth to the screened opening, his lips drooling saliva. Then he mumbled something I couldn't understand.

"What was that?" I asked, raising my voice and leaning closer.

He mumbled again.

"Louder, Bobby! What did you say?" I turned my head to one side and placed my ear against the opening.

Slowly, he whispered, "I love you too, Chuckie."

"Time's up!" ordered a guard, abruptly entering on Bobby's side. The burly man leaned over from behind Bobby and wrapped his muscular arms around him, lifting him out of his seat and carrying away his near-lifeless body.

Sobbing a bittersweet scream, I jumped up. "No, no, not now! Mister! Please wait . . . wait! That's . . . but that's . . . that's the first time he ever told me he—"

The steel door slammed shut. The visit was over.

ENDNOTES FOR CHAPTER TWENTY-NINE

1. See Appendix C.1.4/Abuse and Mistreatment; "Code of Silence"/2002. A Justice Department investigation of a Kentucky facility revealed a "code of silence" among staff regarding abuse and neglect due to fear of retaliation by other employees.

2. See C.2.1 The Dangers of Psychiatric Drugs/1994. Tranquilizers, such as Thorazine, are among the most dangerous of psychiatric medications. They were often used at psychiatric institutions for the convenience of doctors and attendants.

   Also see Appendix C.1.8/Failure to Manage Psychotropic Medication/2004. A Justice Department investigation of an Arkansas facility revealed a failure to properly prescribe and monitor adverse effects of psychotropic medications.

   Also see Appendix C.1.9/Improper Use of Psychotropic Drugs/2002. A Justice

Department investigation of two Iowa facilities revealed psychotropic medications were often used to address staff complaints about individuals with challenging behaviors.

3. See Appendix C.2.2/Shock Therapy Makes a Comeback/1996. Electroshock therapy, which has become more popular in recent years, can cause confusion, memory loss, and even death.

4. See Appendix B.5/Failure to Lock Medicine Cabinet; Patient in Coma/1994. A patient at Trenton Psychiatric Hospital fell into a coma after ingesting medication from a cabinet left unlocked by a nurse.

Also see Appendix B.6/Failure to Supervise; Patient Attempts Hanging/1993. A Trenton Psychiatric Hospital employee was charged with neglect when a patient under his "arm's length" supervision attempted suicide.

5. "[Electroconvulsive therapy] consists of electricity being passed through the brain with a force of from 70 to 400 volts and an amperage of from 200 milliamperes to 1.6 amperes (1600 milliamperes). The electric shock is administered for as little as a fraction of a second to as long as several seconds." Lawrence Stevens, JD, *The Antipsychiatry Coalition*, "Psychiatry's Electroconvulsive SHOCK TREATMENT, A Crime Against Humanity," http://www.antipsychiatry.org/ect.htm (accessed July 6, 2005).

6. "Patients generally receive a one- or four-second electrical charge to the brain, which causes an epileptic-like seizure for 30 to 90 seconds." Dennis Cauchon, "Shock Therapy: Patients often aren't informed of full danger," *USA TODAY*, December 6, 1995: A1, http://www.ect.org/news/series/informed.html (accessed July 7, 2005).

7. See Appendix C.1.7/Failure to Protect Children from Harm and Sexual Abuse; Excessive Use of Restraints and Seclusion/2003 and 2004. The Justice Department's investigation of a California state hospital revealed excessive use of physical restraints without proper monitoring.

CHAPTER THIRTY
Flight into Dignity

WHEN I RETURNED from Trenton after seeing Bobby, I was beside myself. I felt numb, as if in a trance. My brother's condition at the hospital left me saddened, tormented, and angry. Instead of heading directly for my cottage, I went to an isolated corner outside the building to be alone in an attempt to pull myself together and make some sense out of it.

Rawbone and Mr. Pring were coming down the sidewalk and noticed me. Mr. Pring had moved from New Lisbon a few months before, one transfer I was actually glad to see. Suspecting something was wrong, he came over to have a word with me; Rawbone accompanied him.

"What happened at Trenton today?" asked Mr. Pring. "How's your brother?"

"They messed him up bad."

"What do you mean by that?"

"Do I have to talk about it, Mr. Pring?"

"Not if you don't want to, but if you decide later that you do, you know where you can find me. Okay, son?"

"Okay."

As Mr. Pring walked away, Rawbone leaned over and whispered, "I hope they fried his brain good."

I jumped up and started to throw a punch, just barely stopping myself when I heard Mr. Pring's voice.

"Hey, hey, hey! What's going on?"

"He started it, Mr. Pring," I answered.

"That mothafucka almost hit me, Mr. Pring. I'm gonna kick his mothafuckin' ass for that."

"Oh, shut up a minute, Rawbone. Carroll, what's your beef with him?"

"He was sayin' shit about my brother."

"What did you say to him, Rawbone?"

"Not a damn thing."

"He's full of shit," I spouted. "He did so."

"Rawbone, I think you're full of shit too. Carroll, you want a piece of this colored boy's ass?"

"He started it, Mr. Pring."

"That's not what I asked you. Do you want a piece of his ass or not?"

I stared into Mr. Pring's eyes, hesitating, fear flushing through me like a bad fever, uncertain I could whip Rawbone—not because I saw him as a heavyweight boxer with a glass jaw, but because he had worn, for years, an armor that I couldn't penetrate. Now it was time to reassess him—if for no other reason than for my brother.

I focused back on the issue and finally answered, "He shouldn't say shit like that about my brother, Mr. Pring."

"What did he say? I want a straight answer."

"He said he hoped Trenton fried my brother's brain."

"Goddamn it! Is that what you said, Blacky?"

"He's full of shit. I'm gonna kick his ass for tryin' to hit me."

"Okay, then, if you got a beef with Carroll, let's take it to the gym. What about it, Carroll?"

"Ah, fuck it. Let's get on with it."

"Good boy! Let's go, you two."

By the time we reached the gymnasium, the whole cottage got wind of it. Everybody hurried over to witness the match. As they entered the gym, I could hear them commenting.

"Carroll's gonna fight Rawbone!"

"Carroll can't fight his way out of a paper bag!"

"Rawbone'll cream that white boy's ass!"

"Carroll? Fighting? I can't believe it!"

The gymnasium had a portable boxing ring that could be set up in minutes. Mr. Pring pushed a button on the far wall, and the electronic bleachers began rolling forward.

Mr. Pring approached Rawbone. "Is it gonna be with or without boxing gloves?"

"Fuck them things!" Rawbone said, snarling. "I don't need that shit. That shit's for sissies."

"Fine. What about you, Carroll?"

"Fine with me, Mr. Pring."

"Okay then, no gloves. Did you hear that everybody? A no-gloves fight!"

Sounds of clapping and stomping feet filled the room. They wanted blood.

"All right, you two, go to the locker room and get on your trunks. No, better yet, I'm going with you. I don't want this fight to starting ahead of time. Somebody set up the ring. We'll be right back."

"I'll do it," someone volunteered.

"Yeah, I'll help too," offered another.

"Good. Get it set up," answered Mr. Pring. "Let's go, you two."

When we came out of the locker room, we headed into the center of the boxing ring.

"You two go to your corners," Mr. Pring instructed. "Listen up, everybody. The Administration Building will hear about this in the morning. I don't care about that. But there's something I want to make clear: the loser is to be left alone. No making fun. No getting back at anybody. When this fight's over, it's over. May the best man win."

"That fruity mothafucka ain't gonna win shit."

"Shut up, Rawbone." Mr. Pring glared at him. "If you interrupt me again, there ain't gonna be no fight. Now go on and open your trap again."

There was only silence.

"Okay, listen up, everybody. This is gonna be a fair fight. There ain't gonna be no low blows, no rabbit punches, and no wrestling. When a man goes down, the other guy goes back to his corner. I'll come out with the count. Any questions outta you two?"

We shook our heads.

"Is everybody here that's gonna be here?"

"Yeah," yelled someone.

"Okay, then, this is a closed session. Somebody get those doors and lock 'em. I don't want any stragglers coming in during the fight. Let's get to it."

"They're locked, Mr. Pring," announced a kid standing by the doors.

"Good. You two boys ready?"

"I've been ready—ready to kick some white ass," threatened Rawbone.

"Shut up, Rawbone. What about you, Carroll?"

"I'm ready."

"On the count of three, come out fighting."

We both nodded.

"Okay, then. ONE . . . TWO . . . THREE!"

I came out with my fists up and swinging. Rawbone landed a solid punch to my jaw. I shook it off and kept swinging, hitting him in the face, bloodying his lip. Everybody got to their feet and howled, throwing their own punches in the air as if participating in the fight. Before I knew what had happened, Rawbone cold-cocked me in the right temple. I went down. But instead of Rawbone going to his corner, he threw himself on me and kept throwing punches.

"Let him up! Let him up!" somebody yelled from the bleachers. It was Niles, Rawbone's rival, who could easily kick Rawbone's ass.

Rawbone got off me and faced Niles in the bleachers. "Fuck you, white boy!" he yelled.

Niles broke from the bleachers and came running over. "Hey, motherfucker, let the boy up!" He climbed into the ring and shadowboxed around Rawbone, stabbing the air with his knotted fists. "Fight my ass, nigger, if you think you're bad enough."

Mr. Pring threw his arms around Niles. "Get back to your seat, Niles! This ain't your fight!"

"But that motherfucker thinks he's bad, Mr. Pring! You saw what he did to Carroll. He's supposed to let the boy up, and you know it. I know I can kick his black ass."

"Sure, sure, Niles. Maybe you can, but not today. Now move it!" Mr. Pring attempted to shove him out of the ring.

Niles resisted.

"Dammit! I said move it!" Mr. Pring was in Niles's face.

"Ah, fuck it!" barked Niles. "I ain't gonna lose my privileges over this shit! Hey, Rawbone," he warned, rubbernecking around Mr. Pring, "you and me later, motherfucker!"

"Go on, Niles, beat it!"

The crowd applauded Niles as he climbed out of the ring and returned to his seat, proudly wearing his huge ego like a cloak. The bleachers quieted.

"Rawbone," ordered Mr. Pring, "you get back to your corner."

"But, Mr.—"

"Now!"

Rawbone headed for his corner, complaining, "This fight ain't shit."

"Carroll, get up."

As I rose to my feet, Mr. Pring turned to the spectators and announced in a deep microphone voice, "Listen up, all of you. The only fight today's gonna be these two boys. As for you, Niles, if you want a piece of Blacky's ass, I'll set something up for ya next week. Have I made myself clear?"

"I know I can kick his motherfucker's ass!"

"Shut up, Niles! It's next week or nothing. Well? What's it gonna be?"

"Yeah, I'll go for that. Next week."

"That's better! Now listen up, you two." Mr. Pring directed his attention to Rawbone and me. "This is the last time I'm gonna tell you the rules, especially you, Rawbone. I don't wanna see no wrestling or body holds. If a man goes down, that's it . . . the man standing goes back to his corner. Then I'll come out counting. Any questions?"

We shook our heads.

"Okay, then, on the count of three, start fighting. Ready? ONE . . . TWO . . . THREE!"

We fought like we were unbeatable. By the end of the fourth round, though tiring, I was determined to stay with it, Rawbone's insults to Bobby ringing in my ears.

It was the fifth round, and we came out fighting with the vigor and intensity of a first round. The room was filled with the shouts of a ringside frenzy, some spectators encouraging me, others taking up Rawbone's side.

"Get 'im, Rawbone! That's it, keep your fists up!"

"You can take him, Carroll!"

"Good jab, Rawbone! Fuck that white boy after you kick his ass!"

I landed a nasty blow to Rawbone's eye, blood spurting from it like a severed artery, but it didn't weaken him. He returned a smashing right hook to my jaw. I went down, falling flat on my back. Mr. Pring broke from the ropes and began the count:

"ONE . . . TWO . . . Get up, boy, get up! THREE . . . FOUR . . . FIVE . . . Dammit, kid, get up! Want Blacky to win? SIX . . . SEVEN . . ."

Half-dazed and drained of all energy, I staggered and stumbled as I tried to stand. I could hardly carry my own weight, but when I finally did manage to get on my feet, the crowd went wild. Applause erupted throughout the room.

Mr. Pring came up to me. "Do you wanna go on, kid? You look shaky."

I slurred an answer.

"What was that?" Mr. Pring asked, his hand cupping his ear.

"I said I'm okay. I'm tired, that's all."

"Do you think you can go on?"

"I . . . I've got to, Mr. Pring."

"Then pull yourself together."

"I'm okay now."

"Okay, we'll do it your way. I just don't want to see you get your brains kicked in. He's a big kid. One thing's for sure, ya got gristle, kid. Get back to your corner."

Less than a minute into the next round, Rawbone clobbered me good, delivering a solid left hook to the side of my head. It left me momentarily stunned, but I managed to shake it off. This time I went back into him with everything I had, landing another smashing blow to the open wound of his right eye, blood again sliding down the side of his face onto the ropelike veins of his neck. Unaffected, he returned a solid punch and bloodied my nose.

The bleachers went wild over the sight of more blood. It was the perfect elixir to assure the madness of the crowd. We continued at each other nonstop, punching and jabbing left and right hooks, some missing, some landing.

We remained merciless. I connected a left hook to Rawbone's jaw. That did it. He went down as if dropped from a two-story building. The roar of the crowd was deafening. Mr. Pring broke from the ropes.

"ONE . . . TWO . . . THREE . . . FOUR . . ."

Though still dazed, the resilient Rawbone came out of it, mumbling to Mr. Pring as he stumbled to his feet.

"I didn't get that," said Mr. Pring. "Speak up."

"I slipped."

"Slipped? Is that what I heard you say?"

"Yeah, I slipped."

"Bullshit! The kid gotcha and you know it."

"No, no, I slipped."

Mr. Pring didn't buy it. He turned to the howling crowd, waving his arms for them to shut up. The room quieted.

"Hey, listen up. Blacky said he slipped!"

The room thundered and swelled with boos and stomping feet.

Mr. Pring turned to Rawbone. "They think you're full of shit, and so do I. Get back to your corner."

Instead, Rawbone stood his ground. Pointing at me, he grumbled, "That pussy-ass mothafucka ain't shit. I'll get 'im this time."

"I said go back to your corner. I'm tired of your lip, and I'm not telling you again."

"Okay, okay, I'm goin'," Rawbone obeyed, returning to his corner with the gait and attitude of a badass hipster.

Moments after we were settled in our respective corners, Mr. Pring gave us the eye. "You two boys ready?"

We nodded.

"On the count of three, come on out with your dukes up. May the best man win."

Near the end of that round, my energy was gone. Rawbone's punishing blows had whittled me down to a sloppy fighter. My arms felt like lead and my legs unsure. Rawbone, catching me off guard, connected. I went down hard. As I laid there, I began slipping in and out of consciousness, only now and then hearing the count: "ONE . . . TWO . . . FOUR . . . SEVEN . . ." I began seeing images of my tormented childhood flickering before me, much like a runaway movie projector operating out of control, rolling hellish clips of a cruel and enduring past. Then the mental images slowed to a trickle and stopped on a 1951 frame, when the nightmare began nearly a decade earlier.

But I wasn't through yet. I came out of it on the count of nine, staggering to my feet.

"He's up. He's up!" said Mr. Pring, excitedly. "I didn't think you'd make it up this time. Should I call the fight, or do you want to go on with it?"

"I've gotta keep goin', Mr. Pring. I've *got* to."

"Are you sure? Hell, boy. I don't want you dead."

"No, no. I'm okay. Look," I said, throwing jabs. "See? I'm ready."

"You've got grizzly bear in you, boy. No brains, but guts."

"I'm tired."

"Take a deep breath and let it out. That's it. Feel a little better?"

"A little."

"Now get 'em up and cut Blacky out a new asshole."

Mr. Pring returned to the center of the ring. "On the count of three, come out with all you've got. Ready? ONE . . . TWO . . . THREE!"

Rawbone and I went back at it again, splashing sweat with every punch delivered into our all-but-naked bodies. I got a good one in his gut, almost knocking the wind out of him. The crowd roared at his hesitation to go on, but go on he did, landing a sharp blow to my jaw. He knocked me down, but I immediately got up, delivering crushing blows to every part of his body, and he returned them with equal tenacity. I aggravated the cut over his right eye again, and the decibel level in the room rose even further.

Rawbone delivered blow after blow in exchange with mine. We went at it like animals, absent any sense of our own humanity. Rawbone landed a punch to my mouth. Now we were both bleeding, blood rolling down our bodies, both exhausted and delivering clumsy punches. My entire body felt heavy and wobbly, but my spirit remained on target. The crowd egged us on, wanting more blood.

"Hold it!" intervened Mr. Pring, coming between us. "Carroll, let me see that lip. That's split wide open, kid."

"I'm okay, Mr. Pring."

"That's enough, Carroll. Let me have a look at you, Rawbone. Your eye needs stitches. I'm taking both of you over to the infirmary." He waved his arms to the crowd. "That's it! That's it, everybody! I'm calling this fight a draw. Nobody wins. Everybody go home!"

I began crying, all but begging, "Please, Mr. Pring. Not now, please. I gotta win, I just gotta."

"No. That's it. Winning isn't always determined by who wins or loses a fight. You won back a lot today, son. You won your dignity. Come on, that's enough. It's over. Let's get you to the doctor. You too, Rawbone. Let's go."

The doctor quickly patched me up and I returned to my room, physically and emotionally spent from my visit with Bobby, the fight—everything. I laid on my bed, feeling numb, reflecting, as that runaway movie projector seemed to start up again with vivid pictures of years of holy hell—images of Richard and the priest molesting me under the bridge, of hopelessly watching Mrs. Johnson drive off with my brother down Sunfair Road. There was the image of that shadow in the cubicle ejaculating its sin down the wall in front of my face. Another clip emerged of the smiling governor looking down at me while I squeezed my buttocks in secret silence and tennis court spectators snapped chewing gum bubbles behind happy-go-lucky smiles. And yet another image loomed of hunchbacks and droolers in worn-out shoes clopping along in the awkward rhythm of their uneven gaits.

My mind's photo procession moved to Mr. Wheeler and my heart shattering into a million pieces—and to the Hendersons, with their concern over souring haystacks—and to Marilyn's womb, her growing baby still whispering from a mouth filled with rotting teeth, "There ain't room for one more."

The past dug deeper, gnawing at me. I saw helpless children receiving their allotments of hard candy—their sole pleasures—only to have the tasty morsels ripped from their tiny hands by a baby with a hammer in its hand and the authority to use it. I saw Biddle's ear in the mouth of a psychotic wretch who tore it from his victim's skull with one vicious chomp of an unconscionable jaw. And I saw that night—that dreaded night—when the arms of darkness wrapped around me in a python's strangling grip, coiling me into a near act of murder with a rock in my hand as Dr. Alprin's echoing whispers of "homicidal tendencies" stabbed at my conscience.

And then there was Bobby and my deep sense of guilt over our failed escape—guilt that I hadn't talked him out of it, knowing full well we were deluding ourselves, merely running away from a hellish existence for a snippet of respite—rather than, in fact, fleeing *to* someone who might otherwise assure our freedom. And worse, there was Bobby's intense need for attention and his acts of injury to himself—acts that earned him a place on the trapdoor of Trenton's psychiatric gallows, where they had now lynched his good mind. The thought of that sank deeper into my psyche, which housed no internal toys and no more make-believe, long ago converting the child in me into a serious thinker with a lost smile. It all came full circle, to a photo finish, emptying like an over-and-done-with movie reel, the snapping sounds of the celluloid finally bringing me to my knees at the doorstep of madness, to the very edge of that precipice I had so painfully avoided for the past decade.

But then a transformation began working its way into my broken system—a sort of internal repair mechanism that took over when all else failed. My anxiety began withering away, my death grip on years of abuse relaxing and the yoke of uncertainty lightening—gently, softly, and ever so slightly—ushering me, at last, into the bright sunshine of romping kids and happy laughter, of friendships that never were, of love I never had, and of kind words I never heard—ushering me into bright sunshine where imagination was allowed to frolic in Buster Brown shoes in the allure of a dance unabated by threats or ridicule, and where it was safe to daydream and play and discover without self-consciousness.

It was a place where little girls wore pigtails knotted at the ends with pretty red bows, where childhood was held sacred and wholly majestic, where innocence was celebrated, and where, whenever I wanted, I could return to the backyard of a Grandma Moses painting to be part of that innocence and play without interference from a cruel world. So hurrah for that grand old lady a century old who, from the end of a soft, camel-haired brush, ingeniously painted my imagination of perfect harmony and childhood bliss.

My face relaxed into a hint of a smile as my reverie receded—the images slowing, fading—and I gradually drifted off to sleep.

THE NEXT MORNING, Mr. Pring came crashing into my bedroom.

"Carroll! Wake up, wake up!"

Annoyed, I raised my head. "What? What? I hurt all over, Mr. Pring. Not now, please?" I buried my swollen face back into the pillow.

"That's quite a shiner you got there, kid."

I turned from my pillow and looked up at the man. "Does it look that bad?"

"Don't worry about it. Where you're going, you're not gonna care."

"What do you mean?"

"Get your ass outta that bed and get your things together."

"My things? What for?"

"Never mind. Wash up, and bring everything with you."

"My clothes too?"

"Everything. Then I want to see you in the office."

I went into the bathroom and looked in the mirror. Mr. Pring was right. I had one hell of a black eye and my lower lip was twice its normal size.

I washed up, headed back to my room to collect my meager belongings, and went directly to the office.

"Ah, there you are, Carroll. Put your things down and come with me."

I followed Mr. Pring to the front door of the building.

"This is your day, son," he said, holding out his hand. "You made it."

"I made what?"

"Freedom, boy. You're getting out today. I want to shake your hand. I'm proud of you, son."

"I don't believe it. You're kiddin' me, right?"

"Believe it, son. Look at this." He withdrew his hand from mine and reached into his shirt pocket. "These are your walking papers. Your release order came through early this morning."

"My release papers?"

"That's right. They're waiting for you at the Administration Building."

"You're joking."

"I am, huh? Read it for yourself." He held the document up to my face. "What's it say?" he asked, pointing to a bold line.

"'Release Assignment for Charles A. Carroll'. Shit, that's me!"

"What did I tell ya? I'm happy for ya, boy. You got a helluva book in ya, kid. Write it. Now get your ugly face outta my sight."

I took off running to the Administration Building and, until now, I never looked back.

EPILOGUE

I WAS RELEASED from Johnstone in late 1959 to work as a custodian for infirm, elderly people at the Sea Breeze Nursing Home in Atlantic City, New Jersey. I earned fifteen dollars a week, plus room and board. About a year later, I was officially discharged as a ward of the state.

Shortly after my visit, Bobby was released from the New Jersey State Hospital at Trenton (now Trenton Psychiatric Hospital), where he claimed to have received two hundred shock treatments. He returned to New Lisbon for a couple of months, but due to continued "bad" behavior, he was then transferred to Annandale Reformatory, a facility for the state's "most unmanageable" kids (also known at the time as the New Jersey Reformatory, and currently called the Mountainview Youth Correctional Facility). A short time later, he was released into a structured farm setting in the community, where he was supervised under Intermediate Care Facilities for the Mentally Retarded (ICFMR). Bobby remained under the ICFMR umbrella for several months before being officially discharged from the state's rosters. He moved away from the farm and left no forwarding address. I didn't see him again for twenty-nine years.

Jackson and Rawbone were released under the ICFMR program in 1960.

Desarino, after the beating incident in front of Birch Cottage, was never heard from again.

The Steeles retired from New Lisbon in good standing.

Birch One and Two were eventually closed down, tagged "condemned" by the New Jersey Department of Institutions and Agencies (now the Department of Human Services). Its break-wind boilers were tagged "Danger," the belly-wrap tagged "Asbestos Contaminates, Stay Out." In the 1960s, Birch was bulldozed to the ground (though several years later, a new cottage at a different site was given the same name).

I eventually located our mother's sister (our aunt), Josephine Shea, the lady who visited us once at New Lisbon from Clifton, New Jersey. She confided, in a letter to me years later, that our mother provided the coats, and the picture she took was used as proof that we received them.

I never found my father, but did learn he was from Goshen, New York.

In 1966, when I was twenty-four years old, I finally located my mother. She was living in Culver City, California, and enticed me to come live with her (by that time, she had been married seven times). Because of my intense need to recapture a family, I left a successful sales position in Pennsylvania to join her. Two days later, it was over. I slammed that door shut and never saw her again. Twenty years later, I received a call from an unknown relative in Bakersfield, California. He reported that my mother had died peacefully in her sleep nine months earlier; she was sixty-two years old. She had been cremated and her ashes scattered in a rose garden at the Odd Fellows Cemetery in Bell, California. There was no grave or headstone.

Upset that I had not been informed earlier of my mother's death, I contacted my estranged aunt, Josephine Shea, having learned from the Bakersfield call that it was she who took care of all the arrangements. When I asked her why she hadn't contacted me, she replied: "Why should I? You didn't care about her."

As for Dr. Alprin, we finally found each other in 1991, after nearly forty years. I wrote him a letter and discussed the baby incident and the testing procedures when he was doing his internship at New Lisbon. This is what he had to say:

December 16, 1991
(Excerpt of letter from Dr. Alprin to Charles A. Carroll)

There is much to respond to: both your present and distant past. I think I have said how much I admire your struggle to survive, to grow emotionally and intellectually, and to express your thoughts in writing. Now I read about your struggle to let go of that past horror; the debilitating feelings, not the recollections. When you can do that—and it seems you are well on your way—your life can only become better and more worthwhile for you.

I'm more than happy to supply you with whatever memories of our past that I can. I went to New Lisbon one summer to do a brief internship so as to meet some New Jersey psychological examiner requirement. I had just come from a school psychologist job in Michigan and I was offered a combined teaching/testing job with a school district in Somerset County [New Jersey]. I think I spent most of my time at New Lisbon giving the Wechsler Intelligence Scale for Children [WISC], The Stanford-Binet, and the Vineland [Social] Maturity Scale. I probably used the WISC with you. You tested in the normal or average range, somewhere between 90 and 110.

I knew you were not retarded before I gave you the test: your thinking and problem solving seemed perfectly normal. You may have been ignorant about things learned in school, but you sure weren't stupid. That was obvious to me and to other staff people. I questioned why you were there and I have no recollection of the answer. I was upset nonetheless by the apparent injustice, and felt a strong inner tug to give you some relief from that place. And so began the occasional trips to my house and visits with relatives . . . So much of

PLATE TWENTY
CHARLES A. CARROLL (LEFT) AND DR. STANLEY I. ALPRIN
JANUARY 13, 2003
REUNION AFTER NEARLY 50 YEARS
NOVELTY, OHIO

what I saw, thought, and felt is beyond ready recall.

January 14, 1991
(Excerpt of letter from Dr. Alprin to Charles A. Carroll)

I recall that incident with my new baby (Susan). The recollections are not very clear any longer, but I remember how my wife's parents were deeply upset and prevailed upon my wife and me to be very cautious. I want you to know that I felt very bad about not seeing you as frequently or not at all after I left New Lisbon. If I had to do it over, I hope that I would be less prone to make a decision based largely on the worries of others. I'm sorry for having given a little boy some new hope and then pulling it away . . .

I understand your commitment to try to bring about change in people's attitudes toward our "residential" institutions. I hope you never relax this commitment. If there is hope for saving the human species from itself, it will be because there are people like you who are willing to give so much of themselves to set things right.

NEW LISBON DEVELOPMENTAL Center remains open today. It is New Jersey's largest state-operated facility for people with developmental disabilities. By the late 1950s, the population had grown to 1,200 (up from 900 when I arrived in 1951). Those numbers, though, have come down again, and the center now houses about 600 residents ranging in age from eighteen to eighty-seven.

The abuses, unfortunately, continue. In 2002, the federal government commenced an investigation of the facility. The Justice Department findings, issued the following year, cited "numerous conditions and practices that violate the constitutional and statutory rights of New Lisbon residents." A settlement was reached with the State of New Jersey in 2004 (see Appendix A.1/U.S. Department of Justice Investigation of New Lisbon).

WHAT'S MY POSITION today? Elie Wiesel, an eminent author and a brilliant, sensitive man, spoke of his past in a Nazi death camp where his world was "composed of three simple categories: the killers, the victims, and the bystanders." Wiesel's words about the indifference of bystanders seem to resonate with my story:

> *What is indifference? Etymologically, the word means "no difference"* . . .
>
> *Of course, indifference can be tempting—more than that, seductive. It is so much easier to look away from victims. It is so much easier to avoid such rude interruptions to our work, our dreams, our hopes. It is, after all, awkward, troublesome, to be involved in another person's pain and despair* . . .
>
> *In a way, to be indifferent to . . . suffering is what makes the human being inhuman. Indifference, after all, is more dangerous than anger and hatred* . . .
>
> *. . . Indifference is not a response. Indifference is not a beginning; it is an end. And, therefore, indifference is always the friend of the enemy, for it benefits the aggressor— never his victim, whose pain is magnified when he or she feels forgotten. The political prisoner in his cell, the hungry children, the homeless refugees—not to respond to their plight, not to relieve their solitude by offering them a spark of hope is to exile them from human memory. And in denying their humanity, we betray our own.*
>
> *Indifference, then, is not only a sin, it is a punishment.*

American Rhetoric, "The Perils of Indifference," speech given by Elie Wiesel on April 12, 1999, in Washington, D.C., http://www.americanrhetoric.com/speeches/ewieselperilsofindifference.html (accessed June 13, 2005).

* * *

AFTER HAVING SHARED this gut-wrenching story with you, I would rather not lean toward censure or condemnation, as I find blaming a waste of time. The past is gone, but today and the future are here, and they're in our hands.

I wrote this book as a voice not only for the dead, the victims who didn't survive the abuse in state institutions, but also for the survivors of similar mistreatment, to give them a sense of identity and to affirm that they are not alone. I also wrote this book for the professionals in social sciences and for the general public, so that they may learn about the ravages of abuse and come away with a better understanding of the varied personality traits so common among victims.

It is my ultimate hope that my forthright portrayal of the events depicted in *HARD CANDY* will cause all who experience this book to develop not only a better understanding of abuse and its side effects, but also more compassion for the victims. Why? Because, at any age, be they young or old, those victims will need it.

While I did not write this book for myself, I must humbly admit I was the first to benefit. The writing experience was cathartic and most rewarding; by the time I finished the last revision, much of the internal resentment and bitterness that I once felt had slowly, and finally, drained from my system. Yes, I am much better off for having written it—but I must also confess that I am far from cured, because there is no absolute freedom from sexual, physical, emotional, or verbal abuse. And also because, with every abused child, there is a life sentence to be served, one that is paid by the innocent for the guilty—a tragic, but true, indelible hallmark of the world's abused children. That is, while we may improve our lives over time, one sad fact remains: Nobody ever flies over the cuckoo's nest. Nobody.

APPENDICES

Prologue to Appendices

In the following pages, you will find highlights from government investigations and a sampling of incidents reflecting current conditions at New Lisbon and Trenton Psychiatric Hospital as well as other mental health institutions, residences for persons with developmental disabilities, and juvenile facilities throughout the country. While the atrocities I've uncovered are too numerous to mention, I've selected a few that have occurred within the last ten to fifteen years. They depict murders, wrongful deaths, abuse of patients (physical, verbal, psychological, and sexual), misuse of drugs and restraints, neglect of duty, falsification of statements, hangings, scaldings, employee theft of government property, "codes of silence" imposed on potential whistleblowers, and other examples of blatant misconduct and violations of residents' rights.

To reprint each case or finding in its entirety would be cumbersome reading, so I have abbreviated and summarized the information. For people who wish to read the complete materials, links to selected full cases may be found at http://www.championpress.com/books/hardcandyebook.htm.

In reviewing these cases and investigations, you will often discover the mindset of the direct care workers, who work closest to the residents, and the civil servants who supervise them—those who, when caught, are often prone to cover up their negligence to save their own skins or ultimately find ingenious ways to better hide questionable incidents that might otherwise tarnish the state's image. Some, however, have not escaped the attention of the media, the local courts, or the federal government.

What follows dispels a public myth that what happened to us so long ago no longer happens in the present. Similar atrocities do live on, and they have already crept into the twenty-first century, producing more victims every day—with no letup in sight.

Appendix A

Abuses at
New Lisbon Developmental Center
into the Twenty-first Century

This appendix is divided into the following sections:

A.1   U.S. Department of Justice Investigation of New Lisbon

A summary of the Justice Department's 2002 investigation of abuses and violations of residents' rights at the facility.

A.2   Legal Cases Brought Against New Lisbon

Synopses of New Lisbon employees' appeals for disciplinary actions imposed upon them due to various charges of abuse and misconduct.

A.3   Other Violence and Death at New Lisbon

A few recent examples of assaults, homicides, and accidental deaths, due partly to inadequate supervision and staff training.

Appendix A.1

United States
Department of Justice
Investigation of
New Lisbon Developmental Center

In May and June 2002, the U.S. Department of Justice conducted two separate visits to the New Lisbon Developmental Center with expert consultants in various disciplines. Some of the abusive conditions and unconstitutional practices are summarized below. This section includes:

    A.1.1   Investigative Findings for New Lisbon

    A.1.2   Complaint and Settlement Agreement with New Lisbon

A.1.1 Investigative Findings for New Lisbon/2003

Note: The following is a summary/abridgment of the U.S. Department of Justice investigative findings letter. Some passages are quoted from the original text, while others are paraphrased to concisely convey the original content. The full letter may be found at http://www.championpress.com/books/hardcandyebook.htm. Please note that pseudonyms have been used to protect the identities of all New Lisbon residents.

On April 8, 2003, the U.S. Department of Justice (DOJ) sent a

35-page report to New Jersey Governor James E. McGreevey. This report detailed the findings of an investigation into the New Lisbon Developmental Center, which, at the time, housed about 600 residents ranging in age from 18 to 87. The report concluded that "there are numerous conditions and practices that violate the constitutional and statutory rights of New Lisbon residents." Serious deficiencies, sometimes resulting in injury or death to residents, were noted in the following areas:

I.   Protection from Harm
II.   Psychology and Behavioral Services, Psychiatric Services
III. Habilitation
IV.   Health Care
V.   Placing Residents in the Most Integrated Setting Appropriate to Their Needs

The report further warned that "in the unexpected event that the parties are unable to reach a resolution regarding our concerns . . . the Attorney General may initiate a lawsuit pursuant to CRIPA [Civil Rights of Institutionalized Persons Act], to correct deficiencies or to otherwise protect the rights of New Lisbon residents."

I. Protection from Harm

New Lisbon fails to protect its residents from harm or risk of harm. Documents reveal a high number of incidents which resulted in an injury to a resident. From June 2001 to April 2002, there were approximately 4,400 recorded incidents involving injuries to residents. From January 2001 to May 2002, there were over 500 moderate or major incidents, including resident-on-resident assaults, abuse or neglect, and deaths. In addition, in the five months preceding the first visit, it appears that incidents and injuries were increasing.

The following are some examples of numerous, and mostly preventable, significant injuries to residents:

- Paul, 4/5/02, needed four staples and three sutures to close a head wound after an altercation with a peer.

- Andy, 4/2/02, injured the side of his head due to self-injurious behavior, requiring five sutures.
- John, 3/26/02, suffered a laceration on his forehead underneath his helmet from an unknown source, requiring three staples.
- Edward, 3/26/02, suffered a right eye laceration from self-injurious behavior, requiring five sutures.
- Anthony, 3/25/02, fell out of his wheelchair and suffered abrasions on his finger, ear, head, a bruise on his back, a fractured thumb, and a fractured right clavicle.
- James, 3/17/02, needed five staples to close his head laceration due to an altercation with a peer.
- Richard, 3/13/02, was struck by a peer and needed seven staples to close the laceration on his head; his fifth finger was also fractured.
- Matthew, 2/9/02, a resident who is required to have constant supervision, was found by staff with a large shoe-shaped bruise on his chest.

Substantiated allegations of staff physical and verbal abuse against residents, as well as neglect, are ongoing. Below are a few examples demonstrating New Lisbon's systemic failure to protect its residents from harm:

- Robert, 4/17/02 - Staff member punched resident in the chest.
- Jennifer, 3/1/02 - Staff member called resident degrading and undignified names.
- Adam, 2/27/02 - Staff member forcefully pushed Adam into his room, causing him to collide with a chair on the other side of the room.
- Angela, 2/24/02 - Staff member was seen holding Angela's faceguard and shaking her head up and down while yelling at her.
- Wilson, 2/9/02 - Staff member intentionally smeared glue

on Wilson's face and failed to remove the glue before it dried; removal of the dry glue was "painful."

- Paula, 1/25/02 - Staff member slapped Paula in the face, pinched her, struck "the heal of her hand on Paula's forehead," and directed profanity at the resident and verbally threatened her.
- From January 1, 2002 through the time of the DOJ visit in early May 2002, over a half dozen New Lisbon staff were caught sleeping while on duty.

New Lisbon's internal investigations of abuse and misconduct are inadequate and their system is unable to correct problems that would prevent further recurrence of injury. In situations where allegations against staff are substantiated, recommended discipline and corrective action is virtually always more severe than that actually meted out. Reduced penalties may promote a culture where it is perceived that abuse and neglect are tolerated.

II. Psychology and Behavioral Services, Psychiatric Services

New Lisbon fails to provide adequate and appropriate psychological services to meet the needs of residents with behavior problems. This is a contributing factor to a significant number of the incidents and injuries discussed above, which often stem from residents' inadequately addressed problem behaviors, such as self-injurious behavior, aggression, and ingesting inedible objects.

A. Behavior Program Development

The current behavior programs do not contain all of the required components and do not comport with generally accepted practice. New Lisbon has problems with completing an adequate behavioral assessment, developing an effective behavior program, and monitoring the program's effectiveness. Many of these problems relate to the failure to collect consistent and meaningful data.

B. Restraints

New Lisbon residents have a right to be free from unreasonable use of restraints. From January 2001 to April 2002, there were over 1,000 instances of restraining a resident using four-point wrist and ankle restraints and, sometimes, a chest belt. (Note: Some figures were found to be underreported.) However, in an effort to reduce use of restraints in anticipation of the DOJ's scheduled visit, substitute restrictions such as psychotropic drugs may have taken the place of mechanical restraints, or mechanical restrictions may have been relabeled as "medical" devices. The use of medication to control behaviors does not comport with generally accepted practice.

New Lisbon also engages in manual contact by staff to restrict residents' movements. This is not being recorded properly (if at all). There is no data on the use of personal control and little monitoring, training, and examination of how to reduce its usage.

A number of New Lisbon residents wear large, padded helmets that appear heavy, uncomfortable, stigmatizing, and unduly restrictive. New Lisbon does not properly assess and monitor use of these helmets. The DOJ's medical consultant characterizes the helmets as "ponderous, sensory-limiting headgear" and added that such helmets are not commonly used for medical reasons, even for persons with severe seizures that cause sudden falls.

C. Psychiatric Services

New Lisbon provides inadequate and inappropriate psychiatric care and services to residents with mental illness. As of April 1, 2002, 377 residents with mental illness (about 62 percent of the population) received psychotropic medications. Over 100 of these residents were in need of review and reconsent for this medication. Over 30 percent of the residents on psychotropic drugs receive three or more medications. Most of the individuals on four and five medications have a history of high and chronic use of restraint as well as many incidents and injuries due to behavior problems. The use of polypharmacy without strong justification and intense oversight is inconsistent with currently accepted practice.

Behavioral and other data from behavior programs are not being used in developing psychiatric interventions. This places residents at risk for incorrect diagnoses, prescription of incorrect medications, and overmedication.

III. Habilitation

New Lisbon fails to provide its residents with adequate habilitation services and supports to make them fit for functioning in society. New Lisbon's individualized planning process fails to meet current professional standards. As a result, the institution does not provide residents with adequate opportunities to enhance their independence.

During the on-site visit, there was a low level of engagement among the residents, even though staffing was often adequate and the residents had the capability to learn. For example, it does not appear that the facility is offering many residents sufficient opportunities to work off-campus in more integrated settings even though many appear capable of benefiting from more stimulating work. Career development planning for such residents is virtually nonexistent. The lack of opportunity is problematic because many residents are not given enough to do during the day, and this can cause regression and exacerbate problematic behaviors due to boredom.

IV. Health Care

New Lisbon is failing to meet the individualized health care needs of some residents. This is especially true of residents with bowel obstructions and residents with nutritional and physical management concerns. Staff physicians appear to have more obligations than they can handle adequately given the large number of residents with special intensive needs, with high-risk health factors, and/or who are medically complex.

A. Bowel Obstructions

New Lisbon fails to provide needed health care for residents with serious gastrointestinal conditions that may lead to bowel perforation and even death. These conditions are preventable. In the most serious cases, the intestines can rupture, causing blood poisoning and, frequently, death. Such high-risk factors demand proactive and priority involvement from staff, but such involvement is often lacking.

These high-risk residents are frequently hospitalized for continuing care of acute medical problems developed while residing at New Lisbon. Most troubling, several residents have died recently following the rupture of their intestines related to the onset of a bowel obstruction. With appropriate care and monitoring, these emergencies should not have developed in the first place.

B. Neurology

New Lisbon fails to provide adequate neurologic health care or adequate time with neurologists to residents with seizure disorders, close to one-third of the total population.

C. Nutritional and Physical Management

New Lisbon fails to provide adequate nutritional and physical management services to meet the residents' needs. In the absence of proper support, New Lisbon residents with dysphagia (difficulty chewing or swallowing) may suffer pain and discomfort at virtually every meal and increase the risk of aspirating food, fluid, or saliva into the lungs. This can lead to aspiration pneumonia and even cause death. At the very least, these residents may suffer by simply choking while eating or drinking.

The facility has identified well over 300 residents—about half of the total population—on its specialized feeding protocol list. Nevertheless, from January 2, 2001 through May 11, 2002, there were 75 hospitalizations relating to nutritional and physical support issues.

Many practices and omissions of care were observed at mealtimes that place residents at risk of harm and fail to comport with generally accepted practices. For example, staff permitted residents to eat and/or drink at too fast a rate, or presented residents with or allowed residents to take large bites, or allowed residents to eat or drink in poor postural alignment. This placed the residents at risk of choking or aspiration. Also, staff served some residents food that did not match their diet orders.

New Lisbon staff do not use appropriate physical assistance supports for residents being transferred or repositioned. In many cases, handling techniques used by staff are not consistent with generally accepted practices and place residents at risk for injury or fractures.

D. Occupational and Physical Therapy; Communication Services

New Lisbon fails to provide its residents with appropriate occupational therapy, physical therapy, and communication services. In fact, some residents have never been given an evaluation in any of these areas. As a result of inadequate therapy, residents' limbs may weaken and become thinner; their hands may become contractured (curled or distorted due to shortening of a muscle or tendon); they may lose the ability to walk or ambulate; and, overall, their physical fitness may deteriorate, which compromises a host of important daily functions such as breathing, digestion, and maintaining strength to fight off illness.

E. Oral Hygiene

A number of residents have unacceptable oral hygiene as reported in their annual dental examinations.

V. Serving Persons in the Most Integrated Setting Appropriate to Their Needs

The Americans with Disabilities Act provides that: "A public entity shall administer services, programs, and activities in the most integrated setting appropriate to the needs of qualified individuals with disabilities." "The most integrated setting" is one "that enables individuals with disabilities to interact with nondisabled persons to the fullest extent possible."

New Lisbon has identified approximately 200 residents (about one-third of the total population) who are not currently living in the most integrated setting appropriate to their needs. The State of New Jersey instituted and funded a program designed to move residents into more integrated, community-based settings. New Lisbon selected 100 residents for inclusion in this program, but as of the DOJ's first visit, only 15 of those 100 had been placed in the community.

The pace and process for identifying residents who are appropriate for community placement are inadequate. Treating professionals routinely fail to adequately assess the appropriateness of placements at New Lisbon, fail to identify barriers to placement in the most integrated setting and/or include action plans to address such barriers, fail to ensure that residents and their families are informed of their right to live in the community, and fail to provide education and support to the families about the community options available or that could be created.

Minimal Remedial Measures

The Justice Department's letter of findings detailed numerous remedial measures for deficiencies in each of the above areas. The

DOJ indicated that New Jersey should, at minimum, implement these remedies promptly to protect the constitutional and statutory rights of New Lisbon residents.

For a summary of the complaint filed by the United States and corrective measures the State of New Jersey agreed to implement in its settlement with the Justice Department, please see the following appendix section.

U.S. Department of Justice, Civil Rights Division, Special Litigation Section, Documents and Publications, Investigative Findings, http://www.usdoj.gov/crt/split/documents/newlisbon_finding_letter.pdf (accessed June 13, 2005).

A.1.2 U.S. DEPARTMENT OF JUSTICE COMPLAINT AND SETTLEMENT AGREEMENT WITH NEW LISBON/2004

Note: The following are summaries/abridgments of the complaint and settlement agreement between the United States and the State of New Jersey et al. Some passages are quoted from the original text, while others are paraphrased to concisely convey the original content. The full complaint and settlement may be found at http://www.championpress.com/books/hardcandyebook.htm.

United States of America, Plaintiff

v.

The State of New Jersey;

James E. McGreevey, Governor of the State of New Jersey;

James Davy, Commissioner, Department of Human Services;

James W. Smith, Jr., Director, Division of Developmental Disabilities;

Jeffrey Schroeder, Chief Executive Officer, New Lisbon Developmental Center;

Defendants

Following the U.S. Department of Justice (DOJ) 2002 investigation of the New Lisbon Developmental Center (see previous appendix section), the United States filed a complaint against the State of New Jersey et al. on July 2, 2004. The complaint alleges that the defendants have demonstrated a pattern or practice of depriving residents of their rights protected by federal law and the Constitution. For example, defendants have failed and are continuing to fail to provide residents:

- reasonable safety and personal security;
- adequate behavioral training;
- freedom from undue or unreasonable restraint;
- adequate health care;
- adequate nutritional management;
- adequate physical, occupational, and speech therapy;
- adequate psychiatric care;
- adequate opportunities for placement in the community and the most integrated setting.

The settlement agreement, also filed on July 2, 2004, addresses the investigative findings and corrective measures set forth by the DOJ in its April 8, 2003, letter to the State of New Jersey and the ensuing complaint.

The settlement covers:

- Voluntary Measures Adopted and Implemented by State of New Jersey
- Efforts to Be Undertaken by State of New Jersey
- Compliance

Voluntary Measures Adopted and Implemented by State of New Jersey

New Jersey reports the New Lisbon Developmental Center has:

- reduced the incidents of resident-on-resident assaults;
- reduced the incidents of self-inflicted injuries;

- established its own Incident Response Unit to conduct investigations;
- trained its psychologists in behavior interventions;
- reduced the use of mechanical restraints;
- decreased the use of large, custom-padded helmets;
- increased the number of staff psychiatrists;
- provided psychiatric consultation for each resident with mental illness and will do so at least annually;
- reduced the number of residents on more than two seizure medications;
- set standards for maintenance of resident records to include information on the resident's care, medical treatment, training, protection, services, and supports; increased its rate of community placements of residents.

(Note: The United States makes no claims as to the validity of the above statements.)

Efforts to Be Undertaken by State of New Jersey

New Lisbon has agreed to implement the following in each area below. (Note: The use of the words "continue to" does not imply that the United States believes New Jersey has already been meeting residents' needs in each area.)

1. Protection from Harm
   a. Provide a reasonably safe and humane environment for all residents.
   b. Continue to ensure that all resident incidents and injuries are appropriately documented.
   c. Continue to ensure appropriate administrative review of all significant incidents, identify systemic issues, make recommendations to address those issues, and implement recommendations to prevent future occurrences.

d. Continue to implement adequate policies and procedures to conduct investigations and prepare reports.

e. Adequately train staff and independent investigators on how to conduct investigations and prepare reports.

f. Continue to develop a quality assurance program to track and analyze trends of incidents and injuries to help prevent future occurrences. Implement remedial measures to address patterns and trends that are identified.

g. Impose appropriate discipline for employees involved in substantiated cases of abuse or neglect, employees who fail to report abuse or neglect, and employees who provide materially false information during an investigation.

2. Psychological and Behavioral Services

a. Provide residents who have behavioral problems with adequate interdisciplinary behavioral assessments to determine the appropriate treatments and interventions.

b. Provide appropriate staff training and certification on how to implement, monitor, and document data for behavior programs.

c. Implement, monitor progress, and, when necessary, revise behavior plans.

3. Restraints

a. Ensure that all mechanical, physical, and chemical restraints are used only pursuant to professional judgment and are not used in lieu of appropriate behavior programs and interventions.

b. Continue to review each use of restraint to determine whether such restraint could have been avoided.

c. Monitor and track use of all restraints. Ensure that chemical restraints only replace mechanical restraints pursuant to professional judgment.

    d. Fully document and track the use of personal control (manual contact by staff to restrict resident's movement) and implement strategies to limit its use.

    e. Ensure that all helmets are the least intrusive possible and track their use.

4. Psychiatric Care

    a. Ensure that each resident with mental illness receives a psychiatric assessment.

    b. Ensure that each resident receiving psychotropic medication is assessed by a psychiatrist at least annually.

    c. Administer psychotropic medication only in accordance with accepted professional judgment and ensure that no resident receives psychotropic medication without an accompanying behavior program, unless otherwise indicated.

    d. Provide adequate behavioral and other data to psychiatrists to better facilitate treatment.

    e. Coordinate psychiatric services with staff psychologists.

    f. Have a qualified professional monitor the effectiveness of all psychiatric treatments and psychotropic medications on a quarterly basis. Revise treatments when appropriate.

5. Habilitation

    a. Have interdisciplinary teams identify needs and develop strategies for training, services, and supports to make residents fit for functioning in society.

    b. Provide appropriate staff training and certification on how to implement and monitor such plans.

    c. Provide appropriate assessment of all residents' vocational and/or day programming needs. Incorporate assessments into each resident's plan.

d. Provide residents with day programming or vocation/employment opportunities to meet individual needs.

e. Provide individualized habilitation and develop additional training and behavior programs for residents.

6. Health Care

   a. Provide routine, chronic, and emergency seizure management to all individuals with seizure disorders.

   b. Continue to ensure that all residents with seizure disorders have assessments, implemented plans of care, and ongoing monitoring.

   c. Place an emphasis on providing assessments and treatments for residents with high-risk conditions.

   d. Provide ongoing follow-up and monitoring of the plan. Revise the plan as needed.

   e. Continue to employ sufficient physicians to meet residents' needs.

7. Nutritional and Physical Management and Therapy Services

   a. Implement policies and protocols to provide each resident with appropriate nutritional and physical management.

   b. Continue to identify residents with nutritional management problems, including difficulty swallowing, chewing, or retaining food and/or liquid.

   c. Continue to have an interdisciplinary team comprehensively assess each resident's nutritional management needs.

   d. Continue to address each resident's nutritional management needs and provide sufficient mealtime supports.

   e. Develop and implement a system to monitor residents with nutritional management difficulties to ensure staff is implementing and modifying plans as necessary.

    f. Continue to provide each resident with appropriate physical and occupational therapy services, communication services, and physical management. This includes appropriate staff training, certification, and monitoring on safe and proper handling/transfer techniques.

8. Community Placement

    a. Ensure that each resident is served in the most integrated setting appropriate for his needs, in accordance with the Americans with Disabilities Act.

    b. Provide community placement for residents, when appropriate, based on resident assessment, when transfer to a less restrictive setting is not opposed by the resident, and when placement can be reasonably accommodated based on the State's resources.

Compliance

A compliance monitor has been appointed to tour New Lisbon every six months and to monitor and report on New Jersey's substantial compliance or noncompliance with all agreement provisions outlined above. The State of New Jersey shall bear the cost of the monitor and up to four independent consultants chosen by the monitor.

If the United States determines New Jersey is in noncompliance with this agreement and has cause to believe that such noncompliance threatens the immediate health and safety of the residents, the United States shall immediately notify the State and compliance monitor of which provisions have been violated and the facts upon which the allegation is based. The United States shall then have the right to move to reopen or reinstate this litigation.

If New Jersey has fully complied with all above provisions, the agreement will terminate at the end of four years and the United States agrees not to reopen the lawsuit on any issue addressed in the findings letter dated April 8, 2003.

U.S. Department of Justice, Civil Rights Division, Special Litigation Section, Documents and Publications, Complaints filed in U.S. District Court, http://www.usdoj.gov/crt/split/documents/complaint_new_lisbon.pdf (accessed July 2, 2005), and Settlements and Court Decisions, http://www.usdoj.gov/crt/split/documents/settlement_new_lisbon.pdf (accessed June 13, 2005).

LEGAL CASES BROUGHT AGAINST NEW LISBON DEVELOPMENTAL CENTER

THE FOLLOWING ARE synopses of appeals brought by New Lisbon employees against the institution. The employees appealed disciplinary actions imposed upon them due to various charges of abuse and misconduct. These cases provide some insight into the alleged inability of New Lisbon and other state facilities to keep their residents safe.

Note: The following are summaries/abridgments of each case. Some passages are quoted from the original text, while others are paraphrased to concisely convey the original content. Links to selected full cases may be found at http://www.championpress.com/books/hardcandyebook.htm.

A.2.1 Shower Scalding and Resident Abuse/1991

Paula Witcher, Appellant

v.

New Lisbon Developmental Center, Respondent

Office of Administrative Law Docket No. CSV 768-91
Initial Decision: July 26, 1991

Before Joseph F. Fidler, Administrative Law Judge
Final Agency Decision: September 23, 1991

Paula Witcher appealed her termination as a cottage training technician at New Lisbon Developmental Center on charges of physically abusing a resident—specifically, burning the resident with hot water.

R.C. was a middle-aged man with a history of mental retardation and a seizure disorder. On the day of the incident in Yucca Cottage, R.C. became agitated and was twice sent out of the day room by Witcher when he threw his colostomy bag and soiled himself. Witcher then took R.C. to the shower room.

A supervisor heard R.C. yelling, and then observed that R.C.'s body was red and that R.C. was rubbing his penis and his face. According to the supervisor, every time R.C. rubbed his penis, some skin rubbed off and the injured area became rawer and rawer. Witcher told the supervisor that R.C. had taken the shower hose and turned it on himself when she walked away to get a washcloth. Witcher said that it was common for R.C. to scream, so she didn't respond at first.

The nurse on duty testified that, within 15 minutes, R.C.'s skin on his head, chest, penis, and thigh started to slough off. R.C. was taken to a burn center where he was determined to have second-degree burns over 20 percent of his body. R.C. was unable to discuss the incident at first, but eventually indicated that he had been "burned" "in the shower" by a "woman" with a blue or black hose.

A plumber tested the system the following day and testified that the shower hoses, which were beige in color, could not be adjusted for hot or cold. Shower water was automatically adjusted and tempered by two backup systems, a mixing valve and another safety valve. The temperature tested properly at 104 degrees. A nearby janitor's closet also had a hose, which was black. The janitor's hose had a manual adjustment to add cold water and, when no cold water was turned on, tested at 140 degrees. Witcher acknowledged she had access to the locked janitor's closet.

The judge determined the following: Witcher's version of events was inherently not credible as well as inconsistent with other testimony and with common experience. For R.C. to burn himself with the shower hose, both safety systems would need to fail at the same time. But they had never failed in the past and were working properly when tested immediately after the incident. On the other hand, it would be relatively simple to cause burns with untempered water from the janitor's closet hose. If no cold water had been turned on to mix with the hot, it would be apparent that Witcher had, at best, a reckless disregard for the resident's safety. The decision to remove Witcher from her position was affirmed.

Witcher v. New Lisbon Developmental Center, New Jersey Administrative Reports, Volume 91, Second Edition (Civil Service), p. 30.

A.2.2 Employee Sleeping While on Duty/2001

Curstina Keesee, Appellant

v.

New Lisbon Developmental Center, Department of Human Services, Respondent

Office of Administrative Law Docket No. CSV 364-00
Initial Decision: July 26, 2001
Before Joseph Lavery, Administrative Law Judge
Final Agency Decision: September 25, 2001

Curstina Keesee, a cottage training technician at New Lisbon Developmental Center, appealed her suspension on charges of sleeping while on duty. On June 12, 1997, she was working from 11:30 p.m. to 8:00 a.m. at Dogwood Cottage, which housed residents who were hyperactive and had behavior problems. At approximately

6:30 a.m., Keesee was in a recliner that had been taken from the nearby lounge and placed in the hallway to observe Side 1 of the cottage. She was covered to her neck with a blanket or bedspread.

Thelma E. Douglas, the head cottage training supervisor for Dogwood Cottage, arrived at the cottage and was able to see Keesee from down the hallway. The supervisor concluded that Keesee was asleep.

Douglas did not go directly to Keesee, but ordered Keesee's immediate superior, Doris Dresslove, to go down the hallway, approximately 22 feet from the office, and awaken Keesee. Although Keesee disputed what followed, Dresslove testified that she walked down the hall toward Keesee and called Keesee's name two or three times before Keesee, startled, dropped the covering bedspread. Dresslove acknowledged that her voice was naturally low in tone and volume, and that the air blowers overhead were loud.

Dresslove submitted a memo to Douglas describing the event, and Douglas subsequently charged that Keesee had been asleep on duty, which resulted in the suspension.

Keesee maintained that she was never asleep and insisted that at no time after 6:00 a.m. did her supervisor, Dresslove, come down the hall and call to her, startling her, and causing her to drop the blanket that covered her. Keesee explained that it was common practice for employees to remove recliners from the lounge. She also said she had been cold and therefore covered herself with a blanket.

Keesee further maintained that Douglas could not have observed her face from her angle and from 22 feet distant down the hallway, and that Dresslove had not seen Keesee's eyes closed.

The judge concluded that Keesee was not credible in her adamant denial that Dresslove had approached her at all. By comparison, Dresslove, supported by the testimony of her supervisor, was fully believable. Applying the legal maxim of false in one, false in all, it could be concluded that Keesee was not truthful in denying that she slept.

Nonetheless, the burden of proof that Keesee had been asleep had not been met since Dresslove and Douglas had not seen Keesee's eyes closed at any time. Consequently, the charges were dismissed.

Rutgers University School of Law-Camden, New Jersey Administrative Law Decisions, Initial Decision, http://lawlibrary.rutgers.edu/oal/html/initial/csv364-00_1.html (accessed August 18, 2005), and Final Agency Decision, http://lawlibrary.rutgers.edu/oal/final/csv364-00.pdf (accessed August 18, 2005).

A.2.3 Sleeping on the Job; Endangering Residents; Assaulting Resident and Coworker/2001

Patrick Stout, Appellant

v.

New Lisbon Developmental Center, Respondent

Office of Administrative Law Docket Nos. CSV 6905-00 and
   CSV 8695-00 (consolidated)
Initial Decision: September 26, 2001
Before Beatrice S. Tylutki, Administrative Law Judge
Final Agency Decision: November 8, 2001

Patrick Stout appealed his removal from his position as human service assistant at Quince Cottage at New Lisbon Developmental Center. He was charged with leaving his assigned work area without permission, creating a danger to persons, and sleeping while on duty. In a separate incident, he was also charged with the physical and verbal abuse of an employee and the physical abuse of a resident.

There were approximately 44 residents in Quince Cottage and most were severely or profoundly retarded. All of the residents needed supervision on a 24-hour basis. On two occasions, Stout left his assigned work area without permission for a significant period of time. On the second occasion, Stout fell asleep during a break and failed to take two residents to the nurse's station for medication at their appointed time.

On a third occasion, Stout got into an argument with a fellow human service assistant. Despite being told by a supervisor to stop the argument, Stout continued and struck his coworker in the face. Resident A.L. was standing next to the coworker during this argument. A.L. was described as nonverbal and sometimes shook his fists at a person, but he was not confrontational. A.L. could be unsteady and he sometimes fell. The supervisor said that Stout hit and knocked A.L. down to the floor in the process of hitting the coworker, which implied that Stout also hit A.L. The supervisor also stated that A.L. was lying on the floor with his hand on his stomach. Another employee gave inconsistent statements about whether Stout hit the resident.

The judge found the following: Stout physically abused a coworker. While there was no convincing proof that Stout hit resident A.L., Stout's action placed A.L. within a zone of danger where there was an increased potential for injury. Since Stout was aware that A.L. was unsteady on his feet and standing next to the coworker, Stout's action was a contributing factor to A.L.'s fall. Stout's complete disregard for the proper duty of care due to A.L. constituted resident abuse.

The judge further found that the two occasions Stout was absent for significant periods of time without notice showed a pattern of disregard for the needs of residents.

New Lisbon's decision to remove Stout from his position was affirmed.

Rutgers University School of Law-Camden, New Jersey Administrative Law Decisions, Initial Decision, http://lawlibrary.rutgers.edu/oal/html/initial/ csv6905-00_1.html (accessed August 18, 2005), and Final Agency Decision, http://lawlibrary.rutgers.edu/oal/final/csv6905-00.pdf (accessed August 18, 2005).

A.2.4 Physical Contact Causing Resident's Death; Falsifying Statements/2002

Charles Popovich, Appellant

v.

New Jersey Department of Human Services, New Lisbon
Developmental Center, Respondent

Office of Administrative Law Docket No. CSV 100-02
Initial Decision: August 7, 2002
Before Robert S. Miller, Administrative Law Judge
Final Agency Decision: September 10, 2002

Charles Popovich appealed his removal from his position at New Lisbon Developmental Center following charges of: (1) inappropriate physical contact, (2) violation of policy or procedure, and (3) falsification and/or intentional misstatement of material fact.

Popovich worked as a habilitation plan coordinator in Birch Cottage. His job did not include direct supervision of residents. His duties were primarily administrative in nature. However, for several weeks prior to June 27, 2001, he and all other staff members at New Lisbon had been working under unusually stressful conditions because federal inspectors had criticized the facility for inadequate staffing and had either withdrawn federal funds or had threatened to do so. He and most other staff had been working 30 or more hours of overtime each week.

On June 27, 2001, Popovich noticed that a resident, J.L., was causing a disturbance by taking the sodas of other residents. No direct care staff were on the scene, so Popovich decided to intervene. He twice remonstrated J.L. and told him he would have to stop the behavior, but J.L. continued. When Popovich began to approach J.L. for the third time, J.L. ran out of the room and toward the exit leading to the backyard.

Popovich gave chase, believing that J.L. was now presenting a danger to himself and to others. J.L. had a medical condition wherein he could become seriously ill if he drank a great deal of liquids. Further, the fence separating the backyard of the cottage from the roadway running through the grounds was only about 3½ feet high and could easily have been climbed by J.L.

Popovich caught up with J.L. and placed his hands on J.L.'s right shoulder and left arm. As Popovich struggled to control J.L., J.L. slipped and fell backward, the back of his head striking the tile floor and rendering him unconscious. Popovich immediately called for assistance, which soon arrived, but J.L. could not be revived and was pronounced dead a few minutes later.

Later that day and the following day, Popovich gave several statements. Each of these omitted the fact that he'd had physical contact, and struggled, with J.L. before J.L. fell backward to the floor. Popovich declared only that J.L. ran around the corner "and slipped backward and hit his head on the floor."

Popovich subsequently told the administration that he "had not been entirely forthright in his initial interview," especially by implying that he had not touched or made physical contact with J.L. He said he *had* put his hands on J.L., that J.L. was "startled," and that J.L. fell backward before Popovich could catch him. Popovich added that he believed at the time that J.L. "was a danger to himself and to others."

The first two charges—inappropriate physical contact and violation of policy or procedure—both refer to Popovich's attempt to stop J.L. as he was running down the corridor toward the backyard and to bring him under control. The judge concluded that circumstances at that time were "near chaotic," and J.L. appeared to be "a danger to himself and to others." Thus, Popovich's belief that an emergency situation existed was reasonable and, accordingly, the physical contact Popovich made with J.L. was neither inappropriate nor in violation of New Lisbon's policy and procedures.

However, on the third charge—falsification and/or intentional misstatement of material fact—the judge concluded that Popovich deliberately "falsified" his account of what had occurred by intentionally failing to mention the crucial factor of the struggle that had occurred between them. The judge therefore concluded that the appropriate penalty in this matter was a suspension of three months without pay.

Rutgers University School of Law-Camden, New Jersey Administrative Law Decisions, Initial Decision, http://lawlibrary.rutgers.edu/oal/word/initial/ csv00100-02_1.doc (accessed August 18, 2005), and Final Agency Decision, http://lawlibrary.rutgers.edu/oal/final/csv100-02.pdf (accessed August 18, 2005).

A.2.5 Theft; Falsification; Conduct Unbecoming a Public Employee/1997

Richard J. Petrizzi, Appellant

v.

New Lisbon Developmental Center, Department of Human Services, Respondent

Office of Administrative Law Docket No. CSV 2204-97
Initial Decision: December 17, 1997
Before Joseph Lavery, Administrative Law Judge
Final Agency Decision: not posted

Richard J. Petrizzi appealed his termination as locksmith at New Lisbon Developmental Center on charges of attempted theft, falsification, and conduct unbecoming a public employee. Petrizzi was responsible for all the locks and hardware in operation at New Lisbon.

Mr. Petrizzi's supervisor, L. Vaughn Lewis, became suspicious of the whereabouts of a code machine used for duplicating keys. Lewis ordered his assistant to find out from Petrizzi where the machine was. Petrizzi first said that the machine was locked in a closet for security. But the next day, when asked again, Petrizzi confessed that he had taken the code machine from New Lisbon to use in his private locksmith business and that he knew doing so was wrong.

However, when the Human Services Police Department (HSPD) investigated a week later, Petrizzi denied all his earlier statements and produced for the officer both New Lisbon's machine and another code machine that was not state property, which Petrizzi said he personally owned. He claimed he had bought the second code machine before the incident, but could not produce a receipt or date. He said he made the purchase from a mail-order company, the name of which he could not remember.

The HSPD officer closed out the case, but the New Lisbon administration believed there were sufficient grounds to terminate Petrizzi.

The judge found that Petrizzi had taken the code machine from New Lisbon for use in his private business and that, after being discovered but before the police investigation, Petrizzi obtained another code machine that he claimed to have been using instead.

The judge affirmed Petrizzi's termination and further stated that Petrizzi had been employed in a position imbued with the need for trust and reliability. A locksmith in an institution responsible for the care and protection of mentally impaired residents carried with it a responsibility no less important, and arguably more crucial, than even personal custody. These acts irreparably weakened the fundamental, threshold level of trust that is imperative in an institutional locksmith.

Rutgers University School of Law-Camden, New Jersey Administrative Law Decisions, Initial Decision, http://lawlibrary.rutgers.edu/oal/html/initial/csv2204-97.html (accessed August 18, 2005).

APPENDIX A.2

A.2.6 Neglect of Duty; Resident Freezes to Death/1996

Joyce Artemus, Appellant

v.

Department of Human Services, New Lisbon Developmental Center, Respondent

Office of Administrative Law Docket No. CSV 8874-95
Initial Decision: July 9, 1996
Before Kathryn A. Clark, Administrative Law Judge
Final Agency Decision: August 6, 1996

Joyce Artemus appealed her removal from her position as cottage training technician at New Lisbon Developmental Center on charges of (1) neglect of duty and willful failure to monitor a resident under her care, (2) leaving her assigned work area without permission, creating a danger to residents, and (3) intentional misstatement of material facts.

R.S. was a 51-year-old resident who had just transferred from Fern Cottage to Yucca Cottage. He was known to try to leave the building and was not aware of his environment. At some point midday on January 22, 1995, while assigned to Artemus's care, R.S. wandered off from Yucca Cottage. He was found that evening, on the other side of the campus, frozen to death.

Artemus claimed she had taken lunch from 1:00 to 1:30 and assigned her group to another coworker, which the coworker denied. Artemus further claimed that she saw R.S. occasionally when she came back from lunch. A supervisor admitted that, at 5:15 p.m., after R.S. was known to be missing, she filled out an attendance sheet on behalf of Artemus, claiming Artemus's lunch break had been 1:00 to 1:30 (the supervisor was later suspended for this action). Artemus testified she had left the grounds to pick up lunch for herself and several other coworkers, but when no one admitted to placing a lunch order with her, she indicated she had gotten only her own lunch.

The judge made the following findings: Artemus was more than likely away from the New Lisbon grounds from about 12:30 to 2:30, she did not fill in the time on her attendance sheet, and she neglected her duty to arrange for the care of residents under her charge when she was away from her post. For approximately two hours Artemus neglected to account for R.S., who was in her care, thereby allowing him to wander off from Yucca Cottage. Artemus falsely stated that she had assigned the care of R.S. to another co-worker, and these actions were intended to cover for Artemus's neglect of duty.

The decision to remove Artemus from her position at New Lisbon was affirmed.

Artemus v. Department of Human Services, New Lisbon Developmental Center, New Jersey Administrative Reports, Volume 96, Second Edition (Civil Service), p. 767.

A.2.7 Duty Neglect and Striking Resident/1999

Elizabeth Cox, Appellant

v.

New Lisbon Developmental Center, Department of Human Services, Respondent

Office of Administrative Law Docket No. CSV 2091-99
Initial Decision: August 6, 1999
Before John R. Tassini, Administrative Law Judge
Final Agency Decision: September 21, 1999

Elizabeth Cox, a cottage training technician in Birch Cottage at New Lisbon Developmental Center, was charged with slapping (abusing) a resident who was more than 60 years old. Cox's disciplinary history included several instances of chronic and excessive absenteeism, absence from work without permission, and abuse of sick leave.

The day of the incident, Cox was assigned to monitor resident S.S. for two hours after he ate, since he was at risk of choking. However, S.S. did not like to be monitored and he sometimes left the cottage and hid from the staff. Cox failed to keep an eye on S.S. after the meal.

Steven Shauger, a vendor working in the building, observed Cox when she was looking for S.S. and later when she found the resident. Shauger testified that Cox was "frantic" and yelled at S.S., and that Cox then slapped the back of S.S.'s head.

S.S. was questioned on various occasions and provided conflicting statements that he had been hit, had not been hit, and didn't want to talk about the matter. A staff psychologist reported that "as a result of [S.S.'s] level of cognitive development paired with his psychiatric symptoms, his ability to accurately report information . . . is . . . highly unreliable."

The judge made the following findings: Cox intentionally slapped S.S., although not hard enough to cause injury. New Lisbon's residents suffered from a range of mental and/or psychological disabilities and it was reasonably foreseeable that they sometimes would be difficult, exasperating, and even dangerous for the staff who were charged with their direct monitoring and care. When confronted with such a resident's intractability and/or uncooperative behavior, a staff member must carefully control his or her own emotions and carefully control the resident to avoid harm. Striking such a resident is like striking a young child and is dangerous. When, as here, the striking was intentional, it was inexcusable and cause for removal.

The judge dismissed Cox's appeal and ordered her removed from her position at New Lisbon.

Rutgers University School of Law-Camden, New Jersey Administrative Law Decisions, Initial Decision, http://lawlibrary.rutgers.edu/oal/html/initial/csv2091-99_1.html (accessed August 18, 2005), and Final Agency Decision, http://lawlibrary.rutgers.edu/oal/final/csv02091-99.pdf (accessed August 18, 2005).

A.2.8 Physical Abuse of Residents; Denial of Privacy/2001

Nathan Johnston, Appellant

v.

New Lisbon Developmental Center, Respondent

Office of Administrative Law Docket No. CSV 2854-00
Initial Decision: July 30, 2001
Before M. Kathleen Duncan, Administrative Law Judge
Final Agency Decision: September 18, 2001

Nathan Johnston appealed his removal from his position as cottage training technician at New Lisbon Developmental Center after charges of physically abusing residents. He was seen striking two residents in the chest with a closed fist because they would not put on their clothing for him. Officials determined that not only was it abusive to strike residents, it was equally abusive to deny residents of their dignity and respect by having them dress in a clothing room without benefit of privacy.

Johnston was also charged with insubordination and falsification, and he failed to appear at both an intradepartmental hearing and a settlement conference. His appeal was dismissed.

Rutgers University School of Law-Camden, New Jersey Administrative Law Decisions, Initial Decision, http://lawlibrary.rutgers.edu/oal/html/initial/csv2854-00_1.html (accessed August 18, 2005), and Final Agency Decision, http://lawlibrary.rutgers.edu/oal/final/csv2854-00.pdf (accessed August 18, 2005).

A.2.9 Employee and Institutional Neglect in Resident's Drowning/1993

Pamela Castillo, Petitioner

v.

New Lisbon Developmental Center, Respondent

Office of Administrative Law Docket No. CSV 1763-92
Initial Decision: November 5, 1993
Before John R. Futey, Administrative Law Judge
Final Agency Decision: December 21, 1993

Pamela Castillo appealed her 60-day suspension as a direct care worker at New Lisbon Developmental Center. She was charged with negligence in the performance of her duties during events surrounding the drowning death of a resident.

During Labor Day weekend 1991, a group of 25 residents were taken on a picnic to Crowley's Landing on the Mullica River. The residents were from Fern Cottage, a locked unit housing people with behavioral problems who were not capable of supervising themselves. For example, many could not identify environmental hazards. The staff consisted of Karen Roberts, the cottage supervisor who organized the trip, and five direct care workers, including Castillo.

L.R. was a 32-year-old male who had moderate mental retardation with an age equivalent of five years old. He also suffered from a convulsive grand mal seizure disorder. A New Lisbon staff physician later testified that L.R. could not swim without appropriate supervision and safeguards to protect him. However, the physician never told any of L.R.'s staff attendants of any limitations or L.R.'s conditions regarding his medical deficiencies.

At some point during the picnic, Roberts announced that residents could enter the water. L.R., instead of staying near the group, went out into deep water where he was drawn into strong currents and drowned. An autopsy revealed the drowning may have been accompanied by an epileptic seizure.

During the commotion, Roberts ordered Castillo to call New Lisbon regarding the emergency. Castillo immediately shouted to other staff members to keep an eye on the residents she was supervising while she made the phone call. Upon returning, she found that one of her residents had gone into the shallow water. Her failure to supervise this resident was the basis for the negligence charge and her suspension.

Pamela Castillo had been employed at New Lisbon for five years and had gone on numerous field trips, to this location and others, where residents had been allowed in the water. She had never received any counseling or orientation regarding field trips, was never trained regarding her responsibilities on trips, and was never told which trips were dangerous. In most of those previous trips, Karen Roberts was in charge. Castillo felt that if a supervisor was at or in the water and authorized residents' entry, then it was okay.

The judge found that Castillo had acted responsibly during the emergency in relying upon other staff personnel to assume temporary supervision of her residents. Castillo's suspension was reversed.

The judge also made numerous findings with regard to New Lisbon's policies and past practices on supervising residents during outings:

(1) At the time of the drowning, New Lisbon had no clear-cut, written policy setting resident-to-staff ratios for water activities. The ratio that day was five residents to one chaperone. New Lisbon has since set a policy of three to one for water-related activities and four to one for other activities.

(2) Crowley's Landing was a totally inappropriate outing site for residents like those of Fern Cottage. It had inadequate fencing along the shoreline, murky water that impeded visibility, and uncertain river currents that constituted serious hazards.

(3) Karen Roberts, the supervisor and trip coordinator, encouraged and authorized swimming, even though New Lisbon prohib-

ited it. Her role in this entire process, and the resulting disaster, was at the heart of the problem. By disregarding the prohibition, she not only subjected residents and staff to potential harm, but exposed staff members to liability. She was the catalyst of a course of conduct for which a disaster was bound to happen.

(4) Unauthorized water activities had become commonplace at many outings. New Lisbon did nothing to prohibit such activity or punish offenders until the death of L.R. The institution's tacit acquiescence was irresponsible, misguided, and contrary to the best interests of all its residents—and this was a major contributing factor to this tragic event. New Lisbon virtually turned its back and closed its eyes and, as a result, knew or should have known that such unauthorized activity took place on a recurring basis. New Lisbon was accountable to its residents as well as its own employees, who were left stranded in the aftermath of the drowning of L.R. The events that transpired on that date represented a time bomb waiting for a place to happen.

Castillo v. New Lisbon Developmental Center, New Jersey Administrative Reports, Volume 94, Second Edition (Civil Service), p. 150.

Appendix A.3

Other Violence and Death at New Lisbon Developmental Center

Overall, the number of violent attacks reported at [New Jersey] developmental centers has been climbing. An examination of state records found reported assaults more than doubled in the past five years, to 275 such cases in 2001. New Lisbon . . . had 1,100 reported episodes of assault, abuse and suicide attempts since 1995—more than any other institution in the state.

Star-Ledger, Newark, New Jersey
November 4, 2002

Note: The following information is taken from several articles in New Jersey's Times of Trenton, Star-Ledger, and Courier-Post. Detailed references may be found at the end of this appendix section.

WHAT HAPPENS WHEN disabled people with violent tendencies live under poorly supervised, crowded conditions with other disabled people who are unable to defend themselves? The results can be dangerous and, indeed, often deadly. A representative of New Jersey Protection and Advocacy, Inc., a legal watchdog agency for the disabled, said quite simply, "There are assaults every day."[1]

The U.S. Centers for Medicare and Medicaid Services threatened to withhold federal funding to New Lisbon. It reported in June 2002 that the facility "failed to comply with the most fundamental protection and failed to take the necessary steps to protect" its residents.[2]

According to New Jersey's *Star-Ledger*, "records show that younger and more violent people—who also happen to be retarded—are coming through the criminal courts into institutions like New Lisbon. An analysis done by the state's non-partisan Office of Legislative Services . . . found that judges are sentencing mentally retarded felons to developmental centers for fear they would be targets for abuse in state prisons. Between 1999 and 2001, judges ordered at least 10 offenders—whose crimes included homicide and drug possession—into state institutions . . . Six were sent to . . . New Lisbon."[3]

Lack of supervision and staff training are contributing factors in assaults, homicides, and accidental deaths. The ratio of staff to residents is a particular problem, and staffing levels can fall dangerously low during weekends and, especially, overnight.

Below are some examples of what can happen when the wrong ingredients come together at the wrong time.

A.3.1 Resident Beaten to Death by Roommate/2001

In January 2001, Richard Fort, a 46-year-old New Lisbon resident, was found bloody and unconscious under his bed. He died two weeks later of a head injury due to blunt-force trauma (no weapon was believed to have been used).

Fort had been brutally beaten by his roommate, 26-year-old Ronald Watts, who was apparently retaliating for an incident between the two men the day before. Watts had a long history of aggression, including the assault of an employee at one of two state psychiatric hospitals where he resided before New Lisbon. It is unknown how Watts, who had been diagnosed with "intermittent explosive disorder," was allowed to share a room with another resident.

Watts was charged with murder, but was later found not competent to stand trial; the charges were dismissed and he was sent to a state hospital. Two employees were suspended for neglect of duty.

A.3.2 Resident Strangled in His Bed/2001

In October 2001, Norman Alfred Gifford, a 28-year-old New Lisbon resident, was strangled to death while sleeping—the night before he was to move to another facility closer to his family. Another resident, Frank Lippincott, was charged with murder. Both men were residents of Grass Cottage, a locked unit reported to have more injuries, accidents, assaults, and other incidents than any other unit at New Lisbon.

Lippincott, 37, had a history of violence during his 22 years of living in institutions. He had been found guilty of assault in 1994 and 1996, and was indicted for arson in 1998. He was at New Lisbon to serve his sentence of five years' probation. Lippincott was deemed not competent to stand trial; the murder charges were dismissed and the judge ordered Lippincott recommitted to a state institution.

A.3.3 Attempted Sexual Assault by Resident/1998

In April 1998, Tywan Eckols, a 21-year-old New Lisbon resident, was charged with attempted sexual assault on a female employee. He had been housed in a unit with 35 other residents with criminal backgrounds.

Eckols had been charged with sexual assault on three previous occasions in 1994 and 1995, though he was deemed not competent to stand trial all three times. For the New Lisbon assault, state psychiatrists determined he was competent to face prosecution.

A.3.4 Resident Suffocates in Police Car/1993

In July 1993, John Episcopo, a 28-year-old New Lisbon resident, had a seizure and suffocated while "accidentally locked" in the back of an unventilated police car. His body was found 12 hours after he had been given permission to take a walk on the institution's grounds. He was considered "high functioning" and was known to like to "hide." Investigators don't know how long Episcopo had been inside the car, but he had removed his clothes in an effort to escape the July heat, and there was evidence he had struggled to get out.

Two Human Services police officers had been assigned to New Lisbon, but both had the weekend off. A spokesperson said the Human Services police were short staffed and didn't have enough people to cover evenings and weekends.

Episcopo had moved to New Lisbon two years earlier because his previous home, the Johnstone Training Center, was closed by the State.

This was the sixth death in a year at a New Jersey facility for the mentally retarded. The previous summer, a New Lisbon resident drowned during an outing (see Appendix A.2.9/Employee and Institutional Neglect in Resident's Drowning/1993) and another was killed in a bus accident. And three North Princeton Developmental Center residents died: two were struck by buses on institution grounds and one choked to death.

A.3.5 Resident Killed by Van Outside Grounds/2001

In March 2001, a New Lisbon resident in his late 30s was struck and killed by a van while walking along the side of a road. Apparently, he had walked away from the institution's grounds unnoticed. The resident was on Route 72, about one mile from New Lisbon, at 8:15 p.m., when he stepped into the path of the van and was instantly killed.

ENDNOTES FOR APPENDIX A.3

1. Susan K. Livio and Ted Sherman, "Living under a violent shadow," *Star-Ledger* (Newark, NJ), November 4, 2002: 1.

2. Ibid.

3. Ibid.

REFERENCES FOR APPENDIX A.3

Carol Comegno, "Retarded man won't face trial for murder," *Courier-Post* (Cherry Hill, NJ), June 27, 2003.

Beth E. Fand, "Man charged with killing roommate," *Times of Trenton* (Trenton, NJ), February 2, 2001: A3.

Donna Leusner, "Retarded man dies trapped in police car," *Star-Ledger* (Newark, NJ), July 27, 1993.

Susan K. Livio, "Resident is accused in New Lisbon killing," *Star-Ledger* (Newark, NJ), November 10, 2001: 15.

Livio and Sherman, "Living under a violent shadow."

Brian T. Murray, "Mentally retarded man faces sex-attack charge," *Star-Ledger* (Newark, NJ), May 9, 1998: 8.

"Van strikes, kills man," *Times of Trenton* (Trenton, NJ), March 25, 2001: A4.

APPENDIX B

ABUSES AT
TRENTON PSYCHIATRIC HOSPITAL
INTO THE TWENTY-FIRST CENTURY

THE FOLLOWING ARE synopses of appeals brought by Trenton Psychiatric Hospital employees against the hospital. The employees appealed disciplinary actions imposed upon them due to various charges of misconduct. These cases provide some insight into the alleged inability of Trenton and other state hospitals to keep their patients safe.

Note: The following are summaries/abridgments of each case. Some passages are quoted from the original text, while others are paraphrased to concisely convey the original content. Links to selected full cases may be found at http://www.championpress.com/books/hardcandyebook.htm.

B.1 Abuse of Patient Causing Broken Arm; Neglect of Duty/2001

Shawn Copeland, Appellant

v.

Trenton Psychiatric Hospital, Human Services, Respondent

Office of Administrative Law Docket No. CSV 4282-00
Initial Decision: August 13, 2001
Before M. Kathleen Duncan, Administrative Law Judge
Final Agency Decision: September 25, 2001

Shawn Copeland appealed his removal as a human services assistant at Trenton Psychiatric Hospital when he was charged with neglect of duty and physical and mental abuse of a patient.

Copeland had been assigned to supervise activities in the day room when R.G., a combative and aggressive female patient, approached him. Another patient, J.Z., witnessed the incident and testified that Copeland swatted R.G. with a towel, trying to get her to sit down, and said in a loud, angry voice, "I've had enough of you." Copeland then pushed R.G. down "quite hard" between two chairs. The chairs separated and R.G. fell to the floor, after which she said that her arm hurt. Copeland did not report the incident and failed to fill out an incident report.

The following morning, another employee noticed that R.G.'s left arm was very swollen, at which time R.G. was taken to an emergency room and diagnosed with a fracture.

Copeland testified that all he did when R.G. became abusive was take her hands and hold them down to her sides. Copeland said he never had a towel and R.G. never fell or said that her arm hurt. He acknowledged that, if R.G. had fallen, he would have had an obligation to report it right away. Copeland was then confronted with the statement he had made shortly after the incident, in which he indicated that R.G. had fallen.

The judge made the following findings: The testimony of J.Z., the patient who had witnessed the incident, was credible. J.Z. had been interviewed in the presence of a staff psychiatrist who indicated J.Z. was alert and oriented and had no symptoms of being out of contact with reality at the time.

Copeland, on the other hand, was not at all credible, and R.G.'s injuries probably occurred when she fell to the floor as Copeland was attempting to push her into one of the chairs. Copeland physically and mentally abused R.G. He physically pushed her with some force, and he repeatedly flicked a towel at her. Such behavior could not be described as anything other than abuse.

Furthermore, no behavior on behalf of a patient could warrant Copeland's response. The patients at Trenton Psychiatric Hospital were there because of the nature of their mental and behavioral impairments. Staff members were trained concerning the proper methods for addressing behaviors. It was clear that Copeland knew the proper methods to apply when a patient behaved aggressively since Copeland testified, untruthfully, that he had simply held R.G.'s arms to her sides until she calmed down.

Even if Copeland had not pushed R.G. and caused the fall, his behavior would nevertheless warrant removal since he walked away and left the patient on the floor and did not help her up and did not make any report of the fall.

The judge affirmed the decision to remove Copeland from his position.

Rutgers University School of Law-Camden, New Jersey Administrative Law Decisions, Initial Decision, http://lawlibrary.rutgers.edu/oal/html/initial/csv4282-00_1.html (accessed August 18, 2005), and Final Agency Decision, http://lawlibrary.rutgers.edu/oal/final/csv4282-00.pdf (accessed August 18, 2005).

B.2 Employee Theft of State Property/1996

Joseph M. Ferrogine, Appellant
v.
Trenton Psychiatric Hospital, Respondent

Office of Administrative Law Docket No. CSV 8864-95
Initial Decision: August 6, 1996
Before Bruce R. Campbell, Administrative Law Judge
Final Agency Decision: September 17, 1996

INITIAL DECISION:

Joseph Ferrogine, an engineer in charge of maintenance at Trenton Psychiatric Hospital, was found with stolen hospital supplies in his possession. The stolen goods were in the garage of a house he was renting on hospital grounds. Criminal charges were brought and he was suspended from his position. Ferrogine claimed he did nothing unlawful and appealed the suspension.

For the criminal charges, Ferrogine entered a pretrial intervention program, which was not yet completed when he brought his appeal. If he were to complete the program, his record would be clear. If he were not to successfully complete the program, he could be tried on criminal charges.

Regardless of the program outcome, the hospital decided to continue the suspension. The hospital determined that, since Ferrogine had complete access to accounts and materials, and was charged with theft of things that were under his supervision, it was not in the best interests of the institution to keep him in his position.

The judge found the following: Ferrogine was in possession of stolen state property and was a custodian of that property. Even though the pretrial intervention program and, therefore, the criminal case were as yet unresolved, the criminal charges, if proven, would establish a crime of moral turpitude. Under these circumstances, the judge dismissed Ferrogine's appeal to lift his indefinite suspension pending resolution of criminal charges.

FINAL AGENCY DECISION:

Upon final review, the Merit System Board noted that, while the appeal was pending, criminal charges were disposed of through Ferrogine's acceptance into the pretrial intervention program. Therefore, the appeal concerning whether the suspension pending the outcome of those charges was in the public interest was dismissed as moot.

Ferrogine v. Trenton Psychiatric Hospital, New Jersey Administrative Reports, Volume 97, Second Edition (Civil Service), p. 470.

B.3 Verbal Abuse and Punching Patient in Face/1991

Kevin E. Willis, Appellant

v.

Trenton Psychiatric Hospital, State Department of Human Services, Respondent

Office of Administrative Law Docket No. CSV 1986-90
Initial Decision: July 23, 1991
Before Beatrice S. Tylutki, Administrative Law Judge
Final Agency Decision: September 23, 1991

Kevin E. Willis appealed his termination as a human services technician at Trenton Psychiatric Hospital on the charge of physical abuse of a patient. Willis had received employee training on how to handle disruptive patients, avoid confrontations, and control reactions to abusive patients. This training included notification that oral or physical abuse of a patient was not permitted and would result in termination.

Willis was part of a group of hospital staff and patients who attended a basketball game at Trenton State College. Patient M.F., part of this group, was a stocky, 5'9" male, approximately 27 years old.

At halftime, patients were allowed to take turns leaving the gym with staff escorts. M.F. left the gym alone, without permission, and was followed by Willis. M.F. became upset and angry about the fact that Willis had followed him and told Willis in a loud and abusive manner that he did not need an escort.

Stephen F. Vandegrift, another staff person, saw and heard M.F. and Willis shouting in the hallway. Vandegrift heard M.F. shout that Willis was not his father and not to touch him, though no physical contact was observed. Vandergrift then took M.F. back into the gym.

When Willis returned to the gym, M.F. started to shout curses and threats at him. Willis then grabbed M.F. by the shirt with two hands, and both of them fell back against the bleachers. Vandegrift saw that Willis appeared to be holding down M.F. and tried to separate them. Vandegrift then saw Willis punch M.F. in the face. Another staff person sitting nearby also witnessed the punch, though Willis denied punching M.F. Three other staff members, sitting further away, witnessed the shouting and cursing, but did not see the punch.

Vandegrift took M.F. into the hall; he noticed swelling over M.F.'s right eye, as did the other staff member who witnessed the punch. M.F. did not complain about being hit by Willis and said he did not want to report the incident since he was afraid of losing his privileges.

The judge found the following: Willis had no reason to grab M.F. and push and hold him down; this action was inconsistent with the hospital's policy of avoiding confrontation with patients. Vandegrift's testimony about witnessing the punch was credible since Vandegrift had the best view of what occurred. M.F. did not initially complain of being hit since his initial concern was that he would be blamed for the incident and would lose his privileges.

Therefore, the judge determined that Willis physically abused M.F. Willis's removal was affirmed as reasonable and consistent with law.

Willis v. Trenton Psychiatric Hospital, State Department of Human Services, New Jersey Administrative Reports, Volume 91, Second Edition (Civil Service), p. 27.

B.4 Soliciting Sexual Favors from Patient/1999

Fred Nwosu-Eke, Appellant

v.

Trenton Psychiatric Hospital, Respondent

Office of Administrative Law Docket No. CSV 945-98
Initial Decision: January 7, 1999
Before Steven C. Reback, Administrative Law Judge
Final Agency Decision: March 9, 1999

Fred Nwosu-Eke appealed his termination as a human services technician at Trenton Psychiatric Hospital following charges of (1) physical abuse and mistreatment of a patient and (2) violation of administrative procedures involving safety and security. Specifically, he had reportedly brought a patient coffee and food in exchange for sexual favors.

L.W. was a 21-year-old woman who had a history of suicide attempts and drug abuse. She had been diagnosed as a severely depressed and borderline personality and was being treated with a variety of medications, though she was characterized by her psychiatrist as alert, well oriented, nondelusional, and nonhallucinatory. L.W. frequently disobeyed the rules and often possessed various types of contraband.

Among the items which L.W. often craved was caffeine. Caffeine was prohibited from use by patients primarily because of its interaction with a variety of medications. The patients and staff knew this, as did Nwosu-Eke.

L.W. testified that she had, on occasion, asked for and received coffee and food from Nwosu-Eke. She related that, on one of those occasions, Nwosu-Eke grabbed her and began kissing her against her will. While she indicated she initially experienced shock, she said that this developed into a pattern of behavior that was physically consensual. Fearing reprisals from other staff members, and perhaps other patients as well, L.W. at first kept the relationship secret. Eventually she engaged in sexual intercourse with Nwosu-Eke over a period of about one to two months. Essentially, L.W. was trading sex for caffeine.

L.W. eventually confided in another patient and an employee, though she did not come forward officially until a contraband search was announced with respect to another patient, and she did not at first admit that the two had had intercourse. L.W. said she kept that secret because of her own shame and because she did not want to jeopardize Nwosu-Eke's employment.

When asked why she finally did come forward, L.W. said she felt compelled because if something like that could happen to her, it could happen to anyone. She was tired of being a victim.

Nwosu-Eke unequivocally denied ever providing L.W. or any other patient with caffeine beverages or other contraband, and he denied any sexual wrongdoing. He indicated L.W.'s lies were motivated by revenge for his previous attempts to deter her from doing improper things.

The judge found the following: L.W. was credible and her testimony was consistent and corroborated by several other Trenton employees. Nwosu-Eke abused his responsibility and trust by forcing a relationship upon a drug-addicted, suicidal, severely depressed, and psychologically disturbed young woman. Nwosu-Eke used L.W. as a prostitute and paid her with caffeine. He physically abused and mistreated a patient by providing her with contraband, mostly in the form of caffeinated beverages, and by soliciting sexual favors from her, including sexual intercourse, in consideration for receipt of this contraband. Such conduct was not only a violation of the administrative rules and procedures of Trenton Psychiatric Hospital, but it clearly and unequivocally constituted conduct unbecoming a public employee.

The decision to remove Nwosu-Eke from his position was sustained.

Rutgers University School of Law-Camden, New Jersey Administrative Law Decisions, Initial Decision, http://lawlibrary.rutgers.edu/oal/html/initial/csv945-98.html (accessed August 18, 2005), and Final Agency Decision, http://lawlibrary.rutgers.edu/oal/final/csv945-98.pdf (accessed August 18, 2005).

B.5 Failure to Lock Medicine Cabinet; Patient in Coma/1994

Elizabeth Lockett, Appellant

v.

Department of Human Services, Trenton Psychiatric Hospital, Respondent

Office of Administrative Law Docket No. CSV 8292-92
Initial Decision: January 14, 1994
Before Paul J. Sollami, Administrative Law Judge
Final Agency Decision: March 8, 1994

INITIAL DECISION:

Elizabeth Lockett appealed her removal from her position as a nurse at Trenton Psychiatric Hospital on charges of negligence in performing her duty and violation of policies and procedures. Specifically, she was accused of failing to secure a medication cabinet, which resulted in a patient gaining access to medication. The patient subsequently ingested the medication and was hospitalized for several days in a comatose condition (she has since recovered).

Prior to the incident, the patient had been classified as a "moderate risk suicide," requiring staff monitoring every 15 minutes. The patient later told a staff psychiatrist that the upper part of the door to the medication room was open and she just reached down and released the latch of the lower door. The patient also indicated she had been watching for the door to be open and that, once inside the medication room, she took five bottles out of an open cabinet and drank their contents. The psychiatrist determined the patient was telling the truth.

Lockett argued (1) there was no substantial lock on the medication cabinet, (2) the cabinet lock "had a reputation of being broken" and was eventually replaced, and (3) these facts showed the hospital was also at fault because it had failed to address the lock problem sooner. Lockett further testified she didn't tell anyone about the lock not working that day because "all the nurses knew that the lock did not work."

The judge made the following findings: Lockett left the door to the medication room unlocked, failed to inform the charge nurse or anyone else that the door on the medication cabinet could not be locked because the lock was defective, and knew the lock on the cabinet was not working four to six weeks before the incident. The defective lock presented a life/safety emergent situation. The patient's classification as a "moderate risk suicide" required vigilance on the part of the staff and, more particularly, Lockett, since Lockett was in charge of dispensing medication. The judge affirmed the hospital's decision to remove Lockett from her position.

FINAL AGENCY DECISION:

The Merit System Board accepted the Findings of Fact from the judge's initial decision, but did not adopt the conclusion and recommendation that Lockett be removed from her position.

The Board concluded the following: Lockett's conduct was negligent, however there were several mitigating factors. The lock on the medication cabinet had been repaired four times in the five months preceding the incident, and medication cabinet locks on other wards were repaired just as often. Moreover, the lock in question was not working for some weeks prior to the incident and the defective lock had been repeatedly reported; however no action was taken to repair or replace the lock. The blame for an unsecured medication cabinet could not, in fairness, be shouldered by Lockett alone. The hospital was primarily responsible for ensuring that appropriate security equipment was provided and properly maintained.

The Board ordered that the previous penalty of Lockett's removal from her position be modified to a six-month suspension.

Lockett v. Department of Human Services, Trenton Psychiatric Hospital, New Jersey Administrative Reports, Volume 94, Second Edition (Civil Service), p. 454.

B.6 Failure to Supervise; Patient Attempts Hanging/1993

Isiah R. Scott, Jr., Appellant

v.

Trenton Psychiatric Hospital, State Department of Human Services, Respondent

Office of Administrative Law Docket No. CSV 8296-92
Initial Decision: September 2, 1993
Before Beatrice S. Tylutki, Administrative Law Judge
Final Agency Decision: October 13, 1993

Isiah R. Scott, Jr., a human services technician (HST) at Trenton Psychiatric Hospital, appealed his 90-day suspension on charges of neglect of duty, loafing, and idleness or willful failure to devote attention to tasks that could result in danger to persons or property.

Patient L.W. had been placed on suicide precaution, one-to-one supervision, at arm's length. Arm's-length supervision was the highest type of supervision, short of placing the patient in restraints. The staff person assigned to such a patient was required to make entries on a supervision/precaution record every 15 minutes regarding what the patient was doing.

On the day of the incident, L.W. left the day room where Scott was supervising him and went into the bathroom where he attempted to hang himself. Another patient screamed for help, and Scott and several others ran from the day room to the bathroom and were able to stop L.W. before he was injured.

The first dispute was whether Scott was informed that L.W. was on one-to-one supervision, at arm's length. The supervising nurse said she specifically told Scott of his shift time and responsibilities regarding L.W. Stanley Patterson was the HST who supervised L.W. immediately before Scott's shift. Patterson also said that, when he turned over the supervision/precaution record at the shift change, he told Scott that L.W. was on one-to-one supervision, at arm's length. Scott also made entries on this record.

Scott testified that he was not told by either the supervising nurse or Patterson that L.W. was on one-to-one supervision, at arm's length. Scott also stated that he was unaware of this assignment until he was given the supervision/precaution record for L.W. by Patterson, and he did not have time to read Patterson's entries on the record.

The judge found that Scott was told by both the supervising nurse and Patterson that L.W. was on one-to-one supervision, at arm's length.

The second dispute was over exactly what happened in the day room before L.W. left to go to the bathroom. Fred Nwosu, another HST who was in the day room, said that when L.W. left the room, Scott did not follow him. Nwosu said that, after the other patient shouted that L.W. was trying to kill himself, Nwosu and Scott ran into the bathroom and found L.W. with one end of a belt around his neck and the other end over the shower pole.

Scott disagreed and said that he started to follow L.W. to the bathroom, but another patient stopped him to talk. After Scott heard the shouting, he ran to the bathroom and found L.W. with the belt only around his neck, not over the shower pole. Scott estimated that he arrived in the bathroom five to six seconds after L.W. left the day room.

The judge found: Scott was stopped and delayed by another patient when he tried to follow L.W. It was more likely that several minutes, not five or six seconds, lapsed between L.W. leaving the day room and the warning shout that L.W. was trying to kill himself.

Scott did not properly supervise L.W. and this could have resulted in L.W.'s injury or death. It was Scott's responsibility to go to the bathroom with L.W. Scott was guilty of neglect of duty. The 90-day suspension was affirmed.

Scott v. Trenton Psychiatric Hospital, State Department of Human Services, New Jersey Administrative Reports, Volume 93, Second Edition (Civil Service), p. 777.

Appendix C

Abuses Across America
into the Twenty-first Century

This appendix is divided into the following sections:

C.1 U.S. Department of Justice Investigations of Public
Residential Facilities

A sampling of recent investigations by the U.S. Attorney
General's office revealing dire, and often life-threatening,
conditions in which institutionalized persons across the
country are forced to live.

C.2 Psychiatric Drugs and Electroshock Therapy

Brief summaries of articles relating the dangers and continued use of antipsychotic medications and shock treatments.

Appendix C.1

United States Department of Justice Investigations of Public Residential Facilities

Protecting the rights of institutionalized persons is a priority of the Department of Justice. Since 2001, the Civil Rights Division has opened 46 investigations—affecting 53 facilities—concerning the terms and conditions of confinement in nursing homes, mental health facilities, residences for persons with developmental disabilities, juvenile justice facilities, prisons, and jails. These figures represent a more than 30 percent increase in such investigations when compared to those initiated over the preceding four years.

U.S. Department of Justice
Press Release, February 22, 2005

THE JUSTICE DEPARTMENT'S recent investigations of state and locally operated residential facilities have uncovered numerous and systemic violations of residents' rights protected by federal law and the Constitution in areas such as:

- Protection of Residents from Harm
    - Physical Abuse by Staff and Other Residents
    - Sexual Abuse by Staff and Other Residents
    - Self-Injurious and Suicidal Behavior
    - Incident Reporting and Follow-up
- Psychology and Behavior Programs
    - Restraints and Seclusion
    - "As-Needed" Medications for Behavior Control
- Psychiatric Care
    - Psychotropic Medications
    - Assessments and Treatment Planning
- Medical and Dental Care
- Nutritional and Physical Management
- Physical, Occupational, and Speech Therapy
- Education
- Habilitation (enabling residents to function in society)
- Placement in the Community and the Most Integrated Setting

Each of the following investigative findings revealed violations in many, if not most, of the above areas. I have selected only a few brief highlights from only a few of these investigations. They serve as necessary reminders of the scope of abuse still taking place today.

For a fuller understanding of the Civil Rights of Institutionalized Persons Act (CRIPA) and details of other investigations by the U.S. Attorney General's office, you may visit the website for the Department of Justice (DOJ) at http://www.usdoj.gov/crt/split/cripa.htm.

Note: Some passages below are quoted from the original text, while others are paraphrased to concisely convey the original content. The full text for related letters of findings, complaints, and settlements may be found at http://www.championpress.com/books/hardcandyebook.htm.

C.1.1 Sexual Abuse by Staff and Youth/2004
Investigation of Adobe Mountain School and
Black Canyon School, Phoenix, Arizona

The Department of Justice investigation revealed that sexual abuse of youth by staff and other juveniles occurred with incredibly disturbing frequency at Adobe Mountain School, and that management did not effectively address this serious problem. It was difficult to assess the full extent of the sexual abuse occurring at Adobe, in part because of the dysfunctional grievance system and ineffective abuse investigation processes.

In addition to sexual abuse committed by staff, the DOJ investigation revealed many examples of youth-on-youth sexual violence. Documentation revealed that sexual intimidation was occurring in the facilities. In numerous interviews, youth revealed their fears and concerns. Some examples are:

- A male staff member was accused repeatedly of inappropriate sexual contact with youth, including touching boys on their buttocks. Reportedly, 13 boys and five staff members voiced complaints about this behavior and three youth filed formal grievances. The allegations were never investigated by a neutral party. At the time of the DOJ tour, this staff member continued to work directly with youth.
- A youth informed a staff member that other youth were threatening him to perform sexual acts or risk being beaten up or raped.
- An investigation includes strong evidence that three Adobe youth attempted to place a pepper shaker in the anus of another youth.
- Another investigation disclosed that a youth engaged in sex with other youth in exchange for their friendship or for such items as soap.
- There are indications of a prevalence of sexual activity among the girls at Black Canyon, including the character-

ization of some youth as "sexual predators." Reports indicated that much of the activity consisted of inappropriate actions between "girlfriends" due to competition among the girls for affection. The DOJ found no evidence of any action taken to address these reports.

U.S. Department of Justice, Civil Rights Division, Special Litigation Section, Documents and Publications, Investigative Findings, Juvenile Correctional Facilities Investigations, http://www.usdoj.gov/crt/split/documents/ariz_findings .pdf (accessed July 2, 2005).

C.1.2 Sexual Abuse and Inappropriate Relations/2005 Investigation of L. E. Rader Center, Sand Springs, Oklahoma

The investigation revealed that the State failed to provide adequate supervision and monitoring to ensure that youth at the juvenile justice facility were not subjected to inappropriate sexual interaction with staff or other residents.

Sexual Relationships Between Staff and Youth. Numerous sexual relationships developed between female staff members and male youth. Other staff members reported some of these instances, but administrators and supervisors failed to take prompt, appropriate action. Examples include:

- In 2004, a resident reported that a female staff member permitted a youth to carry her into his room and place her on his bed where the youth and others fondled her.
- In 2003, a female staff member and a male youth engaged in a sexual relationship. Rader staff found correspondence between the two that confirmed the relationship.
- In 2003, a female staff member engaged in a sexual relationship with a male youth who was classified as a sex offender and permitted a different youth to fondle her in front

of other youth. At least eight staff members voiced their concerns to supervisors, one of whom indicated the female staff member was a "sexual predator." Documents confirmed the sexual abuse, but the DOJ was not provided with requested documentation regarding any discipline or corrective action.

- Between July and October 2003, a female staff member and a male youth engaged in inappropriate sexual relations. Staff reportedly noted the relationship early on, yet failed to report it to administrators. Action was taken after a security staff member intercepted a sexually explicit letter from the staff member to the youth. Documents confirmed the sexual abuse and the staff member resigned.

- For six months in 2002 and 2003, a male youth and female staff member engaged in a sexual relationship. During this period, three different staff members spoke with the female staff member and other employees wrote memoranda setting forth their concerns about her behavior. Nevertheless, it took six months for administrators to address the relationship. Documents confirmed a finding of sexual abuse against the female staff member, and her employment was terminated.

Sexual Relationships Between Youth. Examples of inappropriate sexual relationships between youth include:

- In April 2004, two male youth reportedly engaged in mutual masturbation while housed on the unit for sex offenders. One of the youth reported that he participated because he feared the other youth would harm him.

- In January 2004, an 18-year-old male youth engaged in anal sex with a 14-year-old male in the restroom of the gym while two staff supervised other youth. One of the youth was on "close observation," which required staff to know of his whereabouts at all times.

- In August 2003, two female youth engaged in sexual activity in their dormitory. There was only one staff member monitoring the housing unit, since the second had broken rules and left the unit for a smoking break. Documents substantiated a finding of caretaker misconduct, and the second staff member was suspended for three days.
- From at least May through June 2003, two male youth engaged in a sexual relationship while housed on the sex offender unit. The two youth regularly paired off and engaged in mutual masturbation and oral sex while staff were preoccupied with other youth. Documents substantiated a finding of neglect against one staff member, who was suspended for three days.
- On January 26, 2003, two youth classified as sexual offenders left the day room of their unit and entered one of the bathrooms where they engaged in oral and anal sex. Although three staff were on duty, two were dealing with a youth in his room and the third was monitoring the day room. An investigation did not confirm caretaker misconduct, but did confirm sexual activity.

U.S. Department of Justice, Civil Rights Division, Special Litigation Section, Documents and Publications, Investigative Findings, Juvenile Correctional Facilities Investigations, http://www.usdoj.gov/crt/split/documents/split_rader _findlet_6-15-05.pdf (accessed July 2, 2005).

C.1.3 Staff and Youth Violence; Unsafe "Lock and Drop" Restraint/2004
Investigation of Cheltenham Youth Facility in Cheltenham, Maryland, and Charles H. Hickey, Jr., School, Baltimore, Maryland

Staff Violence. Evidence indicated a deeply disturbing degree of physical abuse of youth by staff at both Cheltenham and Hickey. The following examples were confirmed by staff and youth to be representative of recurrent problems:

- In January 2004, four Cheltenham staff members allegedly restrained a youth and beat him after the youth resisted going to bed early. The unit supervisor held the youth while the other three punched the youth in the face and kicked him in the ribs and back. By the end of the incident, staff had dragged the youth back to his room and his pants and underwear had been ripped and pulled down to his ankles.
- In January 2004, two Hickey staff members assaulted a youth, who was left injured in his room for three hours before being seen by the nurse.
- In May 2003, a Hickey staff member grabbed a youth around the neck and threw him against the wall when the youth refused to leave a classroom. After the youth threw a chair, the staff member threw him to the ground, choking, punching, and kicking him.
- In March 2003, a Hickey staff member, breaking up a youth-on-youth fight, hoisted one youth in the air and "slammed him to the floor," injuring his left arm, which was later put in a cast.

Youth Violence. Both Cheltenham and Hickey experienced unacceptably high levels of youth-on-youth violence. Contributing factors were a lack of sufficient staff, inadequate training of staff, and a failure to report incidents.

Examples of incidents are:

- In May 2003, a youth assaulted another youth who was sleeping in the day room, resulting in a fracture of the second youth's left orbit. The staff member supervising the day room had fallen asleep.
- In April 2003, a group of youth assaulted another youth for a period of several minutes without staff intervention. The staff did not refer the injured youth for medical care or report the incident.
- In April 2003, a youth suffered a broken jaw after another youth attacked him with a stick.

Unsafe "Lock and Drop" Restraint. Methods used by Hickey staff to restrain unruly youth created grave risk of harm to youth. In a technique called "lock and drop," staff would force a youth to the ground lying on his stomach, placing weight on the youth's upper torso to hold him down. This could prevent the youth from breathing and cause asphyxiation. Another commonly reported method was described as being "slammed on the neck and arms bent way back" or "they put a knee in your back, one hand on the back of your neck and the other hand bends your arm up in back." Some incidents involving dangerous restraint are:

- A restrained youth vomited and appeared to have inhaled some of the vomitus, triggering a loss of consciousness due to transient asphyxia.
- A youth suffered neck and shoulder injuries.
- A youth suffered a seizure and required hospitalization.
- A 300-pound staff member sat on a youth and mocked the youth when he complained he couldn't breathe.

U.S. Department of Justice, Civil Rights Division, Special Litigation Section, Documents and Publications, Investigative Findings, Juvenile Correctional Facilities Investigations, http://www.usdoj.gov/crt/split/documents/cheltenham _md.pdf (accessed July 2, 2005).

C.1.4 Abuse and Mistreatment; "Code of Silence"/2002 Investigation of Oakwood Developmental Center, Somerset, Kentucky

Oakwood had numerous and recurring incidents of abuse and mistreatment by staff members over the past several years. The sheer volume of incident reports of harm was unacceptably high, especially recurring incidents with specific individuals over long periods of time. Examples of incidents are:

- In August 2000, a staff member stomped on a resident's head and rendered the resident unconscious. An investigation uncovered three further instances of this staff member physically abusing residents.
- A staff member was observed pushing, slapping, and cursing at a resident on a daily basis for four months in 2000. An internal investigation revealed a "code of silence" among staff regarding reporting allegations of abuse/neglect on other employees. Staff were afraid to report resident abuse because of retaliation by other employees.
- A resident was beaten with a coat hanger, but investigators could not confirm allegations identifying certain staff members.
- During a three-month period in 2001, one resident unit had 30 reported incidents of harm, another had 20 incidents, and a third had 16 incidents. During the same period, there were 24 residents with an unacceptably high number of recurring incidents of harm.

U.S. Department of Justice, Civil Rights Division, Special Litigation Section, Documents and Publications, Investigative Findings, Developmental Disability and Mental Retardation Facilities Investigations, http://www.usdoj.gov/crt/split/documents/oakwoodfindings.pdf (accessed July 2, 2005).

C.1.5 Staff Abuse; Neglect and Inadequate Supervision/2004 Investigation of Woodbridge Developmental Center, Woodbridge, New Jersey

The DOJ investigation found that residents were subjected to a pattern of staff abuse and neglect. Particularly disturbing was that confirmed abusers were sometimes reassigned to resident care. The following are representative examples of staff abuse:

- In August 2002, a staff member twisted a resident's arm with substantial force, causing a fracture. Less than six months later, a second staff person grabbed the resident shook the resident by the neck, then lifted the resident from his wheelchair and pushed him back into it several times.

- In July 2002, a resident was hit by a staff person with her purse strap and buckle, receiving multiple red marks on her neck, torso, arm, and leg.

The DOJ also found that residents suffered many serious injuries because Woodbridge failed to supervise them adequately, further indicated by the fact that residents routinely suffered injuries of unknown origin.

- In December 2002, a resident entered the kitchen through a door staff had failed to lock, then stuffed his mouth with bread and choked to death. Investigation notes indicated there were actually staff present during the incident, but no one could explain how it happened. Further, the staff had never been trained regarding the patient's tendency to put choking hazards in his mouth, despite abundant documentation about this during the patient's 37 years at the facility.

- In October 2002, a resident was bitten repeatedly on the face, neck, and arms by another resident, requiring 15 sutures. The aggressor had a known history of biting others; this was amply documented. Nevertheless, the staff did not intervene when they observed the aggressor entering the victim's bedroom.

U.S. Department of Justice, Civil Rights Division, Special Litigation Section, Documents and Publications, Investigative Findings, Developmental Disability and Mental Retardation Facilities Investigations, http://www.usdoj.gov/crt/split/documents/split_woodbridge_findings_nov11_04.pdf (accessed July 2, 2005).

C.1.6 Inappropriate Use of Restraints and Seclusion/2004 Investigation of North Carolina's Public Mental Health Hospitals:
Dorothea Dix Hospital, Raleigh;
Broughton Hospital, Morganton;
Cherry Hospital, Goldsboro; and
John Umstead Hospital, Butner

The investigation revealed that restraint and seclusion policies and practices departed substantially from generally accepted professional standards throughout all four hospitals. Justification for restraint was rarely documented, and patients were placed inappropriately in restraint and seclusion more often than necessary, longer than necessary, and when alternative, less intrusive interventions were available.

There were particular concerns about the inappropriate use of restraints and seclusion for children and adolescents.

- A patient was placed in four-point restraints for over two hours, despite the fact that, according to notes in his record, he was calm the entire time.
- A patient on a children's unit had 16 restraint and seclusion episodes in less than one month, with vague release criteria, often no postincident debriefing information, and no analysis of precipitating factors that might facilitate a more proactive treatment approach.
- A 17-year-old and 12-year-old were repeatedly placed into seclusion for not following staff instructions.

Medical/surgical restraints were being used inappropriately on geriatric wards as a way to address ambulation and gait issues. For example, a patient was strapped to a geri-chair around the clock for six days, except for required two-hour breaks, even though he had no difficulty walking.

U.S. Department of Justice, Civil Rights Division, Special Litigation Section, Documents and Publications, Investigative Findings, Mental Health Facilities Investigations, http://www.usdoj.gov/crt/split/documents/nc_mh_hosp_findlet.pdf (accessed July 2, 2005).

C.1.7 Failure to Protect Children from Harm and Sexual Abuse; Excessive Use of Restraints and Seclusion/ 2003 and 2004
Investigation of Metropolitan State Hospital, Norwalk, California

Harm and Sexual Abuse. Metropolitan's child and adolescent program served approximately 100 patients.

Between May 1, 2001, and March 31, 2002, there were:
- 131 patient-against-patient assaults;
- 169 incidences of patients abusing themselves;
- 74 accidental injuries.

Between May 1, 2001, and April 30, 2002, there were:
- 27 allegations of staff abuse;
- six allegations of rape;
- an additional 28 instances of inappropriate sexual contact between children and adolescents. An aggressor and/or victim was identified in 21 of these instances, indicating they were not consensual.

In one case, a young patient who had made a documented claim that he had been raped had no evidence in his chart that a physician had examined him physically, and no responsive interventions were undertaken, apart from moving the involved boys to separate bedrooms.

Metropolitan's incident tracking and trending system was at odds with generally accepted professional standards of care. Incident trending reports did not track important types of incidents, such as allegations of patient abuse by staff, neglect, rape, or other inappropriate sexual incidents. Furthermore, although the summary reports provided some information regarding patterns or trends, there were a number of other potential trends and patterns that were not included but that were fundamental to identifying potential problems and formulating solutions, such as which patients most often were victims or aggressors.

Excessive Use of Restraints and Seclusion. Metropolitan overused seclusion, restraints, and as-needed medications in the absence of adequate treatment and, in some instances, as punishment. Numerous episodes had no documentation indicating that the team adequately assessed the patient, developed and/or reviewed the treatment plan, or considered alternative interventions.

- A patient was in walking restraints 24 hours a day for almost the entire month of March 2002, and was in restraints another 41 times between April 7 and November 11, 2002.
- A patient was placed in wrist and ankle walking restraints continuously for three days and then for ten days, with one day off restraints in between.
- A patient was placed in seclusion and/or restraints on 25 occasions during a nine-month period, with restraint episodes lasting between 30 minutes and 23 hours.
- A patient was kept in walking restraints 24 hours a day for 33 days, and, beginning nine days later, for three more days.
- For over six months, a patient was kept in walking restraints during waking hours and placed in a locked seclusion room to sleep.

Metropolitan failed to conduct face-to-face assessments of patients placed in seclusion or restraints within one hour of the initiation of the episode. This did not comply with generally accepted professional standards of care. Some examples are:

- A patient was placed in seclusion and/or restraints at least five times in one month without a physician's order denoting a face-to-face assessment within the required time frame. On another occasion, the patient was kept in seclusion and/or restraints for more than 11 continuous hours without a timely assessment.
- A patient was placed in physical restraints seven times over six weeks, without a physician's assessment, including one episode that lasted 24 hours.
- A patient was placed in seclusion and restraints at least 14 times between February 25 and September 8, 2001, without evidence of any face-to-face assessments.

U.S. Department of Justice, Civil Rights Division, Special Litigation Section, Documents and Publications, Investigative Findings, Mental Health Facilities Investigations, http://www.usdoj.gov/crt/split/documents/metrol_findings_let428 .pdf (accessed July 2, 2005) and http://www.usdoj.gov/crt/split/documents/ metro_hosp_findlet.pdf (accessed July 2, 2005).

C.1.8 Failure to Manage Psychotropic Medication/2004 Investigation of Conway Human Development Center, Conway, Arkansas

In many cases, Conway either did not assess or ignored serious adverse effects on cognition, motor functioning, behavior, and physical health caused by psychotropic medications. Some of these effects were irreversible and disabling movement disorders. Examples are:

- A resident was treated with a combination of two drugs, neither of which was appropriate to her condition, and her symptoms worsened. One drug was continued for almost four months, despite repeated tests suggesting serious and life-threatening pancreatic dysfunction, well known to occur with that drug.

- A resident was treated with two antipsychotic medications, both of which had the potential to worsen one of his diagnoses. After more than two years, the psychiatrist noted that there was a safer, equally effective medication, but six months later he still had not prescribed it. There was also no indication that Conway was monitoring the resident's condition that may have been worsened by the drugs.

- A resident was treated with an antidepressant appropriate for depression or panic attacks, but nothing in his record indicated these conditions. The antidepressant had a known side effect of aggression. But when the resident exhibited increasingly aggressive outbursts, the psychiatrist added another medication without any indication that the first drug may have been causing the aggression. The second drug then caused the resident to develop tremors, which resulted in a third drug being prescribed. The psychiatrist's notes indicated the resident was "tolerating treatment well" and did not indicate any monitoring for serious risks associated with the third medication.

U.S. Department of Justice, Civil Rights Division, Special Litigation Section, Documents and Publications, Investigative Findings, Developmental Disability and Mental Retardation Facilities Investigations, http://www.usdoj.gov/crt/split/documents/conway_find_let.pdf (accessed July 2, 2005).

C.1.9 Improper Use of Psychotropic Drugs/2002 Investigation of Woodward State Resource Center, Woodward, Iowa, and Glenwood State Resource Center, Glenwood, Iowa

The investigation determined that psychotropic drugs were often used without medical justification. For example:

- Psychotropics were prescribed to address staff complaints about individuals with challenging behaviors—that is, prescribed for the convenience of staff.

- Polypharmacy (using multiple drugs to treat the same condition), was not justified on any of the charts reviewed by investigators.
- Some residents received powerful psychotropic medications that did not improve their psychiatric or behavioral problems, but caused them to develop seizures and other permanent physical side effects. In some cases, residents were then placed on additional medications that would facilitate the onset of further seizures.
- Drugs were administered for conditions that were not diagnosed.
- Drugs were repeatedly administered without any indication as to why, what results were expected, or whether the drug was providing effective treatment.

U.S. Department of Justice, Civil Rights Division, Special Litigation Section, Documents and Publications, Investigative Findings, Developmental Disability and Mental Retardation Facilities Investigations, http://www.usdoj.gov/crt/split/documents/ia_findings_wsrc_gsrc.htm (accessed July 2, 2005).

APPENDIX C.2

PSYCHIATRIC DRUGS AND ELECTROSHOCK THERAPY

C.2.1 The Dangers of Psychiatric Drugs/1994

Psychiatric medications are known to be unpredictable and can sometimes cause violent—and deadly—behavior.

Tranquilizers (antipsychotics), introduced in the mid-1950s, are considered the most dangerous. Some of the most common are Haldol and Thorazine. These drugs were often used at psychiatric institutions for the convenience of doctors and attendants. Today, they are commonly prescribed to elderly residents of nursing homes to keep them in a calmed state.

A common negative side effect is akathisia, a drug-induced inability to sit still, often characterized by restlessness and pacing. Another side effect is nerve damage that affects muscle control of the face and body, causing involuntary contortions and spasms. This can become permanent.

Studies have shown that psychiatric drugs cause violent behavior, often in people with no history of aggression. The increase in violent behavior is often attributed to akathisia.

Minor tranquilizers or anti-anxiety agents—such as Xanax, Halcion, Valium, and Ativan—are the most commonly prescribed psychiatric drugs. They have also been known to cause an increase in acts of aggression.

Antidepressants such as Prozac, Pamelor, and Elavil are also widely used. Prozac has been particularly linked with violence and suicidal behavior.

Tanya Bibeau, "The dark side of psychiatric drugs," *USA Today Magazine*, May 1, 1994, http://www.stopshrinks.org/reading_room/drugs/dark_side_1.htm (accessed July 6, 2005).

C.2.2 Shock Therapy Makes a Comeback/1996

Electroshock therapy, known by many today as electroconvulsive therapy or ECT, first gained popularity in American mental institutions in the 1940s. There are many documented accounts of its use to subdue and punish difficult patients. ECT fell off in the 1960s and 1970s, but then it began making a comeback. By the mid-1990s it was being administered to an estimated 100,000 patients per year in the U.S.

This resurgence hasn't come without controversy. While some call it an effective treatment for depression, others say it's only a temporary fix that can cause confusion, memory loss, and even death. In elderly patients, common recipients of ECT, it can cause severe confusion, lung problems, irregular heartbeats, heart failure, and aspiration pneumonia.

Many psychiatrists, psychiatric organizations, and patients say ECT is effective in treating depression and preventing suicide. But patients commonly complain about losing memories of events in the distant past, and even claim their ability to learn is adversely affected. And ECT has not been proven to prevent suicide. In fact, critics say quite the opposite, that the confusion and loss of memory from ECT may even *create* suicidal tendencies.

Little high-quality ECT research has been done, and there are many contradictory results, including huge discrepancies in ECT's mortality rate. Though there are improvements in patients with severe depression, critics say the improvement is temporary and relapses are frequent.

Sandra G. Boodman, "Shock Therapy . . . It's Back," *Washington Post*, September 24, 1996: Z14, http://www.ect.org/news/post.html (accessed July 7, 2005).

C.2.3 Patients at Risk from Shock Treatments/1995

On October 14, 1994, 72-year-old Ocie Shirk received shock therapy at a for-profit psychiatric hospital in Austin, Texas. Her medical history included one heart attack and atrial fibrillation, a condition causing rapid heart quivers, but her hospital records did not include a current medical history or physical.

Shirk had a heart attack in the recovery room and died four days later of heart failure, the leading cause of shock-related deaths. Shock therapy is mentioned nowhere on Shirk's death certificate, though the medical examiner indicated it should have been listed.

Electroshock treatments have gained popularity in recent years, and are frequently performed on elderly women suffering from depression. Most are not told of the dangers and risks involved, and many are losing memories, suffering heart attacks and strokes, and dying. The American Psychiatric Association claimed electroshock's death rate was one in 10,000. But according to reports from Texas, the mortality rate for elderly patients was 50 times higher, about one in 200.

And shock therapy is a profitable business. Psychiatrists, anesthesiologists, and hospitals can command huge reimbursements from Medicare and private insurance companies. Critics say this too often influences treatment decisions.

Dennis Cauchon, "Shock Therapy: Patients often aren't informed of full danger," *USA TODAY*, December 6, 1995: A1, http://www.ect.org/news/series/informed.html (accessed July 7, 2005).

APPENDIX D

NATIONAL CHILD ABUSE HOTLINES AND REPORTING INFORMATION BY STATE

EACH STATE DESIGNATES specific agencies to receive and investigate reports of suspected child abuse and neglect. Typically, this responsibility is carried out by a child protective services (CPS) group within a department of social services, department of human resources, or division of family and children services. In some states, police departments also receive reports of child abuse or neglect.

If you cannot reach the number in your state, please contact Childhelp USA (see below) or your local CPS organization. You may also call information and ask for the child abuse reporting number (or the police or sheriff's department) in the county and state where the abuse occurred.

National Child Abuse Hotline (Childhelp USA)
Serves the United States, Canada, U.S. Virgin Islands, Puerto
   Rico, and Guam
800-4-A-Child or 800-422-4453 (24 hours)
http://www.childhelpusa.org

Alabama
Report by County
334-242-9500
http://www.dhr.state.al.us/page.asp?pageid=304

Alaska

907-269-3400 (out of state) or

800-478-4444 (in state) Division of Family and Youth Services
   Regional Office

http://www.hss.state.ak.us/ocs

Arizona

888-SOS-CHILD or 888-767-2445

http://www.de.state.az.us/dcyf/cps

Arkansas

800-482-5964

http://www.state.ar.us/dhs/chilnfam/child_protective_services.htm

California

Report by County

800-540-4000 (in state)

916-445-2832 (out of state)

http://www.dss.cahwnet.gov/cdssweb/FindServic_716.htm

Colorado

Report by County

303-866-5932 Division of Child Welfare Services

http://www.cdhs.state.co.us/cyf/Child_Welfare/cw_home.htm

Connecticut

800-842-2288

800-624-5518 (TDD/hearing impaired, in state)

800-842-2288 (nationwide)

http://www.state.ct.us/dcf/hotline.htm

Delaware

800-292-9582

302-577-6550 (out of state)

http://www.state.de.us/kids

District of Columbia
202-671-7233 (nationwide)
http://cfsa.dc.gov/cfsa/cwp/view,a,3,q,520712.asp

Florida
800-962-2873 (nationwide)
800-453-5145 (TDD/hearing impaired, in state)
http://www.dcf.state.fl.us/abuse

Georgia
Report by County Division of Family and Children Services
706-227-7000 Clarke County
478-553-2350 Washington County
http://dfcs.dhr.georgia.gov/portal/site

Hawaii
Report By Island
808-832-5300 Child Protective Service Hotline
http://www.state.hi.us/dhs

Idaho
Report by Regional Office of Child Protective Services
800-600-6474 Boise (24 hours)
860-926-2588 Care Line (business hours)
208-332-7205 (TDD/hearing impaired)
http://www.healthandwelfare.idaho.gov/site/3333/default.aspx

Illinois
800-252-2873 (in state)
217-524-2606 (out of state)
800-358-5117 (TTY/hearing impaired)
http://www.state.il.us/dcfs/child

Indiana

800-457-8283 (in state)

800-800-5556 (24 hours)

317-233-0800 (all counties)

http://www.in.gov/fssa/families/protection/dfcchi.html

Iowa

800-362-2178 Child Abuse Hotline

http://www.dhs.state.ia.us/reportingchildabuse.asp

Kansas

800-922-5330 24-hour Hotline

http://www.srskansas.org/services/child_protective_services.htm

Kentucky

800-752-6200 Child/Adult Abuse Hotline

http://cfc.state.ky.us/help/child_abuse.asp

Louisiana

Report by Parish/County

225-342-6832 (business hours only)

225-342-2297 State Office of Community Services

http://dss.state.la.us/departments/ocs/child_welfare_services.html

Maine

800-452-1999

207-287-2983

http://www.state.me.us/dhs/bcfs/protection.htm

Maryland

Report by County

800-332-6347 (in state)

410-361-2235 (24 hours)

410-822-3107 (State Police)

http://www.dhr.state.md.us/cps

Massachusetts
800-792-5200
617-232-4882
http://www.state.ma.us/dss
(click on Report Child Abuse or Neglect)

Michigan
800-942-4357
517-373-3572
http://www.michigan.gov/dhs
(click on Protective Services)

Minnesota
Report by County
651-291-0211
http://www.dhs.state.mn.us/CFS
(click on Child Protection)

Mississippi
800-222-8000
601-359-4991 (out of state)
http://www.mdhs.state.ms.us/fcs_prot.html

Missouri
800-392-3738
573-751-3448 (out of state)
http://www.dss.state.mo.us/dfs/csp.htm

Montana
800-332-6100
406-444-5900 (out of state)
http://www.dphhs.mt.gov/aboutus/divisions/childfamilyservices

Nebraska

800-652-1999

402-595-1324 (out of state, business hours only)

http://www.hhs.state.ne.us/cha/chaindex.htm

Nevada

800-992-5757

775-684-4400 (out of state, business hours only)

http://dcfs.state.nv.us/page24.html

New Hampshire

800-894-5533 or 800-852-3388

603-225-9000 (out of state)

http://www.dhhs.state.nh.us/DHHS/BCP

New Jersey

800-792-8610 (nationwide, 24/7)

800-835-5510 (TDD/hearing impaired)

http://www.state.nj.us/humanservices/dyfs

New Mexico

800-797-3260 (24/7)

505-841-6100 (out of state, 24/7)

http://www.cyfd.org/reporters.htm

New York

800-342-3720

518-474-8740 (out of state)

http://www.ocfs.state.ny.us/main/cps

North Carolina

Report by county

919-733-3055 Raleigh

336-593-2861 Stokes County

800-627-2851 Emergency
http://www.dhhs.state.nc.us/dss/cps

North Dakota
Report by Regional Office
701-328-8888 or 888-326-2662 West Central Human Service
Center
701-328-8879 or 888-326-2112 24-hour Crisis Lines
701-222-6622 Prevent Child Abuse Alliance
http://www.state.nd.us/humanservices/services/childfamily/cps

Ohio
Report by County
614-229-7000 Franklin County 24-hour Child Abuse Hotline
http://jfs.ohio.gov/ocf

Oklahoma
800-522-3511 (nationwide, 24 hours)
http://www.okdhs.org/dcfs

Oregon
800-854-3508 ext. 2402 (in state, business hours only)
503-378-5414 (TTY, hearing impaired)
503-378-6704 (nationwide, business hours only)
http://www.oregon.gov/DHS/abuse/main.shtml

Pennsylvania
800-932-0313
717-783-8744 (out of state)
http://www.dpw.state.pa.us/Child/ChildAbuseNeglect

Rhode Island
800-RI-CHILD or 800-742-4453 (nationwide, 24 hours)
http://www.dcyf.ri.gov/chldwelfare

South Carolina

Report by County (in state)

803-898-7318 (out of state, business hours only)

http://www.state.sc.us/dss

South Dakota

Report by County

877-236-9858 Hughes County, Pierre (toll free)

605-773-3227 (local toll)

http://www.state.sd.us/social/CPS

Tennessee

Report by County

877-237-0004 (toll free)

http://www.state.tn.us/youth/cps

Texas

800-252-5400

512-834-3784 (out of state)

512-832-2020 (after hours)

http://www.tdprs.state.tx.us

Utah

800-678-9399 (nationwide)

http://dcfs.utah.gov

Vermont

Report by County (business hours only)

802-479-4260 Barre District Office

802-649-5285 (out of state, after hours)

800-649-5285 (in state, after hours)

http://www.path.state.vt.us/cwyj/cabuse/tnrpt.shtml

Virginia

800-552-7096
804-786-8536 (out of state)
http://www.dss.state.va.us/family/cps

Washington
800-END-HARM or 800-363-4276 (toll free)
http://www1.dshs.wa.gov/ca/safety/abuseReport.asp?2

West Virginia
800-352-6513
http://www.wvdhhr.org/bcf/report.asp

Wisconsin
Report by County
608-266-3036 (nationwide, business hours only)
http://www.dhfs.state.wi.us/Children/CPS

Wyoming
307-777-3570 State Department of Family Services
307-637-8622 Prevent Child Abuse
http://dfsweb.state.wy.us/menu.htm

Appendix E

Books of Interest

Abused Boys: The Neglected Victims of Sexual Abuse
by Mic Hunter (New York: Ballantine Books, Reprint, 1991)
Mr. Hunter debunks the myth that abuse of males is rare. His book explores the serious consequences that boys face as a result of abuse.

Allies in Healing: When the Person You Love Was Sexually Abused as a Child
by Laura Davis (New York: Perennial Currents, 1991)
Based on in-depth interviews and her workshops for partners across the country, Ms. Davis offers practical advice and encouragement to all.

Beyond Betrayal: Taking Charge of Your Life after Boyhood Sexual Abuse
by Richard B. Gartner, PhD (New York: John Wiley & Sons, 2005)
Dr. Gartner shares insights from years of working with male survivors of abuse in his clinical practice. The book includes many examples of problems and solutions on the path to healing.

Broken Children, Grown-up Pain: Understanding the Effects of Your Wounded Past
by Paul Hegstrom (Boston: Beacon Hill Press, 2001)
This book addresses both the abuser and abused with in-depth cov-

erage of guilt, shame, and the helper-vs.-rescuer theory.

Child Abuse Trauma: Theory and Treatment of the Lasting Effects

by John N. Briere (Thousand Oaks, CA: SAGE Publications, 1992)
Geared toward the practitioner, Dr. Briere's book explores many aspects of the abuse experience, both in childhood and adulthood.

Leaping upon the Mountains: Men Proclaiming Victory Over Sexual Child Abuse

by Mike Lew (Berkeley, CA: North Atlantic Books, 2000)
Drawing insights from men from 45 countries who survived childhood sexual abuse, Mr. Lew presents a powerful picture of how it's possible to not only survive but overcome.

Memory and Abuse

by Charles L. Whitfield, MD (Deerfield Beach, FL: HCI, 1995)
Dr. Whitfield brings to the reader his clinical experience and knowledge about traumatic memory, exploring and clarifying the experience of trauma survivors.

Opening the Door: A Treatment Model for Therapy with Male Survivors of Sexual Abuse

by Adrienne Crowder (New York: Brunner/Mazel, 1995)
This book is based on current research and evolved techniques of 41 therapists who have developed expertise in working with sexually abused males.

Our Fathers: The Secret Life of the Catholic Church in an Age of Scandal

by David France (New York: Broadway, 2004)
Mr. France, who covered the Catholic church sex scandal as an investigative editor at *Newsweek*, has compiled a compelling story sweeping a 40-year history.

Outgrowing the Pain: A Book For and About Adults Abused as Children
by Eliana Gil, PhD (New York: Dell, Reissue edition, 1988)
Dr. Gil's book is designed to help adults survive, cope, and understand.

Sexual Abuse of Males: The SAM Model of Theory and Practice
by Josef Spiegel, PhD (New York: Brunner-Routledge, 2003)
This book, aimed primarily at professionals, discusses treatment approaches and intervention strategies.

The Sexual Healing Journey: A Guide for Survivors of Sexual Abuse
by Wendy Maltz (New York: Perennial Currents, Revised edition, 2001)
Ms. Maltz covers details of what constitutes abuse while providing victims with a guide toward healing.

Thou Shalt Not Be Aware: Society's Betrayal of the Child
by Alice Miller (New York: Farrar, Straus and Giroux, 1998)
Ms. Miller's book offers a fresh take on how the unconscious retains memories of childhood and, without appropriate intervention, generates emotional ills and destructive behavior.

The State Boys Rebellion
By Michael D'Antonio (New York: Simon & Shuster, 2004)
In 1949, eight-year-old Fred Boyce was committed to the Walter E. Fernald School for the Feebleminded in Waltham, Massachusetts. Even though IQ tests showed Boyce was normal, he was labeled a "moron" and remained institutionalized for eleven years. Aside from receiving little education and suffering physical and sexual abuse, Boyce and others were, without their knowledge, given radioactive oatmeal as part of an experiment conducted by MIT

and Quaker Oats.

The Trouble with Secrets
by Karen Johnsen (Seattle: Parenting Press, 1986)
This book helps children understand the difference between when they should keep a secret and when they should not.

Understanding Child Abuse and Neglect
by Cynthia Crosson-Tower (Boston: Allyn & Bacon, 5th edition, 2001)
This book explores the issues surrounding abuse and neglect from several vantage points, addressing both the problems and possible solutions that are crucial to the proper protection of our children.

Victims No Longer: The Classic Guide for Men Recovering from Sexual Child Abuse
by Mike Lew (New York: Perennial Currents, 2nd edition, 2004)
One of the first books written specifically for men, this is an invaluable resource. It's filled with compassionate advice and information from male survivors.

Wounded Boys Heroic Men: A Man's Guide to Recovering from Child Abuse
by Daniel Jay Sonkin, PhD (Cincinnati, OH: Adams Media, 1998)
Wounded Boys Heroic Men is a workbook for transformation, specifically written for and about men.

Appendix F

Websites on Child Abuse and Support for Victims

Websites are divided into the following categories:
- F.1   Websites about Male Sexual Abuse
- F.2   Websites for Male or Female Victims of Abuse
- F.3   Resources for Helping an Abused Friend
- F.4   Websites for Child Abuse Awareness and Prevention
- F.5   Information on Reporting Abuse

F.1   Websites about Male Sexual Abuse

Aardvarc.org
Male Victims of Sexual Assault
http://www.aardvarc.org/rape/about/men.shtml
This project was supported by the Office for Victims of Crime, U.S. Department of Justice. According to their 2002 statistics, "over 31,000 males over the age of 12 reported being the victim of rape or sexual assault." The site delves into the topics of sleep issues, male victims, obsessions, statistics, and more. It also posts a valuable listing of sexual assault resources categorized by state.

MaleSurvivor.Org
Overcoming Sexual Victimization of Boys and Men

http://www.malesurvivor.org
In October 1988, the first professional Conference on Male Sexual Victimization was held. As more conferences ensued, professionals worked together to create an outreach for male victims. MaleSurvivor is part of this outreach program. Their website contains support, resources, and articles that dispel common myths surrounding abuse.

MenStuff.Org: The National Men's Resource
Sexual Abuse of Boys
http://www.menstuff.org/issues/byissue/abusedboys.html
This compilation contains many links and articles on what Karl Tripple calls "the secret epidemic." The site links to additional books and resources covering topics of sexual abuse.

Sexual Abuse of Males: Prevalence, Possible Lasting Effects
http://www.jimhopper.com/male-ab
This is one of the most comprehensive websites I have found covering the abuse of males. Content, written by psychologist Jim Hopper, PhD, covers controversies and biases, prevalence methods and studies, possible lasting effects, recommended books and articles, female perpetrators, hotline resources, and men's stories of recovery.

F.2 WEBSITES FOR MALE OR FEMALE VICTIMS OF ABUSE

Self-Injury, Abuse, and Trauma Resource Directory
http://www.self-injury-abuse-trauma-directory.info
This serves as a portal to many websites covering topics of physical abuse, sexual abuse, protective parents of abused children, family crisis after an abuse disclosure, depression, anxiety and panic attacks, bipolar disorder/manic depression, family crisis during legal processes against perpetrators, and more.

Focus Adolescent Services
Abuse: Physical, Emotional, Sexual, Neglect
http://www.focusas.com/Abuse.html
This comprehensive site contains information for helping teens suffering from all kinds of abuse. There are ideas for working with schools and reporting abuse as well as helpful phone numbers.

F.3 Resources for Helping an Abused Friend

Survivors and Friends
http://www.survivors-and-friends.org
This nonprofit organization was founded by a sexual abuse survivor to provide hope and encouragement. The site contains an area where survivors can anonymously share their trials and experiences. A comprehensive reading room offers articles on recovery written by fellow survivors.

UCLA Center for Women & Men
How to Help a Friend
http://www.thecenter.ucla.edu/friend.html
This website offers a checklist of symptoms and questions you can ask yourself if you think a friend has been sexually assaulted. It contains basic guidelines for helping a friend in need.

F.4 Websites for Child Abuse Awareness and Prevention

Stop It Now!
The Campaign to Prevent Sexual Child Abuse
http://www.stopitnow.com
Their resource guide offers links to many of the most reputable support organizations for child abuse prevention. The main page

links to their newsletters, groups, and more. This nonprofit organization was founded to "call on all abusers and potential abusers to stop and seek help, to educate adults about the ways to stop sexual abuse, and to increase public awareness of the trauma of child sexual abuse."

HelpGuide on Child Abuse: Types, Signs, Symptoms, Causes, and Help

http://www.helpguide.org/mental/child_abuse_physical
  _emotional_sexual_neglect.htm

An in-depth, well-done resource by the Rotary Club of Santa Monica and Center for Healthy Aging. This site covers: the definition of child abuse, types of child abuse, signs and symptoms, causes, results, help for children and teens, and how to report suspected abuse.

Safe Horizon: Child Abuse and Incest

http://www.safehorizon.org

This is an outstanding website emphasizing the effects of child abuse and where you can find help for yourself as a victim or for others currently being abused. Learn that: "Being abused is one of the most traumatic things that can happen to a child. Telling someone about the abuse, especially when it has been committed by a family member or someone the child trusts, can also be a frightening, difficult experience. Children need different support and services than adults. Safe Horizon has programs that are specifically designed to meet the needs of children and of adult survivors." Safe Horizon's Child Advocacy Centers are "child-friendly, safe spaces that provide prevention, intervention, emotional support and treatment services to physically and sexually abused children and their families by using a child-focused team approach."

Parents Anonymous

http://www.parentsanonymous.org

Founded in 1991, Parents Anonymous is the country's oldest child abuse prevention organization and currently has 11 support groups for adult survivors of physical, sexual, and/or emotional child abuse or neglect. They encourage victims to do something positive with their abuse.

Psychological Self-Help
Relationships within the Family

http://mentalhelp.net/psyhelp/chap9/chap9k.htm

This webpage explores the dynamics and roots of abuse within families and offers links to other websites with information on sexual abuse.

F.5 INFORMATION ON REPORTING ABUSE

Note: Please see Appendix D for national and state-by-state phone numbers and websites.

While all available websites for reporting child abuse are too numerous to mention, the following list has been chosen so that, no matter where you live in the United States, you'll be able to report suspected abuse.

U.S. Department of Health and Human Services
Administration for Children and Families – Children's
Bureau

http://www.acf.dhhs.gov/programs/cb/publications

This website has several fact sheets and publications on child abuse and neglect. Topics include prevention, how to report suspected abuse, and state liaison officers. The website points out that federal agencies have no authority to intervene in individual child abuse and neglect cases. Each state has jurisdiction over these matters and has specific laws and procedures for reporting and investigating. In some states, citizens are mandated by law to report suspected child abuse or neglect.

Mandatory Reporting of Child Abuse and Neglect
Susan K. Smith, Attorney at Law
http://www.smith-lawfirm.com/mandatory_reporting.htm
Here you can access information about mandatory reporting statutes and child abuse prevention laws in all 50 states. The site posts links to specific state resources and to more information on what constitutes abuse.

About.com
Child Abuse Prevention, Recovery, and Reporting
http://incestabuse.about.com/od/childabuse
This has a solid collection of articles that "will provide information and action plans to detect and prevent child abuse. Learn the signs of child abuse, what you can do, how to heal, recover and become a survivor." You can also learn about "dealing with the courts, police and legal and medical systems."

International Child Abuse Network
The Reality of Abuse
http://www.yesican.org/suspect.html
This lists phone numbers and websites for states to assist with reporting abuse. It also posts a checklist of information you should record if you suspect abuse.

Appendix G

Websites Listing
Registered Sex Offenders

Megan's Law

The parents of seven-year-old Megan Kanka didn't know that a twice-convicted sex offender was living across the street until he was charged with the brutal rape and murder of their daughter. The 1996 federal law inspired by this tragedy is commonly known as "Megan's Law." It requires convicted sex offenders to register with local law enforcement agencies, which, in turn, provide information about the offenders to the public. Some national databases are listed below, followed by individual state websites.

National Databases

Sex Offender and Violent Criminal Databases
http://www.sexoffender.com
This website has more information on Megan's Law and links to state sex offender registries and violent criminal background checks.

Parents for Megan's Law
Nationwide Registry and Links
http://www.parentsformeganslaw.com
"Parents for Megan's Law recently conducted two national surveys.

The first survey evaluated sex offender registration compliance. Our results indicate that approximately 24% of the nation's sex offenders are failing to comply with state registration requirements." This site offers a report card on Megan's Law, how many offenders have registered by state, and a grade for each state. More importantly, it offers advocacy toward improving the reporting system.

Darkness Against Child Abuse

http://www.magickalshadow.com/daca

This has a comprehensive listing of state and county resources for reporting child abuse and locating sex offenders. Australia, Canada, and the United Kingdom are also listed.

Rob's SearchEngineZ

http://searchenginez.com/sex_offenders_usa.html

This is another valuable resource that includes links to state registries, maps on where sex offenders live, and more.

National Registry Service

http://www.nationalalertregistry.com

This site allows you to quickly search by entering your ZIP code and e-mail. It will then tell you if there are any registered offenders in your immediate area. If there are, you may purchase a report that details their names, addresses, last offenses, and more. The reports are inexpensive and, if you're seeking a quick way to find the information, this is a good source. (There are often unique guidelines for each state—and information, though public, isn't easy to access.) You may also register to be notified by e-mail if a sex offender moves to your area.

Sex Criminals

http://www.sexcriminals.com

This is a comprehensive site covering abuse, reporting, and Megan's law at a national view and by state.

State Websites Listing Registered Sex Offenders

Alabama
http://www.dps.state.al.us/abi

Alaska
http://www.dps.state.ak.us/nSorcr

Arizona
http://www.azsexoffender.com

Arkansas
http://www.acic.org/soff

California
http://meganslaw.ca.gov

Colorado
http://sor.state.co.us

Connecticut
http://www.state.ct.us/dps
(click on Sex Offender Registry)

Delaware
http://www.state.de.us/dsp/sexoff

District of Columbia
http://mpdc.dc.gov
(click on Sex Offender Registry, under Services)

Florida
http://www.fdle.state.fl.us

Georgia

http://www.ganet.org/gbi

(click on Sex Offenders)

Guam

http://www.guamcourts.org/sor

Hawaii

http://sexoffenders.hawaii.gov

Idaho

http://www.isp.state.id.us/identification

(click on Central Sex Offender Registry)

Illinois

http://www.isp.state.il.us/sor

Indiana

https://secure.in.gov/serv/cji_sor

Iowa

http://www.iowasexoffender.com

Kansas

http://www.accesskansas.org/kbi/ro.shtml

Kentucky

http://kspsor.state.ky.us

Louisiana

http://www.lasocpr.lsp.org

Maine

http://www4.informe.org/sor

Maryland
http://www.dpscs.state.md.us/sor

Massachusetts
http://www.state.ma.us/sorb

Michigan
http://www.mipsor.state.mi.us

Minnesota
http://www.doc.state.mn.us
(click on Level 3 Sex Offender Locator)

Mississippi
http://www.sor.mdps.state.ms.us

Missouri
http://www.mshp.dps.missouri.gov
(click on Sex Offender Registry)

Montana
http://svor.doj.state.mt.us

Nebraska
http://www.nsp.state.ne.us/sor

Nevada
http://www.nvsexoffenders.gov

New Hampshire
http://www.egov.nh.gov/nsor

New Jersey
http://www.nj.gov/njsp/info/reg_sexoffend.html

http://www.state.nj.us/lps/njsp/spoff

New Mexico
http://www.nmsexoffender.dps.state.nm.us

New York
http://criminaljustice.state.ny.us/nsor

North Carolina
http://sbi.jus.state.nc.us/DOJHAHT/SOR

North Dakota
http://www.ndsexoffender.com

Ohio
http://www.esorn.ag.state.oh.us

Oklahoma
http://www.doc.state.ok.us/DOCS/offender_info.htm
(click on Sex Offender Lookup)

Oregon
http://egov.oregon.gov/OSP/SOR

Pennsylvania
http://www.pameganslaw.state.pa.us

Rhode Island
http://www.paroleboard.ri.gov

South Carolina
http://www.sled.state.sc.us/default.htm
(click on Sex Offender Registry, under Services)

South Dakota
http://www.sddci.com/administration/id
(click on State Sex Offender Registry)

Puerto Rico
Puerto Rico does not maintain an online sex offender registry.

Tennessee
http://www.ticic.state.tn.us

Texas
http://records.txdps.state.tx.us
(click on Sex Offender Search)

Utah
http://www.cr.ex.state.ut.us

Vermont
http://www.dps.state.vt.us/cjs/s_registry.htm

Virgin Islands (U.S.)
The Virgin Islands does not maintain an online sex offender registry.

Virginia
http://sex-offender.vsp.state.va.us

Washington
http://ml.waspc.org

West Virginia
http://www.wvstatepolice.com/sexoff

Wisconsin

http://offender.doc.state.wi.us

(click on Wisconsin Registered Sex Offenders)

Wyoming

http://attorneygeneral.state.wy.us

(click on Wyoming Sex Offender Registration)

ILLUSTRATION CREDITS

Plate 1   Charles A. Carroll and Robert L. Carroll
            Original photo sent anonymously to Charles A. Carroll
            in 1989 from Brooklyn, New York. The source was later
            discovered to be his foster parents' biological child.

Plate 2   New Jersey State Colony for Boys Sign
            From a 1968 public relations brochure for the recently
            renamed New Lisbon State School, which later became
            the New Lisbon Developmental Center. Brochure con-
            tributed in 1984 by Ruth Wurtzel, wife of Charles
            Wurtzel, vice president of the New Jersey Association
            for New Lisbon Boys.

Plate 3   Charles A. Carroll
            Original photo sent anonymously to Charles A. Carroll
            in 1989 from Brooklyn, New York. The source was later
            discovered to be his foster parents' biological child.

Plate 4   Governor's Day Annual Picnic
            From a 1968 public relations brochure for the recently
            renamed New Lisbon State School, which later became
            the New Lisbon Developmental Center. Brochure con-
            tributed in 1984 by Ruth Wurtzel, wife of Charles
            Wurtzel, vice president of the New Jersey Association
            for New Lisbon Boys.

Plate 5   Birch One and Two

From a 1968 public relations brochure for the recently renamed New Lisbon State School, which later became the New Lisbon Developmental Center. Brochure contributed in 1984 by Ruth Wurtzel, wife of Charles Wurtzel, vice president of the New Jersey Association for New Lisbon Boys.

Plate 6   Birch One Dormitory

Original photo contributed in 1984 by Ruth Wurtzel, wife of Charles Wurtzel, vice president of the New Jersey Association for New Lisbon Boys.

Plate 7   Charles A. Carroll and Robert L. Carroll

Photo taken of the brothers, Charles and Robert Carroll, by their aunt, Josephine Shea. Original photo contributed by Ms. Shea in 1966.

Plate 8   Birch One Day Room

Original photo contributed in 1984 by Ruth Wurtzel, wife of Charles Wurtzel, vice president of the New Jersey Association for New Lisbon Boys.

Plate 9   Robert Carroll with Wiggie

Original photo sent anonymously to Charles A. Carroll in 1989 from Brooklyn, New York. The source was later discovered to be his foster parents' biological child.

Plate 10   Robert L. Carroll

Original photo sent anonymously to Charles A. Carroll in 1989 from Brooklyn, New York. The source was later discovered to be his foster parents' biological child.

Plate 11   Charles A. Carroll
            Original photo sent anonymously to Charles A. Carroll
            in 1989 from Brooklyn, New York. The source was later
            discovered to be his foster parents' biological child.

Plate 12   Hanukkah Dinner
            Original photo contributed by Dr. Stanley Alprin.

Plate 13   12th Annual Invitation Tennis Tournament
            Original photo contributed in 1984 by Ruth Wurtzel,
            wife of Charles Wurtzel, vice president of the New Jersey
            Association for New Lisbon Boys.

Plate 14   Outside Birch Two
            Original photo contributed in 1984 by Ruth Wurtzel,
            wife of Charles Wurtzel, vice president of the New Jersey
            Association for New Lisbon Boys.

Plate 15   Charles A. Carroll with Wiggie
            Original photo sent anonymously to Charles A. Carroll
            in 1989 from Brooklyn, New York. The source was later
            discovered to be his foster parents' biological child.

Plate 16   Charles A. Carroll and Robert L. Carroll
            Original photo sent anonymously to Charles A. Carroll
            in 1989 from Brooklyn, New York. The source was later
            discovered to be his foster parents' biological child.

Plate 17   Melvin Wheeler
            Drawing by Charles A. Carroll

Plate 18   Johnstone Training and Research Center Sign
            Photo taken by Charles A. Carroll in September 2002.

Plate 19   Johnstone Administration Building
           Photo taken by Charles A. Carroll in September 2002.

Plate 20   Charles A. Carroll and Dr. Stanley I. Alprin
           Photo taken by Karen Dribben.